THE NUMBER

Dear Daneel R. Olivaw,
I had to shank Peter
for this book. Stay strong
down in the Cape.

MR

THE NUMBER

One man's search for identity in the Cape underworld and prison gangs

JONNY STEINBERG

JONATHAN BALL PUBLISHERS
JOHANNESBURG & CAPE TOWN

Published in 2004 in trade paperback by
JONATHAN BALL PUBLISHERS (PTY) LTD
P O Box 33977
Jeppestown
2043

ISBN 1 86842 205 4

Cover image by Adam Broomberg & Oliver Chanarin, England
Cover design and reproduction by
Triple M Design & Advertising, Johannesburg
Typesetting and reproduction of text by
Alinea Studio, Cape Town
Printed and bound by
CTP Book Printers, Duminy Street, Parow, Cape

Set in 11 on 13 pt Palatino

A NOTE ON NAMES

My contract with the Department of Correctional Services, which gave me access to Pollsmoor Prison, forbade me from naming any person I interviewed who is currently serving a prison sentence. I have thus given pseudonyms to several of the inmates who appear fleetingly in this book. There are also several other people whose names I have changed in order to protect their identities. The following is a list of the pseudonyms that appear in this book:

Andrew Bosch, Rashid, Serfontein, Natalie, Jake Williams, Farieda, Gareth, Peter, Stan Landman, Jack, Josephina, Fi, Isaac, Florence, Wayne, the Marais Brothers, Pieter Brink, Diamond, Malan, Miriam, Mr Smit, Heunis, Cups, Humphrey, One Touch, Howard Jacobs, Fred, Alfred, Gerald, Benjamin, Mr Kloppers, Mr Arendse, Joshua Saul, Ishmael, Nikki Cupido, Robin and Helen Morris, the Sampsons – Harry, Norman, Denise, Stephen and Joanne – Zubeida, and the Benjamins – Faranaaz, Leila, Hassan, Jumat and Shamil.

AUTHOR'S NOTE

I have accumulated many debts of gratitude over the last two years.

The Centre for the Study of Violence and Reconciliation found funding for the research and provided an institutional home for the writing of this book. I am particularly indebted to the Centre's Executive Director Graeme Simpson, whose tolerance for my projects seems endless, and to Amanda Dissel, who accommodated my work in the Centre's Criminal Justice Programme. Many thanks to the Development Cooperation Ireland which funded this book.

I suspect that Chris Giffard has little idea just how valuable he has been to me. He smoothed my path to Pollsmoor Prison at the beginning, lent me his ear every time I needed to talk through problems – and there were many times – and then read several draft chapters with great care. Many thanks.

Christopher Glenn Malgas, the senior Pollsmoor warder whom I shadowed for nine months, was a study in graciousness. He manages, against all odds, to combine intense seriousness about his trying, often thankless work, with unfaltering levity. Most warders would have seen me as an unwanted appendage; Chris made me a welcome companion.

Jeremy Vearey, currently station commissioner at the Elsies River police station, lent me a great deal of his time and his considerable knowledge. The crash course he gave me on street and prison gangs proved invaluable. He also allowed me to read a copy of a monograph he has written on prison gangs, which was extremely useful.

Kelly Gillespie was a much-needed peer whose own research has taken her to several of the Western Cape's prisons. It was with her that I shared my excitement when I discovered that the Goliat-One is the Man of the Light, and that Pomabasa took the truth with him to the grave.

I am indebted to all the authors from whose primary research I learned and drew. In particular, Don Pinnock's and Wilfried Schärf's respective master's theses, both more than twenty years old, were manna from heaven. Together, they gave me an introduction to the origins of the post-removals Cape Flats without which I would have stumbled around the ghettos blind. I also benefited enormously from the work of Dirk van Zyl Smit, without whose extraordinary scholarship much of the history of prison law and practice in South Africa would have remained unchronicled.

Vanessa September and Chris Giffard both read draft chapters with a sharp and critical eye. Many thanks.

I am particularly indebted to those who read and commented on the entire manuscript: Ivan Vladislavič, Ben Carton, Carol Steinberg, David Jammy and Isobel Dixon.

Mark Gevisser also read the whole manuscript, but he did so much more than that. He lent the entire enterprise the care, scrupulousness and passion he gives to projects of his own. I have lost count of how many problems – stylistic, journalistic and ethical – he worked through with me.

Lomin Saayman graciously subjected himself to being read to, talked at, shouted at, and ignored by turn for almost two years. Such is the stuff of which heroes and madmen are made.

PROLOGUE

It happened more than two decades ago, and prison gangsters are not wont to keep records, so fixing the date and time is at best an educated guess. Some say 1976, others swear it was '78. Still others hurry back to their cells to consult the yellowing scraps of paper that were their makeshift secret diaries back in the seventies. Perhaps the story is apocryphal. But it is legendary; the old Number veterans talk of it with pride – the day the coloured man in the gallery stood up and began shouting at a witness in prison language, the white prosecutor and judge staring at him in bewilderment, the meaning of their own trial suddenly unintelligible to them.

I'd hazard a guess that it was August 1978, at the Supreme Court Building in Keerom Street, Cape Town: *The State v Pietersen and two others*. It was a murder trial. The victim, a young coloured man by the name of Marthinus Hollander, had been an inmate at Victor Verster prison in Paarl, one of the picturesque rural towns scattered across the Cape's famous wine farming districts. On the night before his death, in December 1977, the prison authorities had moved Hollander to a large communal cell in the maximum security section of the prison. The following morning, when the warders did their rounds, they found his dead body curled up under his blanket. His throat had been slit with a razor blade and he had been disembowelled.

Normally, the prospect of handling a case of this nature would have made the prosecutor and investigating officer jittery. Prison murders were notoriously slippery: state witnesses would sign lengthy affidavits only to contradict themselves in court; new witnesses would appear mid-trial to rubbish the evidence of others; those in the dock would suddenly change their testimony in sync with the changing evidence. Months of meticulous pre-trial work could be unstitched, out of sight, in the prisons, during the opening days of the court proceedings.

But in this particular case, the prosecutor and investigating officer must have been quite relaxed. Hollander had spent his last night with 17 cell-mates. When his body was found the following morning, three of them had blood smeared on their clothes; two of the three had wounds on their fingers. It was almost as if things had been set up to make the investigation easy.

Although the two accused with cuts on their hands pleaded not guilty, they conducted a dispirited, half-hearted defence; it seemed that they were just going through the motions. The court would sentence both of them to death.

'Can you tell us how you got those cut marks on your hands?' the prosecutor asked Pieter Hendriks, the first of the two men who were to die.

'What I want to say to the *Oubaas*,' Hendriks replied, using an obsequious term of racial diffidence perhaps best translated as 'Master', 'the *Oubaas* will not believe.'

'Did you sleep the whole night?' the prosecutor asked.

'Yes.'

'When you went to sleep, was there anything wrong with the deceased?'

'He slept on his bed and there was nothing wrong with him.'

'Can you explain how you got blood on your shirt?'

'It's not my shirt.'

The second man who was to hang, Frans Linders, was equally unenthusiastic in his self-defence.

'I know nothing about the case,' he told the court. 'I slept. I woke in fright during the evening. I saw that Accused Number One was busy with the deceased. He had already cut his throat.'

'Can you explain how you got blood on your trousers?' the prosecutor asked.

'The blood is from my own finger,' Linders replied.

The other 14 occupants of the cell had been questioned. Prisoners make for extremely reluctant state witnesses, but after months of cajoling and threatening, several came forward. At first, their testimony was somewhat puzzling. Questioned about the motive for the murder, they spoke vaguely of horrendous conditions in Victor Verster, of being 'caged up like dogs', of going mad. But gradually, as the investigation proceeded, a coherent story started coming together. It emerged that a joint parliament of 26s, 27s and 28s, South Africa's three national prison gangs, operative in every jail around the country, had decreed that an informer be killed; not a particular informer, the witnesses said, but any informer. It was to be something of a cleansing ritual. And so, on the night Hollander arrived in his new cell, word went round the room that he was a member of The Big Five, a gang whose self-appointed task is to spy on the Number gangs on behalf of the authorities. Before the night was through, the joint parliament's order had been executed; an informer was dead.

It was probably during the latter stages of the trial that the famous incident happened. A state witness took the stand at the start of the morning session. He answered questions diligently for about half an hour until a middle-aged man, who had been listening to the proceedings from the gallery, stood up and began shouting at him. Judge and prosecutor strained to understand what was being spoken. Some of the words spewing from the court spectator's mouth were clearly Zulu, others derived from Afrikaans. Still others were entirely unintelligible. He was emphatic and angry. The witness stood still in the witness box, staring at his hands, listening intently. The man sat down and the witness tried to resume his testimony, until the judge interrupted him and asked what the hell had just happened.

What had just happened was that the state witness had strayed from the script written for him by the gangs that controlled Victor Verster prison. The court got a rare glimpse of a practice usually rendered invisible; the parliaments of the Number gangs had done more than just order the murder: they had decided who would stand trial after the killing, who would appear as state witnesses, and what they would say in court.

This shed some light on the vague testimony about the motive for the murder – the constant talk of 'horrendous conditions', of being 'caged like animals'. The prison gangs regarded the courts as their only public platform. They believed that, behind the mute walls of South Africa's jails, black prisoners were being subjected to a holocaust. They thought that if the world knew, it might be stopped. So, the witness stands of South Africa's courts were their press galleries, the witnesses their spokespeople.

What were Number gangs up to? What, precisely, was being staged in apartheid's courtroom? Thanks to the research of an enterprising young criminology student, Fink Haysom, supplemented by interviews with former Victor Verster inmates I conducted more than two decades later, the motives for Hollander's murder can be placed in their correct context. Between the beginning of 1974 and the end of 1977, a fierce war was fought in the prisons of the Western Cape between the 26s and the 28s. The conflict was euphemistically referred to as a 'general election', a violent contest to rule the prisons. Much of the war was fought at two jails: Victor Verster and Brandvlei, another prison in the Cape hinterland. During that period, 21 prisoners were murdered in the two jails.

The meeting of the three parliaments in Victor Verster in late 1977 was an extraordinary and unusual event. It was convened to end the war. The murder of Hollander was to seal a peace pact. He was chosen on somewhat arbitrary grounds; he was a fairly anonymous, and certainly powerless, member of Victor Verster's prison population. It is possible that he was named an informer simply for the purpose of killing him; he was a convenient surrogate for the enactment of a symbolic ritual. He was decreed to be a *vuil mpata*, a 'dirty nothing', and the spilling of his blood was to symbolise the cleansing of the prison.

More important, though, was the question of who was to hang for the murder. During the trial, Hendriks told the court that he was a 28, while Linders claimed to be a 26. Yet every prisoner I have spoken to who was at Victor Verster at the time insists that both men were leaders of the 27s. The difference is important, since the primary function of the 27s was then, and remains now, to keep the peace between the 26s and the 28s by 'righting wrongs'. The fact that the war had dragged on for four years pointed to a terrible dereliction of duty on the part of the 27s, a failure to perform its leadership function adequately. That two 27 leaders were chosen to die points to the severity of the war and to the extremity of the measures the gangs deemed necessary to end it. The two men chosen to hang were almost certainly present at the meeting of the three parliaments.

The war did indeed end with the killing of Marthinus Hollander and the state execution of the two 27 leaders. During the following four years, only three prisoners were murdered on the premises of Victor Verster and Brandvlei, compared with 21 during the previous four years. The gangs had ended the war by sentencing two of their leaders to death; but they had outsourced both the passing of sentence and the execution of punishment to the apartheid state.

*

Throughout much of the twentieth century, this is how news of the world inside South Africa's prisons emerged – from court records, judicial enquiries, prison department statements. Needless to say, they were hopelessly inadequate. Slivers of the hidden world appeared in the courtrooms and judicial hearings, disembodied, severed from the complexity of their context. Part of the problem, of course, was the spokespeople and the enquirers: prisoners whose testimonies were determined beforehand by the gangs; warders who in reality knew little of these secretive organisations, and filled the gaps with their own prejudices; judicial officers tasked with finding evidence rather than understanding human relationships.

Yet many of these disembodied slivers hinted at the strangeness of the society behind the bars. Much of it had to do with the politics of sexual relationships. In one murder case conducted in Cape Town's courts in 1977, the accused implicated his *wyfie*, 'wife', so that he could have 'her' with him on death row. Does a man not take his furniture with him when he moves house, he remarked.

News from the jails also hinted at what must have been a perverse and disturbing relationship between inmates and warders. For instance, a committee of enquiry into an attempted escape from Barberton Maximum Security Prison in September 1983 reported some harrowing practices. 'It was established,' the committee members wrote, 'that for many years there has been a tradition at the prison of "greeting" new arrivals or "warming" them. After they are stripped naked, they are forced to run in a circle in the courtyard past a number of warders, both white and black. The warders are armed with clubs or pieces of rubber pipe, and hit the prisoners as they run past.'

More disturbingly, it appeared from the committee's report that warders took sides in gang conflict in the most cruel and insidious manner. On 19 April 1983, a senior warder rounded up 24 leaders of the 28s and 12 leaders of the 26s, and sent them to work at a stone quarry near the prison. Each prisoner was issued with a 4-pound hammer to do his work. Inmates testified to the committee that the warder had deliberately armed the men with lethal weapons and deliberately outnumbered the 26s by a ratio of two to one. His aim, it was contended, was to decimate the 26s in the jail. Not surprisingly, the warder himself was attacked in the battle that ensued and spent several weeks in hospital.

*

Between 1975 and 1983, four documents were written which together shed a great deal of light on South Africa's prison gangs, indeed far more than the whole history of judicial proceedings and government papers combined. The first was an unpublished manuscript written by a certain Major Rodney Keswa who had spent more than twenty years in the prison service and had just been appointed Commissioner of Transkei Prisons. The second was a biography, penned by a brilliant young historian, Charles van Onselen, of an early Johannesburg bandit by the name of 'Nongoloza' Mathebula. Then there was Fink Haysom's honours dissertation completed at the Institute of Criminology at the University of Cape Town. And finally, Morg Lötter and Willem Schurink, social scientists at the Human Sciences Research Council in Pretoria, wrote a book, having conducted dozens of interviews with prison gang members.

The story the four books told was extraordinary. It emerged that the 26s, 27s and 28s all originated from bands of outlaws that had plagued late-nineteenth- and early-twentieth-century Johannesburg. The most memorable of these gangs was called the Ninevites; its rank-and-file were lumpen proletarians – young black men who had left their ancestral land in the countryside but had refused to take up wage employment for white bosses in the early mining town.

The Ninevites were led by a charismatic young Zulu migrant, 'Nongoloza' Mathebula. Imbued with a crisp and feisty imagination, which had been instilled by the injustices that lay in his own past, Nongoloza shaped his crew of outlaws into a paramilitary hierarchy. It borrowed its rank structure and its imaginary uniforms from the Natal Colony's judiciary and the Transvaal Republic's military. Perhaps most interesting of all, Nongoloza imbued his bandit army with a political purpose. 'I reorganised my gang of robbers,' he reported to his white captors in 1912. 'I laid them under what has since become known as Nineveh law. I read in the bible about the great state Nineveh which rebelled against the Lord, and I selected that name for my gang as rebels against the government's laws.'

The Ninevites lasted nearly two decades. At their height, in the early 1900s, they had absorbed scores of the vagrants and drifters of early Johannesburg into their ranks. They had also infiltrated the labour compounds where Johannesburg's gold mine workers lived, and they had taken control of the inmate population at many of the Transvaal's prisons. They were famous for launching their sorties of robbery and plunder from a series of caves and warrens that stretched across the south-western perimeter of Johannesburg. Had they chosen to practise their profession differently, they might have been remembered as an African pedigree of Robin Hoods, taking from the victors of South Africa's colonial order and giving to the downtrodden. As it was, the Ninevites showed little discernment when it came to their choice of victims. Among their favourite pastimes was to rob black labourers as they made their way home on payday.

And so early Johannesburg's black proletarians remembered Nongoloza with a mixture of fear and awe. It was said that he and his bandits established an underground world in a disused mineshaft, complete with shops, beautiful white women and a Scottish bookkeeper. It was also said that Nongoloza himself was imbued with magic, that the bullets of white policemen and soldiers bounced off his skin. In early proletarian lore, he was something of a Janus-faced monster: horrible because he was undiscerningly brutal, enticing because he showed that even the poor can inspire terror.

The Ninevites were crushed in the mid-1910s, and Nongoloza himself slipped into a life of obscurity that I will recount to you later. But by then, most of the gang's leaders had spent time in jail and had begun to recruit there. Thousands of young black men, criminalised by white South Africa's racial laws, drifted in and out of the prisons of the early twentieth century. By the 1930s, gangs derivative of the Ninevites had a presence in almost every prison across the country. They have been there ever since, the memory of Nongoloza and the paraphernalia and legends of his life passed down from one generation of prisoners to the next.

*

It is quite remarkable how much of Nongoloza's imagination has been preserved in the prison gangs of today – the 26s, 27s and 28s. The uniforms copied from the early Boer Republic are still there – imaginary of course, worn only in prisoners' heads. So are the .303 rifles and bayonets that the Boer commandos took into battle with the British in 1899. Nongoloza's original rank structure, dividing members between soldiers and judicial officers, and dividing the judicial officers themselves between an upper and a lower court, is still extant.

Most interesting of all, the Number gangs have held onto Nongoloza's original ideology. All three are organised around a largely mythical narrative of the great bandit's career. Indeed, they place the origin of their own division into three rival gangs in Nongoloza's times. And yet, while they disagree about episodes in his life, and about decisions he made in regard to the nature of banditry, all agree that he became a bandit because blacks were being disinherited of their land and forced to work like slaves in the mines. In other words, throughout the century, South Africa's prisons have incubated a fiercely anti-colonial ideology.

But it is an ideology of the most disturbing kind. Indeed, the very idea of banditry has always been a deeply unsettling phenomenon; it tampers with the boundary between acquisitive crime and political nobility; it hovers ambivalently between an aspiration to social equality and anti-social violence, between a disdain for the current order and disdain for social order in general.

*

In early 2002, I visited the Pollsmoor prison complex in Cape Town for two weeks on assignment for a magazine. Pollsmoor is by no means South Africa's oldest prison complex – the maximum security jail it houses was just 25 years old when I first visited – but it is certainly among the most legendary. One reason is that Nelson Mandela spent six of his 27 years in jail there. He lived in an isolated cell on the roof of the prison, his 'penthouse', as he referred to it in his autobiography. Another reason is that the Pollsmoor complex is breathtakingly enormous and jarringly visible. It gobbles up a giant swathe of Cape Town's most beautiful and valued real estate, under the eastern flank of Table Mountain. Its five prisons host more than seven thousand prisoners on any given day. Finally, Pollsmoor is legendary because it is the central railway station of the Western Cape's criminal underworld. Located less than twenty kilometres from the endless drug wars of Cape Town's ghettos, it is the prison in which most of the city's suspected criminals await trial. Everybody who is anybody in the city's underworld passes through there; it is the nerve centre of the Western Cape's illicit economy.

Two weeks is not nearly enough time to get to know a place like Pollsmoor, but it was enough to find out that Nongoloza's legacy was in great flux. To be sure, the prison was full of 26s, 27s and 28s, and it was clear that, after lockup time at 4 pm, they ran many of the sections. But it was also clear that much had changed since Keswa, Haysom, Lötter and Schurink penned their books. For generations, the Number gangs had been obsessively secretive organisations, their activities strictly confined to prison. But it was obvious that all that had changed in recent years, and dramatically so, certainly in the Western Cape at any rate.

The Western Cape's street gangs, which had transmogrified into massive criminal empires in the later apartheid years, had taken Number lore and spread it all over Cape Town's ghettos. The Firm, one of the region's two largest criminal organisations, had begun calling itself the 28s, recruiting and initiating new members with bastardised 28 rituals, and honing an organisational structure based vaguely on the 28s' original hierarchy. The Americans, the other of the two mega-gangs, had done much the same with the 26s.

In Pollsmoor itself, the relationship between the 26s and the 28s was more and more resembling the war between the Americans and the Firm on the outside. Old-time Number men, who had begun serving their sentences back in the 1970s and 1980s, grumbled that the sacred traditions of their gangs were being corrupted by the super-gangs on the outside. It seemed that an eccentric and intriguing response to apartheid's demise was being played out in the prisons, one that was not immediately intelligible to me. I wanted to know more. So, with the blessings of the Department of Correctional Services, I returned eight months later to write a book.

*

Why write such a book?

South Africa talks incessantly about crime, but dares not think about it much. For all the gallons of ink devoted to gruesome tales, few have ever attempted to write a serious history of South African lawbreaking. Why not?

The reason, I believe, is that such an attempt would unsettle too many shibboleths, in regard both to how we understand the past, and what we expect from the future. South Africa's old rulers never looked at crime too closely because doing so would illuminate the revolting underbelly of white domination. It was in its relationship with black criminals that white South Africa cultivated a great deal of its decrepitude and perversion. In the jails, white men played out their fantasies that blacks were animals, and in the process brought out the animal in themselves.

Yet South Africa's new rulers are also more than a little shy when it comes to thinking about crime, and the reasons are far more interesting. Read left-wing social histories of South Africa and you will see that they tell a series of brutal tales; a rural peasantry wrenched from its land and into the frontier towns of early industrial South Africa; an urban working class criminalised by a succession of pass laws; the forced removals of the high apartheid era, creating abandoned communities on the far-flung sand dunes of the Cape Flats and in the hinterland of the interior. In short, South African social history is a story of human beings shunted around the modern landscape and forced to live their lives in the most precarious and depraved of settings.

Yet read the left's political histories of anti-colonial resistance and they are, with few exceptions, about an almost angelic dignity. A genteel, mission-educated African middle class raises a polite voice of protest in the early years of the twentieth century, culminating in the formation of the African National Congress in 1912. As the century wears on and the gentlemanly voices of protest continue to fall on deaf ears, so the African intelligentsia hardens. Rationally, and in sober knowledge of the gravity of its decision, it turns to violence. As it does so, it reaches out to the popular classes – the industrial working class, the urban youth, the peasantry – and by the last quarter of the century, most of black South Africa is galvanised behind the liberation movement's moral authority.

It is as if the South African masses rose above their wretched circumstances and found an essential nobility which transcended time and place. The morbidity and violence of social life which finds such lucid expression in the left's social histories finds no expression in its political histories.

The reality, of course, is both more complicated and less comforting than that. Twentieth-century South Africa bore witness to a host of political and social movements that will never find a place in the lexicons of political orthodoxy; movements both politically articulate and chillingly anti-social; movements enraged by, and yet symptomatic of, the psychological damage inflicted by South African industrialisation.

Prison gangs are precisely that. They are a century old, avowedly political and yet horribly pathological. They illuminate the fact that crime too has a history and a future, a canon of myths and legends by which its practitioners understand what happened in the past and decide how to act in the present. As such, they get too close to the bone. They show us why generations of young black men lived violent lives under apartheid, and why generations more will live violently under democracy.

*

This book has ended up taking the form of a single life story. The man introduced to me as William Steenkamp joined the 28s in the late 1970s while still in his teens. By the time I met him, in October 2002, he was at the tail-end of a fraught but ultimately clean exit from the prison gangs.

The prospect of recording his story was attractive, not only because his time as an active 28 encompasses a long period of prison gang history, but also because the cornerstones of his life coincide with so many of the beacons of modern South African history. In the late sixties, for instance, his family was forcibly removed from its home in inner-city Cape Town's District Six; more than ten years later, he went to prison for the first time, not on a criminal charge, but as a detainee, picked up off the streets in the great uprisings of the late 1970s; another decade on, and he was making a living off the debris and confusion of South Africa's popular anti-apartheid insurrections. Within the confines of a single life, he demonstrates the proximity of the history of crime to the central fault lines that shape the world.

But this is a history of a peculiar kind. Prison gangs leave no record of their own activities. Things that happened twenty and thirty years ago are borne only in people's heads, the most unreliable repositories of truth. So, this book is as much about memory as it is about history. Indeed, a good deal of it is about how a particular human being has come to understand his own past and why.

PART ONE

POLLSMOOR PRISON, 2002-2003

1

THE PRISON AND THE MOUNTAIN

I first visited the Pollsmoor prison complex in February 2002 on a freelance writing assignment with Benetton's *Colors* magazine. The 50th issue of the publication was to be devoted to prisons, and its launch was to coincide with a Benetton campaign to reform Italy's penal system; the design house's champagne activism was at its finest. They sent writers and photojournalists to 12 prisons around the world. My task was to visit Pollsmoor with two photographers and an editor, every day for two weeks, and to write a 5 000-word essay on the institution.

We stayed at a holiday apartment block in Camps Bay, one of Cape Town's most upmarket suburbs, its California-stucco homes terraced along the western flank of Table Mountain. I woke at dawn each morning to an awesome view of the Atlantic Ocean; our flat was high up, close to the mountain road that links the City Bowl to the western suburbs, and the sea filled my large bedroom window.

Having grown up in Johannesburg, 1 400 km north of Cape Town, I had visited the city for holiday and relaxation several times. But I had never really absorbed its most remarkable feature: the way its social geography follows the contours of its natural geography; the way white supremacy has fashioned racial segregation around the presence of Table Mountain.

Yet this time, perhaps because visiting a maximum security prison makes you think about these things, it struck me in the face every morning on the drive to the jail: this unsettling congruity between mountain and people.

Table Mountain lies on its stomach, its face staring down into the city centre, its back stretching south about fifty kilometres into the long, narrow peninsula for which Cape Town is famous. The city's bourgeoisie lives along its slopes: below its face, the old, tastefully restored neighbourhoods of the inner city; along its eastern flank, the oak-lined streets and whitewashed double-storeys of Newlands, Claremont and Rosebank; on its western flank, a string of luxurious Atlantic Ocean settlements, built into the slopes, facing the sea.

That is bourgeois Cape Town, the most beautiful city I have ever visited. On our 30-km journey to Pollsmoor every day, we traversed its length. Our car climbed the back of Kloof Nek, then dropped into the City Bowl and sped south along the urban freeway, the ivy-clad buildings of the University of Cape Town on our right; then the southern suburbs, the early morning sun hitting the slopes of Devil's Peak; then further south, onto the M3, which takes you into the peninsula.

As you drive along the M3, the long spine of the mountain lies to your right, and the forests and vineyards of Constantia and Tokai roll gently into the valley. Wedged between the farmland and the luxury gated villages, circled by some of the most valuable real estate in Cape Town, is the Pollsmoor prison complex. It is the most unlikely setting for a jail. The first you see of it from the M3 are the flat-topped turrets, poking their heads out of the vineyards, an intimation of the ugliness below. You exit the highway, and from the elevation of the off-ramp the full catastrophe of the maximum security prison parades itself before you. Long blocks of light brown face brick, shaped into a digital figure of eight, stretch across the greenery of Tokai.

Once inside the gates, you realise that you have entered a little city. In the shadows of the turrets and the face brick of the maximum security prison, four smaller prisons stand: the female prison, the juvenile prison, and the medium and minimum security prisons for men. Each is a bare, single-storey structure surrounded by two layers of barbed wire.

Deeper inside the complex are triple-storey blocks of flats and small square houses, each enclosed by a waist-high fence, summer flowers on proud parade in the little gardens. It is the village where warders and their families live. Adjacent to the village lie the institutions of the warders' communal life: rugby fields and a swimming pool, a club house and recreation halls.

Right at the bottom of the grounds, up against the highway, are strips of farmland, where some of the pre-release prisoners work, and a caravan park for holiday-makers from South Africa's interior;

Pollsmoor is less than a ten-minute drive from the beaches of False Bay. 'Safest place in Cape Town,' a large-bellied vacationer told me on my first day at the prison. He smiled unconvincingly and stole a glance at the turret in the background.

Reading through the various prison diaries of people who have been interned in Pollsmoor, I discovered something of a dispute among them. Did they see the magnificence of their surroundings from the cells of the maximum security prison? 'The natural beauty was invisible to us from behind Pollsmoor's high concrete walls,' Nelson Mandela wrote in his autobiography. 'At Pollsmoor I first understood the truth of Oscar Wilde's haunting line about the tent of blue that prisoners call the sky.'

And yet Breyten Breytenbach, the writer and painter who was interned at Pollsmoor in the late 1970s for his work in the anti-apartheid underground, was haunted by the incessant presence of the landscape. 'Always,' he wrote in his memoir, 'at the turn of a corridor, dimly observed, or when you were out in the yard like an enormous voice standing over you – the mountain. The mountain with its richness of clothes as the seasons came and went.'

After a couple of days inside the walls, I discovered that Breytenbach was right. Through the jail's high windows, above the flat roof of the courtyard, peering in from the top of the wide staircases – each corner of the prison shows you a different segment of the mountain, and each segment stands in for a universe. The inmates I was to talk to in the coming two weeks displayed a sensory awareness – about the play between shadow and light, about the texture of colour – unavailable to those who live on the outside.

*

Pollsmoor is a journalist's paradise; it is an interminable labyrinth of pure story. You walk down a corridor, a journalist clutching a notebook, and you are assailed by a thousand groping hands. Everyone wants to stop you, to own you, to unload his tales into your notebook.

Our daily excursions through prison had to proceed at a snail's pace. In each communal cell we entered, prisoners would assemble to tell their stories like patients queuing before some special doctor who carries in his bag a rare and vital medicine. By the end of each day I was exhausted, countless threads of life stories tangled in a great knot in my head.

After you have heard a few tales, though, you realise that there is something wrong with them, but you can't put your finger on it. You are aware that something of the madness of the place has been transmitted into the narratives its inmates weave; but what, precisely?

About midway through our Pollsmoor tour, I sat up through the night reading *Cold Stone Jug*, the prison memoir of Herman Charles Bosman, South Africa's most celebrated short story writer. In the late 1920s and early 1930s, Bosman spent eight years in Pretoria Central Prison, having been convicted for murdering his stepbrother. 'Touch a long-term prisoner anywhere,' he wrote in his memoir, 'and a story would flow from him like a wound. They were no longer human beings. They were no longer people, or living creatures in any ordinary sense of the word. They were merely battered receptacles of stories, tarnished and rusted containers out of which strange tales issued, like djinns out of magic bottles.'

Transcribing Bosman's words now, having spent some time observing the politics of Pollsmoor, I think I understand why I found prisoners' tales so unsettling during that first trip to the jail. It is not that the prisoners who told the stories were dead, or no longer human, as Bosman suggests, but that the stories themselves had died during their transmission from the jail to my notebook. By the time they were safely in my satchel, they had absolutely nothing to do with the world from which they were uttered. Indeed, they were a screen between us journalists and the prison.

I would come to learn that prison is a world nourished by stories. It would be no exaggeration to say that the master story – that of Nongoloza, the God of South African prisoners – organises life behind bars. A prisoner's capacity to imbibe and retell that tale is probably his most potent weapon.

But that is precisely the point. Stories in prison are weapons, tools, the stuff of action; they are insinuated into the exercise of power. Severed from their practical functions, regurgitated in the contextless context of a journalist and his interviewee, their meanings drain away.

It was only much later, when I came to understand something of the prison's internal world, of the ancient, elaborate and often violent game between captors and convicts which animates prison life, that the remarkable power of tales prisoners weave came home to me.

Back then, on my first trip to Pollsmoor, I got just an inkling of this internal world, second-hand, thanks to the insightful commentary of Andrew Bosch, one of the warders who shepherded us around the prison. At about noon one day we were passing the kitchen wedged between B section and D section. Jets of hot air carrying the acrid smell of overcooked vegetables and boiled meat hit our faces. The air was milky and humid, the vinyl beneath our feet wet. The Rastafarians had already come and gone, their plastic lunch boxes crammed with carrots and cabbages, and the food teams were milling about the doorway, waiting to distribute meals to every corner of the prison.

Bosch and I leaned against a wall in the corridor and watched.

'That's the nerve centre of the prison,' he murmured quietly in my ear. 'This is the point from where inmates exercise power.'

I looked at him and smiled at the drama of his announcement.

'All 3 300 prisoners must be fed every day,' he said. 'And all the food comes from the same place – the kitchen. It is the only place that connects every point of the prison with every other. So those trolleys,' he said, pointing to the food team waiting in the doorway, 'they don't just carry food. They are the prison's telephone lines; they carry information and instructions.'

'What sort of information?' I asked.

'There is a high-ranking position common to all three major prison gangs called the Glas,' he replied, not really answering the question. 'He has two imaginary tools: a pair of binoculars that hang from his neck, and a bunch of 16 keys tied to his waist. The binoculars mean he can see everything that happens in the prison. The keys mean he can go anywhere in the prison; he can open any door.

'What this really means,' Bosch continued, 'is that he controls access to the kitchen. His job is to see to it that the right gang member is appointed to the food team.'

'But warders appoint inmates to the food teams,' I said gingerly; I didn't know Bosch well enough to talk easily with him about corruption.

He stepped closer and put his mouth to my ear. 'You can't keep the gangsters off the food teams,' he said. 'If you cut off the ability of gangs in your section to communicate with other sections, they get nasty. We have the safety of our members to think about.'

I thought about this for a while. 'Seems to me it's a big game,' I said. 'Your job is meant to be to keep the prison closed, the sections separated from each other. Theirs is to keep the prison open. But if you won, if you really kept the prison closed, they would stab you. So you lose on purpose.'

He warmed to the provocation. 'It's actually not that simple. If we really lost, if the prison was really open, this place would be so dangerous we would not have allowed you to come in. Weapons would pass between the sections every day, death sentences would pass between the sections. We would have to patrol the corridors with automatic weapons. It's about striking a balance. The sections must be mainly closed, but a little bit open.'

'Otherwise the gangsters will hurt you?'

'And each other. You see, prison gangs are paranoid, and if the prison is too closed, if they can't communicate with each other, there will be too much intrigue.'

'For example?'

'Take the 28s. Something terrible happens on D section. Some 28 breaks a serious rule. Now, say there is only one 28 Judge in the prison, and he is on B section. He must be part of the decision, he must have the final say in handing down sentence. So, a message passes from D section, through the kitchen to B section, and the Judge is informed of the offence. He thinks about it, sends a message back, and the messages pass back and forth until the highest structure of the gang has met, via the messengers in the kitchen, and sentence is passed.

'Now, in this situation, you would say that our task is to keep the sections closed. If the Judge can't pass sentence, it can't be carried out. But say the kitchen is closed, and D section makes a decision all on its own, and punishes the offender without the consent of the Judge. Rumours come to the Judge about what has happened, and he thinks some *laaitie* on D section has staged a coup, assumed the power of a Judge. Or the Judge hears a rumour that some upstart on D section has appointed himself treasurer and is hoarding all the money from the drug trade. Then the next thing that passes from B section, via the kitchen, is a knife, an order to kill.

'So, on the one hand you want to keep the sections closed, so the Judge can't order a stabbing. But then, you want to keep the sections open a little, otherwise the Judge will definitely order a stabbing.' He smiles at his paradox. 'It's difficult to know where the line should be drawn.'

*

The most interesting time of every day was lockup time, mid-afternoon. You needed neither a watch nor the use of your eyes to know when it was coming; were you to be blindfolded, sound and smell would inform you. If the staccato lyrics of American West Coast rap echoed from the cells around you, you were walking through territory dominated by the 26s and 27s. If you heard East Coast gangsta music, you were in 28 territory. I asked countless prisoners where this split in allegiance originated. They all laughed at me, as if I wanted access to a secret I had no right to know.

Accompanying the sound of the music, the sweet-sour fragrance of Mandrax fills your nose. It is a mid-afternoon smell; no warder is going to bust an inmate for smoking drugs after lockup. To find the master key, to open up the cell, to begin to search, takes too long. By the time the warder is in the cell the drugs are gone. So the odour of drugs tells you that you are on the seam separating night from day, lockup time from open time: the moment in the daily cycle when power shifts from warders to inmates.

Take off your blindfold, peer through the high barred window of a communal cell, and you see six men in the centre of the room talking in hushed tones. It is a daily meeting the gangs call the Valcross – two 26s, two 27s and two 28s: it inaugurates the end of the warders' day, the beginning of the gangsters' day. They are discussing how life is going to be organised for the next 15 hours.

The 28s are not allowed to talk directly to the 26s; the 27s mediate the flow of information. So, watching carefully, you notice that two of the six men remain in the centre of the room all the time. The other two couples step back and forth in turn, waiting patiently for their counterparts to finish.

What are they talking about? I asked many prisoners what life is like after lockup, and prisoners, being the compulsive storytellers they are, told me many things. But nothing could substitute for being there.

And so I tried to get inside after lockup. I struck up a friendship with a General in the 26s called Blitz. He was reputed to be volatile, unpredictable and mad, and it didn't take long to see why. I asked him why he was inside. He told me he had committed a triple murder in the early 1970s. He had been running an illegal shebeen in the Cape Flats ghetto of Bonteheuwel. The local street gang came round one afternoon and demanded protection money. He said no and closed his door in their faces. That night, his shebeen was fire-bombed.

The following morning, he locked up what remained of his shebeen and walked across Bonteheuwel, in broad daylight, with a pistol in his hand. He arrived at the house that headquartered the gang that had been bothering him and knocked on the door. One of the gangsters opened, and Blitz shot him in the face, walked into the living room, shot two more people, left the house and walked home, his pistol now tucked into the waist of his trousers. He immediately started packing a bag for prison.

It wasn't so much the content of Blitz's story that made my hair stand on end as the indignant self-righteousness with which he told it. I didn't want to begin to get inside the world in which his ethics made sense.

During that two-week visit to Pollsmoor I had a heavy cold. Meeting with Blitz, sitting on the edge of his bed, my nose ran constantly, and my questions were interspersed with uncontrollable coughing and spluttering. Blitz, who had nasal and respiratory problems of his own, immediately took pity. He barked instructions across his communal cell, and soon the cell's entire population was organised into a conveyer belt, delivering reams of toilet paper and mugs of water to his bed.

I told him how unsatisfactory my visit was proving to be, and he frowned like a host whose guest has just pronounced the food inedible.

'What can I do?' he asked.

'If I spend a night in your cell,' I asked, 'would I be safe?'

'You'd be my guest,' he replied. 'If anyone touched you, they'd regret they'd been born.'

I told Bosch the story and he threw his shoulders back and laughed. 'If Blitz says you'll be safe, you'll be safe,' he smiled. 'But if anyone found out I locked you in a cell, I'd lose my job.'

So I was left only with prisoners' interminable stories, which had everything and nothing to do with the place.

*

At the end of that first tour of Pollsmoor with *Colors* magazine, the head of the maximum security prison, Johnny Jansen, called us into his office to say goodbye. 'So,' he said, once we were all seated, 'I'm sure you've had a ball, wandering through my prison collecting horrible, sensationalist stories.'

Jansen was a heavy coloured man in his early fifties, a serious rugby player in his youth, and the residues of his once-powerful frame were still discernible beneath the layers of a sedentary middle age. Looking at his body, and the expression on his face, I was reminded that black and white South Africans share far more than they care to admit. His languid movements, his slow gestures, the patriarchal authority with which he carried himself, brought to mind the white Afrikaans *paterfamilias* of the suburbs. I could picture him at a Sunday braaivleis, a beer in one hand, a pair of barbecue tongs in the other, a coterie of other middle-aged men around him, talking rugby. Church on Sunday mornings and daughters home by nine.

The first time we met him, during our introduction to Pollsmoor, he had said something that made me wary.

'Many years ago,' he told us, 'I was called into this office by the head of the prison and I was racially abused. A white warder had called me a *hotnot* and I had given him a piece of my mind. You know what is a *hotnot*,' he said, for the benefit of our editor, who was European. 'It is a derogatory word for a coloured. It means you are a filthy little liar, that your dishonesty is in your blood. The head of the prison called me into this room, and all the senior managers were here. He told me I was a liar, that nobody had called me a *hotnot*. He said I must go back to my parents, because they had not brought me up properly.'

Jansen smiled to himself, then gestured round the room: 'Now I occupy this office. It's strange how things change, isn't it?'

At the time, Jansen's anecdote had unsettled me. He was among the first generation of black South African bureaucrats to run the post-apartheid administration. To my mind, the ones who were struggling, those who found themselves at the helm of a bureaucracy they could neither understand nor manage, they were the ones who told the kind of stories Jansen was telling us. They distracted themselves from their own drowning by incessantly rehearsing the grand narrative of their ascension to power.

So, throughout that two-week visit to Pollsmoor, I had this image in my head of a fumbling middle-aged man, charged with managing this inferno, collapsing under the burden. I imagined him sitting in his office steeped in memory, the story of how he came to run this place a heavy opiate transporting him away from the present.

I was wrong, very wrong. In the months to come, I was to discover that Jansen had begun an experiment of breathtaking audacity in Pollsmoor; he was one of those invisible heroes of the civil service, working his corner of the administration on home-grown wisdom and with little assistance, and performing small wonders.

When he took over Pollsmoor's maximum security prison in 1997, it was quite literally a battle zone. Warders patrolled the corridors armed with tear gas canisters and dogs. Gangsters, in turn, beat and sometimes killed any of their peers whom they suspected had spoken privately to a warder. It was an internecine war which had begun in the prisons of early-twentieth-century South Africa and had never abated.

Jansen, who had been recruited into the prisons service in the early 1970s as a lowly coloured employee, spent the dying years of apartheid organising coloured and African warders in open rebellion against the old guard. When he and his peers in the Pollsmoor prison complex finally came to office in the mid-1990s, the white men who had run the place for the past generation left in droves. Working-class men with little managerial experience, Jansen and his peers were administrators now, in charge of one of the most violent and chaotic institutions in the country.

He came armed with a philosophy as laudable as it was naïve: an evangelical belief that all men's souls are naturally gentle, that only the cruelty of history had made them bad. He identified with the gangsters behind the bars. The humiliations he had suffered as a coloured warder working in apartheid's jails were the same humiliations, he thought, that had turned many Cape Flats men into monsters. He believed that violence was born from self-loathing, that if he showed the Generals of the Number gangs how to respect themselves, their innate humanity would shine through.

A few months after he came to office, the dogs disappeared from Pollsmoor's corridors. And then the tear gas canisters too. For the first time in the institution's history, gang leaders watched warders walk into their cells unarmed.

In the awaiting-trial section of the prison, an anarchic place jam-packed with the soldiers and the generals of Cape Town's drug wars, Jansen identified the leaders of the Number gangs and walked into their cells to chat with them. They sat there aghast, wondering whether the new head was charmingly naïve or barking mad. He told them he needed their help in running the prison; he asked them to elect cell representatives to take complaints to warders, a representative to monitor the quality of food, and another to ensure that sick prisoners received adequate attention from the medical staff. He expressed his intention to start sports and recreations, and asked for the election of recreation officers. And then he spoke to the gang leaders about their lives on the outside, about being fathers and husbands. He asked them to describe their children and to volunteer their thoughts on what the Cape Flats would look like a generation from now.

Within a year of coming to office, Jansen had convened a forum of gang leaders and had invited several NGOs to run workshops. Motivational speakers talked of self-respect. There were workshops on aggression and on the nature of conflict. The forum's meeting room was host to bizarre scenes, awe-inspiring to the credulous, laughable to the cynical: a battle-scarred 26 dropping backwards off a table, caught inches from the ground by the hands of his foes in the 28s; hardened old assassins weeping hysterically for forgiveness.

Did Jansen succeed? That is still to come. It is a complicated story, part sad, part redemptive. The relationship between Christianity and Cape Flats gangsterism has always been an unsettling one. The ghettos are deluged with preachers and saviours; they have all saturated the Flats with their discourse, and the gangsters have happily imbibed their words. It is not unusual for a gang leader, facing trial for murder and rape, to step out of the dock and read a psalm to the packed court. There isn't a soldier on the Cape Flats who is not well versed in the morality of redemption, nor a Number gangster in Pollsmoor who cannot speak with conviction about the conditions of rehabilitation. Jansen had chosen to fight the most unforgiving of battles, one in which his enemy could regurgitate his discourse with eloquence and panache.

Suffice it to say, though, that if Jansen had not taken over Pollsmoor's maximum security prison in 1997, I would probably not have written this book. I entered the prison in the wake of his unlikely initiative; it cleared the space, among other things, for a journalist to walk the corridors collecting stories in his notebook. And I do know for certain that were it not for Jansen, the prisoner whose life this book will recount would not even have bothered to greet me.

Back on that day in February 2002, the last day of the *Colors* magazine crew's Pollsmoor tour, we sat in Jansen's office and the old patriarch scolded us for the gruesome stories he was sure we would write.

'No,' I protested. 'This is not going to be a horror story. We have heard what this prison was like a few years ago. We have seen the work you have done. That is the story we will write.'

Jansen stared back at us suspiciously. 'Nonsense,' he replied. 'It will all be sensationalism. Who have you been speaking to? Have you spoken to William Steenkamp?'

'We've spoken to Diamond,' I replied, 'the old 28 who is trying to leave the gang.'

'He's full of shit,' Jansen snapped back. 'Who else have you spoken to?'

'Farouk from the 27s,' I replied.

Jansen put his head in his hands and sighed deeply. I don't think it was bad PR that was troubling him: it was bad journalism. He knew that his prison housed the Western Cape's master bullshit artists; he himself had been bullshitted by them all in times past. He was concerned that the bullshitters had filled our young heads with misguided romance; seduced by the imaginary uniforms and the codes and the history, we would, he believed, turn these monsters of self-denigration, these perverse creatures of apartheid, into glorious icons.

'Why,' he asked, his head still in his hands, 'why on earth did nobody introduce you to William Steenkamp?'

2
WILLIAM-MAGADIEN

Eight months after the *Colors* assignment I was back in Pollsmoor, this time to write a book. The name William Steenkamp had stuck in my head. It was just a name; we had not met during the *Colors* assignment. But the circumstances in which I had heard of him, the irascible Jansen scolding us for not talking to William Steenkamp, seemed to tell a story in itself, and a man came to life in my imagination.

He was in his late forties or early fifties, I imagined, a veteran of the Number gangs. And he was Jansen's treasure, the one man those workshops of his really turned. I imagined that he had spent his entire adult life in the Western Cape's jails, steeped in Number history and law, a great deal of blood on his hands. At the approach of middle age, battle-weariness and the feeling of bones growing old crept up on him with stealth and menace, and robbed him of his faith in his own cult. He found himself, I believed, at the helm of an organisation for which he no longer cared. He was stuck; he had no way out.

And then Jansen came along, his gateway from hell. I had read several accounts of the classic scenario in which the enlightened warder turns the long-term prisoner. The key to the warder's genius is his capacity to listen. He is silent, refuses to judge, and for the prisoner, the benign silence makes the warder a blank canvas. The rich colours pour out of the wells of his humanity, all the suppressed fears and wishes he had ever entertained, and he paints his new identity all over the canvas the warder has become. The prisoner's experience is one of life-changing epiphany. His life is divided into before and after, and the warder is the seam dividing the two; the prisoner loves him deeply.

He was the sort of man I wanted to write about. I was frightened of penning a story about hell; I wanted to find a redemptive tale, to write about someone who had journeyed to the heart of the inferno but had come out the other side. I was also wary of developing a relationship with somebody who had not come out the other side. Pollsmoor was full of the most sophisticated tricksters; I didn't want to tie myself to someone who would haunt me.

There is a sense in which the William Steenkamp of my imagination tallies with the real man, but only in the most banal and uninteresting ways. Journeys are interesting for their detours; they are never as simple as the narrative I conjured. I met him on my third or fourth day back at Pollsmoor. I was walking through the entrance of the maximum security prison along with a warder I had been shadowing. Three prisoners, dressed in the bright orange overalls inmates must wear when outdoors, filed past us.

'That's the man you've been looking for,' the warder said. 'That's Steenkamp.'

One of the three men turned round. The warder introduced us.

Steenkamp was small and balding, in his early to mid-forties perhaps, and he was astonishingly thin. The bone structure of his face was strikingly visible, high cheekbones and a pointed, protruding chin. He appeared to use his chin in the way other people gesticulate with their hands, pointing it this way and that as he spoke or listened, the movement of his head darting and nervous.

He spoke with studied politeness, apologised for the brevity of our meeting, said he had a workshop to attend. As if to compensate, he rummaged through his satchel and handed me a few pages of typescript.

'This is my speech for the event on Saturday,' he said, 'when the Minister of Correctional Services is coming to Pollsmoor. Read it and tell me later what you think.'

I went to the administrator's office at the front of the prison, sat on one of the chairs that lined the walls, and read.

The speech began with a striking apology: 'I would like to ask you to be silent for a moment to pay tribute to all the victims and families of those who died in prison for the struggle and those who were killed on the outside, by the hands of myself and my fellow brothers. We hope that their families will find it in their hearts to forgive us for all the pain and suffering we have caused.'

Suddenly, he veered off in another direction: 'I salute the 26, 27 and 28 groups for showing courage. They stood up and fought for our rights under the apartheid regime, for us to be treated in a humane way. But when democracy came to South Africa everyone forgot the blood that we shed in prison for the sake of democracy. Instead we were labelled as gangsters. Let me put the record straight: we were never gangsters. With our souls and our minds we were freedom fighters. We put our bodies and lives on the line for democracy, and we are doing it yet again for change.'

Then came what appeared to be a threat: 'Please don't disappoint us yet again, for the results will be irreversible.'

Finally, Steenkamp went on to write what every prisoner feels, and what I too would write were I a prisoner: that the world is conspiring to keep inmates behind bars the rest of their lives, that there is no path out of jail.

'We know that jobs are scarce, but we can make bricks, blocks, tables, chairs. We can renovate state institutions. To be honest, we can do anything. Business Against Crime complains so much about crime, but why don't they do something constructive instead of spending R25 million on surveillance cameras in the Cape Town city centre to monitor the movements of blacks and coloureds, who are all suspects …

'It is no use us prisoners changing,' he continued, 'if the world outside is still the same. You are still labelled a criminal when you leave, which means you don't get a job. And inside here, we are told when to eat, sleep, walk, exercise, play sport, when to watch TV and when to phone our families. How can you expect a person enslaved in this mentality to have responsibility on the outside? That is why we always come back.'

It was not what I had expected from the man Jansen had begged us to talk to. It was orthodox Number gangs propaganda, and I had heard it countless times during the *Colors* tour of Pollsmoor.

Since the end of apartheid, journalists, social workers, NGOs and government officials had begun speaking to members of the Number gangs, which for the past century had been entirely mute. The gangs, in turn, wove a single discourse, with impressive speed, and offered it to the world. The mythical history around which they were organised was never spoken about, nor the rank structure, the arcane labyrinth of rules and codes, nor the famous inter-gang disputes known to every gang member.

Instead, the gangs offered a press conference history of themselves. They would begin with the conditions of apartheid prisons: no beds, only a scrawny mattress and two blankets so thin, an old Number veteran told me, 'that when you put them together and held them up to the morning sun, the light would still blind you'; watery porridge for breakfast, served outdoors, even in the rain, so that 'water from the sky would merge with the water in your bowl and the little flakes of porridge would float to the surface like drowned fish'; the medieval torture racks on which prisoners were lashed; the 'carry-ons' – where warders would encircle a prisoner and beat him senseless with bats and sticks; the 'spare diet solitary confinement' – 15 consecutive days in a windowless cell, fed a diet with no salt.

Then the official history would move to the story of resistance: how the Number gangs fought for beds, for television sets, for the right to wear watches so that prisoners could retrieve their control of the passing of time, for decent meals. It was the simplest of struggles, for rudimentary human dignity, and countless people died for it. There are bodies in the fields surrounding farm prisons, the history states, and bodies in the Atlantic Ocean from the prison on Robben Island. The authorities killed us in droves and in secret, because of our simple struggle for beds and watches and decent meals.

Finally, the narrative would arrive at the present. Why do we still exist? Apartheid is gone, we have the privileges we fought for. We wear watches, sleep in beds, eat healthy meals. Why not close shop? Because, the answer goes, you do not abandon a century-long struggle on the grounds that you appear to have won. You hang around to defend your victory. Democratic South Africa is a volatile place. Each new parliamentary session sees some politician launch a populist campaign against criminals. Just three years ago, they wanted to take away our television sets on the grounds that we did not suffer enough for our crimes. And we stopped that. We made these prisons ungovernable until they reversed their decision. So we are still here, waiting, and the moment anyone tries to take away the gains we took a hundred years to win, we will strike back.

That is the story, the press conference history any senior Number member will recount if you ask him about his organisation. And Steenkamp's speech was an abbreviated version. Was this Jansen's man, the reformed gangster? I wondered about the politics of this prison, which was still indecipherable to me. I wondered to whom Steenkamp's speech was addressed, what it meant to those who knew this place well.

*

I met him in his cell later that afternoon. He had a room of his own, an unusual privilege in this overcrowded prison. I would learn later that Jansen had given him this precious solitude, and that there were people who were not happy about it.

His cell was perhaps two-and-a-half metres by one-and-a-half metres; there was just enough space for a double bunk, a toilet, a basin and a waist-high cabinet. His window overlooked the exercise courtyard and was high up near the ceiling; he had to stand on the basin to look out. There were a handful of family photographs on the wall, and a calendar poster of Celine Dion. An assortment of jewellery boxes and ornamental tins were arranged across the top of the cabinet, and an old black bible, on which was written 'Magadien: JR'.

I handed the speech back to him, told him I found it interesting and then said nothing. He looked at me, then at the speech, and began talking, as if he was delivering the speech, as if he was on a podium.

'Journalists have been spreading a lot of lies about the Number,' he began. 'I hate people who do not do their jobs properly. Where is your research? Why can't you tell the truth?'

'What sort of lies do we tell?' I asked.

'Like that the 26s and 28s are at war. It's not true. We sit side-by-side in the same cells and laugh and talk together. Go to the communal cells on B section. Will you see people fighting there?'

'Where do the lies come from?' I asked.

'The problem is that people who do not have the authority to speak, talk in front of the television camera. Like Mogamat on Special Assignment,' he said, referring to *Cage of Dreams*, an award-winning documentary on Pollsmoor's gangs that had recently been made, 'and Skaapkop on Fokus. Neither are Generals; both claim to be. Both claim that the 28s sodomise people. They are lying.

'And look at Mogamat and Skaapkop now. Mogamat was beaten up in his home. Skaapkop is walking around this prison waiting for a knife in his back. That's what happens when irresponsible journalists talk to liars.'

'You're saying people are not raped in prison?' I asked.

'Ja, there are those who break the rules and sodomise. Eight, nine years is a long time to be inside, without a woman, and there are prostitutes on the inside, so a 26 might pay somebody for sex. Or, if they have no money to pay for sex, they may use force. But people are not sodomised the way you read about in the newspapers. It is not true that to join the 28s, you must be fucked in the arse. That is propaganda spread by our enemies. I am a 28, a proud 28. Don't come here to spread rumours about us. If a member rapes somebody he is severely punished. Write that. Write the truth.'

*

Steenkamp did not get to deliver his speech the day the Minister of Correctional Services came to Pollsmoor. The event was held in the central courtyard of the prison, a bold move, the prison's managers believed. Taking a host of dignitaries into the bowels of this notorious place was to be a sign of how things had changed since the end of apartheid.

The prison's corridors, usually jammed with idle prisoners and enveloped in a cacophony of noise, were empty and silent, the prisoners locked in their cells for the day. The guests shuffled through the labyrinth, photocopied direction arrows posted at every twist and turn, the stiletto-footsteps of the important men's wives echoing back to us from the walls. It was the first time I had heard an echo in these corridors, the only moment during my visit that the noise ceased.

A giant marquee stretched across the length and breadth of the courtyard. It was strange to see the place so transformed. The stylised choreography of prisoners' exercise time had given way to the stiff formations of the official event. The VIP table on the stage was almost as wide as the courtyard itself; the uniformed officers and suited politicians sat there, some stiff and glum, others leaning back luxuriously in their chairs. The minister himself sat on a wide, cushioned chair. He was a very big man, his bulk encased in a black, dog-collared robe.

The audience was divided into three groups: invited guests at the front, inmates' families in the middle, dense rows of orange-overalled prisoners packed into the back. Out on the periphery and above us, hundreds of faces stared intently from the cell windows that overlooked the courtyard. I was seated in the family section. I lit a cigarette, and a moment later a hand touched my ankle. I looked down to find a prisoner on the ground, squeezed between the chairs. 'Please, brother. Pass us a smoke.'

The minister spoke at great length, and what with the heat and the distractions of all the people around me, it was difficult to follow him. He spoke of rehabilitation, of employment, of growing vegetables for impoverished children within prison grounds. At one point he said, addressing the prisoners at the back: 'You are here because you have done terrible things to people on the outside. Don't do terrible things to people on the inside. Don't rape people here. The gangs are unacceptable and must go.'

The prisoners listened in polite silence. They always listen. They always imbibe the words of authority and churn them around with their own words, making a strange mixture of the two; Number Generals talk of the imperatives of reintegration, and their soldiers speak of growing vegetables for the children of the poor.

I observed the minister's bodyguards – three flanking him on the stage, two watching the audience from the sides of the marquee – and I wondered whether his office had been informed of what had happened at Pollsmoor during the preceding week. Five days before the big event, a rich crack dealer from Tamboerskloof, Rashid was his name, had been interned at the maximum security prison. A drug lord who arrives at a prison brings with him the prospect of a great deal of money, and everyone wants a piece of him. Warders carry his merchandise into jail in their tog bags, and prisoners returning from court carry it in sheaths stuck up their anuses. A rock sells in prison for about double its street value – what with the bribing of warders, the increased risk and the conditions of scarcity – and the group that entices the crack dealer has done well.

On his second day in prison, Rashid was recruited into the 26s, and by evening the gang's rank and file were threatening open rebellion. For Rashid's admission into the gang had bypassed all its ancient mores of initiation. You are meant to begin by committing an act of violence, you must spill blood, and when the warders beat you for your transgression, you must not cry out in pain. Once you have come back from solitary confinement, you are passed from one senior member to another, and slowly taught gang language – *sabela* – aspects of the history of Nongoloza, the arcane rules of your position in the gang.

Recruitment is meant to take place only in the sentenced section of the prison. It has always been considered too risky to induct an awaiting-trial prisoner. Should he be acquitted in the middle of his training, he is released into the world a half-caste. Lingering in this no-man's-land, the law of the Number not properly internalised, he is considered dangerous.

Rashid's recruitment broke all the rules – his instant taking of rank without learning or violence, the fact that he was awaiting trial – and the leadership of the 26s soon saw that they were not going to get away with it. So they improvised, shored up some of the old initiation rules, and made a ruling; Rashid would stab somebody at the minister's gathering – a warder or a *frans* (a prisoner who is not a member of a gang), I am not sure – in front of all the invited guests. And if Rashid himself was not permitted to attend the event, if he was stuck in his cell, another 26 would stab on his behalf.

A warder I had been shadowing called Chris Malgas got wind of the plan shortly after it was hatched; the faction in the 26s that disapproved of Rashid's recruitment had whispered in his ear. Before the 26s parliament could meet to make formal the decision to stab, he transferred six of its members to a prison on the Boland. They were to return to Pollsmoor the following Monday, two days after the minister and his marquee had gone.

Sitting with the inmates' families, I observed Chris standing watchfully at the periphery of the marquee. I left my seat and went to join him.

'What's up?' I asked.

'Nothing,' he replied, not looking at me, his eyes scanning the rows of prisoners.

*

When the VIPs had finally finished speaking, the meeting was opened to the floor. A representative of one of the warders' unions took the microphone, turned his back to the VIPs on the stage, and addressed the prisoners. You could see from the excitement in his body language that he was going to play to the crowd.

'You go to prison on a charge of common assault,' he began, 'and actually, it was just self-defence; you were saving your own life. But the judge wasn't interested because you don't dress nice, you don't speak nice.' The sea of orange overalls stirred, and a murmur of approval rose from the back of the marquee. 'When you get out,' he continued, 'that's it; your record says you're a criminal. Nobody will ever give you a job. So you become a criminal, because that's all that's left to you.' Some prisoners in the audience began to shout their assent, and, emboldened now, the warder turned to face the minister. 'The system, sir,' he shouted, 'is a factory for criminals. It makes criminals out of decent people.'

The orange overalls exploded into noise and dance. Every prisoner rose from his chair. Packed together, with no space for movement, they danced by hopping on the balls of their feet, spinning their bodies in tight circles. The minister rested his chin on the palm of his hand and watched this strange performance of human spinning-tops until it ceased. Then he gazed into the distance impassively.

A number of the other invited guests spoke. Some took their cue from the excitable warder and whipped the prisoners up into their awkward dance. Others spoke in long monotones, and the prisoners sat upright and attentive in their chairs, as they had done when the minister delivered his speech.

Finally, the floor was opened to the overalled men. They left their neat rows, gathered in two groups, and all, as one, pointed their fingers at the master of ceremonies. I saw Steenkamp in the centre of one of the two groups, clutching his speech in both hands, his chin pointing nervously in the direction of the stage. In the middle of the second group, also clutching his papers and shuffling around, was an inmate I would get to know well: Joshua Saul. He was 60 years old, positively ancient by prison standards; I was to see him walking the corridors of B section every day on failing hips.

He had come to prison in 1969 for housebreaking and theft, and had been due for release in 1972. About nine months into his sentence he joined the 26s, and within a year had been sentenced to death for murdering two inmates. ('Why did you kill?' I asked him some time later. 'The warders were taking control of the prison,' he replied. 'They were using a group of inmates to destroy us: so we had to destroy them. The spies had to go.') He spent two years on death row, then was granted a reprieve: 25 years, followed by a long period of parole. He was released in 1996, but returned to jail two years later, having been convicted on a charge of drug possession.

The master of ceremonies recognised the sea of hands around Joshua, and the old man rose to address the ceremony. He had a deep, mesmerising voice and an extraordinary gift for using the power of silences and pauses: when he began speaking, a hush came over the gathering.

'I entered the prisons of this province in 1969,' he began, and prisoners around him gasped and whistled. 'I have been told that I am being freed early next year.' He paused and twisted his mouth into a rictus of sarcasm. 'Freed,' he repeated. 'What civilised man would describe the fate that awaits me as "free"? What man who knows the conduct of this department's parole officers would call the condition that awaits me "freedom"?

'I will be housebound. I will not be able to look for work. The meals in my stomach will come from the generosity of my sister's husband, a decent working man. He will be feeding an old criminal, giving him a bed and shelter. This department's parole officers will come banging at the door of his family home at two in the morning, three in the morning, four in the morning, to see if I am there. This is a decent man's house. He must go to work in the morning. The kids must go to school. How long will he tolerate the banging on his door in the middle of the night? How long will he feed the caged old criminal I am until he throws me onto the streets? Do you know a respectable family man who wants the law banging down his door in the night, for all the neighbours to hear?'

'No,' the sea of orange overalls murmured in response. 'He will throw you out.'

'Mister Minister,' Joshua continued, 'I am watching the world through a sheet of glass. I am not in it. The glass is invisible, sir, the glass of parole. I do not want my freedom, I want my life.'

He sat down and the inmates erupted once more. This time, the noise was deafening; the minister twitched uncomfortably, and the master of ceremonies looked at his watch. Before the commotion had died down, the meeting had been closed, the VIPs readying themselves to file off the stage. The group of inmates around Steenkamp began remonstrating, waving their arms and shouting at nobody in particular. Steenkamp himself was gesticulating with his hands, the text of his speech flying all over the place.

Johnny Jansen, who had been sitting anonymously in the audience, suddenly appeared among the demurring prisoners in his crisp uniform. I was about fifty metres away and could not hear what he said. His body language was calm, his face serene, and he gestured with open hands, his palms turned to the ground. Within a few minutes, the prisoners had quietened and began to drift away. Jansen and Steenkamp were left alone, in the middle of the empty marquee. I started walking towards them, and as I did so I heard Steenkamp's angry, plaintive voice. He was screaming at Jansen for his life's worth, a torrent of abuse and cursing so fast I could not make out what he was saying.

Jansen waited politely for Steenkamp to calm down, then looked at him closely. '*Moenie so emosioneel wees nie, Steenkamp*,' he said gently. '*Dis niemand se skuld nie*.' 'Don't be so emotional, Steenkamp. It's nobody's fault.'

Steenkamp stared at Jansen gravely, folded up his speech, put it in his pocket, and kicked the ground. Jansen watched him patiently. The image that came to mind was of a father and his spoiled son.

*

The next time I met Steenkamp was in the contact visit room at the maximum security prison. There had been a hitch in the process of getting my research application approved somewhere in the bowels of Correctional Services head office in Pretoria. I was not allowed into the prison proper again until the problem had been sorted out.

The visiting room resembled the classrooms of my childhood: rows of government-issue desks and diminutive wooden chairs. The desks were tiny, and Steenkamp and I sat close together, his breath brushing my face every time he spoke.

He was agitated and began muttering about conspiracies that were being hatched against him.

'Last week, a warder caught me smoking dagga,' he explained. 'It was seven in the evening, long after lockup. I was all alone in my cell, hurting nobody. He sprang on me. Now the institutional committee wants to downgrade my privileges.'

I was not sure what to say. I said I was sorry.

'I have many enemies in this prison,' he continued in his

impeccable English. 'There are warders here who do not like what Mr Jansen is doing. They believe that if they destroy me, they will destroy Mr Jansen: show the world that his achievements are nonsense. When I was caught with ganja, the news spread like wildfire. It was a propaganda victory for them.'

I asked him why there were warders who wanted to destroy Johnny Jansen.

'Two reasons,' he replied immediately. 'First, they don't like treating prisoners as human beings. They prefer running warehouses: taking us out in the mornings, locking us up in the afternoons, going home. Jansen's trying to make them do their jobs.

'And second,' he said. 'Some of them make money smuggling drugs. They prefer the old way, Number on one side with its knives, warders on the other with their dogs and their tear gas. When there is total war, it is easier to work for the Number.

'Their prize would be to push me back into the 28s. That would show the world that Mr Jansen's vision is a pipe dream, that all this talk is bullshit, that the only way to deal with a prisoner is to smack him.'

I asked him what position he held in the 28s.

'It is supposed to be a secret,' he replied, 'but since I am no longer in active service, I will tell you: I am a Magistrate.'

'You preside in the 28s court and pass sentence on the accused?' I asked.

'Perhaps if we get to know each other better,' he replied, 'I will explain to you one day.'

'Did you train someone to take your place as Magistrate after you retired?' I asked.

He frowned. The question appeared to make him irritable: 'Why train somebody for the post when there is no use for the Number any more? After democracy came in 1994, the reason for the Number disappeared.'

'That is a minority position,' I replied. 'The Number is very strong in here.'

'Gangsterism is strong in here,' he sneered, 'not the Number. The Number is dead. What we have now are drug lords using our history in vain. Look at what happened with Rashid. It's sick. These young boys with their drugs and their guns pretending to know about Nongoloza. This place is rotten to the core.'

*

I was considering giving up on Steenkamp. I suspected that he was what prisoners call *tronk mal* – 'prison crazy'. On the three occasions I had met him, he had offered three rival identities, and I suspected that he had lost control of the vicissitudes, that they dragged him from one persona to another. First, he was the ardent defender of the Number, in combat against the enemies at the fortress walls. Next, the Number had long ago died an ignominious death. He himself embodied the memory of its heyday: he was a monument to a dead colossus. And finally, there was Steenkamp the tantrum-prone child, stamping his foot before his warder-father.

Asking others about Steenkamp didn't help much either. In this world of shadows, no story was consistent with the next. One 28 I spoke to brushed Steenkamp aside with a dismissive wave of the hand. 'Every word he speaks to the *boere* is mandated by the 28s,' he said. 'He is the gang's puppet, dangled in front of Jansen on a set of strings.' Another 28 told a conflicting tale: 'For as long as the Number has existed,' he said, 'there have been people like Steenkamp. They set themselves up as intermediaries between the *boere* and gangs. They think they can live in both worlds. They can't. They are on no-man's-land. They get killed.'

*

It was at my fourth meeting with Steenkamp that we finally made a connection and I began to understand. He was no less sane than I; the vicissitudes I had witnessed spoke to something far more compelling than madness.

We were sitting in his cell, Steenkamp on the bed with his head bowed under the double bunk. I pointed to the bible on the dresser, with the inscription 'Magadien: JR'.

'What does that mean?' I asked.

'JR is my gang name,' he replied. 'I got it when I joined the 28s in the 1970s. Go to any prison in this province and ask who is JR. It's me.'

'And Magadien?'

He looked at me with what I took to be a wounded, indignant expression. 'That is my name,' he replied. 'Magadien Wentzel.'

'And William Steenkamp?'

'There is no William Steenkamp. Well, there is. He is some white man living in Paarl. We took his ID book when we stole his car. I was using that name when I was arrested this last time.'

'How long have you been Steenkamp?'

He shrugged. 'I will make a request for my conviction record. Then you will see. I have served five or six sentences over the last 20 years. Each time under a different name.'

I laughed quietly. 'How does it feel,' I asked, 'to be called by some strange white man's name?'

He stared at me deadpan. 'You joke,' he said. 'It's no joke. What would happen if I died in this prison tomorrow? They would see the name "Steenkamp", and they would think "Christian", and they would hold my body for a week. "Magadien" is a Muslim name. A Muslim must be buried before the sun sets.'

He stopped and stared at the wall for some time, thinking of his grave. 'There would be this tombstone that says "Steenkamp",' he continued. 'Would there be any evidence that a man called Magadien Wentzel had walked this earth? I would vanish with my death. As if I had never existed.'

'Magadien is a Muslim name,' I said. 'But you have written it on a Christian bible.'

'You're confused,' he smiled. 'Let me warn you, the deeper we get into my life, the more confused you will get. Even I am confused. My mother, she is the Wentzel in my life; she is a Muslim. My foster-mother, in whose house I grew up, her name is Mekka; she is a Christian. When I was a child I went to church. I sang in the choir. When I was told who my real family was, I was sent to mosque. So you could say I am confused.

'My father was a Christian. But I am not sure if he was really my father. If he was my father, why didn't they give me his surname? Why Wentzel? Why my mother's name?

'When I get out of jail, I am going to ask my mother for forgiveness for the things I have done to her. I will cry in front of her, and then I will sit her down and ask her some difficult questions. I want to know who my father is, and when I find out, I want to take his name. And then my sons must take his name. JR and Steenkamp must disappear. I owe it to my children that they know who they are. And to their children and the children after that. I have fucked up my life. Why must I also fuck up the lives of children who have not yet been born? Why must they wander around nameless like me?'

'Does so much hinge on a name?' I asked.

He looked at me in astonishment. 'You have never had to question that you are Steinberg,' he said. 'There are Steinbergs as far back as you can go. And there will, God willing, be Steinbergs way into the future. So you don't understand.

'Last time I was released from jail was 1996. I swore to myself I was going to become a family man. I was offered a house in Betty's Bay by the Firm, the biggest gang in the Western Cape. They wanted me to sell drugs. I said no, thanks very much, I have unfinished business in Cape Town. I went back to my wife, even though I had serious problems with her, because I wanted my kids to see their mother and father together. And then I went to the employment office and waited in a line for days.

'I finally got a job as a driver for a glass outfit in town. I was good. I am a quick learner and a hard worker. Soon I learned how to be a glazer, to work with glass. But I had this ID in my pocket that said William Steenkamp and the boss, Mr Morris, called me Steenkamp, this man who does not exist. I could not work under my real name. You don't get a job when you have a record like mine.

'At home, the phone would ring, one of my kids would answer and someone would ask to speak to Steenkamp. I couldn't open a bank account. I couldn't get a real driver's licence. One day, my kids would grow up and marry. How can they introduce their new wives to this Steenkamp? Where would they go to get the name Wentzel: their real name?

'So you know what I did, I started stealing from Mr Morris, one of the kindest men I have ever known. I used his invoice book to get thousands of rands worth of glass and I set up my own business after hours. I think I destroyed him. I think he went bankrupt because of me. It is one of the many things I must find out when I get out of prison. Anyway, I knew I would get caught. I wanted to get caught. I couldn't live this life. I wanted to be in jail where I was JR. And you know, when they found me out, when the police came looking for me and I left my house and started my life on the run, I was quite relieved. I wanted to go back to jail so this lie would end.

'And I came back here. I was JR, a Magistrate in the 28s, a very big deal. I was back where I was before 1996. My life goes round in these circles. You ask why a name is so important. I am telling you why. I need to be Magadien Wentzel to live a proper life.'

*

As I write these words, a tall pile of transcripts lies on my desk: more than fifty hours of conversation with Magadien Wentzel, conducted over a period of six months in late 2002 and early 2003. It is difficult to know where to begin.

My initial fantasy about Magadien and Johnny Jansen, the prisoner who is turned by and grows to love the enlightened warder, was more or less correct. When Magadien came back to Pollsmoor in 1998, having robbed Mr Morris blind, he did indeed resume his position in the upper echelons of the 28s. Several months into his stay at Pollsmoor, he and Jansen clashed after an instruction came from Correctional Services head office to remove the television sets from prisoners' cells. Magadien had written a letter to the head warder, telling him that the corridors of the prison would flow with warders' blood unless the televisions came back. That was their first substantive encounter: the warder facing down the violent gangster, negotiating the safety of his staff.

The timing was fortuitous. The gangster was tiring of JR; he was in the early, still inchoate stages of his search for Magadien Wentzel. And Jansen was new and energetic, full of hope and ideas. When he began speaking of families and children and the future, and of the barren nihilism of those who think only of the here and now, the gangster began to melt: it was what he had been wanting to hear for some time.

The seduction of a gangster by a smart warder makes for compelling drama; but that is not, I would venture, the most interesting aspect of the story.

The agents of change at Pollsmoor are Christians. At their worst, they understand change as a great rupture. The old self mired in sin is swept away by the new self touched by God. It is a rebirth; history vanishes; the infinite complexity of a human being's past is washed away like shit in a sewer.

It is never like that, of course. The changed one is stuck with his past. He tries to rework it, to reinterpret, but he is not fully in control, he is no alchemist; there are ghosts that refuse to go away.

Nor is he sure whether it is better to remember or to forget. Entire episodes of his life lie buried. He feels he must retrieve them to move forward, that he must recall, for instance, how his mother betrayed him if he is to forgive her. Yet he is not sure that he has the stomach to remember. He wonders whether stepping into the dark zone will not make him a monster. And as for his future, it does not yet exist; he is trying to invent it. But that too is not entirely within his control; those who must people his future also peopled his past, and they have been hurt; they are not quick to forgive.

When I met Magadien Wentzel, he inhabited a no-man's-land far lonelier than the one that separates Pollsmoor's gangsters and warders. It was this no-man's-land I mistook for madness – a hell of identities not yet erased, and identities not yet formed. He was not sure what do with the 25 years he had spent in the vast universe that is the cult of the 28s. Sometimes he would draw a line between the present and the past. The camp was a true brotherhood when he joined, he would say, but the end of apartheid and the invasion of the drug trade has made it rotten and meaningless. He wanted to erect plaques in every prison, naming those who had died, and making public the secret history of the gang for all to see. He wanted to destroy the 28s' future by reifying its past; he wanted to give meaning to his own future by dignifying his own past. At other times, the Number still existed in its pure form, but always somewhere else – in the prisons of the Western Cape hinterland, in the heads of veterans who still wandered the Cape Flats, but never at Pollsmoor. 'Those people in the 26s who were transferred when they tried to recruit Rashid,' he told me, 'there is a terrible fate waiting for them where they are going. The Number is still pure in Brandvlei Prison. They will be punished for corrupting the Number.'

As for his future, away from prison and from the Number, he was trying to create it on the telephone in the corridor outside his cell, the credit on his R20 Telkom card stretched far too thin. From the debris of a wretched past – estranged children mothered by different women, a bitter mother, a foster-mother who had long given up hope – he was attempting to make a family. The voices at the other end of the telephone line were hauntingly ambivalent; they wanted to believe, but they were not sure.

When I met Magadien he was eight months away from having

served his sentence, and he was terrified. There were times when I too was scared. Our relationship took us places a subject should probably never go with a journalist. We would sit in Magadien's cell and he would shore up those fragments of his history he could remember. Then I would go out into Cape Town, searching for the spectres of his past, and return with news.

It is no joke to have your memories tested by the memories of others, relayed second-hand, by a journalist. You lie on your bed, waiting for ten o'clock, the hour of your appointment, and you wonder which piece of your past the journalist will bring you now. Will it be something that betrays the unreliability of your sense of who you are and who you were? Will the journalist bring an event long buried, buried because you cannot afford to remember?

During the months of our conversations in his cell, Magadien and I revisited his past a hundred times, and it changed on each occasion. We would discuss the days of his mid-adolescence in the Cape Flats township of Hanover Park, the very beginning of his life as a gangster, and it would yield a colourless narrative, dulled by years of forgetfulness. A month later, I would return with a map of his Hanover Park neighbourhood, as it was when he was young, divided into rival territories. He would follow the gang turf boundaries with his finger and suddenly things would come back to him, viciously alive and horribly painful. He would curse himself for having buried vast tracts of his story, pacing his cell in frustration. 'I have forgotten my own life,' he would say. 'I was too fucking angry to take notice of my own life. I'm scared I will never get it back.'

The chapters that follow recount my and Magadien's journey into his past. But before we get there, I want to tell you two stories. The prison-gang world Magadien inhabits is truly arcane, and I want you to get inside it, to begin to understand it. The best place to start is with a tale Magadien and several other prisoners told me. It is the master-tale that shapes the world behind bars, and that animated Magadien's understanding of the world for the first two-and-a-half decades of his adult life; the mythical story of Nongoloza and Kilikijan, the two original bandits, that has been passed down from one generation of prisoners to the next throughout the twentieth century.

3
NONGOLOZA AND KILIKIJAN

There are two Nongolozas. The first is a real-historical figure who walked the actual streets of early Johannesburg. The second is the mythical Nongoloza, whose story was invented and transmitted by thousands of South African prisoners. I will start with the first, the flesh-and-blood man who beguiled and frightened early industrial South Africa with his banditry. For the most part, I recount his story as told by the historian Charles van Onselen, who gathered the scant evidence of his real existence into a slim biography – *The Small Matter of a Horse*. Were it not for Van Onselen, we would know next to nothing about him.

'Nongoloza' is a name the bandit adopted at the height of his underworld reign. He was born Mzuzephi Mathebula, the son of Zulu-speaking parents, in 1867, either in Zululand or in the British colony of Natal, 12 years before the British defeated Cetswayo, the last independent Zulu monarch.

All we know of Nongoloza's youth is what he himself has left us. In the 1912 Department of Prisons annual report, there is a thin, three-page memoir which the outlaw dictated to his captors from his prison cell in Pretoria. He tells us that during his teens, he and his family lived on a white-owned farm 'near to where the river Tugela takes its course from the mountains', probably the Bergville district of Natal. The farmer's name was Tom Porter.

It was the early days of South African labour tenancy. White farmers like Porter would allow black families to live on and farm small sections of their properties. In return, the tenant patriarch would give the white farmer the labour of some of his family. Mzuzephi's elder brother and mother worked the white man's fields. Nongoloza himself tended his father's cattle.

At the age of 16, he left the Porter farm to look for wage work in the town of Harrismith, about sixty kilometres north of the

Bergville district. He does not tell us whether he left on the instructions of his family, in order to remit his wages home, or whether he had began to feel the tug of independence. The young black men of the time who left their ancestral homes to work for whites did so for many reasons.

He drifted from job to job during the next three years, and finally took up employment as horse groom for a Mr Tom J in Harrismith. 'Before I had finished the first month of this employment,' Nongoloza said from his prison cell 24 years later, 'one of the horses got lost. On informing my master of this he accused me of being negligent and blamed me for it and told me to go and look for it. I told him I was working in the garden on that day; he could not hold me responsible for the loss, as all the horses were out grazing alone. He then threatened to place me in gaol if I did not go and look for the horse that was missing, so I searched but could not find it. He told me to go back to my kraal and work for Mr Tom P again, and added that Tom P would then bring to him the value of the horse that was lost. This would represent my wages for about two years.'

Mzuzephi went back to Tom Porter, but not for long. He raged against what amounted to his own enslavement. A few months into his employment, Porter sent Mzuzephi to the young mining town of Johannesburg with a wagonload of sugar and flour. He never returned.

Severed from his family and his ancestral home, and with no desire ever to go back, Mzuzephi abandoned his name and called himself Jan Note. The first name, 'Jan', is Dutch, the second, 'Note', is English. He had, at least nominally, discarded his Zulu roots for the languages of the mining town's commercial and administrative bourgeoisie; he wandered the streets of this wild cosmopolitan town in search of work.

In 1888, two years after the discovery of Johannesburg's gold, the new Jan Note got a job as a groom 'to four single men', he tells us, 'who were living in a house at the foot of a hill near a small railway station ... The "boss" of these four men was named Tyson,' Nongoloza recalled, 'and another was named McDonald, but the names of the other two I can't remember.'

He did remember that right from the start, his four employers kept strange habits. They would stay at home all day and then disappear on their horses at dusk. They would return at around midnight, always carrying money, and Jan Note would watch them counting it in the small hours of the morning.

'I had been with them for several months when they asked me if I would like to go out with them and see how they obtained their money,' the 45-year-old Nongoloza was to tell his captors. 'We had ridden as far as the Jukschy [Jukskei] River where we dismounted, and I was told to look after the horses. A coach was coming towards us, and the men pretended to be busy examining their horses' feet until the coach came up to us. The men then held up the driver of the coach with revolvers and some of them mounted the coach and threw all the boxes and trunks belonging to the passengers into the road. These were broken up and searched and all valuables and money taken by the four of them.'

On other occasions, Note's employers would pose as policemen on the outskirts of Johannesburg, stop young black miners who were returning to their rural homes with their savings in their pockets, 'ask to see their passes' and then 'handcuff the lot of them. After searching them and taking any money they possessed they would release them.'

'Until this time,' Nongoloza said in his 1912 statement, 'I did not know what robbery was and I was surprised to learn how easy it was to get money by this means ... I decided to [leave my employers and to] start a band of robbers on my own.'

It was not long before the learner-bandit found others of his kind – young black migrants, severed from their rural families, unwilling to take up employment for whites at meagre wages, wandering the periphery of Johannesburg. By the early 1890s, he had established contact with a group of outlaws, 'a loosely organised community,' Van Onselen writes, 'of approximately two hundred male and female vagrants, dislocated migrants, petty thieves, burglars and armed robbers.'

They based themselves in the Klipriversberg hills south of Johannesburg. Go there today and you will see triple-storey stucco houses on the summits of the hills, and electric-fenced cluster homes in the valleys. Back then, though, the Klipriversberg was well out of town, and its caves, ditches and disused mine-shafts constituted excellent terrain on which a bandit might make his warren.

Were it not for Note's charisma and his honed, articulate sense of injustice, the Klipriversberg outlaws would probably have remained 'a shapeless riff-raff drawn from the fringes of the underworld', as Van Onselen describes them. But Note had other ideas, and his ideas were very powerful indeed. By the late 1890s, he had shaped his band into a quasi-military regiment, its rank structure a hybrid of the Zulu hierarchies of Note's youth and the echelons of the Transvaal Republic's and colonial Natal's judiciary and military. The ideology that breathed meaning into this mongrel army was fiercely anti-colonial.

'I reorganised my gang of robbers,' Nongoloza recalled. 'I laid them under what has since become known as Nineveh law. I read in the bible about the great state Nineveh which rebelled against the Lord and I selected that name for my gang as rebels against the Government's laws. I had learned to read in my association with white people,' he added, probably in response to a question from his bemused captors.

'The system I introduced was as follows: I myself was the *Inkoos Nkulu* or king. Then I had an *Induna Inkulu*, styled lord and corresponding to the Governor-General. Then I had another lord who was looked upon as father of us all and styled *Nonsala*. Then I had my government who were known by numbers, number one to four. I also had my fighting General on the model of the Boer *vecht generaal*. The administration of justice was confined to a Judge for serious cases and a *landdrost* for petty cases. The medical side was entrusted to a chief doctor or *Inyanga*. Further, I had Colonels and Captains, Sergeant-majors and Sergeants in charge of the rank and file, ... the soldiers.'

There is something else about the ranks Nongoloza styled that is worth mentioning. 'As to the practice of *hlabonga* which you complain of as existing among the Ninevites in gaol,' Nongoloza told his captors in 1912, 'in that the soldiers subject the *piccanins* to immoral practices, that has always existed. Even when we were on the hills south of Johannesburg, some of us had women and others had young men for sexual purposes.'

In Van Onselen's book, these thin remarks are elaborated into a fleshier story. In the early days of Nongoloza's incipient Klipriversberg army, the historian writes, 'there was a constant stream of men leaving the camp and making their way to some of the less salubrious haunts of the nearby mining town. This movement threatened control and discipline in the regiment and, given early Johannesburg's preponderance of prostitutes, produced a rank and file considerably weakened by the ravages of venereal disease.'

Confronted with this crisis, Van Onselen continues, Note reached for a severe remedy. 'Pointing to women as the source of the "poison" of venereal disease,' he writes, 'the King of Nineveh instructed his troops to abstain from *all* physical contact with members of the opposite sex. Instead, older men of marriageable status within the regiment ... were to take the younger male initiates in the gang – and keep them as "boy-wives". It was after this startling decree that the Ninevites [in the Klipriversberg], and more particularly those who found themselves in the even more receptive host cultures offered by the prisons and mine compounds, became closely associated with the practice of homosexuality.'

Van Onselen is probably right. In 1912, the Director of Prisons noted in his annual report that 'a counter-movement has started in gaol in an organisation styled the Scotland Gang which was apparently established in self-defence and to preserve the members ... from having to submit to the immoral practices resorted to by the Ninevites.'

*

It was, ironically, thanks to the brutal labour regime, the very system Nongoloza had spent his early adult life skirting, that the Ninevites were able to grow into a formidable force, a veritable army of working-class and unemployed men. During the early years of the new century, in the aftermath of the great South African War, the new British administration developed a tight labour regime, enforced by a host of laws restricting the urban movement of black migrants. The result is that thousands upon thousands of working-class men lived their urban lives being shepherded from prison to compound, compound to prison. In the jails of early Johannesburg, these nominal criminals, their only offence to have been caught walking the streets without papers, were housed in the same cells as career criminals – Nongoloza's men. And in the compounds, the Ninevites would infiltrate and recruit among the ranks of the gold mine workers. As vast numbers of men were shuffled from one total institution to another, so the law of the Ninevites spread.

By 1908, Van Onselen tells us, the Ninevites had gathered an army more than a thousand strong. Its warrens stretched from the hills of Benoni to the east of Johannesburg, right round the back of the city to Roodepoort in the west; from the mining compounds of the East Rand to the Johannesburg Prison just north of the city centre.

Nongoloza himself was first jailed in the closing year of the nineteenth century, and spent the better part of the following thirteen years interned in several of South Africa's upcountry prisons. From what evidence we have, his status among black prisoners was that of a brutal god; he was worshipped and feared.

Reading through a commission of enquiry conducted in 1904 into conditions at Johannesburg Prison, I come across the evidence of a nameless black prisoner. 'I wish to ask,' the prisoner begins his testimony, 'how many Governors there are here in this jail, because I find there are a lot of officers besides the Governor who punish.'

'Who punishes?' a commissioner asks.

'Prisoners here get tried by other natives, who draw their teeth out,' the witness replies.

'Do I understand you to say,' an incredulous commissioner asks, 'that Kaffir prisoners are tried by other Kaffir prisoners and punished by them?'

'Yes, sir,' the prisoner replies, 'and have their teeth knocked out.'

'Have you had your teeth drawn out?'

'Yes, sir. I was tried by other prisoners, who drew my teeth out.'

'Who were the other prisoners?'

'Jan Note.'

'I would like to know for what reason Jan Note punishes [prisoners].'

'Jan Note accuses the prisoners of being detectives,' the witness replies.

'What sort of punishments have you seen awarded by Jan Note?' the commission asks.

'Jan Note tries the prisoners. I have seen them throw natives up to the roof and let them fall on the floor of the cell ten and fifteen times; otherwise he draws out their teeth.'

It is truly strange reading these words, and absorbing the fact that they were spoken several generations ago. They embody so much of the next hundred years: these parallel, quasi-judicial structures, warders on the one side, gangs on the other, vying to control the prison population.

*

What sort of outlaw was Nongoloza? Was he one of the great bandits in the Robin Hood tradition, drawn to crime in defence of the poor? Are the Ninevites reminiscent of the folk-tale heroes described by Eric Hobsbawm, the grand old historian of social banditry? 'The social bandit,' Hobsbawm writes, 'shares the values of his … community, commits his acts in the defence of that community, and is not regarded by his community as a criminal … He rights wrongs. He takes from the rich and gives to the poor. He never kills but in self-defence or just revenge. He is admired, helped and supported by his people. He dies invariably and only through treason, since no decent member of the community would help the authorities against him.'

Nongoloza, alas, fits none of these descriptions. If the black working classes of early times were fascinated by him, they feared him in equal measure. For the second crime that Jan Note learned during his apprenticeship to the four white men – robbing black workers for their pay packets – became a favoured habit of the Ninevites. At the onset of the South African War, when black workers fled the city for their rural homes, Nongoloza and his comrades followed on their heels, waylaying the stragglers on quiet country roads and relieving them of their worldly possessions. And in years to come, the Ninevites would rule the mining compounds with an anti-social ferocity that sends cold shivers down the spine.

Nongoloza was no Robin Hood. He is closer to what Hobsbawm called 'the avengers'. 'They are not so much men who right wrongs,' Hobsbawm tells us, 'but … the exerters of power; their appeal is not that of the agents of justice, but of men who prove that even the poor and weak can be terrible.'

In the late 1970s and early 1980s, when Van Onselen was writing a mammoth history of the early Witwatersrand, his researchers tracked down a handful of old men and women with living memories of the Ninevites. Many of the interviews they conducted were lost when Van Onselen vacated his position at the University of the Witwatersrand in Johannesburg. But some are still to be found – the interviews recorded on ancient tapes, the transcripts and translations bound in musty-smelling brown folders – lying in the basement of Wits's William Cullen library, less than a kilometre from the old Johannesburg Prison that once housed Nongoloza.

One of the people whose testimony survives is Mankailang Maria Molokoe, her thin voice battling with the crackles and hiss of a timeworn recording. She came to Johannesburg in 1914, as a domestic worker, two years after Nongoloza gave up his title as King of the Ninevites. But in her memory, he was still there when she arrived, and the Nongoloza of her imagination is precisely the 'avenger' of Eric Hobsbawm's world: cruel, but tantalisingly powerful, a figure who quite literally resided underground, coming out only to taunt Johannesburg's white rulers.

'They stayed in old, disused mineshafts,' the old woman tells her interviewer. 'Nongoloza was the king of the gang. He had a very big home underground there. The day he was taken out there by the police they found white women as well as black women. They found shops and butcheries underneath there.

'[The gangsters] were just ordinary gentlemen and ladies during the day,' she continues. '[During the morning hours] they were not supposed to do anything.' They were anti-colonial avengers disguised as ordinary folk.

'And what did they do when they were not in disguise?' the interviewer asks. 'What deeds did they commit?'

'After killing a policeman and decapitating him,' the old woman replies, 'they would take his helmet and put it where his head was supposed to be, let the hands hold the bridle and prick the horse ... The horse would stop where the police usually get off at the stables ... The onlookers would wonder where the rider's neck is since it looks like the man on the horse has got only a head, no neck ...'

'Were you afraid of them?' the interviewer asks.

Oh yes, Molokoe, replies, and I picture her eyes widening. 'Between three and four in the afternoon, they would block all the paths and roads and nobody would go anywhere. They would kill anyone who walked around in the street whether white, black, coloured or Indian ... The people would start cooking and going to the shops earlier so that when the raid starts there would be no fires.'

*

By the end of the 1910s, the Ninevites had been rooted out of the peri-urban warrens, and crushed. Nongoloza himself, extraordinarily enough, had renounced his gang and agreed to work for the prison authorities. The king of the underworld became a prison warder. But by then, the Ninevites had retreated into South Africa's jails where they spread right across the country, from Cape Town in the south to Barberton in the north. And as the memory of the great outlaw was passed from mouth to mouth, across the country and over the generations, so his life became myth, and his myth became law.

At the very time that the mythical Nongoloza was becoming the God of South African prisoners, the real-historical Nongoloza was drifting into an unhappy and anonymous old age. He died in 1948, was given a pauper's funeral, and was buried in a shared grave.

*

Here and now, in the early twenty-first century, Nongoloza's story is told, in the prisons of the Western Cape, as an odd hybrid of Homeric and Talmudic tales. A figure journeys through a stylised landscape; he meets people along the way, and his encounters throw up challenges and questions about how he ought to live his life. By the end of the story, he has lived his life, lived it in the right way, and developed a following. From now on, the decisions he made at each crossroads are formalised into philosophy and law, the philosophy and law of banditry.

As with all oral histories, there are countless variations in the story. Any Western Cape prison gangster who reads what is written here will quibble with at least part of it. But aside from the inevitable vagaries in any story that is not written down, there are rival versions, each allied to a competing doctrinal position; the 26s, 27s and 28s disagree about certain things Nongoloza thought and did, about decisions he made. Aligned to this disagreement about the story, there is disagreement about practice in the here and now, about how prisoners ought to live their lives in 2003.

The story begins in an African village somewhere in South Africa, on the brink of industrialisation. The 28s say it is a Zulu village. The 27s don't specify where it is, but they insist the village is not Zulu, anything but Zulu. There is an elderly man: the 28s call him Nkulukut, the 27s call him Pomobasa, or Paul Mobasa, or just Po. He is a wise man and a seer, and he embodies the interests of all black people.

During Po's autumnal years, the young men of his village begin leaving their kraals to look for work in the gold mines of the new cities that the whites have built. Oddly, time and place have changed. The year is 1812, 74 years before gold was discovered on the Witwatersrand. And the place of the gold mines is Delagoa Bay, on the far north of the eastern coastline, near current-day Maputo, not Johannesburg.

The young men leave their kraals for the gold mines, but they never return. And so the seer, wondering what has happened to the bearers of his village's future, journeys to the mines himself. He spends time in the single-sex mine compounds where the young black men stay, and he soon discovers why they do not return. The work beneath the ground is not fit for brutes; the young men are dying digging up the white men's gold.

So Po leaves Delagoa Bay and retreats to the outskirts of the town of Pietermaritzburg, where he finds a cave which is to serve as his lair, and gives thought to what he should do. His cave is *agter die berge*, behind the mountains, a place of solitude and contemplation. He spends the first weeks in his retreat inventing a secret language, for he knows that if the young men are to be saved, the whites must not understand the talk between the men who are to become his followers.

Po's cave is a short distance from a vantage point. Sitting there one morning, he looks out over the roads that lead from the hinterland to the mining town. He sees a cloud of dust on the road that comes from Zululand. He descends from his lair, goes out onto the road, and finds a young man in the cloud of dust. He asks the stranger his name. 'Nongoloza,' the young Zulu replies.

Po asks him where he is going.

'To the mines,' Nongoloza answers, 'to look for work.'

The old man shakes his head. 'I have been to the mines,' he advises, 'and I have seen what happens there. The work will kill you in the years to come.'

Nongoloza asks the wise man what he should do instead.

'The gold of the white man is good,' Po replies. 'You must take it, but not from the ground. You must rob it from the white man himself.'

Po takes Nongoloza up into his cave, and the following morning, sitting at his vantage point, he sees another cloud of dust, this one on the road from Pondoland. Again, he goes down onto the road to intercept the traveller. This youngster says his name is Kilikijan and that he is a Pondo. Po entices him up to his cave, and so things go on until the old man has gathered 15 young migrants around him. He instructs them in the secret language he has invented, tells them of the pay wagons that roll into the mine compounds on Fridays, and teaches them the art of highway robbery.

The young bandits are successful at stealing wages, but holed up in their cave they need other provisions as well, like food and clothes. So Po directs them to attack the colonial army camps that mark the perimeter of the mining town, and this they do. As with the pay wagons, they have success. In addition to pillaging food and supplies, they also bring back with them the accoutrements of warfare: .303 rifles, bayonets, army uniforms, and the rank structure of the colonial military.

By now, Po's men are wanted and hunted. The whites advertise rewards for their capture. They must change their ways to avoid detection. So they become nomads, moving from cave to warren, using the hills outside the mining town as their camouflage. They also divide themselves into two groups. Kilikijan takes seven men and robs by day. Nongoloza takes six men and robs by night. For a long time, working in this way, they terrorise the whites, taking their gold and hounding their army.

*

At this point, Po turns his attention from tactical concerns about the present to the question of the future. What is to become of banditry? How are his two bands of men to prepare the ground for the years ahead?

Since the beginning, Po has been instructing Nongoloza and Kilikijan to keep a diary. There is a large rock in the vicinity of one of the caves to which the men periodically retreat. He has told them to inscribe their activities as bandits onto the rock, to record how they go about their business and live their lives. This they have done. The rock is covered with the record of their short history as outlaws.

Po now brings Nongoloza and Kilikijan together and instructs them to go to a white farmer called Rabie. He tells them that they must buy a bull that grazes on Rabie's farm, and he is very specific in his instruction: there is a particular bull the men must bring back – its name is Rooiland ('Red Earth').

The two bandits arrive at Rabie's front door and offer to pay for Rooiland. The white man is suspicious. He has heard of the bandits who are roving the outskirts of town. He refuses to sell his bull and instructs the men to leave his property. But they will not go until they have carried out Po's order. So they kill the farmer with the bayonets they have plundered from the white army. They find Rooiland in Rabie's fields and herd him back to the cave where Po is waiting.

The 15 bandits throw a tremendous feast as they slaughter Rooiland. Po presides over the slaughter. He tells the men to preserve particular parts of the beast: the hooves, the legs, the eyes, the ears, the tail, and, Po says, more important than anything else, the bull's hide.

Once the animal has been dismembered, Po calls Nongoloza and Kilikijan to his side. He tells them to take one of Rooiland's horns and to fill it with a mixture of the beast's blood and gall. He then instructs both men to drink from the horn.

Kilikijan is the first to drink. He grimaces, spits it out, and then exclaims: 'There is poison in here; this stuff will kill me.' Then Nongoloza takes a sip, swallows it and smiles. Kilikijan stares at him in horror: the Zulu drinks poison.

In another version of the story, it is Rabie's gall that the two men taste and that Kilikijan cannot drink. In years to come, Nongoloza's followers – the 28s – will argue this goes to show that Kilikijan didn't have the stomach to take on whites. Kilikijan's followers, on the other hand, – the 27s – will say that Nongoloza drinks poison – that he is thus a muti man, capable of betrayal and of evil.

In any event, Po smiles to himself as he observes Nongoloza enjoy the gall. He lets the matter pass without comment, and turns the discussion to Rooiland's hide. He instructs the two bandits to drape it over the rock on which their diaries are recorded, and to press it against the rock, until the diaries are imprinted on the animal's skin. The words of the diary, now duplicated, one on the rock, the other on the hide, are to become the law of the gang. Whenever there is a dispute about what bandits ought to do, Po says, consult the hide or the rock, because they are a record of how things were done at the beginning, and how things ought to be done in the future. Nongoloza rolls up the hide and takes it with him. Kilikijan is left with the rock.

*

It is a strange tale, isn't it? For the thinking of the old African seer is somewhat unfathomable. A man of his village and the embodiment of its interests, you would imagine that his task is not merely to save the young men for their own sakes; his initial concern was the village itself – the disappearance of those who were to secure its posterity.

Bandits who protect their peasant villages from extinction surely live alongside their communities, sheltering them from the forces that threaten to tear them apart. They are an adjunct to a way of life. But not in our story. Po's young men have no plans to return to their villages. They are a new breed, an eternal army that apes the one they fight, and they work for themselves, one another and the posterity of their band. Right at the beginning of their bandit lives, they have already forgotten their villages and have become embroiled in making the laws and mythology of their own cult-like future.

It would not be unfair to say, then, that the path Po chose was as corrosive of traditional life as the white men's gold mines. Just as the whites stole the villages' progeny, so has Po, swallowing up the young migrants who leave their ancestral homes, never to return.

And how, it is fair to ask, are the outlaws to acquire their own progeny? There are no women and children. Who is to pick up the shield when Nongoloza dies? Surely, in the background to the pillages and murders that are the heartland of the tale, there will be future generations of migrants and drifters, young men who abandon their families and take to the hills. The ravages of colonialism must continue if the band is to survive. Their ancestral homes must be torn apart in perpetuity if the outlaws are to have a future.

And so there is an incoherence at the heart of the tale. The survival of colonialism is the band's primary nourishment. They have become bandits for the sake of being bandits. If the band is to live, so must injustice.

And if this secret society is indeed to be sealed within the mores of its own world, if it is to become its own universe, other, difficult questions arise: such as love and companionship, sex and romance.

*

As you might expect, this business of the duplication of the record of the law was soon to cause trouble. The old rock on which the diaries were written was large and cumbersome; Kilikijan's outlaw band was always on the move; they had to take the wretched thing wherever they went. One day, high up in the hills, one of the rock's carriers stumbled and it rolled down the side of a valley. Somewhere on the slopes, the boulder crashed into a tree and broke in half. The part of the rock that hit the tree imprinted its content on the bark. The rest rolled down into the river and floated downstream to be lost forever. Kilikijan made has way down to the tree, peeled off the bark and took it with him. The bandit was now in possession of only half the law. The rest had drowned in the stream. Nongoloza, though, possessed the whole law, for he had Rooiland's hide.

*

At some point after the rock had been lost, the two bands – Nongoloza's and Kilikijan's – went out pillaging together. I am not sure why. The usual practice was for Kilikijan to work by day, Nongoloza by night. Just as the bandits were about to leave their hideout, Nongoloza announced that he was ill and wanted to rest. He asked that one of Kilikijan's men, a youngster called Magubane, stay behind to tend to him. So thirteen went out to plunder and two stayed behind.

Kilikijan returned during the course of the afternoon, and stumbled upon Nongoloza making love to Magubane under a cow hide. Incensed, he raised his sabre and told Nongoloza to get up and fight. Nongoloza demurred. He said it was written in the law that what he and Magubane were doing was permitted. It says on Rooiland's hide, Nongoloza explained, that women are poison and that soldiers must choose wives from the young men in their ranks.

This only enraged Kilikijan more, since he had only half the law in his possession. He could never distinguish between what had been written on the original hide, and what Nongoloza had added later. Indeed, in years to come, the 27s were to deny that there ever was a hide, claiming that it was invented retrospectively by self-interested sodomites.

So Kilikijan took a swipe at Nongoloza with his sabre and the two men fought, until, it is said, Nongoloza was ankle-deep and Kilikijan knee-deep in blood. Po, who had come down from his lair at the sound of the clashing sabres, appeared on the scene. Horrified that the two bandits had hurt each other, he ordered them to put down their weapons and enquired about their dispute.

Being a sage and a seer, the old man did not resolve the disagreement in a simple manner. Instead, he issued the terms of a riddle. He told Kilikijan to go to the mine compounds at Delagoa Bay to see if sex between men was practised there. He refused to be drawn, though, on the significance of the meaning of Kilikijan's findings, whatever they might be. If the gold miners did indeed have sex with one another, what precisely would this mean? He did not say.

Po also said something else. Should the two bands of men ever return to his lair, they would find a rock at its entrance. Under the rock, they would find an assegai. If the blade of the assegai was rusted, it would mean that Po was dead. Upon entering his cave, they would find his skeleton. Needless to say, that is precisely what came to pass. Neither of the bandits was to see the old man alive again. The adjudicator of the law went to his death without ever pronouncing on the legitimacy of sex between bandits.

Having listened to Po's instructions, Nongoloza and Kilikijan went their separate ways. Kilikijan went to Delagoa Bay to enquire about the sexual practices of the miners. He left Magubane behind; his band was now composed of seven men. Nongoloza headed to a place called Germiston on the Moliva River. He took Magubane with him; his band now had eight men. That is one of the explanations for the numbers 28 and 27. There are others, but this one was repeated to me most often. I am not sure where the '2' in 28 and 27 comes from. Perhaps the '2' signifies the two original bandits: Kilikijan and Nongoloza. Or perhaps, as some who tell the tale today insist, there were 55 bandits, rather than 15.

In any event, they agreed that Kilikijan would keep working by day, Nongoloza by night. 'You will recognise me,' Kilikijan said as he set out for Delagoa Bay, 'by two rays of dawn sunlight: one over my right shoulder, and the other in front of me.'

The two men were never again to talk of their dispute about what happened between Nongoloza and Magubane under the cow hide. They next met several years later in the cells of Point Prison, Durban. Both had been captured and tried for their crimes; they had been given indeterminate sentences, and faced the prospect of spending the rest of their lives in jail.

If the two pioneers never again spoke to each other of their dispute, their respective followers talked about it all the time – quietly, and among themselves, for generations, spreading rumours and casting aspersions about the other camp. Both camps agree that Kilikijan did, in the interim, find his way to the mine compounds at Delagoa Bay, and that he discovered that the men there did indeed sleep with one another. The 28s say that this vindicates Nongoloza, that the legitimacy of sex between bandits had always been written on the hide. The 27s disagree. Kilikijan's discovery, they argue, only confirmed that sex between men is a foreign practice, one alien to those initiated into bandit life. It arose at the compounds because the work underground was so hard: weak men needed help from stronger men with their picks and shovels, and they gave them sex in exchange. Sex between men is a pollution, a symptom of the unnaturalness of the work white men forced blacks to perform.

The dispute, of course, is incapable of resolution. The rock on which bandit law was written has long been eroded by the waters of the Moliva River. And all that remains of Po, the sage, is a mute skeleton. In years to come, this irresolvable quarrel is to shape relations between the gangs. It is bound up with the question of why Nongoloza was able to drink poisonous gall and smile. And it was to frame the immediate events that arose in those first weeks when Kilikijan and Nongoloza found themselves together in Point Prison.

There were six inmates in Point Prison – *voels* or *franse*, that is to say, members of neither camp, non-gangsters – who sat in a circle and flipped a silver coin. Their leader was a man by the name of Grey. Among the first practices to emerge among the 27s and 28s of the prisons was the confiscation of a *franse's* possessions. A portion would always be returned, but it was to be the *ndotas* – a corruption of *ndoda*, which means 'man' in Zulu – the Number gang members, who determined the distribution. When Nongoloza's men demanded from Grey that the six inmates hand over their possessions, coin and all, he refused. Troubled by this disobedience, Nongoloza approached Kilikijan and asked what was up with these recalcitrant men. Kilikijan explained that the flipping of the coin was a form of gambling, that these men were trained in the arts of smuggling and acquiring valuables.

During his first days in prison, Kilikijan continued, before Nongoloza arrived, he had stabbed a troublesome warder. As punishment, he was placed in a tiny dungeon and was fed a spare, saltless diet; the warders' aim was to make him weak. The six gamblers, led by Grey, who was skilled in the art of smuggling, and had the cunning to enter into prudent allegiances, slipped him salt and bread and other nourishment under the crack beneath his door.

Impressed and curious, Nongoloza asked Kilikijan to bring him Grey's coin. He handled it carefully, then bit it, then dropped it on the floor. 'It is hard, like a nail – a *spyker*,' Nongoloza said, 'and when it drops to the ground it makes the noise of a nail. I will call it a *spyker*. It will be useful in the years to come. I can use it to button my uniform.'

'It is called a *kroon*, a crown,' Kilikijan replied, 'not a *spyker*. It is useful because it brings wealth.'

The disagreement between the two men extended beyond the question of what names to give things. 27s and 28s offer rival versions of what happened next. According to the 27s, the two men fought over the six gamblers. While the stakes were never spoken of openly, it was quite clear what was going on; Kilikijan wanted to protect Grey and his colleagues from the appetites of the sodomites. Absorbed into the 28s, they would be used, he believed, not just to smuggle, but for sex.

According to the 28s, there was no such dispute. They say that Nongoloza said to Kilikijan: 'I give you permission to constitute these men as the third camp of bandits, but on several conditions.

First, they will be called the 26s, to show that they will never rise above us. Second, they will be the last camp to form. There will never be a fourth camp in this prison. Every other inmate is a *frans*. And finally, you will be responsible for their conduct. You will be answerable for them. When they commit a wrong, I will not come to them, I will come to you.'

'That is all well and good,' Kilikijan replied, 'but when you wrong them, I will come to you.'

And so the three camps were formed, each with their self-made philosophies of banditry and their collectively assigned roles. The 26s were to accumulate wealth, which was to be distributed among all three camps, and acquired through cunning and trickery, never through violence. The 28s, in turn, were to fight on behalf of all three camps for better conditions for inmates. They would also be permitted to have sex, in their own ritualised manner, among themselves. They were never to touch a 26.

As for the 27s, they were the guarantor of gang law; they were to keep the peace between the three camps. They would learn and retain the laws of all three gangs, as well as the laws of the relationships between gangs. And they would right wrongs by wreaking revenge; when blood is spilled, they would spill blood in turn.

But there is an important caveat in regard to the role of 27s. All three camps are camps of bandits; they are brothers and must thus never spill one another's blood. So, when a 28, for instance, commits a wrong, blood must be spilled to make things right, but never the blood of a bandit. The blood of a warder, or of a *frans*, must substitute. For the world is divided into *bandiete* and *boere*, and the *boer* is always the enemy.

While the camps insist their enemy is the *boere*, and that they themselves are all brothers, the question of what happened between Nongoloza and Magubane under the cow skin, out on the hills around the mining town, comes back to the bandits in endless relays; it is a collective obsession. Within each camp, a series of private myths evolve. The 28s, for instance, say that after Nongoloza and Kilikijan took their respective men separate ways, Mugubane turned into a con artist. He stole from his fellow bandits in the 28s, tricked them, and when he was discovered, fled and disappeared. They claim that Grey, the founder of the 26s, the man gambling with a coin in Point Prison, Durban, is actually

Magubane, that the original sodomite is alive and well among the 26s. The intimation, of course, is that, under cover of darkness, the 26s and 27s break their most sacred rule; they too make men into wives.

In years to come, the bandits will fight bitter wars over who does, and who does not, give succour to Magubane.

4
THE FATE OF DOGGY DOG

'If there is one story that encapsulates for you what Nongoloza means today,' I ask Magadien during one of our morning meetings in his cell, 'what would it be?'

He does not have to think for long. 'Doggy Dog,' he replies. 'Go and find the Doggy Dog story in newspapers and court records. Then come back to me and I'll tell you the other Doggy Dog story – the one I saw with my own eyes here in prison.'

In the late 1990s, much of South Africa was talking about the Doggy Dog story. It concerns a triple murder that took place in the spring of 1996 in the isolated Namaqualand hamlet of Niewoudtville. The killings became famous across the country overnight as the Flower Gang murders.

A group of five men, four of them ex-convicts who had spent time in Pollsmoor, the last a Zambian immigrant, broke into a farmhouse on the outskirts of Niewoudtville on the evening of 24 September 1996. They interrupted a foursome who were eating dinner: Hendrina Louw, the middle-aged woman who owned the farm; Johan Viviers, her fiancé; Julia Fairbanks-Smith, a young mother; and Emma, her three-year-old daughter. Fairbanks-Smith and her daughter were guests; they had come to see and photograph Namaqualand's springtime daisies. Hence, the 'Flower Gang', as the press was to dub the murderers in the months to come.

By the time the five men left a couple of hours later, they had stabbed and beaten the two women and the young girl to death. The stolen goods they took with them were of pitifully low value: some jewellery, a few household goods, a gun. Viviers they had left for dead, buried under a mattress in the main bedroom, several stab wounds in his neck. He survived to tell a disturbingly eloquent story in a Cape Town courtroom several months later.

In the public imagination, the murders were shocking primarily for what they intimated about the future. The victims were not only white: they were landed. The perpetrators were black and were self-styled outlaws. And the killings appeared to be gratuitous, utterly unrelated to the purpose of stealing household goods, jewellery and guns. The crime appeared to toy with the boundary that separates acquisitive crime from politics, racial hatred from banditry. For those of a gloomy and pessimistic bent, murders like these suggested that we were to pay dearly for the ordered political settlement that ended white minority rule; the price would not be open civil war, but an endless relay of quiet, inarticulate sniping from the margins of the new democracy.

For all the copy written in the wake of the Flower Gang murders, the South African media missed what is perhaps the most disturbing moment in the story: the things Doggy Dog did with his newfound status as a famous killer when he walked into Pollsmoor Prison in the wake of the murders. Magadien was a witness to his extraordinary performance. He was the head of the 28s on Pollsmoor's D Floor in the late 1990s, Dog the head of the 27s. They were to get to know each other well.

*

The transcripts of the Flower Gang trial are over 5 500 pages long. But there are just two testimonies that interest us. The one is Laston Chavulla's. He is the most forthcoming of the five killers; much to the chagrin of the judge, he insists on recounting the minutest details of the gang's deranged journey. The other is that of Johan Viviers, the sole survivor of the attack.

I wonder whether Viviers's memory is ordinarily photographic, or whether the horror of that evening etched every event of the preceding 12 hours in his mind. The prosecutor's questions are hyperbolically detailed; she gives the impression of a mindlessly fastidious person, gathering facts with the arcane fascination of a stamp collector. In Viviers she has a soul mate; you can hear the prosecutor warm to her witness's extraordinary powers of recall.

Viviers, who is in his fifties, tells the court that his fiancée, Hendrina Louw, the owner of the farm, had been recently widowed. 'Her husband passed away on 16 February 1995,' Viviers explains.

Asked about his own relationship to the deceased, he replies in the wonderful euphemisms of church-going Afrikaans: *Dit was 'n baie goeie verhouding gewees, meer as vriendskaplik op daardie stadium*. 'It was a very good relationship, more than friendship at that time.'

Viviers was in the middle of an extended stay at his fiancée's farm. He was a policeman and worked in a town some distance away. He does not say why he was away from his job for so long, but it appears that he was running Louw's farm. He explains that the other two members of the household that day, Julia Fairbanks-Smith and her three-year-old daughter, Emma, were guests who had come to see Namaqualand's springtime daisies.

Viviers describes the morning activities, and as he does so, the coordinates of more than a century of white South African farming fill the courtroom. The farm employed one permanent worker, a middle-aged man named Job. He and his wife, Vytjie, lived in a simple home some two-and-a-half kilometres from the main house. During September of 1996, Viviers was busy with *skaapwerk*, 'sheep work', and had hired four temporary labourers for the job. The first three he knew as Kerneels, Alfred and Koenaas. He never learned the name of the fourth.

Viviers and the five workers went out to do *skaapwerk* in the morning. They broke at 11.45 for lunch and planned to be back at work at 2.00. Viviers went into the farmhouse for his lunch; the workers retreated to a *skerm* somewhere in the farmyard, a wind shelter, under which they ate their own meal.

It began to rain during lunch and the *skaapwerk* planned for the afternoon was postponed. The five workers remained under the *skerm* staring at the rain, waiting for it to stop. At four o'clock, Viviers decided to call it a day; he summonsed the workers to round up the sheep. The work done, he instructed the day workers to come to the house to collect their pay; then they climbed into the back of his bakkie and he took them to the village of Niewoudtville where they would sleep the night.

He dropped them at the bottle store in the village's main street, and, while they were climbing out of the bakkie, he saw a brown-coloured BMW parked outside the Niewoudtville Hotel. It had tinted windows, Viviers said, and he noticed immediately that the car's paintwork was a 'back-yard job'. 'I know it was a back-yard job because I spent three years at a Technical High School,' Viviers explained, 'where I learned car repairs and paintwork.' He noticed that three men were standing around the car. He drove off and arrived back at the farm at 4.50.

*

By the time Viviers returns to the farm in the late afternoon, Fairbanks-Smith and her daughter are back from their tour of the daisy fields. He sees them unpacking their car in the driveway in front of the farmhouse. Fairbanks-Smith tells him she wants to go for a jog. He offers to look after her child, and points out the road that leads to Job's house – a five-km run there and back, he tells her. From now on, the register of his testimony changes subtly. He recalls details that betray a gentle fondness for the young woman and her daughter. And he appears to feel the weight of a sacred duty to recall the idiosyncrasies of the two strangers in their last living moments.

Fairbanks-Smith arrives back at the house shortly before dusk, and Viviers notices that her clothes and her hair are wet; it had rained again while she was out. 'Her shoes were caked with mud,' he says. She took them off and 'I took them from her and banged them together twice to get the clay and the mud off.' She went to take a shower, Viviers continues, 'and when I saw her again she had on fresh clothes and a new pair of shoes. Her hair was in a ponytail. She went to bath her daughter.'

Half an hour or so later, Viviers is now in the dining room. *Klein Emma*, 'Little Emma', is at the head of the table with a plate of mixed vegetable soup in front of her.

'What sort of vegetables?' the prosecutor asks.

'Potatoes, onions, split-beans and rice,' the witness answers promptly. But she does not eat them; she is not feeling well. Her mother puts her to bed.

Next, Viviers joins Julia in the study. He reads a copy of *Die Burger*, the Cape's Afrikaans daily, and she writes letters. They are waiting for dinner, which Mrs Louw is preparing in the kitchen. They have two whiskies each, Viviers recalls.

Viviers excuses himself to go to the bathroom. Fairbanks-Smith asks if he will check up on Emma. He goes to her room and finds her sleeping on her right side, clutching a little teddy bear. The duvet has slipped to her waist. He quietly picks it up and covers her.

Now Viviers is at the dining room table with Julia. On the table in front of them is a shoulder of mutton, baked potatoes, grilled sweet potatoes, rice, gem squash filled with sweetcorn. Viviers is cutting Julia's meat. Mrs Louw is standing at the stove behind Viviers's back.

'Johan,' Viviers hears Julia ask, 'what is wrong with Gansie?' He turns round to find his fiancée frozen in front of the stove, staring into the passage. He asks her what's wrong and tells her to come and sit at the table. Then he hears a voice, *Hei!*, 'Hey!' from his left.

'I looked to my left and saw a brown man in the passage leaning against the wall. He was holding a 9-mil. pistol in his right hand. He was short, wore a little black cap, the peak turned the wrong way round.

'"What the hell are you doing in the house?" I asked.

'He raised his left index finger and signalled for me to come to him. Then he winked at me.'

*

If the testimony of Johan Viviers is solidly grounded in the traditions of more than a century of white farming, Laston Chavulla is his opposite. He is rudderless; he belongs nowhere, not in any of the three African countries he has inhabited during the 26 years of his life, and certainly not in the Flower Gang.

In September 1996, Chavulla was living with his girlfriend, Sandra, in a house in the coloured settlement of Atlantis. The house belonged to a woman called Angira. How he got to be living there is an odd story. His father was Malawian, his mother Zambian. They met and married in South Africa, but they were expelled in 1961, nine years before Laston's birth, when the apartheid government decided to expatriate black foreigners. He came to South Africa for the first time in 1992 because he had an aunt in Atlantis and he was struggling to find work in Malawi or Zambia. He spent much of his four years in the country in unsteady work as a bricklayer, battling to learn Afrikaans, moving from one temporary job to another.

Atlantis, Chavulla's South African home, is among the most chilling of apartheid's constructions. Erected in the early 1970s on a barren, sandy wilderness close to the western seaboard, it was a dumping ground for tens of thousands of coloureds who were being removed from Cape Town's inner city. Unlike the townships of the Cape Flats, which were to become satellite towns feeding the white city with labour, apartheid's engineers envisaged Atlantis as a 'self-sustaining, coloured economic hub'. It was too far from Cape Town – about fifty kilometres – for workers to commute. Prosperous factories were meant to emerge in Altantis's industrial zone, and the coloureds there were meant to live happily ever after, sealed off from white South Africa.

They were indeed sealed off, but the jobs and the factories did not last long. Driving past there today, you can see the rows of identical matchbox houses standing on the sand in the middle of nowhere, like a mirage or a hallucination.

So there was Laston Chavulla, among the most marginal members of one of the most peripheral settlements in South Africa, living with his girlfriend Sandra in Angira's house.

To say that he is the outsider among the Flower Gang is to understate things. He is Zambian, was brought up in Malawi, and speaks poor Afrikaans, the mother tongue of the other four. He is thus not privy to much of their conversation, both in the planning of the crime, and during the strange ideological debate that ensued between the killers in Hendrina Louw's house. He did spend a few months in a Western Cape jail some time before the murder, awaiting trial for housebreaking, but was later acquitted; he has never been a member of a prison gang and knows next to nothing about them. His relation to the crime is thus doubly removed, not just with regard to language, but with regard to the labyrinths of prison-gang symbolism. He is witness to exchanges between his peers he does not begin to understand; all he can do is listen carefully and report, like a foreigner who masters the memory of phonetics and tone without ever grasping their meaning.

*

André Solomons, accused number two in the Flower Gang trial, had recently been released from jail and had shacked up with Angira, Chavulla's landlady. The entire Flower Gang had recently been released from prison. With the exception of Chavulla, they were all prison gangsters, three of them members of the 26s. If Chavulla's testimony is to be believed, his trouble began when he found Solomons lying asleep one evening in a drunken stupor on the couch in front of the television set. He rifled through the sleeping man's pockets, found a wad of money stashed in a wallet, took it and spent it.

All hell broke loose when Solomons woke up the next morning to find his pockets empty. Chavulla was bundled into a brown BMW, where he found the other members of the gang – David Ruiters (Doggy Dog's real name), Charles Adams and Johannes Bruintjies – sitting on the back seat. He recognised Bruintjies and Adams at once; they had both been at Goodwood Prison while he was there awaiting his trial. In jail, they had been *ndotas* – prison gang members, he a *frans* – a nothing. He remembers Adams in particular for having mugged him in the prison corridor. What he does not know is that three members of the gang had stolen the BMW he has found himself in, and that its owner has been murdered.

Solomons, Dog, Adams and Bruintjies drove Chavulla around Atlantis trying to retrieve the money he had stolen. They went to his aunt's house, then to a friend's house, but nobody was prepared to lend him anything. So Dog took out a gun and pointed it at Chavulla's head. The four tied him up, put him in the boot of their BMW, and headed north along the coastal road, driving through several of the stark, beautiful fishing villages on the western seaboard.

Who knows whether Chavulla's story is true? 'I was only at the scene of three gruesome murders because I was kidnapped.' It sounds like the desperate fabrication of a man who knows he is sinking. And yet there is a ring of poetic truth to his story, even if some of it was pieced together in the holding cells and on the hoof. He is so thoroughly alien to the other four, so unlikely a candidate to be present at a ritual Number slaying; it seems appropriate that he was only there because he stole a drunk man's wallet and was bundled into the boot of a stolen car.

In any event, at some point along the journey, the four stopped the car, took Chavulla out the boot, and told him that he need not repay them, so long as he helped them in the robberies they were about to commit. He assented gratefully, he claims, and took his place on the back seat.

It was a deranged, maniacal road journey. The BMW zigzagged its way northward, sometimes hugging the coast, sometimes veering inland onto the N7, the regional artery that takes you to

Namibia. The gang was in search of three things: alcohol, Mandrax and armed robbery. At Laaiplek, a tiny West Coast village some hundred kilometres north of Atlantis, they staked out a roadside canteen. Two white men with guns on their hips kept wandering in and out of the little shop, and the gang took fright and left.

A little later, they picked up a hitchhiker carrying an old satchel on his back. They robbed him of his meagre possessions (there was only R300 in his wallet), and threw him into the road. Rifling through his rucksack, they found a well-thumbed set of house plans. Chavulla stared at the familiar sketches. He imagined that, like him, the hitchhiker was a bricklayer. He looked back out the window as they drove off, hoping that somebody on this forlorn and empty coastal road would drive past soon and help the man.

The search for Mandrax and alcohol is an interesting tale. No matter that they were travelling through one of the remotest regions of western South Africa, they were always within an hour or two of somebody they knew, some *ndota* they had met in prison, someone who made a living trading contraband. Prison is the great networking centre of criminal South Africa. Spend four or five years of your life in the 26s, and wherever you go after that you will always find a brother with whom to do business. Prison has taken the illicit market to every village in the country.

Throughout the quest for drugs and alcohol, Chavulla observed something unusual about his travelling companions. Dog was in charge. It was he who insisted that they spend their time searching for Mandrax and drink. He was also the one with the most connections on the West Coast, and it was he who directed the journey. Yet Dog himself did not touch liquor or Mandrax. He led the others to the contraband, he was intimately involved in the trading, but he refused to allow anyone to smoke buttons or drink liquor in the car; he couldn't stand the smell.

I have always wondered about the association of Western Cape crime with Mandrax. It is a downer, not an upper; it first came into the world as a prescription sleeping pill. Users quite literally pass out during their third of fourth pipe of the day. It is an odd drug on which to pump oneself up for the commission of a murder.

*

There are many other details of the journey with which I will not detain you. Let us move to the evening of the 24th. The five have made their way to Mrs Louw's Niewoudtville farm, and climbed through an unlatched window and into her house. They have interrupted dinner and informed Viviers that they are after money and guns. Fairbanks-Smith and Louw have been led to rooms at the back of the house. Emma is still asleep. Dog is with Viviers.

The white man declares that he has money but no guns, takes Dog to the main bedroom and pulls a wallet out of a clothes cupboard. Dog grabs it and searches through it. He looks up, grimaces and tells Chavulla that this man is a *mphungwuthu*. Chavulla does not understand what it means, but in prison language it is one of the many words for policeman. Dog must have seen Viviers's badge in his wallet. He instructs the rest of the gang to tie Viviers up, 'because the man is a pig,' he explains.

Henceforth in his testimony, Chavulla complains that there is much he does not understand. The other four spoke a mixture of Afrikaans and prison gang language; he could only grasp snippets of their conversation. And the symbolism of the things that passed between them confuses him. His narrative is fragmented, jumping from one scene to another. But his observational powers are good enough; his fragments tell a coherent story.

Adams, Chavulla tells us, is growing nervous. He appears to have sensed what some of the others are planning, and he keeps muttering that this is just an armed robbery; nobody must die. The others ignore him. Solomons has something different in mind. He keeps going into the room where Fairbanks-Smith is being kept. He comments on how pretty she looks in her tight white pants. Finally, Chavulla tells the court, Solomons 'held the young woman tight and got an erection. He wanted to rape her. Dog said we must not make friendship with white women; we must kill them. [Solomons] threw the young woman on a bed and opened his pants and pulled out his private parts. It was long. She cried and spoke the name Emma. I thought Emma was the elderly woman.' Dog pulled Solomons off her. 'We do not love white women,' he repeated, 'we kill them.'

So there was this debate among the armed robbers, an ideological debate, if their reasoning deserves the dignity of that description, about what to do with their victims. Adams wanted to leave them unharmed. Solomons wanted to rape the young woman. Dog wanted to kill them all because they were white.

Dog resolved the dispute. He did so with an instruction. 'Adams came back with the old woman,' Chavulla tells the court. 'She was crying and the young woman was crying. The young woman said she wanted to help Emma. Dog said "Up bayonet!" and Solomons took out his knife.' A few minutes later Fairbanks-Smith was led to the bathroom from where Chavulla heard a thumping noise; she had been beaten over the head with a toilet jug. She was then repeatedly stabbed.

Neither the prosecutor nor the court stops to ask Chavulla what 'Up bayonet!' means, and it is doubtful that Chavulla knows. But it is, in fact, the first clue to how Dog understood the murders. 'Up!' is the command a fighting General in any of the Numbers – 26, 27 or 28 – gives his soldiers to signal the commencement of battle.

But 'bayonet' signifies something more specific. It is among the weapons Nongoloza and Kilikijan plundered from the colonial army camps on the outskirts of the mythical mining town. And it is the weapon they used to kill Rabie. None of this symbolism is pertinent to the 26s, to which Dog, Bruintjies and Adams belong. The 26s, remember, were formed in prison, long after the Rabie killing. *Ons is manskappe van die vier hoeke,* is one of their mottoes. 'We are men of the four corners [of prison].' As arcane as this may sound at first blush, Dog was instructing his gang to re-enact the most sacred crime of the 27s – the murder of a white farmer, on a farm, outside 'the four corners' – and thus to induct the gang as 27s.

You can see by the following chain of events that Solomons and Adams understood precisely what Dog had in mind. Solomons walked into the passage with his bloody knife, and wrote something on the wall, using the blood as ink. Chavulla is illiterate and does not understand what was written. Solomons stands back to admire his artwork, and says, *bloed het salute,* 'blood has saluted'. Now, the 27s is the only one of the three gangs in which every new recruit is required to take blood upon acquiring membership. Solomons is declaring that he has performed the work of a 27. Adams affirms this. He stares at the markings on the wall, makes a sign with his fingers and says, 'General, Salute.' Chavulla does not understand the sign, but he describes it well; thumb and 'pointing finger' raised, the other three digits clenched against the palm. It is the sign of the 27s.

Chavulla aside, who is now witnessing the workings of an entirely alien world, it is only Bruintjies who dissents. 'Dog ordered Bruintjies to kill the child,' Chavulla tells the court. Bruintjies protested. 'The child knows nothing,' he said. Solomons scowled at Bruintjies, muttering that he does not like whites. He walked up to Emma, 'stabbed her twice in the neck,' Chavulla tells the court, 'and hit her on the head with a flashlight'.

It is an hour or so later now. The two women and the young girl are dead. Each has been stabbed at least twenty times. The gang believes that Viviers is dead too. He has been stabbed several times, a knife blade left protruding from both sides of his neck, and is lying unconscious under a mattress. The newly recruited 27s are searching the house for valuables.

The last event to take place in the house that Chavulla describes causes some confusion in the court.

'Dog walked into the kitchen,' Chavulla tells the court. 'He ordered Solomons to take Rooiland. I did not know what he meant when he said Rooiland, but when …'

'Rooiland?' the judge interjects.

'Rooiland,' Chavulla replies.

The judge repeats his question: 'Rooiland?'

'Yes, Your Worship, and when I went to jail, I learned that Rooiland meant meat. Solomons went to the fridge, took out the meat and put it in a bag. And he took some cold drinks too.'

*

I should tell you about another of Chavulla's observations before we move on. The murders are six or seven hours old now. The gang is driving south, in the direction of Cape Town, in Louw's car, which they have stolen, and dawn is breaking. 'As the sun came up,' Chavulla tells the court, 'Dog looked out the window and said that this sun is the sun of the Hollanders [another name for the 27s]. He said, "The first ray is Kilikijan".'

At this point, the judge loses his cool. He has heard too much about secret hand signs and pieces of meat called Rooiland and the name for the first ray of the sun. He turns to Chavulla and instructs him sharply to stick to relevant facts. Chavulla protests. 'I want to tell everything,' he says. 'Before the court and before God, I want to tell absolutely everything.'

If the judge had known something of prison gang history, he would have been struck by the murderers' obsessive, evidently maniacal fidelity to signs and symbols. Recall the myth: Nongoloza works by night, Kilikijan by day. Recall that, when they parted after the fight over Magubane, Kilikijan said: 'You will recognise me by two rays of dawn sunlight.' Dog is adding yet another symbolic layer, reminding his accomplices that they are in the process of becoming 27s. Why does the performance continue even now, on the journey back to Atlantis? The gang's relationship to its own myth appears credulous to the point of madness.

*

Magadien arrived at D Floor Pollsmoor in early 1998, more than a year after Dog and the rest of the Flower Gang. During his previous sentence, in the early 1990s, the 27s had been, as they always were, on the point of extinction, leaving a brittle modus vivendi between the 28s and the 26s. But on his return to Pollsmoor in early 1998, the prison was full of 27s, and they had all been recruited by Doggy Dog. Dog was Lord of the Hollanders, the highest rank in the Pollsmoor gangs.

'Why?' I asked Magadien. 'How can a rank-and-file 26 waltz into Pollsmoor and reconstitute an ancient gang?'

'Because of the Niewoudtville murders,' he replied.

'You're not serious.'

Magadien sighed and muttered that there are things about prison that 'civilians' like myself will never understand. Then he smiled mischievously and advised me to commit a terrible crime. 'You must get to live here night and day,' he said. 'Then you will get to understand things like why Niewoudtville made Dog Lord of the 27s.'

'Is that why Dog committed the crime?' I asked. 'Did he know he was going to get caught? Did he do it in order to rule Pollsmoor?'

'It's complicated,' Magadien replied. 'I'm sure he was hoping he'd never get caught, but by the time he had been here a year, he wasn't so sure any more. We shared a cell during 1998. Dog stayed up till late every night smoking one pipe after another. I'd sit with him and talk. He'd fall over after his third or fourth pipe and I'd laugh at him. We were close, in a way.

'I asked him why he killed that little girl. At first he said it was for the money and the guns. I said to him, "Bullshit, you don't kill a little girl for money and guns." And he said, "Ja, okay, *ek het dit gedoen om die nommer vol to maak* – I did it to make the Number complete," to do what Kilikijan did years back, to get the power, to get the blood of the white man, to become king of the 27s.

'Because, you see,' Magadien continued, 'Dog was in a lot of shit in the 26s ...'

'What was his rank in the 26s?' I interrupted.

'I don't know, and it doesn't matter. It doesn't matter to Dog's story. The point is that when he was in Helderstroom Prison in the early 1990s, he was in love with another man, with a 28. And the 26s caught them fucking and they punished him bad. They beat the shit out of him. And from that day on he was dirt in the 26s. Whatever prison he went to after that, anywhere in the Western Cape, he was going to be dirt. Because prisoners circulate in this province. Whatever prison he went to, there would have been somebody there who knew, who was there at Helderstroom. That's why the gangs work. Everyone circulates, so everyone knows.'

Magadien looked at me closely and smiled. 'Are you following the story, are you understanding Doggy Dog? I don't think so.' He laughed a little patronisingly. 'You see, there comes a stage in your life when you know you will be spending more of your life inside than outside. So when you plan for your future, you plan for prison, like I used to. Dog knew that a future in the 26s was going to be a *kak* life. So he planned. He did what he did outside to plan for the inside. To make his life here better. Only, he wasn't thinking straight. He was thinking the next five years. If he'd thought about the next 50, he wouldn't have done what he did.'

*

Magadien's theory of Doggy Dog's motivations was intriguing enough, but it didn't answer the most important questions. Like why Dog knew that the Niewoudtville murders would be interpreted the way they were in Pollsmoor, why indeed they *were* interpreted the way they were.

Everything I had come to know about the 27s during the previous months made no sense in the face of the Doggy Dog story. The 27s were the upholders of the law that shapes the peace between the three gangs. Their recruitment and training was a long, tedious process, stretching over several years. In theory, at any rate, they carried the law of all three camps in their heads, as well as the entire record of how disputes had been resolved by their forebears over the last century.

More pertinently, their job was to take blood, often warders' blood, every time a wrong had to be put right. To rise through the ranks of the 27s is to commit oneself to a lifetime in jail, to be sentenced again and again for violent crimes committed within the four walls. To be a 27 is to be beaten senseless and thrown in solitary confinement every time you use your knife. That is why the 27s have always been so few in number, I was told. It takes a maniacally Talmudic man, one given over entirely to the world of the Number, to make a genuine 27.

So how was it that Dog could slaughter three innocents, a toddler among them, and claim this revered mantle? And how did he get the authority to recruit others, who had neither spilt the blood of a warder nor learned the interminable layers of gang law, into the 27s? I was intrigued by the gap between what the Number says about itself and what actually animates it.

'So Dog walks into Pollsmoor after the Niewoudtville murders and everybody knows immediately that he has done what Kilikijan did?' I asked Magadien.

'Almost,' he replied. 'There were other things Dog had to do. The whole country was talking about Niewoudtville, it was on the front page of every newspaper. And then Dog walks into prison and starts talking as a 27. It means the whole country is talking because Kilikijan is back. Because the Number is powerful. Every time he walked down the passage, 26s would ask him for advice. They made him a god. And once that happened, the 28s had to accept him too. All that mattered to us was that when he was at the Valcross, he could stand as a 27 without making a mistake. He could *sabela* the whole history of the Number on the Valcross, just like an old and experienced 27 does, and so we could not question him. Nor could we deny the blood he took at Niewoudtville.'

'So if any old idiot, like some *frans*, had committed the Niewoudtville murders, come to Pollsmoor and announced that he was Kilikijan, what would have happened?'

'He would have been stabbed. He would have walked onto the Valcross as a 27 and not been able to *sabela*, not been able to answer questions about the history, and the others on the Valcross would have taken out a knife and stabbed him there and then, on the Valcross itself.

'You see, Dog has a brain, and it is his brain, not just his knife, that worked for him. While he was in the 26s, he, how can I say, he observed. He learned the language of the 27s like he himself was a 27. He learned and he learned and kept it all to himself. And when he came back after Niewoudtville, it was all there in his head. If he had been unable to act like a 27, he could never have pulled it off.'

'But there are still many things that puzzle me. Like how Dog could recruit others into the 27s without training them properly, without them taking blood.'

'Pollsmoor is notorious for closing its eyes,' Magadien replied. 'Anyone who knows the history and has a silver tongue can talk his way into anything. Dog knew enough to know that the 27s are nearly extinct because they took blood and they got punished and sentenced; they never leave prison. They were beaten, some were disabled, hobbling around on crutches. The sickness of what they did had got the better of them. They became afraid of blood.

'Dog knew that. He knew Pollsmoor wanted its 27s back. He knew they could never come back the old way. So he used Niewoudtville as an alternative, a pretend alternative, as something so powerful, so strong in terms of the history, that people would close their eyes to the fact that he was breaking the rules. This new breed of 27s, those Dog made, they are just there to – how can I put it – to fill the gap.'

'So Dog understood the power of stories? He knew that if he acted out the most powerful story of all, he could do anything?'

Magadien threw me a proud smile, like a teacher acknowledging a bright pupil. 'I think you are beginning to understand,' he said.

I thought of Herman Charles Bosman's remark about prisoners and stories. He was right to say that tales issue from prisoners like djinns from magic bottles. But it is, perhaps, not true that the prisoners themselves 'are merely battered receptacles of [the] stories'. The prisoners *are* the djinns. They emerge from their tales transmogrified, haloed by the magic dust they gather from the myths. And with this magic they garner real power in the politics of the here and now.

*

Is it possible that the Niewoudtville murders carried the force they did because they happened in 1996, two years after the beginning of democracy? Two years was just enough time for the Number gangs to have absorbed and understood that the South African revolution had disappointed them terribly: it would not bring any storming of the Bastille in its wake.

Gangsters have always loved revolutions. They love them because authority evaporates, rules are suspended, and there is much to accomplish during the anarchy of the interregnum. Yet South Africa's revolution turned out not to be a gangster's revolution. It was too orderly, too civil. There never was a gap between the old regime and the new.

When the ANC was unbanned, prisoners across the Western Cape were convinced that the liberation movement would declare a general amnesty. They were sure that the prison doors would be ripped from their hinges. When they discovered it was not to be, when, indeed, they learned that many of them would not even be allowed to vote in the first democratic election, the Number gangs took a collective decision to burn down the prisons themselves. It was a ghastly debacle; prisoners were burnt alive in their locked cells while warders looked on, too afraid to let them out. Magadien was there and you will hear a lot about it later.

And so, perhaps the Niewoudtville murders carried a symbolic weight in 1996 that would have been absent several years earlier. To say, in 1996, that Kilikijan is roaming the countryside once again, that he has killed Rabie, is to say that nothing has changed, that authorities are still authorities, and bandits are still bandits.

*

There is a final twist to the story of Doggy Dog, an unhappy one for the protagonist. Recall Laston Chavulla. Recall how his attention locked onto the fact that Dog neither drank alcohol nor smoked Mandrax during that manic road trip. Recall also Magadien's late-night sessions with Doggy Dog on D Floor: he smoked his pipes until he fell over. What had happened in the interim?

During the Flower Gang trial, a psychiatrist who evaluated the accused on behalf of the state diagnosed Dog and three of his four accomplices as psychopaths. He said that Chavulla was the only one who felt remorse; the rest felt nothing. In the courtroom, the behaviour of the accused seemed to confirm his evaluation. 'Except for Chavulla, [the accused] seemed to view the trial as a bit of a joke,' the journalist Judith Soal wrote in the *Cape Times* the morning after sentence was passed. 'They slumped into the court with their trendy, shaved hairdos and coloured sunglasses, waving to their friends and relatives in the public stands ... One of them, "Moonlight" Bruintjies, claimed to have converted to Christianity and waved a bible in the air, telling anyone who would listen how the Lord forgives your sins and Jesus forgets your crimes, much to the amusement of his accomplices.'

Yet there is a fine line between bravado and genuine jest, too fine, it seems, for the psychiatrist to have noticed. Perhaps if he had been privy to the late-night conversations between Magadien and Dog, he would have thrown away his report and written it all over again.

I asked Magadien why Dog smoked so much Mandrax. 'I don't believe in ghosts,' he replied, 'but sometimes you need to believe in something like that, in spiritual powers. Doggy, that guy could not sleep. He would scream at night. Every time his eyes closed he would wake up and shout. It happened four or five times a night. I told the guys many times, that is the people from Niewoudtville who come to visit him at night, because of the way they were killed. Because they did not know him, they did not do anything to him; they came to ask him why.

'So Dog had to tranquillise himself with Mandrax. He started to smoke more and more. And I knew he is either going to go crazy, or he is going to kill himself. He's not going to live with this thing. He couldn't sleep at night. He needed to fill himself with Mandrax until he was knocked out.'

So there was Doggy Dog, jester of the Keerom Street courtroom, Hollander King in the corridors of D Floor, tormented wreck late at night, trying to smoke his demons away. Magadien was not the only one who noticed. Pollsmoor is full of eyes, full of brains ticking over. There were others who quietly watched Dog fall apart, and they had plans for him.

Among the many quirks of Pollsmoor is this: you may be king of the 27s, but that doesn't mean you have ready access to the drugs that are smuggled into the prison. Out on the Cape Flats there are other gangs, not prison gangs, but street gangs, and it is they who control the province's illicit economy. The relationship between street gangs and prison gangs is a subtle and fascinating one. It has changed quite dramatically over the years and it is changing still.

In the mid and late 1990s, a fierce battle raged in the streets between the Western Cape's two biggest gangs, the Americans and the Firm. The battle had everything to do with the end of apartheid, and the way the opening up of South Africa's economy to the world had changed the country's drug market. Scores of new people were buying new drugs, provided by new market players. The big coloured gangs were scrambling to lay down turf outside the ghettos of the Cape Flats, all over the Western Cape.

For decades, the relationship between the Number gangs and the street gangs had been an oblique one. In the 1970s, many gangsters who were 26s on the inside were Born Free Kids on the outside, and many who were Cape Town Scorpions on the outside were 28s on the inside. But that is as far as the connection went. When a Born Free Kid was finished his sentence, he left the 26s behind in jail, and when he came back to prison he left the Born Free Kids on the streets.

By 1998, that had all changed. The turf battle between the Americans and the Firm was too volatile, too consuming to leave prison out of the picture. And, unlike their small-time forebears in the Scorpions and the Born Free Kids, the drug lords of the Firm and the Americans were multi-millionaires, genuine mafiosi, backed by street armies and arsenals of automatic weapons. When these men went to jail, they were vulnerable; prison was always full of the foot soldiers of their enemies. They needed jail to look more like the streets; they needed to begin to tamper with the century-old Number gangs.

In the early 1990s, something strange began happening on the streets. The Americans took scraps and pieces of ancient 26 ritual – recruitment, rank structure, and so forth – and began to emulate it, in a cobbled, bastardised fashion. The Firm did much the same with the legacy of the 28s. Nongoloza would probably have been pleased. The old Ninevites, who had been crushed on the streets of Johannesburg in the 1910s and had had to retreat into the prisons, were back on the outside.

And in the prisons, the 26s began to look more and more like the Americans, the 28s more and more like the Firm. For decades, successive white governments had been unable to destroy, or even weaken, the Number. And yet, within a few years of apartheid's demise, drug capitalism and drug barons were wreaking havoc with the gangs' ancient traditions. The orthodox old men of the Number, like Magadien, who had little time for street gangs, frowned upon the things happening around them. In their eyes, the 26s and the 28s were brothers, bound together in their anti-colonial struggle. The prospect of a war between the two prison gangs, a war brought in from the outside, was nothing less than a travesty.

As far as the story of Doggy Dog is concerned, what is important is that neither the Firm nor the Americans had been able to gain control of the 27s. It was simply too difficult. An aura of sacredness surrounded the dying Hollanders; the legend of their austerity and their taste for violence was too powerful to emulate. Which rising star in the drug market of the streets is going to sacrifice his life on the outside for the sake of his gang? Which foot soldier is going to agree to spend the rest of his life in jail in order to accrue power for his bosses? The 27s kept wilting away, the force of their legacy growing stronger as they grew weaker, the drug barons of the streets unable to take possession of their authority.

Until Doggy Dog came along, that is.

Many savvy and watchful pairs of eyes observed Doggy Dog. They saw the growing dissonance between the Hollander King of the daylight hours and the mangled being of the night. They noticed in particular the breathtaking quantities of Mandrax he was beginning to consume in order to rest.

It was not long before the drug dealers of Pollsmoor were queuing up to service Dog's habit, and the Americans got in first. 'They stuffed the man with drugs,' Magadien told me. 'They made sure that every night he had enough to feed ten hungry men. They knew if they could keep him in the sky another few months, keep him from going insane until he was sentenced and taken to a prison up country, their work would be done.'

When Dog was sentenced in February 1999, even the cunning Americans were surprised by its severity. The Flower Gang was expecting to be sentenced to life, which meant 25 years, much less if they got out on parole. Instead, the judge dusted off a law that had never been used; he gave them all an indeterminate sentence. Dog, Solomons, Adams and Bruintjies were told to return to court in 50 years, Chavulla in 30. Until then, they were to be housed in the C-Max prison in Pretoria, an ultra-maximum security jail where prisoners spend 23 hours a day alone in a single cell. The Flower Gang would appeal and their sentences would be commuted to life imprisonment. But they did not know that then.

'I didn't see Dog after his sentence was passed,' Magadien told me. 'And it is probably better that way. It is better that Pollsmoor did not see their Hollander King all broken and fucked up.'

Instead, Pollsmoor was left with his legacy. The prison was full of 27s now, and they were all Americans. Dog had recruited them during his final months, a tacit and unspoken quid pro quo: face-saving for power – relief from his nightmares for the Hollander King, possession of the 27s for the Americans.

PART TWO

MAGADIEN BEFORE I MET HIM

5
DISTRICT SIX, TAMBOERSKLOOF

Magadien's cell, Pollsmoor, early December 2002. It is about noon and I am preparing to leave after a marathon session. Magadien fiddles with my dictaphone. He has given himself the responsibility of changing tapes every time one comes to an end, a procedure that has taken on the character of a solemn ritual.

'This thing's fucked,' he says, peering disparagingly into the dictaphone's interior. 'You must go digital. I am worth some decent technology, don't you think?'

I smile at him wearily – it has been a long morning – and turn my back to leave.

'Wait,' he says. 'I've got something for you.'

He rummages through the jewellery box that lives on the cell's narrow table-top, and retrieves a tiny coin.

'Look,' he says. 'Look closely.'

It is a half-cent piece. They were discontinued when I was five or six years old. It is dated 1961, the year in which South Africa's new currency was first minted, and is thus a rare collector's item.

'I thought about it last night,' he says, offering me the coin. 'I decided I want to give it to you.'

'I couldn't possibly,' I say. 'You've been keeping it since your childhood.'

'I'm trying to tell you I'm fond of you, you idiot.' He smiles generously. 'You must keep it. When you go home, you must show it to your dad or mom, see if they remember it.'

I thank him and put my hand on his shoulder, but he darts away, moving about his cell on the balls of his feet. He crouches and throws open the door of his waist-high cabinet.

'I have an apartheid collection,' his voice echoes as he rummages through the cabinet. 'I like to hoard things.' He emerges from the floor with a small bundle, and unwraps it. There is a very formal postcard depicting Cape Town's parliament buildings, a collection of 1960s stamps, another landmark postcard, of the Castle, if I recall correctly.

'I must have something to show my kids,' he explains, 'not because I want to bring back the past. Most of my life was in prison. I have nothing to show the generations to come. Even if it is something small, that will make me happy.'

Walking back to the entrance of the prison, I clutch Magadien's half-cent coin in a tight fist. He is obsessed with posterity and with roots; he fears he will have no posterity if he does not retrieve, or at least improvise, his roots. A couple of postcards, a few stamps, a coin; it is a sparse collection of tools with which to put together one's childhood. Then I recall his fantasy of me, my dad and my mom, sitting around the family table, fingering this coin; the memories of one Steinberg generation are rekindled, shored up in the heart of the Steinberg home, transferred to me. Magadien has a wonderful propensity to project the things he never had onto others, as if the richness of other people's lives will fill up the holes in his own.

*

Magadien was born in the Somerset Hospital in the inner-city suburb of Green Point on 8 March, probably in 1960, possibly 1959; like much of the South African working class, his family is a poor keeper of records. He spent the first seven years of his life in the midst of a large extended family on Cowley Street in District Six.

It is very hard, given what has come to pass, for anyone to think clearly about District Six. Built in the heart of nineteenth-century Cape Town, and host to generations of that dazzling creole culture peculiar to port cities, it was razed to the ground by apartheid's masters between the late 1960s and early 1980s, ejecting tens of thousands of its coloured and African inhabitants onto the Cape Flats – a stretch of windswept scrubland on the city's south-eastern flank. The removals were among apartheid's most spine-chilling ventures, blistering evidence of its indifference to the memories and public spaces of those who are not white.

It is unsurprising then that today, at the beginning of the post-apartheid era, the old neighbourhood has been canonised as a dreamy myth. The still images on display in the District Six Museum on Buitenkant Street – narrow terraced streets, *fin de siècle*, double-storey houses, teeming street life – appear to be bursting with an exotic vitality. 'The apartheid government did not like us living under democracy,' a museum tour guide, who grew up in District Six, told her audience the day I visited. 'We were a little rainbow.'

The truth, of course, is a lot harsher than that. District Six was a place where aspirant petit bourgeois had to share their space with an aggressive underclass, where priests had to walk past brothels and through gang turf on their way to Sunday services. Everybody was crammed together, and so everyone tried to distinguish themselves. A minute filigree of social distinctions, quite illegible to an outsider, traced itself across the district. And at the centre of it all was the vexed question of colouredness, an identity that had been raped and disfigured by three centuries of white supremacy. District Six was a place where those of too dark a skin were barred admission from sports and social clubs, where those who claimed to trace their ancestry to the proud Malay Muslims disparaged those with allegedly bastardised roots as *hotnots* and *boesmans*.

'The Half-caste has multiplied and now forms a more or less distinct section of society,' the celebrated novelist Olive Schreiner wrote of coloured identity in 1923. 'Nevertheless, socially his position remains much what it was. Without nationality, tradition, or racial ideals … robbed of racial self-respect … The Englishman will swear to you on the word of an Englishman, and the Bantu on the word of the Bantu, but no Half-caste ever yet swore on the honour of a Half-caste. The world would break into cackling laughter did he do so: "*The honour of the Half-caste!*"'

District Six absorbed much of this cruel, historically erroneous jibing. The bustling street life of the museum photographs conceals a lot of pain, a lot of confusion.

Magadien's own lifelong quest to find his origins is buried deep in the malaise of coloured identity. His dilemmas, though, are far more difficult than most; right from the start, the question of his ancestry, indeed, the question of his very name, was something of a puzzle.

*

Magadien's memories of early childhood are potted but wonderfully vivid, animated as they are by his deep fascination with objects. He grew up in the household of Johnny and Annie Mekka, a respectable, working-class, Christian family. 'We lived in a huge house on Cowley Street,' he recalls. 'The floors were planks and the stairs too. Lots of families lived there. We were upstairs because I remember we had a balcony. Most of the properties then were owned by Jewish guys who lived elsewhere.' The photographic books on District Six are littered with pictures of such houses: turn-of-the-century double-storeys, boasting tasteful wrought-iron trimmings.

He recalls the crèche on Cowley Street where he spent his days – 'we were given huge ginger biscuits and milk there' – and the corner shop at the end of his street. 'Remember that half-cent coin you took home,' he reminds me. 'Before that there were pennies and tickeys and sixpence. Annie would give me a couple of pennies. There was a big sweet with a star you could get in the corner shop; you got four for a penny. And then there was also a big pinball machine full of sweets.'

I wonder about Magadien's recollections of the pennies and sixpence. He was, at most, two years old when they were removed from circulation. What he is giving me, I suspect, are memories of memories, a childhood glimpsed through the tapestry of four subsequent decades.

The pennies and the sweets trigger rounder recollections, the beginnings of a narrative. 'The shop owner was an Indian, a Muslim guy. Bapi, we called him. My granny lived further along Tennant Street, past Hanover Street. The National bioscope was there and a barber, Jackie Oakers. His son was married to one of Annie's sisters, so I went to him for haircuts. All our people were in and around Hanover Street.'

At first blush, it appears to be a typical District Six childhood. Throughout the first half of the twentieth century, the district had been host to wave upon wave of immigrants from the countryside. The newcomers sought out near and distant family in the neighbourhood. Extended families began to live in close proximity, shared domestic responsibilities, helped one another into the job market, patronised one another's modest businesses. Through their mutually supportive networks, Don Pinnock wrote in the early 1980s, a few years after the last structures in District Six were demolished, extended families found livelihoods 'in the crevices of economic activity, in micro-commerce and hawking – all with extremely limited access to capital'.

Magadien's most sensate memories of early childhood are of Johnny Mekka, the first of several father-figures in his life. His recollections of Johnny are idealised, almost dreamlike – this gentle, angelic figure, the exotic scents of his trade in his clothes and in his hair.

'He worked at sea,' Magadien tells me. 'He was a fisherman. My memories of him are strange; what I remember most clearly are his tools. Like the leather thong that was strapped to his hand. I cleaned all his stuff: that was my job.'

The memory of Johnny's tools sits with him for a while, other recollections gather around them, and when he speaks again his voice is quiet and wistful.

'He took me out on the boat once. Remember, in the early days we lived near the docks. It was one of my most exciting days. I watched everything he did so closely. And there was the wind and the sea and the sight of Cape Town from the sea.

'He always had time. He took us for walks, through the Gardens, to the bicycle shop. He would buy us ice creams. I am by his side in all my early memories of town.'

'Your postcard of parliament,' I say, 'that is right next to the Gardens ...'

'Yes,' he interrupts. 'I was with Johnny when I saw parliament. You know you could never tell when he was cross. I can't recall that he ever hit someone or talked badly about somebody. He was respected. He was everything wonderful, everything you could wish for in a dad.'

About Annie, Johnny's wife, Magadien is less enthusiastic. 'She loved me in her own way,' he says, 'and she still does. But her mind was always somewhere else. She only saw me out of the corner of her eye. She was busy with other things.'

There is no such thing as pure memory. Everything we recall is filtered by the things we learned later. It is quite possible that if Johnny had not died an early death, if he had been around when Magadien learned the truth about himself and the Mekkas, his memories of the idyllic boat man would have been sullied. He has attached Johnny to the days of his innocence, Annie to the trauma of his experience. That is how things have come to sit in his mind.

But right from the start, something was awry. Magadien's three older brothers were called John, Victor and Anthony Mekka. Yet his own birth certificate named him Magadien Darryl Martin

Wentzel. His younger sister, Anne, was also a Wentzel at the beginning. But then her name was changed to Mekka. The Mekkas were Christian and Afrikaans-speaking. Yet 'Magadien' is a Cape Muslim, Malay name. And, in the racial classification that adorned every birth certificate and identity document during the apartheid days, Magadien was designated 'Cape Malay'. The rest of his family was 'Cape Coloured'.

The Mekkas called him Darryl. They never referred to him as Magadien. And in the first eleven years of his life, he never asked himself or anyone else why his surname was Wentzel. 'At school,' he recalls, 'I was very active in athletics – javelin, high jump, everything. We would have these big inter-school tournaments and you would have to bring your birth certificate. The teachers would look at it and say, "Why Magadien?" I could not answer. I did not know the story of my name.'

But there were people who called him Magadien. Sometimes on weekends Annie would take him to visit a friend of hers in Tamboerskloof, a white middle-class, inner-city suburb on the slopes of Table Mountain. The friend was a coloured woman called Gadija. She was employed as a domestic worker by a young white family, the Sampsons, and she stayed in the servants' quarters on the roof of the residential building where her employers lived. Norman Sampson was a young lawyer in private practice. Magadien's earliest memories of him are of a reclusive, withdrawn man, glimpsed furtively through the open door of his study. His wife, Denise, Magadien barely recalls at all. She is merely an absence. But he remembers their two children – Stephen and Joanne – very well. Joanne was a little younger than Magadien, Stephen about two years older.

Upon arriving in Tamboerskloof, 'Darryl' would be sent to the children's room to play, while Annie chatted to Gadija in the kitchen. In his memory, Stephen and Joanne are barely interested in him, or in their expensive and exotic toys. Instead, they fight viciously with each other, and they keep abandoning their bedroom for the kitchen. They are competing for Gadija's attention. They call her 'mommy'.

Another figure is present in those early visits to Tamboerskloof. His name is David Cornelius and he is the janitor of the building. David is also coloured; he also lives in the servants' quarters on the roof; he appears to be Gadija's lover. 'Darryl' is very fond of him. He recalls that David takes him through the streets of the inner city to a dry cleaners just off Kloof Street. A group of David's friends are always already gathered there when he arrives. They are smart, smooth men, and they wear Stetsons and tailor-made trousers. They take a keen interest in the young boy; they give him small change, and he asks them questions about their clothes. He will learn a little later that they refer to themselves as members of the Globe, District Six's most legendary gang.

Sitting in his Pollsmoor cell, I press him for early memories of Gadija. She must have been keen to develop a relationship with him right from the beginning. But his responses are thin and scant. He remembers her as the mommy of the two quarrelsome white children. And he remembers that she called him Magadien.

There were other oddities in his childhood. Every Christmas, an expensive present would be waiting for him under the Mekka household tree. Yet there were no expensive presents for Victor, John or Anthony, nor any for his younger sister Anne. On his third Christmas Day, a state-of-the-art pram was delivered to the Mekkas' doorstep. 'Whenever my parents pushed me through the streets,' Magadien tells me, 'everyone stared. Nothing like it had ever been seen in District Six. So they sold the pram. It was drawing too much attention.' It is unlikely that Magadien has first-hand memories of the famous pram. He is probably recalling Mekka folk lore.

'I only found out when I was ten or eleven where the presents came from,' he recalls. 'They told me they were from the people in Tamboerskloof.'

'From Gadija and David?' I ask.

'No, from the Sampsons.'

There were other weekend visits too, to the Strand, a town on the Indian Ocean about forty kilometres from Cape Town, cradled in the giant arms of False Bay. The Strand is home to one of the Cape's oldest Muslim settlements, and Annie would lead him through the town's coloured township, Rusthof, past the neighbourhood mosques, to a modest house on Webb Street. There they would be greeted by a pious old Muslim man and his wife. The old man was known as Bapi, and he would beam at the young boy and address him as Magadien.

*

In 1967, the double-storey house on Cowley Street was demolished and the Mekkas were forced to move to the distant Cape Flats estate of Heideveld. They were among the first wave of families to be moved from District Six. By the early 1970s, Cowley Street had become a derelict lane overgrown with weeds and lined with the stumps of amputated houses.

'We were the first or second among the extended family to be moved,' Magadien tells me. 'Our section was the first to be bulldozed. Where my granny lived, they survived a couple of years longer. Then they bulldozed that too.

'We were split up. The other family that moved at the same time as us only had a daughter and they wanted Anthony to go with them. They went to Hanover Park. We went to Heideveld. Daphne Court, number 12. I'll never forget that name. It was strange; the sand dunes, the veld, the nearby farms. No more extended family. Lots of strangers. I spent every afternoon with the others kids in the courtyard. We became a little group.'

Shortly after the move to Daphne Court, Johnny Mekka died of heart problems. 'I must have been nine years old. I was there at his death bed. He told me to look after the family. I guess that's just something some people say when they are dying. But after he died, everything changed. We had to leave Daphne Court. With Johnny gone, we were told the flat was too big for us, that we had to make way for a larger family. So they moved us to another building in Heideveld, Grace Court, number 33, opposite the hospital. I never felt at home there. Annie worked at a printing works. She would pick me up from school on her way home. I would go straight to Daphne Court. That's where I had made friends, in the courtyard. The new place was not my home.'

Magadien's most vivid memory of the events surrounding Johnny's death is an incident at the funeral. 'Remember,' he tells me, 'coloured funerals are quite different. We party and drink.

'I was sitting on the floor, surrounded by these adults sitting in chairs. David Cornelius was there. Everybody was drinking and talking and somebody pointed at David and said to me, "That's your new dad." So I went to sit in his lap. He played with me and I was happy to be there. You see, I had just lost Johnny. I was very sore. I was worried about where love was going to come from. And I said to Annie, "He's not really my dad, is he?" And she said,

"Yes, he is." And everybody laughed. It seemed to be some sort of adult joke. But I liked the thought. It made me feel happy and grateful.'

There soon was to be a new man in Magadien's life, but it wasn't David. Shortly after Johnny died, Annie brought home a man called Quinton. 'When we met him for the first time he was wearing a Stetson and a leather jacket with the collar turned up. Like a gangster, like the old Globe Gang. His trousers were always cut at the tailor. He was out of a different class.' Magadien hated him instantly.

'He sounds like David's friends at the dry cleaners,' I comment.

He shrugs.

'What did he do for a living?'

'I don't remember exactly. He had recently been released from jail. He got a good job and he held onto it; one job, the whole time. I must respect him for that.'

That is all Magadien is prepared to say about him. In his memory, or at least in those quarters of his memory he chooses to verbalise, Quinton has no face, no gestures, no voice. He is an icy, menacing presence: just his Stetson, his upturned collar, and his fists.

'We didn't see eye-to-eye from the very beginning,' Magadien says. 'I'm not sure whether I drove him to beat me, but I know that I made his life as difficult as I could right at the start. I missed Johnny, and I didn't like the way he made Annie behave. After Quinton came into her life, he was priority number one. It was always about him. Not about me and my sister any more. During that time, me and my sister became inseparable. We had this telepathy between us. We developed this second instinct, to look out for each other.'

But his sister Anne was not an adequate defence. Magadien would steal from Quinton – the money from his wallet, any portable valuables – and the dark Stetson man would beat him with his belt buckle and his fists. The way Magadien relates the story now, it was almost as if he willed Quinton's violence, as if he knew exactly where to find it and sort it; it is as if he was acting out a set-piece of the relationship between the cruel stepfather and the rebellious stepson. If he did seek beatings from Quinton, it was mostly to remind himself that Annie was not a proper mother. 'She just stood by,' he tells me. 'She let him beat me. What sort of a mother allows a man to come into her house and do that to her son?'

Then there were John and Victor, who were in their late teens by the time the family moved to Heideveld. They were wild, intemperate boys, among the first recruits of the Cape Flats' emerging street gangs. Victor was later to go to prison and join the 26s; and he was to die a violent death on the streets. But when Magadien's older brothers were at home, they terrorised him.

'I wouldn't call it bullying,' Magadien says. 'That word is not heavy enough. They would hit me hard, very hard, and for no reason. Coming home was a nightmare. I wouldn't know where the next fist would come from, or why.

'And nobody stopped them. When Johnny was alive, they did not dare put a finger on me. Nobody raised his voice or used his fists when Johnny was around. It was just unthinkable.'

It is difficult for Magadien. He speaks these words now, more than thirty years later, on the brink of his release from prison. He is trying to start a new life, one centred around a family. He needs to make amends with the adults of his childhood. He needs to ask their forgiveness for the things he subsequently did, to tell them that however badly they brought him up, he is responsible for all his actions.

'When they read this they will feel hurt,' he says. 'But these are things I must say to their faces, with forgiveness in my voice, forgiveness for them and myself.'

*

About two years after Johnny died, Magadien asked Annie to help him with a school assignment. 'We had to go and find out about our family roots,' he tells me. 'Where we came from, where our parents and our great grandparents lived, what they did for a living, how things have changed. I took the assignment very seriously. I was still thinking a lot about Johnny. I wanted to know where he came from, who he was. I didn't want him to slip away from me.

'So I asked Annie to help me, and she said to me, she said, "I can't answer these questions. I don't know. You must go and ask your real mother. You must ask Auntie Gadija from Tamboerskloof. And your father, David."

'It should never have come out that way. It was a mistake. I will never be able to describe how I felt when I heard that. Even now, when I am thinking about it, I am so fucking confused.'

What he felt was indeed complicated, but it is not impossible to put it all together. Strange as it may sound, one of those feelings was relief. He had discovered, among other things, that his maternal heritage was Muslim and Malay, and he liked that a lot.

'When we were still in District Six, the Mekkas used to take me to church. They were Anglicans. Annie's late brother was one of the choir boys at St Mark's. We went there on Christmas day, and for Sunday school. In Heideveld, we went to the Holy Cross, and later, after we moved to Hanover Park, my sister and I went to St Dominic's and sang in the choir. But I got bored and dropped out. It meant nothing to me.

'You see, I always had this sense I did not belong. It wasn't a conscious thing. I didn't ask myself, "Is Annie really my mother? Why is my surname Wentzel?" It was just a feeling inside, starting mainly from when Johnny died, that I did not belong.

'I was proud to discover I was a Muslim. You can understand that, can't you? For the first time in my life, I discovered where I came from, what my history was. The first time I went to mosque, at the Strand, with my grandfather, I felt comfortable there. I listened to the sounds, and smelt the smell, and to me it was something special. I had a feeling I belonged.'

He was proud to be a Muslim boy, certainly, but his pride was tinged with rage. He had had to discover his roots by accident, by a careless slip of Annie's tongue. And he hated the adult world for the things it kept from him. He walked through his foster-family's cramped Cape Flats home, a place of cruel men's fists and a distracted mother, and he felt, with unsuppressible fury, that he never did belong there, never should have been there, that he had been tricked into living this miserable life.

Yet he saved most of his bitterness for Gadija, and, by proxy, for her two surrogate children, Stephen and Joanne. 'She gave me away when I was a baby,' he says, 'so that she could look after some white cunt's children. She lied to me so that she could spend her life being some white cunt's servant maid. That's how I felt for a long time. I hated her guts. I hated her for all I was worth. Now, things have changed. Now I'm a little confused. I think, Jesus, she must have done her best. She was a servant maid who loved her children so much that she put them all in different places so they could pursue what they wanted.'

Magadien hated his mother, but he clung to her nonetheless. She haunted him, and he made a mission of coming back, again and again, to haunt her in turn.

'I kept going to Tamboerskloof,' he tells me. 'Sometimes it was because I was in trouble in Hanover Park, but mainly it was to make trouble for my mother. I wanted to hurt her any way I could. She would give me money and I would spend it on dagga, just because it was *her* money; I believed it should be wasted on something destructive. When she wasn't looking, I would steal her money. I needed her to know how much I hated her. I tried my best to make her hate me back. My whole life was centred around making her hate me.'

He also kept on playing with the Sampson children, carefully masking his jealous rage. 'They didn't notice me,' Magadien comments bitterly. 'They only noticed my mother. They were fighting each other for her attention. I was this plaything, this little coloured plaything. When their toys weren't good enough for them any more, I would get them. When their clothes got holes in them, they would arrive on my doorstep.'

Magadien hated Gadija well into his adulthood. In his early twenties, during a three-year spell in jail, Gadija, his sister Anne, and his foster-mother Annie would visit him from time to time. When he asked after David Cornelius, the man he had been told was his biological father, he was told that David was fine, that he sent his love and his greetings.

A few days after he was released from prison, he discovered that David had been dead for more than two years. 'He was murdered by his own brother,' Magadien recalls. 'He was beaten to death with a spade.

'They didn't want to tell me because they were worried about what I would do. I was a crazy, fucked-up guy. They thought I would try to kill my uncle. But that's not how I saw things. I exploded. I thought, "When are the lies going to stop? When the fuck is this bitch going to stop hiding my life from me?"'

By then, Gadija had long since parted company with David, and the Sampsons no longer lived in Tamboerskloof. She had married and was living in Hanover Park with her husband. This union was to give Magadien two new half-siblings.

'I wanted to kill her and her husband,' Magadien says. 'I went to their house in Hanover Park in broad daylight, in the afternoon. I stood outside the house and shouted and screamed and started to cry. She appeared at the window and I shouted at her. I called her a bitch. Then I took out my gun and I started shooting. She ducked under a table, but the bullets flew through her house. The TV was smashed and many of the windows. When the magazine was empty I sat down in the road and cried.'

The fury that the news of David's death unleashed in Magadien was quite complicated. It was not that Gadija had concealed his father's murder from him. He felt that the deceit and the dissembling went much deeper than that, that a whole host of precious truths about his parentage remained shrouded.

For Magadien never believed that David was his biological father. 'Why is my surname Wentzel?' he wonders aloud. 'Wentzel is from my mother's side; it is her father's surname. If David was my father, why didn't they call me Cornelius? And David was a Christian. Why were they so quick to call me a Muslim?

'David never treated me as a son, you know. He always acted like a friend. I loved him, and I always remembered that day at Johnny's funeral when I sat on his lap; but he was never like a father. He would take me to the dry cleaners off Kloof Street and his friends would joke around with me. I loved their attention. I loved the things they spoke about – girls and clothes. But his interest in me was not the interest a father takes in a son. He was just fond of me.'

There was another man who did take an extraordinary interest in Magadien, precisely the sort of interest a father might take in a son: Stephen and Joanne's dad – Norman Sampson. His presence in Magadien's memory is odd: always withdrawn, always at a remove from the life of his family, but always there, in Magadien's life, long after the other Sampsons had retreated, right until his death in the early 1990s. It was not just the expensive presents that lay under the Mekka Christmas tree every year, nor the fact that there were no gifts for young Anne, even though she too was Gadija's biological child.

Long after Gadija stopped working for him, Norman kept a benign eye on Magadien. He bought him school shoes when he began high school; he monitored Magadien's academic development with interest. And he appeared to be elated when it became apparent that Magadien was very clever, that he always finished first or second in his class. In Magadien's and Gadija's memories, Norman was determined that Magadien was going to become an attorney like him.

Later, when Magadien's life of crime began in earnest, Norman would appear again. At the commencement of his first three trials, Magadien would climb up the stairs from the holding cells into the courtroom to find Norman there, talking in a huddle with prosecutors and other lawyers. Thanks to Norman, three of his sentences were commuted: one to a warning, a second to a fine, a third to a caning. 'I was much too old for a caning by then,' Magadien tells me. 'It was meant to be for juveniles. Norman must have pulled a lot of strings.'

It is one of those tantalisingly ambivalent tales. The 'servant girls' of the townships brought their souls, their bodies and their troubles into white suburbia. The family hearth is seldom a stable place; it is often the scene of unpredictable adventures; it is not a place where the line between master and servant is easily patrolled. And so actions and gestures become ambivalent. The difference between a guilt-ridden benefactor and a wistful lover is not always easy to detect. Nor indeed is the difference between a sentimental patron and a secret father.

The relationship between Norman and Magadien could go either way. It is possible that Norman was an unusually sensitive man, prone to strong and painful bouts of empathy. It could be that the figure of the servant who gave up her children in order to care for his touched a chord. He might have watched the decline of young Magadien despairingly, aware that he himself was indirectly complicit, that a woman who is forced to spend her life in his kitchen gathers a great deal of tragedy about her.

But if this is indeed the case, Norman was an extremely unusual man. Ever since Nongoloza's times, young black adults have been abandoning their children to others in order to work in white businesses and homes. It was a dominant signature of twentieth-century South Africa, and it imprinted itself on the lives of generations of black children. Most whites did not notice. The colonial imagination did not stretch very far. The 'servant girl' would spend 11 months of the year in the kitchen and then disappear to her 'home' for Christmas or Easter: some dimly imagined ghetto or countryside where whites did not venture.

So it could be that Norman only thought about the ghettos and the prisons because his own blood was wandering its side streets and its corridors. Everything Norman did for Magadien he did in the utmost secrecy: his family knew nothing of it. And he failed miserably. Magadien hated Norman for all he was worth; he wasn't going to accept the white man's helping hand.

*

Magadien is impressively philosophical about the question of his parentage. 'I would be a fool to say I know that Norman is my father,' he tells me one summer morning in his Pollsmoor cell. 'But then again, I would be a fool to say I know he isn't. He and my mother had something strange between them. And then he took this interest in my life, right until the end, like he was trying to save me.

'I need to know why. I need to know who I am. If David is my father, I will have my name changed to Cornelius. And my children too: they must become Corneliuses. I have been through too many false names: Magadien, Darryl, William Steenkamp, JR. What will they write on my tombstone? I need the truth written on my grave. Not just for my sake, but for my children. I owe it them that they find out where they come from, that they carry the family name of their blood.

'It is the first thing I must do when I get out of here. I must repair things with my mother. I will ask for her forgiveness, but I will also ask her difficult questions. She needs to come clean with me about who my father is. I need to explain to her, gently and carefully, why it means so much to me.'

I look at Magadien closely. There is nothing Negroid about his facial anatomy. His thin mouth is Arabic or Caucasian. His hooked nose is positively Semitic. But that does not tell me very much. Gadija's parents are from the Strand, one of the oldest Muslim settlements in South Africa. They could well be the direct descendents of Dutch East Indian slaves imported to the Cape in the seventeenth and eighteenth centuries. There is no reason for there to be a drop of Negroid blood in his veins.

I mutter something to him about apartheid, about how his mother was forced into choices no human being should have to make. He responds with anger. 'I am so fucking tired of people blaming apartheid,' he shouts. 'Every time some community on the Cape Flats fucks itself up, people shrug and say, "apartheid this, apartheid that". It's pathetic.

'Long ago, I stopped blaming apartheid for who I am.' He thumps a long digit into his chest. 'It's me, just me. I made all the choices. I fucked up. And I'm sorry, but the same applies to my mother. During the Holocaust, the Jews died alongside their children. In the camps. On the trains. They died with their children, for fuck's sake. We didn't have a Holocaust here. My family was not slaughtered in a concentration camp. So where were they? Why couldn't they take responsibility for their children?'

As Magadien speaks these words, Gadija is just twenty-odd kilometres away, somewhere in the maze of Heideveld. I want to get into my car and drive straight from Pollsmoor to her home; I want to sit down with her, cultivate a relationship with her, slowly tease out her past, eventually get to the point where I can ask her about the circumstances of her son's conception. But I restrain myself. It is too meddlesome. Magadien's release date is a few months away, and he needs, perhaps more than anything, to mend his relationship with his mother. I fear the damage I might do.

So we agree that I will only meet Gadija after his release, that he himself will introduce me to her, that he himself will ask her the tough questions. In the mean time, I poke around in safer places.

*

I try to make contact with the Sampsons. Norman is long dead. His daughter Joanne has emigrated. I search the telephone directory of the town in which I am told she lives; I make a dozen phone calls; I cannot find her. Norman's wife, Denise, has moved to the other end of South Africa. My messages go unanswered.

Stephen, though, is easy to find. He still lives in Cape Town. It is simply a question of looking up his name in the phone book, dialling the number.

I tell him my business and he responds with enthusiasm. 'Of course I remember Miriam,' he says. 'I will never forget her.' (Yet another person with multiple names in Magadien's life. 'Miriam' is Gadija's servant name; the pronunciation of her real name is too difficult for white, English-speaking employers. So she thinks up something common and English for the Sampsons.) 'And yes, I remember Darryl. He was a little older than Joanne, a little younger than me. I knew him well.'

I ask if we can meet, and suddenly his demeanour changes. 'The story I have to tell is of the utmost importance,' he says. 'You cannot possibly write your book without it. And nobody else will tell you. My mother will never speak about Miriam, and my sister has emigrated. We have not spoken in ages. I am the only one.'

By now I have grown quite excited. I ask when we can meet.

'Like I say,' he replies, 'I am the only one who will talk.'

'And so?'

'And so I am wondering about money. My story is worth a lot.'

I bristle with anger. Magadien, the penniless prisoner, about to be released into the world without a cent, without a definite prospect of a job, has insisted that there be no exchange of money. And yet this spoiled bourgeois man, whose father paid Gadija's wages from a fraction of his income, he is the one scrounging, right from the start.

I tell him curtly that there will be no money, that it is not even worth talking about. He hops and dances. 'If the book is successful …? An agreement about a percentage of royalties …?'

'No,' I say.

He agrees to meet me anyway, says he will 'consult with friends' in the mean time. We arrange a time and a place.

*

We meet on a Saturday afternoon in one of Cape Town's spectacular public spaces. It is late summer, the sun is on our backs, and there are families and young lovers and solitary strollers about.

I have changed his name on his request. I will not describe the setting of our meeting. Nor will I describe his physical appearance except to say that he is an obviously tragic figure. He wears an odd assortment of clothes: well-worn blue jeans with a smart shirt and a tie, an old-fashioned sleeveless jersey, a sweat-stained baseball cap. He makes little eye-contact, pointing his head down and to the side; but the stories flow out of him, sad and largely unsolicited.

He tells me he is unemployed at the moment, although he gets work from time to time. He is university-educated, articulate and erudite. His difficulties in conducting a successful life clearly stem from emotional trauma; a man of his education and background should not struggle to find a job. He hints that he is supported by a controlling, meddlesome mother, and he does so with resentment. 'At the age of 45, I don't take kindly to being told whom to see and where to go,' he says. 'I am not a happy chappie.'

At first he protests that it was all so long ago that he cannot remember much, but the protests are merely a formality, a clearing of the throat. He is, in fact, quite anxious to talk about his childhood; he has clearly been looking forward to our meeting.

'It would be no exaggeration to say that I loved Miriam,' he tells me. 'And equally, it is no exaggeration to say that my mother handled her problems with Miriam very badly.'

'What sort of problems did your mother have with Miriam?'

'It was about us,' he says. 'About Miriam's relationship with me and my sister. My parents' marriage was a messy one; it didn't leave one with good feelings. My best memories are in the kitchen with Miriam. She encouraged us to be more lively. My mother was quite a disciplinarian when it came to bedtime and eating habits. I would say that I owe – how shall I put it? – my comforts to members of the previously disadvantaged community. To Miriam. She would always have people of that background round visiting her. I got to meet people from all different walks of life. She taught me Afrikaans. We used to sing together.'

I marvel at his euphemisms as he dances around the fact his surrogate mother was coloured. 'Previously disadvantaged ... people of that background ...' And I grimace to myself when I imagine Magadien listening to this. He would not take kindly.

'I remember her with great affection,' Stephen continues, in his formal, very Anglophone manner. 'More affection than my mother would care for me to express. Miriam substituted for my mom when she was busy with charity work and other good works. And when my mother was on one of her lengthy trips overseas, we would stay up late at Miriam's parties. We got up to all sorts of naughty but nice things.'

He smiles broadly for the first time; his commentary has brought with it a cherished memory.

'We had lovely Christmases with Miriam. One Christmas we had a huge, 13-foot tree on the balcony. My parents had gone somewhere for the night and weren't expected back until the next morning. Miriam invited all her friends to come up. I suppose there was a lot of drinking and smoking – I don't remember. We were five or six, up well past our bedtimes; it was wonderful. When my parents came back the next morning and we were still up, having not gone to bed, there was hell to pay. My father took my mother's side in order to keep the peace, but I don't think his heart was in it.'

'Was your mother quite as strict as you remember?' I ask. 'Are you perhaps making her more extreme, in opposition to Miriam?'

'Oh, no. No, not at all. I was not allowed out alone until I was well into my twenties. Only when I got a car could I go out by myself, but even then there would be restrictions, and if I disobeyed there would be terrible consequences.'

Miriam drifted in and out of his life until he was 12 or 13. Her absences were painful, her presence exhilarating. 'Sometimes she would leave to have another child,' he says, 'and I guess for other reasons. She had a terribly stormy relationship with her husband, David, the janitor. And then with her next husband; Khan was his name, I think. Very stormy relationships.

'Then, when I was 12 or 13, my mother cut all ties with Miriam. I was very angry, very angry indeed.'

'Your mother cut ties because ...'

'Because we were too close to Miriam, too close to the so-called coloured community. She still feels the same way, by the by. I, on the other hand, can mix in all sorts of communities. I attribute that to Miriam. She was very liberal. Her influence was positive, not negative.

'At one of my birthdays she got a top coloured band to perform. They were the rage at the time. The Rockets, I think they were called. It was a huge affair. Three hundred people. Anybody and everybody came: all the top people in Cape Town.'

He didn't lay eyes on Gadija again for another seven or eight years, he tells me. As far as he was aware, she and her son had vanished from the Sampsons' lives for good. I begin, gently, to broach the question of Norman's relationship with Magadien, which was at its most interesting during the years in which Stephen's surrogate mother was banished, the years during which, he believed, there had been no contact. I tell him that Magadien became a career criminal in early adulthood, that he has spent the better part of his adult life in jail.

'Good grief. I had no idea, absolutely no idea. Crumbs, what a terrible story. I remember Darryl as a little boy in his little clothes. He was a pretty baby. He used to come to visit with other people.'

He digests the information I have given him, and it is not long before he has regurgitated it in the form of white guilt. 'I liked to share, when I could,' he says. 'My mother used to give me all the latest toys from overseas, and I would share them with Darryl. When I had my birthday parties I'd invite all my friends to come. If Darryl happened to be there he would be invited too and get his slice of cake.'

I tell him of the things Norman did for Magadien, from the Christmas presents under the District Six tree, to the academic coaching and encouragement, to the legal assistance when Magadien was in trouble with the law.

He responds immediately, without pondering. 'Certainly if he had been assisting Darryl when Darryl was 18, I can't recall him mentioning it to me one way or the other. He probably did it surreptitiously. My mother certainly would have known nothing about it. She would have been horrified. She would have freaked.'

He pauses and thinks for a while. 'My father was inclined to charity. He was a kind-hearted man. He understood Miriam's circumstances far better than my mother. She had a typically middle-class, upright upbringing.'

'He must have been very fond of Miriam,' I say.

'It would be no understatement,' he repeats, mistaking the subject of my question, 'to say that I loved Miriam deeply.'

'What was your father's relationship with Miriam like?'

'He was a very strange fellow. He interacted very little. He wanted supper to be ready. We would listen to the radio or sit around the table. Unfortunately, my recollections of Darryl are vague. It was long ago.'

Gadija appeared in the Sampsons' lives again, when Stephen was in his early twenties, under the oddest circumstances. Norman and Denise had recently divorced. 'It should have happened much sooner,' Stephen tells me. 'It would have been better for everyone involved, including the two of them. They were utterly incompatible.

'My father was becoming increasingly quirky. And Joanne and I decided that our mother needed our support. So we chose to live with her, in the southern suburbs. And Miriam came to work for us, briefly.'

'That's extraordinary,' I say. 'Your mother seems to have regarded Miriam as her enemy.'

'She needed someone she could trust, and she knew Miriam. She does not trust people, my mother. Somehow, contact with Miriam was remade. The two of them had a long talk, and it seems mother came to terms with the past.'

Soon after Gadija returned, Denise went on one of her extended overseas trips, leaving the coloured woman in charge of the household. Stephen's face mellows with sweet memories. He begins, for the first time, to speak of Gadija as a mother, quite literally as a mother, without realising it, it seems, and the profundity of her place in his soul is both moving and unsettling.

'I remember that period as wonderful. Miriam did everything she could to make our lives comfortable. Joanne had boyfriends my mother did not take kindly to, and Miriam would say it is quite all right. My own preferences are not the point, but suffice it to say that I had callers of a different persuasion. And Miriam understood and accepted my choices as she would her own child. She spoke to me about it, made it clear she wanted me within certain boundaries, but within those boundaries, things could work well. It was a lovely, carefree time.'

Then Miriam disappeared again, this time forever. He has not seen her in 20 years. 'I miss her terribly,' he says. 'As to whether I would go to great lengths to re-establish contact is another question.'

There is a long silence during which we both take in the world around us. Stephen has transferred some of his sadness to me; the people about seem far away; their shouts and their chatter appear to echo.

A group of teenaged boys are playing soccer. Their ball bounces towards us and I punch it back to them. Stephen watches and giggles. He has been thinking about his father.

'In a way, he was a very gentle, very kind man, who ended up very badly from promising beginnings. He did not die a particularly good death. He was not a good role model, to put it plainly. Although a good man, he was a weak man. I might have done things slightly differently if he had been a good role model. I never became a lawyer. People say, why didn't you follow in his footsteps? Nothing would have filled me with more horror.'

'Why?'

'He did not need to go it alone. He could have joined a successful practice. Many of his friends went on to join the ranks of the finest practitioners in the country. I visited their offices as a boy: all the books, a magnificent desk. My father's office was the complete antithesis. I don't know why. He could have been great. Instead, he had this hole-in-the-wall practice. Many of his clients did not pay him.'

There is a long silence again.

'Perhaps I've let the boat pass me by in some respects. But I've always been a romantic and an optimist. Maybe the ship is still in the harbour somewhere waiting for me to board. Realistically, I think I have missed my chances and I will make do with what I have got. But I am comfortable with that.'

Later, as we are preparing to part, I remind him of the things he said on the phone. 'Why did you tell me my book would be impossible to write without your story?'

'I was being facetious,' he replies, with some embarrassment. 'I hadn't had a particularly good day myself, so forget about it.'

'I'm sorry I can't offer you money for your help.'

'I'm sorry I had to ask,' he replies. 'I'm not a wealthy man. Most people would have responded similarly. I'm not making excuses for it.' He looks up and laughs. 'Any offer of semi-permanent employment would not go amiss.'

I am about to walk off and he calls me back. 'When are you seeing Darryl again?' he asks.

'Monday morning.'

'Monday morning, you say, Monday morning. We were close once, a long time ago. I've recollections. They're very distant memories, like an echo you hear at the bottom of a well.

'It's awful that he's ended up in the big house. Miriam sometimes discussed problems but we never went into much detail. I had problems of my own with my mother, and she would counsel me through those.

'Darryl in the big house. I certainly wouldn't be out there to judge him any more than I would want someone to judge me. Please give him my fondest regards.'

He ruminates on what he has said. It is not enough. 'I wish I had something of mine for you to take with to give him.' He takes the cap off his head. 'Give this to him. Tell him I sent it. A memento: I care about you. If he needs some help, some guidance, after he is released, please tell him he is welcome to contact me. I have had education and experience.'

*

It is Monday morning, Magadien's cell. I recount the whole meeting with Stephen, to the point where he gives me the cap. I take it out of my bag and offer it to him. He grabs it, looks at it indifferently, then tosses it aside. 'Tell me more,' he says.

He asks me to repeat my account of Gadija's final episode with the Sampsons, in the house in the southern suburbs. I tell him again how the twenty-something Stephen would bring boys to his bed, how he would seek Gadija's approval, how he recalls that she was gentle with him, telling him that everything is all right.

'I rest my case,' he says bitterly. 'My mom was not at my wedding and I married twice to the same girl. And I invited her. She didn't tell me about the birds, the bees, the flowers and the trees. She didn't give my wife her blessings. Yet she gave Stephen's lovers her blessings. If she had just said, "This girl is no good for you," she would have shown that she cares. I could bring any girl home and sleep with her in the house; she didn't mind. I could even have slept with one of her friends in the house, she wouldn't have minded.'

He looks at the cap lying on his bed and smiles to himself. 'You say he's fucked up. Strange, I never thought of him that way. He was a happy boy, very in control of himself. I'm not pleased he's fucked up. There's enough pain, isn't there?'

He laughs cynically. 'I guess we're both fucked up. It's not that funny, is it?'

6
THE NEVER WORRY BASTARDS

Magadien was among the first generation of teenagers who lived their lives in the half-moon streets and tenement blocks of the post-removals Cape Flats. A mere 15 minutes' drive from the heart of District Six, the new housing estates of Cape Town's hinter-world constituted a different planet. The drearily symmetrical tenement blocks rising from the sand dunes, the distant blue outcroppings of the Peninsula's mountain range, the nameless public spaces filled with strangers: it was the sort of place one comes to in the depths of a troubled sleep. Indeed, Magadien was a guinea pig of the most far-reaching project of spatial engineering in the Western Cape's history, and a casualty of its catastrophic failure.

In pre-removals Cape Town, the boundaries dividing black and white, rich and poor, were porous and haphazard. Tens of thousands of the city's coloured and African populations lived their lives at the foot of Table Mountain, crammed into dense pockets of the inner city and the suburbs. There was the old neighbourhood of District Six, just inland from the harbour, and the Malay district of Bo Kaap, on the slopes of Signal Hill. Beyond these two ghettos, Cape Town's racial demographics were more complicated. The band of suburbs stretching south of the city – from Woodstock to Retreat – was largely white, but pockets of coloureds, some middle-class, others much poorer, were scattered throughout. In suburbs like Plumstead, it was not unusual to find a white middle-class block, with its prim hedges and pretty gardens, adjacent to a coloured working-class street, densely packed, lined with hawkers and shebeens.

Above the inner city, on the slopes of Table Mountain, middle-class coloured families lived in the suburbs of Vredehoek, Oranjezicht and Gardens. Many were involved in the messy, complicated business of passing for white.

Out in the city's hinterland, the Cape Flats, a vast expanse of scrubland and sand dunes that flanks the city's south-eastern perimeter, hosted a motley collection of outsiders. There was scattered farmland, but the sand dunes and the beach scrub was good for neither grazing nor cultivation. There were recent and older immigrants from the countryside, both African and coloured, banging on the city's doors with more or less success: a peri-urban underclass. And then there was the spill-over from the inner city, the poorest of Cape Town's poor, ejected from the cramped quarters of neighbourhoods like District Six.

It is often said that it took the madness of apartheid, and thus, by implication, the madness of the Afrikaners, to re-engineer Cape Town. It is often English-speaking writers who say these things. In fact, plans to reinvent the city began a decade before the National Party came to power. And the wellsprings of inspiration were to be found not in the obstinacy of a parochial nationalism, but in the giddiness of European modernism; remanufactured Cape Town sprang from the imaginations of cosmopolitans and futurists – English-speakers, all of them.

In the late 1930s, the radical modernism of Le Corbusier was the rage among South Africa's more erudite urban planners. There were circles in which his new book, *The City of Tomorrow and its Planning*, was something of a bible. 'The city of today is dying,' Le Corbusier wrote, 'because it is not constructed geometrically. To build on a clear site is to replace the "accidental" layout of the ground, the only one that exists today, by a formal layout. Otherwise, nothing can save us.' Forty pages on, he declared that 'surgery must be applied to the city centre. Physic must be used elsewhere. We must use the knife ...'

Le Corbusier's South African disciples took out their knives in 1940. The Cape Town city council began planning its Foreshore Project: a grand overhaul of the inner city, the pinnacle of which was to be the construction of a Monumental Approach to Cape Town – a boulevard so wide it would 'take five minutes to cross it in a stiff south-easter' – stretching from the harbour into the heart of the city. The Approach was to be lined with sky-scraping office blocks, welcoming the visitor to South Africa's shores with a dizzying spectacle of the modern. Among the confidential papers in the city council's sketches were plans for three slum clearance projects: District Six, the Malay Quarters and the Dock areas.

The Foreshore Project ended in disaster, but that is another story for another time. The point is that plans to move coloureds from the inner city had long been in the air by the time the apartheid state got to work. If the reinvention of Cape Town had taken place along pure Le Corbusian principles, coloureds would have found themselves in 'vertical cells': tall residential buildings ringing the outskirts of the inner city. But plans seldom travel well, especially to the colonies, where the questions of fear and control are bound to shape the organisation of people and space. White South Africa was not about to build spanking new homes for coloureds in the heart of the city. So, instead, the fate of Cape Town's coloureds was inspired by another modernist idea, that of the Garden City; the coloureds were to be moved to 'the countryside'.

The Garden City was the invention of late-nineteenth-century England, a society which, like mid-twentieth-century South Africa, was wondering what to do with its workers and its industry. The idea was to move both from the city into self-contained satellite towns on the urban periphery. Young working-class lads and lasses were to grow up in quaint, quasi-rural 'clusters', surrounded by lush meadows, vast stretches of common land, and farms.

Mutilated in ways both comic and chilling, this is the idea that animated the building of the cluster-like townships on the Cape Flats. Flying over the Flats on the descent into Cape Town International Airport, you can see the clusters in all their glory: concentric layers of streets, turned in upon themselves, forming tight, hermetic circles, each surrounded by a barren wilderness of no-man's-land.

With some imagination, you can just make out some of the benign intentions behind the original Garden City idea. The notion of the inward-looking cluster was meant to foster a village-like sense of community. Yet driving through Manenberg, or Heideveld or Hanover Park, one feels as if one has been locked into a maze, as if the ghetto is a dense universe. The idea of buttressing the clusters with greenbelts was intended to create open spaces in which the cluster-children would spend their afternoons. But the 'greenbelts' of the Cape Flats are intraversable scrublands; the kids are locked inside the labyrinth.

From the aeroplane window, you see six-lane highways linking the Flats to the city; in theory, the satellite towns are 15 minutes from downtown. But this is premised on the universality of the family car; the working-class families of the Flats have no cars. Moving in and out of the satellites is a costly expedition.

Most important of all, perhaps, the Flats neighbourhoods were built on the premise that coloureds lived their lives in nuclear families. Indeed, it was a conceit of modernism that the nuclear family was synonymous with the twentieth century, that other forms of kinship were the residues of more primitive times. Yet the coloureds of the inner city had lived their lives in extended families. You saw from Magadien's earliest recollections how the boundaries of the Mekkas' world traced a jagged, invisible circle around Hanover Street: between granny's house, Jackie Oakers's barber shop, St Mark's Cathedral where Annie's brother sang in the choir. The extended family was not just a source of emotional support: it was the structure through which people like the Mekkas negotiated their way into Cape Town's economy.

And so, between 1966 and the early 1980s, tens of thousands of people were wrenched from their lives in the inner city and dumped in the satellites on the edge of town. Extended families were dispersed to all four corners of the Flats, and everybody shared their cramped streets with strangers. The more well-to-do moved into districts of square, free-standing houses: Surrey Estate, Ravensmead, Uitsig. The poor made their new lives on the crescent-shaped streets and in the squat residential buildings of places like Valhalla Park, Bonteheuwel, Manenberg and Heideveld.

The Mekkas found themselves in 12 Daphne Court, Heideveld, a short, wide tenement block surrounded by two others just like it. Together, the three structures formed the walls of an open courtyard. One stepped from one's front door into a common space shared by dozens of families.

The Mekkas' extended family, which had once lived within a small radius around their Cowley Street home, was scattered across Cape Town. The city was a mirage of lights on the evening horizon. In Heideveld itself, life was lived in a sharp dualism between the very private and the very public: within the curtained windows of their cramped flat, and in the courtyards formed by the tenement blocks. There was nothing in between.

And so townships like Heideveld became crowded, public worlds of strangers, effectively severed from the rest of the universe. If the people of the inner city built their lives around extended family networks, the people of the Flats, thrown into an alien world, were to organise their lives around their immediate neighbours. The whole of life was lived in the tenement courtyards, and each courtyard became a world.

The new neighbourhoods of the Cape Flats were to become deeply insular. Each block came to constitute a territory, its defenders possessive of insiders, aggressive to outsiders. 'The boy from across the road married Annie's sister,' Magadien tells me when he describes the Hanover Park neighbourhood where the Mekkas finally settled. 'And the next-door neighbour married my cousin. My sister is married to Brian van Rooi, who lived at the end of the block. My older daughter is Brian's niece. Few people left our block. And few new people arrived. We have lived our lives together for the last 40 years.'

And yet the people from just three or four blocks away were like foreigners. A few hundred metres from his house, Magadien would find himself in a world of strangers, sometimes indifferent, often hostile. The ghettos of the Flats were divided into hundreds of micro-turfs, each given life by a micro-identity. It was not only about who married whom. It extended to who did business with whom, how one earned a living, and, perhaps most important of all, the politics of the street gangs, which drew entire communities into their wars.

*

The Mekkas' stay at 12 Daphne Court, Heideveld, was a short one. When Johnny died, less than a year after the move from District Six, Annie was told that her flat was too big for her family: they were assigned a smaller place, in Grace Court, opposite Heideveld's hospital.

When Magadien first told me about the move, it sounded as if his new home was miles away from Daphne Court. We were in his Pollsmoor cell and I had not yet visited the places of his childhood. 'I was a stranger in Grace Court,' he told me. 'I knew nobody and nobody knew me. So, after school, I wouldn't go home; I would go to Daphne Court. That was my block.'

When I did go to Heideveld, I was surprised to discover that Grace Court is about 150 metres from Daphne Court, on the same side of the same street. And yet it looked out over a different courtyard and thus formed part of a different universe.

The family's stay at Grace Court proved almost as short as the Daphne Court interval. Magadien's memories of it now are almost blank; they consist more of scattered emotions than images or events. He simply remembers that he felt alien there, and spent as little time there as possible.

It is puzzling that he remembers so little about Grace Court. For I was to discover later that it was during his brief stay there that Magadien, at the age of ten, began to commit his first crimes. They were of a piece with the crimes he was to commit for the next three decades: beguiling, clever, and horribly manipulative.

Sitting at her kitchen table in Hanover Park, Magadien's younger sister, Anne, the first eye-witness to his germinating career as a fraudster, grins broadly as she remembers her brother's early cons. 'Annie used to give me and Magadien our rent account, together with the rent money, and we would march down the street, this six-year-old and this ten-year-old, to go and pay the rent,' she tells me. 'We would arrive at the rent office and Magadien would tell me to wait outside. He would come back out with this proud smile on his face, and say to me, "Look what I've done."' He had scratched out the figure in the 'money due' column and replaced it with a smaller one. 'His copying was brilliant. The new figures look exactly like the typewriter figures. He would split his little profit with me, and we'd spend it on pinball and sweets.'

It was to be a constant refrain throughout Magadien's life. The minute anyone gave him money to deliver or keep safe, he would, as a matter of reflex and instinct, work out a way to keep some of it.

'He was ten years old,' I remark. 'That's so young. Where did this desire to steal come from?'

'From Johnny's death,' Anne replies, without missing a beat, 'and from Quinton's arrival in our lives. First we had this wonderful father, earning a good living and spoiling Magadien rotten, with love, toys, gifts. Then he dies, and Quinton comes. Suddenly, there is this new father figure, but he brings no money and no love. It has all gone with Johnny.

'The rent money was just the start of it,' Anne continues. 'He would find hundreds of ways to steal money from Annie, most of them clever, most of them in a way he'd never get caught. He'd bribe me; offer me some of the spoils in return for keeping quiet. And I would go along with him, not because I was scared of him, but because I loved him. He was my big brother, and we hated Quinton together.'

Anne is 40 years old now. She does not look at all like her older brother. Her face is broad and solid, his long and bony, the face of a man prone to ruminating, mooning. There is a hint of mischief in Anne's eyes, as if she would rather be jibing and joking than reflecting on the past. The kitchen in which we sit is squeakily domestic and wholesome. She is the mother of three clean-cut kids, and she has a solid career as a manager in a small business. Her husband, Brian, who grew up a block away from Magadien, is a hard-working, modestly successful carpenter. Like so many of the women who have surrounded Magadien, she is all work and family ethic, this solid woman living on a sturdy foundation.

I ask her when she found out that Gadija was her biological mother.

'When I was 13,' she replies. 'This lady used to come and visit us from Tamboerskloof, and she brought us nice things. I used to like her; I liked Aunty Dija. One day, Annie put me down and said, "You know that lady who always comes and brings nice things? She is your mother."

'I didn't take it badly. I didn't feel betrayed or abandoned. I stopped calling her Aunty Dija and started calling her Dija, and I made a bigger effort to get close to her, and to David. But she never became my mother. She was, and still is, like a big sister. Annie was my mom. She brought me up. And that's that.

'Once, Dija came to me and said, "Jesus, Anne, can't you call me mommy? I'm your mom, for God's sake." I had to be honest. I said: "I love you. But Annie is my mom."'

'It's funny,' I say, 'how different people respond to the same situation. Everything about your family setup made Magadien feel angry and betrayed. Nothing made you angry, even though you were in the same situation.'

'I took it differently,' she replies. 'We are brother and sister, but very different people. He gets angry, I don't. Not because I was a girl, but because I don't bear grudges. Even Quinton. I hated him when I was growing up. He was terrible to me. But I forgave him, he mellowed with age, and I look out for him now that he is old and lonely.'

*

It was because of John and Victor, Magadien's foster-brothers, whom he remembers for having beaten him without provocation, that the family left Grace Court soon after they arrived.

'One day, Annie told me it was not safe to stay at home, that I must go and stay with friends,' Magadien told me. 'She said that some men were after Victor, that they wanted to come to the house and kill him. I thought, fine, I prefer Daphne Court anyway. I'll hang out there.

'So I was not at home when it happened. When I arrived back in the evening, the house was smashed. The furniture was broken and all over the place. Victor was not at home when they arrived, but Annie was: so they beat her up. She was crying, she had marks all over her. Her clothes were torn. She kept saying how Heideveld was not a nice place, not a safe place, that she was going to die if we stayed, that she couldn't look after her kids here.'

Anne, who had been at home that day, was seven at the time. Her mother locked her in a wardrobe when she heard the men coming. The young girl listened to her mother's screams, all the while obeying Annie's instruction to remain absolutely silent.

Annie Mekka was in trouble. Recently removed from her extended family in District Six, freshly widowed, the new man in her life silent and uninterested in her children, her boys were running wild, and they were bringing the wildness of their lives into her home. A few months after the incident, she moved her family, Quinton and all, from the gangland of Heideveld to the newer and remoter ghetto of Hanover Park. And that's where Magadien became a teenager, and where much of his family still lives today.

*

Hanover Park is just four or five kilometres south-west of Heideveld. When the Mekkas moved there, it was wedged between a large industrial zone to the east, the respectable and genteel coloured suburb of Lansdowne to the west, and a vast stretch of scrub and dune land to the south. The Mekkas' new home was in the south-east corner of Hanover Park, right on the edge of the empty 'greenbelt'. In years to come, Magadien would get to know and use the ghetto's terrain as a gangster does: to the east, the clothes factories where he stole everything from ladies' bermuda shorts to babies' shoes; to the west, the middle-class kids in their chinos and collared shirts 'who shat perfume and pissed me off'. But back in his first months in Hanover Park, it was the south and its empty scrublands that grabbed his attention. 'There was a farm up the road with milking cows,' he tells me. 'And there were the sand dunes and the big, empty pieces of land. Heideveld was strange, but this was very strange. Like we'd ended up in the middle of nowhere.'

There is a long-held myth in the Mekka and Wentzel families. They say that Magadien's trouble with the law started at the tender age of 12, that during his first year in Hanover Park he was hauled by the scruff of the neck before a magistrate and sentenced to spend time in a reformatory. 'Magadien was already behind bars before he had hair under his arms,' I was told several times. It is extraordinary how families read their histories backwards, as if everyone's life path was always already destined. The true story is far more interesting than the family legend.

When Annie moved her kids to Hanover Park, her son John went his own way, settling into a new home with a new wife. He was flush, living from the combined income of a day job as a bus driver, and his moonlight life of drug peddling. He would help out with his mother's household; every couple of weeks, Annie would send one of the kids to John's place to collect money.

She should have known by then that Magadien was not the sort of boy to whom one entrusts cash. One Thursday afternoon, on his way back from John's house, his pocket full of bank notes for Annie's grocery shopping, he wandered into a street corner café. By the time he came out, several hours later, Annie's money was gone, half of it in the pinball machine, the other half in the cash register. It was shortly after Magadien's discovery that Annie was not his biological mother.

'I knew I was in shit,' Magadien tells me, 'so I didn't go home. I went straight to the child welfare office and told them that my family was about to beat the shit out of me. I made up a whole story, about how I was neglected, how they were not my proper family, how there was this vicious man at home called Quinton, and that he was not even married to my mom, and that she was not even my mom. I said I don't want to go home. I want to go to a place of safety, for children.

'So welfare took me to the child court, on the very same day, and I told them there was no way I was going home. They put me in Bonnytown, a place of safety, in Wynberg, with a good school, good food, a dormitory for boys, and a dormitory for girls. Abandoned kids from everywhere around the country lived there, kids found in the rubbish heap, orphans. When Annie found out I was in Bonnytown, and came to see me, I told her I didn't want to go home. So I stayed, for a whole year, and Jesus, I was happy there.'

It is perhaps understandable that the family, and Annie in particular, fiddled with their memories of this event; it must have been excruciatingly embarrassing, and it was cruelly unfair. But it remains one of the most fascinating courses of action Magadien has ever taken, a shameful tribute to the subtlety and the tactical savvy with which he read the world around him.

When I first heard Magadien's account of the tale, it put me in mind of an essay by Richard Rive – District Six's most eloquent and observant prose writer. 'During school vacations,' Rive writes of his District Six childhood, 'social workers, both white and black, would invade us and smother us with love, good will and dripping-wet charity. They would assemble us on the nearest stony, vacant lot, hand out second-hand bats and balls, and watch us whooping and desporting, their eyes tinged with pity and understanding. We masked our resentment but deliberately and calculatedly shocked them by hurling invectives at one another and discussing sexual details as loudly as possible. We would side-spy them for any reactions. And indeed soon enough these would come. Raised eyebrows and sympathetic clicking of tongues.'

Like many boys before and after him, Rive was playing the coloured *skollie*, a performance for the benefit of outsiders. This ambivalent mocking, this double-sided laugh, is a venerable old motif of the coloured working and underclasses. The coloured boy plays out the white stereotype, enacting Olive Schreiner's bigoted caricature – the sarcastic, guttural honour of the half-caste. He is taking the piss out of the observer, but he is also taking the piss out of himself; by the end of the performance, it is no longer clear which of the two has been humiliated.

Magadien, too, was taking the piss, and, by the end of his own performance, it was also unclear who had won and who had lost.

Whoever the final victor, it remains that, at the age of 12, he had read the apartheid state's fraught relationship with coloureds masterfully.

Afrikaner nationalism's relationship with the coloured population was always a charged and confused one. For some, like the early apartheid ideologue Geoffrey Cronjé, who spoke of racial mixing as a degenerate disease, the very existence of coloureds was a cruel reminder that the founding fathers of the Afrikaner *volk* had practised widespread miscegenation, that the *volk* had been contaminated at its very roots. He spoke of coloureds as *'n kultuurlose massa*, 'a cultureless mass', that had been *verswelg*, 'swallowed up', by the process of westernisation. He feared that the poor whites of the cities and countryside, who lived their lives far too close to heathens and bastards, would also degenerate into a cultureless mass. The coloureds were a curse, a rudderless hodgepodge of pathetic beings, against whom whites had to be quarantined.

Yet for others, particularly in the gentler 'Cape stream' of Afrikaner thought, the coloureds were an object of pity and empathy. Afrikaans-speakers – and thus brothers and sisters of sorts – they were marooned between black tribalism and white civilisation; they had to be reeled in from the dastardly no-man's-land they inhabited.

And so, curiously enough, at the very moment the apartheid government dumped thousands of coloureds onto the periphery of Cape Town, it also subjected the coloured population to a torrent of paternalistic welfare programmes. Most of these were animated by an obsessive project to save coloured children from growing up in households dominated by drunken men. Social workers invaded the Cape Flats, teaching women the rudimentaries of home-craft and child-rearing. And scores of homes were declared unfit for the raising of a child; thousands of coloured kids were removed from their families and placed in institutions of shelter.

When Magadien marched himself off to the local welfare office, he came armed with apartheid's very own discourse on coloureds. He told them that his stepfather was a drunken bastard who was not even his legal stepfather, that his mother was not really his mother, that if he went home he would be welcomed by physical abuse. And he omitted that he had just emptied Annie's precious grocery allowance into a pinball machine.

But it was true, of course, that Quinton was an unworthy stepfather, that Annie was not his mother, and that if he had gone home it would have been to a beating. Magadien went off to the welfare office to conduct a consummate performance of a *skollie*-in-the-making. And that is, in fact, precisely what he was.

During his year in Bonnytown, the 12-year-old did not miss his family for a moment. 'The schooling was better than in the ghetto,' he tells me. 'There were ten or eleven in a class, compared to thirty or forty in Hanover Park. We weren't locked in. We could run away and go home if we wanted. I didn't even consider it. There were also lots of girls there.

'Even my relationship with my family was nice while I was in Bonnytown,' he adds. 'They came to visit. Not Gadija,' he says pointedly, 'but Annie. They would spoil me, my family. They brought wonderful sweets, a bucketful of popcorn, chips. I would have preferred to stay there. But Annie wanted me to come home.'

Gadija's memory is very different, and sadly so. She may not have gone to visit her son, but, in her memory at any rate, she was monitoring the situation closely, and making all the crucial decisions. 'Yes, he could have stayed there,' she told me when we finally met. 'But he was such a bright boy, so good in school, that the place was unsuitable for him. I instructed Annie to take him back. I wanted him to have a normal childhood.'

He was a very bright boy indeed. On his return to Hanover Park, he enrolled at Crystal High, a school up the road from Annie's new house. Despite his persistent discontent, and his hair-raising extra-curricular activities, he was, for the next four years, seldom lower than second in his class, defeated only by a goody-two-shoes girl called Fatima.

*

Annie's move to Hanover Park was a flight from violence. She wanted her family to live, in Magadien's phrase, in 'the middle of nowhere'. Yet if she believed that the edge of the Flats constituted a safe haven from the gang wars further north, she was wrong. Within a year of the family's move, the Mongrels set up shop in the north-east corner of Hanover Park. They were to become one of the largest and fiercest of the Cape Flats gangs, led by the legendary Bobby Mongrel and his formidable mother. And they changed the social geography of Hanover Park; in each zone of the tiny neighbourhood, defence gangs emerged to keep aggressors out. By the late 1970s, Hanover Park was home to the Vultures, the Genuine School Boys, the Fancy Boys, the Gipsy Kids, the Sexy Boys, the Wild Cats, the Nice Time Kids, the Laughing Boys, the New York Yankees, the Cape Town Scorpions, the Three Bob Kids, the Sexy Rexies and the Dynamite Kids. Each owned a little patch of the ghetto. Each entered into a loose alliance with others. Residents needed to know the intricacies of these alliances well if they were to make a safe passage from their homes to the railway station. Straying onto enemy turf was no joke.

Decades later, in Magadien's Pollsmoor cell, I show him a gang-map of Hanover Park, circa 1982. It divides the neighbourhood into 16 pieces of rival turf. I had been anticipating this meeting with some excitement. I thought the map would draw buried memories. Instead, he looks at it dispassionately for a long time, then frowns. 'This map is wrong,' he finally declares. 'Zone 1 was not the Vultures' turf, it was New York Yankees territory. Who the fuck drew this thing?'

*

In the early 1970s, when Magadien moved to Hanover Park, crime in his corner of the ghetto was in something of an interregnum – between the residues of old District Six formations and the embryos of the new Cape Flats gangs. The blocks around the Mekkas' house were the turf of the Dynamite Kids, the DKs, run by the legendary Pang DK. Everybody remembers Pang with nostalgia; nobody refers to him by his real name, which was Arendse: he was, simply, the patriarch and the embodiment of the DKs, and everyone, it seems, loved him dearly.

A decade earlier, District Six had been littered with gangs, but they were not, as the scholar and journalist Don Pinnock has shown, anything like the mega-gangs that came to own the Flats. The largest of the inner-city gangs were, in essence, petit bourgeois defence associations: groupings of entrepreneurs who came together to defend their businesses against the *skollies* – destitute members of the underclass who poured into District Six from the countryside to scavenge at the margins of the urban economy. The most legendary of these gangs, the Globe, began as a typical defence association, but soon grew drunk on its own power. By the 1950s, its leaders had become small-time thugs, extorting protection money from District Six businesses, and ruling the streets like a bunch of cowboys.

There was another category of gang in District Six, somewhat distinct from the defence associations. Pinnock called them 'family mafias'. 'They are,' he wrote in the early 1980s, when such formations were still in existence, 'the remains of an earlier form of social organisation, of a time when large extended families operated a wide range of "informal sector" activities in the old working-class areas of the city ... Powerful families could call on the contacts, capital and physical strength of their kin in any undertaking. But after the massive population relocations from the inner city, most extended families fell apart.'

The DKs was one of the few extended family formations that did not fall apart, at least not initially. Having conducted business for a generation in a radius around Hanover Street, District Six, Pang somehow managed to convince the apartheid authorities to move much of his extended family to the same corner of the Cape Flats. So the DKs relocated, root and branch, out into the city's hinterland. Crammed into a few blocks of a new ghetto, they set up shop.

Pang understood the residents of his new Cape Flats neighbourhood well. They were stranded on the periphery of the city; the six-lane highway linking the Flats to Cape Town was inaccessible to them – poor people, they would fork out the return fare to town only for work and necessity. And beyond the few blocks of their micro-neighbourhood, the rest of the Flats was filled with forbidding strangers. So people lived their lives in little capsules, drinking, smoking, performing and fighting among their immediate neighbours. It is in this context that Pang, and thousands of entrepreneurs like him, earned a living.

The front of Pang's home was a shebeen, an informal drinking and drug house where people had their beer and smoked. In his courtyard was a makeshift cinema – a 16-mm projector, a whitewashed wall, a few scattered chairs.

Anne smiles broadly when I mention Pang's name. 'My, that was a fine family,' she says. 'Hundreds of uncles, brothers, cousins: they were all in different strands of the business. And they were good people, very good people. Pang is dead, and his drinking house died with him, but I am still friends with his sons and daughters. He would throw dances, show movies. Everyone spent their time there, the young and the old. Me, Magadien, my husband Brian, all of us – we spent our lives at Pang's place.'

Pang's various businesses were, of course, illegal. He bought his liquor on the black market and his drugs from out-of-town men who would visit him after dark. Indeed, in the early 1970s the Cape Flats was serviced by just 20 licensed liquor outlets, part of apartheid's obsessive project to keep coloured households dry. Each was confined to regular business hours, and was allowed neither to offer entertainment nor to extend credit to their clientele.

It is difficult to believe that the authorities ever expected their regulations to be obeyed. For one, the Western Cape's wine industry was never going to allow it. About 75% of its bottom-of-the-market wine was consumed by Cape coloureds.

Vast quantities of alcohol were sold to the handful of legal outlets, and they in turn wholesaled to literally thousands of illegal shebeeners. By 1980 there were about 3 000 shebeens on the Cape Flats. Social life became synonymous with underground trade.

And so, as with the thousands of shebeeners like him, there were no regulatory authorities or police officers to protect Pang's enterprise from rivals. He had to do it himself, and he nurtured a veritable little army of men around him. Magadien's block was DK turf, his neighbours were DK clientele, and Pang held onto them with violence. When a rival gang crossed the invisible boundary of Pang's territory, the whole neighbourhood became honorary DKs. Behind the front line of DK fighters, residents would set up barricades with trash cans, and use dustbin lids as makeshift shields.

*

From the start, I was sceptical of the benign, nostalgic image of Pang that people painted for me. I know that many of the neighbourhood shebeen owners of the early 1970s were not good men. They sold liquor and drugs on credit; they dished out loans to their poverty-stricken clientele at horrific interest rates; they cultivated a devilish relationship of patronage and dependence, ensuring that their entire community was in debt to them. Many turned the armed youngsters that surrounded them on their own clientele, beating debtors senseless, extorting protection money from nearby businesses. So I cross-examined everyone I spoke to, searching hard for the old mafioso's dark side.

But Pang, it seems, really was the genuine article – the benign gangster-patron of comic books. In mid-2003 I spoke to Faya Jacobs, a woman Magadien's age, who has lived in the neighbourhood since the late 1960s.

'Did Pang ever lend people money?' I asked.

'Goodness no,' she replied. 'He made a lot of money from his shebeen, and he helped people out. He never lent money. If you were in trouble, you must ask him for help. If your problem is genuine, he picks you up.'

'Did you ever get money from Pang?'

Faya smirked mischievously. She is a middle-aged spinster, somewhat prim, sitting very formally on her living room couch. The question seemed to have awakened a naughty memory.

'Just once,' she grinned. 'Only once. It was a Friday afternoon, and that is the point of the story. I just casually went up to him and asked him to lend me R20. He hardly even noticed. He said, "Fine, pay me back next week."

'The next week, on wage day, I went straight from work to his house to pay him. I offered the R20 to him and he laughed his head off. He said, "You went dancing, didn't you! Keep it. Please keep it."'

'And had you gone dancing?'

'Oh yes: right through the night, into Saturday morning.'

*

Pang's greatest legacy in his small corner of Hanover Park is not his shebeen, nor the small change he gave to youngsters to go dancing, but the Broadway Coons. Quite literally everyone I have interviewed about Pang begins talking, without being prompted, about 'Pang's *klopse*'. It is the single cultural artefact around which the neighbourhood was organised, and through which its residents now remember the 1970s and '80s.

In June of each year, Pang would order reels of black, red and white material, and set a host of tailors to work. Shortly before year-end, he would be selling the garish and outrageous uniforms coming off the sewing machines to the members of his troupe, no doubt at a healthy profit. Beginning in August, the brass band would meet for rehearsals every Tuesday and Thursday evening, members of the choir every Monday and Wednesday. In mid-December, a dress rehearsal would convene in the south-west corner of Hanover Park. Members of the *klopse* would paint their faces black and white, the band would fire up its wind instruments, and the *moffies* – the transvestites – would don their makeup and their dresses. The choir would polish its *moppies* – slapstick, rhyming lyrics sung to popular tunes. Magadien was there, and so was his sister Anne, Faya Jacobs, his neighbour Stan Landman, and everyone else.

And then, on New Year's Day, the Broadway Coons would join the main procession, constituted by dozens of troupes from around the Cape Flats, and thousands of troupe members would make their gaudy way through Cape Town, heading for the Hartleyvale Stadium in Observatory. In the stadium itself, a huge crowd and a panel of judges would await their arrival. There were prizes for the best band, the best choir, the best costumes, the cleverest *moppies*.

The Coon Carnival is the coloured poor's oldest and most striking contribution to the culture of Cape Town. It embodies all the ambivalence and sarcasm and drama of a creolised minority. For generations, the coloured middle classes have heaped scorn upon it with a degree of anger and revulsion that truly astonishes. In popular myth, the Carnival was born in the mid-nineteenth century, when an American ship, the *Alabama*, docked at Cape Town harbour. A group of black American minstrels disembarked; for the next few weeks, they treated Cape Town to their clownish, obsequious, Uncle Tom performances of self-denigration. Sadly, the myth insists, the coloured poor, freed from slavery not a generation ago, were immediately seduced by these slapstick ex-slaves. And so it was not long before they themselves started painting their faces black and white, and became self-loathing jesters, aping the apes, revelling, perversely enough, in their collective memory of slavery.

'Why do the Europeans not have Coon Carnivals and Moffie Concerts?' a letter-writer, who signed himself as 'Coloured Student', wrote to *The Cape Standard* in January 1940. 'Is it because they do not feel happy and gay at this time of year? Have they not also sexually abnormal people? ... You may have many answers but mine is this – they have more race pride than we have! They think more of themselves than we do of ourselves. Why do they then patronise Coloured Coon Carnivals? Because it amuses and pleases them to think of the Coloured people doing what they themselves are too proud to do. It gives them a satisfying feeling of superiority over us. And can we blame them in that respect? Are they wrong? No.'

The Carnival's defenders tell a very different story. For them, the annual processions are nothing less than a heroic act of cultural preservation, achieved in the most hostile of circumstances. Cape Town, they argue, is a typical port town; it is naturally creolised, having played host, across the generations, to a limitless hybrid of people – Madagascans, Malaysians, Tanzanians, Mozambiquans, and many others beside – each carrying a different heritage of self-expression. The Afrikaners, driven by a project of racial purity, have suppressed every trace of the creole that has touched Cape Town's shores. It was left to the coloured poor, uninhibited by the smothering currents of racial supremacism, to preserve Cape Town's dazzling cultural legacy.

And so, cultural historians like the Frenchman Denis-Constant Martin have sifted through the Carnival's artefacts with a fine-tooth comb, finding traces of a thousand lost heritages, from Arabic percussion to Madagascan choral music. It is the Coons, they argue, that embody Cape Town's cultural history – and they do so with unselfconscious levity, and indeed with honesty.

Moreover, defenders of the Carnival argue, if the revellers and troupes are jesters, the joke is not on them, but on their detractors. For one day every year, the marginalised of Cape Town, their culture ridiculed, their very lives uprooted and dumped on the outskirts of town, march triumphantly through the centre of the city. And if they are smirking, it is because they are taking the piss – a giant, raucous fuck-you to whites and to the bourgeoisie – deflected by the disarming lightness of laughter.

The Carnival's champions are, alas, hopeless romantics. Life is more interesting and sadder than that, not least the life of coloured Cape Town. Richard Rive playing the *skollie* for social workers, Magadien playing the boy from the broken home for the child welfare office – the Carnival embodies the same unsettling ambivalence. On the 3rd of January every year, when the revellers have returned home to nurse their hangovers, it is equally unclear who has lost and who has won. The following is an extract from a joke, written by Stompie, a once-well-known coloured humorist, and altered, where necessary, to non-colloquial English:

> Now, Jan van Riebeeck did mos land here in early April hey? According Jan van Riebeeck Day. So de first ting dose Hollanders does when dey lands are to pallie up to de Hottentot girlies in de super-miniskirts ...
>
> So, okay, you count nine months from the beginning of April, and see where you comes out. Right! Beginning of Janneware. New Year ...
>
> So dat de special meaning of New Year are dat it are really de time of de birth of de Coloured People. Dat's why de Coloured People did always have a special feast time dose days ...
>
> We got to start a campaign. Like de Afrikaner. He are always starting campaigns. Now we start a birthday campaign.
>
> We collecks money to build a monument. Somma here, byre Castle Bridge, byre start of District Six. An we puts up a plate on which read:
>
> 'Here (or very nearby) de first Coloured Person were born on New Year (or very near) in 1653.'

Who, indeed, is the butt of this joke?

*

Magadien never joined the DKs. Nor did any of the other boys on his block. It was a generational thing. 'We were like chickens in a coop,' Magadien explains. 'We wanted to spread our wings.' Or, as Magadien's peer and neighbour, Stan Landman told me, 'Pang was the boss, and the point is that we did not want a boss.'

Instead, Magadien and his friends started their own corner gang, just like thousands of other boys on the Cape Flats. They spent every afternoon together on the streets, and they stamped their identity on their environment with a name, a code, a hodgepodge of borrowed rituals. They were, initially, the Peaceful Cats.

At first, they were mostly into eating, hanging out and, above all, playing soccer. Magadien has been a sports fanatic for as long as he can remember. His uncle was a groundsman at Newlands, home to Western Province's first-class rugby and cricket teams. He used to take Magadien to matches on weekends, and the youngster learned the names of every batsman to play for Western Province for a generation, every fly-half to don a Western Province jersey.

There were a dozen or so Peaceful Cats, and they all played in the local soccer team. 'The club nearest our block was called Lags Eleven,' Magadien tells me. 'The owner had a fancy job, and he would go to America from time to time, for long periods. When we became seniors, when we were all in the first team, we got involved in the running of the club. One of us was appointed secretary. When the owner went travelling, we took it over. He came back and said, "You guys are doing a great job." So it became our club. We picked the team, set practice time, drew up a constitution.'

Several years later, in the early 1980s, when Magadien was becoming a proficient career criminal, he would invest a fair chunk of his criminal earnings in Lags Eleven. 'I remember my first successful cheque fraud,' he tells me. 'When I cashed the cheque, the first thing I did was buy new goalkeeping gloves, an expensive leather ball, and kit. I went straight to Hanover Park and dished everything out.'

Back in Magadien's early teens, the Peaceful Cats were, by all accounts, much loved by the adults on the block. They hung out at Pang's place, and attended weddings, funerals and 21st birthday parties together, invading the gatherings as a single group and demolishing all the food on the tables. 'The adults were startled at how much we ate,' Magadien tells me. 'There was this joke that you must hide all the food when we arrive. They renamed us. They called us "The Hungry Boys". At first it was fun, this new name. It was a joke. But as we got older, it started to embarrass us. Who wants to be known as a bunch of little boys who stuff themselves at weddings? So we changed our name, quite dramatically, in fact, to the Never Worry Bastards.'

Why they dubbed themselves the Never Worry Bastards has become the subject of legend. I have interviewed four of the original Bastards and each tells a rival story. The dispute is an important one, since it sheds light on a much larger tale.

From early on, the Peaceful Cats' signature was the wild afro hairstyles they wore, an oddity in Hanover Park, and bait for the members of other corner gangs. Whenever any of them wandered off their turf, they were jibed by the boys on the neighbouring territories. The older they got, the more menacing the jibes became. When Magadien was about fifteen, one of the Hungry Boys was stabbed while making his way to the railway station.

So the Hungry Boys were faced with a choice: they could

disband and be absorbed into one of the neighbouring gangs, or they could defend themselves. They chose the latter: they renamed themselves the Never Worry Bastards, they grew their afros even bigger and wilder, and they began to carry knives.

'We invented the name one afternoon while we were smoking dagga on the corner,' Magadien recalls. 'The philosophy behind the name was – you're not going to live long; either you will get killed by another gang, or the police will *moer* you, or something. So never worry. Just be a bastard.'

There is another tale, and it goes along similar lines. 'One Sunday evening,' a peer of Magadien's told me, 'someone in the Cape Town Scorpions came onto our turf, broke into the home of a man we called Barbarian, tied him up and raped his wife before his eyes. That same night, we decided that every evening, we would stand in twos and guard our turf. We needed a new name, a very heavy fucking name.'

There is a third explanation which strays from the logic of the first two, and is perhaps more illuminating. 'There was a boy in our gang called Baliekop,' Stan Landman told me. 'Everything changed when Baliekop's uncle came out of a 30-year prison sentence. He didn't live in our area, but he came to visit, and when he arrived it was like the coming of God. He was a big shot in the 26s.

'One afternoon, we were all sitting in the yard at Baliekop's place. His uncle laughed at us. He said, *Peaceful Cats klink soos mossies* [Peaceful Cats sounds like little birdies]. He gave us our new name there and then: The Never Worry Bastards. Then he'd say to us, "So-and-so is full of shit. Fuck him up." And we'd do it.'

This is a variant of a classic story, one that was to shape the future of the Cape Flats. The government of the early and mid apartheid eras locked itself, as I mentioned earlier, into a welfarist relationship with Cape Town's coloureds. There was an obsession with families, with kids growing up among lazy, drunken men. The women of the Flats were bombarded with advice and child welfare cheques; scores of young boys were taken from their homes to reformatories, industrial schools and places of shelter; many young men were imprisoned. Reading through the figures of incarceration rates in the 1960s and 70s is an astonishing experience; coloureds were incarcerated at twice the rate of Africans.

And so a whole generation of youngsters was touched by a collective experience of institutionalised care. You can see it in Magadien's life. He himself spent a year in Bonnytown. His older brother, Victor, went to jail and became a 26. And, if Stan Landman's story is correct, the Never Worry Bastards received their name at the feet of a prison gangster.

The government's project to save young men by putting them in institutions backfired spectacularly. As Stan Landman put it, they came back from the reformatories and the prisons and their arrival was like a god's descent. If the kids of the new ghettos were stranded in their isolated pockets, the one thing that brought them together, that created allegiances crossing ghetto boundaries, highways and deserted scrublands, was the magical tales and exotic initiation rites of the reformatories and the jails. All the mega-gangs that were to emerge in the 1970s were born in correctional institutions. The Born Free Kids, which was to become one of the three province-wide gangs of the late seventies and eighties, was conceived in the reformatories. The Mongrels, which began as an old District Six family mafia, wove together strands of 26 ritual, and established branches across the Cape Flats. Members of the Cape Town Scorpions, the richest and most authoritative gang of the 1980s, were said to go to prison 'to pick up 28 poison for the stings in their scorpion's tails', a reference to the bile Nongoloza drank after the slaughtering of Rooiland.

By the late 1990s, going to prison was a prerequisite for taking a leadership position in any street gang. There are many young men who have sought a prison sentence in order to prepare themselves for life on the streets. And some of the millionaire drug lords of today are forced to claim that they are Number Generals, even when they are not, in order to garner credibility.

*

Magadien and his friends found themselves at the margins of this new movement. The Never Worry Bastards were not absorbed into one of the emerging super-gangs. And they kept their distance from Pang's DKs. They were, for the most part, a parochial group of boys, confined to their corner of Hanover Park; Magadien is the only one of his contemporaries ever to go to prison.

Indeed, the Never Worry Bastards is perhaps best understood

as a hybrid of three sorts of gangs. First and foremost, they were a corner gang, a group of boys who grew afros and ran a soccer club. At this level, all its members participated. Next, they were a defence gang, protecting the integrity of their turf, invading the territory of others, doing ritualised battle with rivals over weekends. At this level, about half of the Never Worry Bastards were enthusiastic participants.

Finally, a small group of them, led by Magadien and a boy from down the road called Jack, were budding career criminals. It is in this role that Magadien 'spread his wings', strayed from his corner of the ghetto, and negotiated his way through the rest of the Flats. To the east was the industrial zone of Epping, with its textile factories and warehouses. Magadien and Jack were amateurs and opportunists; they stole from whatever warehouse they could access. Babies' socks, cheap t-shirts, bottom-of-the-market sports shoes – they took what they could. To the west was the coloured middle-class suburb of Lansdowne, whose residents Magadien hated for all he was worth. 'You walk down one of their streets,' he told me, 'and they gather outside their homes to watch you. They see by your clothes you are poor. They think: "*Skollie*: this one is here for trouble."'

'And what did they wear?' I asked.

'Fucking chinos. Fucking polished stupid shoes. Even fucking bowties. Like they don't shit in the toilet like you do. Like they shit perfume.'

They were also among the global wave of 1960s and 70s consumers who filled their homes with the new electronic appliances of the age, and that is why Magadien went to Lansdowne. He does not recall his first housebreaking. 'It must have been in Lansdowne,' he says. 'Where else could it have been?'

Magadien and Jack seldom took their stolen goods back to Hanover Park. They would cross the railway track into the coloured ghetto of Bonteheuwel, then cross a vast, desolate field, and walk into the African township of Guguletu. 'It was a dangerous journey,' Magadien recalls. 'You would have to walk through dozens of gang territories, and there were dangerous people walking around at night. We went armed with bush knives.'

'Why go to Guguletu, of all places, to unload your stuff?' I asked.

'Because there was a huge market for stolen goods in black townships,' Magadien replied. 'And because blacks don't talk.'

Magadien's attitude to Africans is tinged with racism, somewhat muted when he was in prison and surrounded by African peers, far sharper when he left jail and moved into the coloured ghetto of Manenberg. 'I am not a black man,' is one of his constant refrains. 'I am a Cape Malay.'

'Ja, Jack and I went to Guguletu,' he tells me one day in his prison cell, 'and your mouth will drop if I tell you who we did business with. The new elite, walking round parliament in their fancy suits, talk so high and mighty against crime. But you know the big secret? They were all criminals. The townships lived off stolen goods and they are all from the townships.'

'Who do you have in mind?' I ask.

'If you write it down we will both be in a lot of shit,' he replies. And then he whispers a story about Guguletu in my ear, and it is true that, had I recorded it here, we both would have been sued.

*

'Did your parents know that you stole babies' clothes and hi-fis?'

I ask this question to every Bastard and all their old friends. The answer is always the same: 'We never brought stolen goods back into the neighbourhood.'

'I know that,' I reply, 'but that is not an answer to my question. Did they know?'

'Of course they knew.'

'And what did they do about it?'

'We never mentioned it to them, and they never raised it with us.'

Like the maniacal fans of a local soccer club, the Bastards' parents were, at times, bigger Never Worries than their sons. They loved the Bastards-as-corner-gang, celebrating their presence at neighbourhood gatherings; they greeted Jack's and Magadien's crimes with complicit silence.

'Once,' Anne told me, 'Magadien got a holiday job at Pick 'n Pay supermarket. He came home with dozens of yellow t-shirts, and we all wore them, all the time. Nobody asked where they came from. People just said, "Ag nice, man: the kids are all wearing the same shirt."'

And their parents supported the Never Worries' defensive battles over turf like crazed hooligans.

'Aunty Annie,' Stan Landman tells me in reference to Magadien's foster-mother, 'was the most serious Never Worry in town. When another gang came onto our turf to make war, Aunty Annie would come onto her balcony, scream the most terrible abuse at them, pick up a brick and throw it at them. We'd say, "Jesus, Aunty, get back inside, man: it's dangerous." And she'd say, "Mind your own fucking business," and she'd throw another brick at them. We called her Ouma Never Worry – Granny Never Worry.

'All the old people supported us. When we were doing battle, we could run into any house. The door would open for us, and then close behind us.'

Even scowling old Quinton pitched in. 'His pigeon coop was our armoury,' Stan tells me. 'There was this huge hollow below the pigeons, with a bolted trapdoor. We kept the key. Quinton knew what was there, but we only spoke about it once. The New York Yankees launched a surprise attack and we rushed to Quinton's house to get our pangas and shields. And then we discovered that we'd lost the fucking key to the trapdoor, and everyone went tearing around the neighbourhood looking for Quinton, hoping to God he had a spare key.'

*

'The nicest thing about gangsterism,' Magadien tells me, 'is that our place is like a library. There are lots of passages. You get locked in and there is no way out. We knew those passages like no-one else. The Fancy Boys, the Mongrels, they'd chase us into our territory and we'd disappear into the maze. Then we'd corner them. We'd appear from over the fences, out of the gardens and beat the shit out of them.'

'How violent was it?' I ask.

'We killed a member of the New York Yankees on their turf,' he replies dispassionately, 'because they nearly killed one of our members the previous Sunday morning. So we retaliated. And we killed one of the Fancy Boys because they killed one of the Gypsy Boys. We were allied to the Gypsy Boys. If they were in trouble, we would step in.'

'What did the police do when these boys were killed?' I asked.

'Nothing.'

'And what did your parents say?'

'Nothing. They were on our side.' He pauses, and when he speaks again, it is in the moralising tone of an indignant crusader. He switches, as is his wont when discussing such matters, from relaxed, colloquial English, to formal, perfectly structured sentences. 'The coloureds complain about crime,' he says. 'They say that gangsterism is the scourge of their communities. They are a bunch of hypocritical fuck-ups. It's not just that you get three generations of one family smoking buttons together. It's that our parents were on our side. The blood made them as crazy as it made us. They'd say, "The gangsters are on the next block. Our boys are just defending themselves." And I have to stop myself from laughing in their faces.'

*

'When you were taking on the Mongrels and the Fancy Boys,' I ask Magadien, 'what did you fight about?'

'Stupid things,' he replies. 'Girls, turf: mainly girls. You see, that was our mentality. Everything on our territory belonged to us, even the girls. Say, somebody from the Fancy Boys worked in the same factory as a girl from our block. They meet every day in the factory, and they fall in love. We say, no, that is not love; love does not cross the boundaries of gang turf. She must fall in love with one of us. So a whole war with the Fancy Boys would start; people might even get killed, all because these two young people met at the factory and fell in love.'

I stumble across an old postgraduate thesis written in the early 1980s by Wilfried Schärf, who is today a professor of criminology at the University of Cape Town. Schärf wrote his dissertation on the Dobermans, an Elsies River gang.

'On weekends,' he writes, 'the gang attended discos if they were held not too far outside safe territory ... Only part of the purpose of attending was actually to dance. The rest was an attempt to establish relative power over rival gangs ... For instance, a member of the Dobermans would ask a woman from rival gang turf to dance, which was really a direct challenge to that gang's possession of her. If she was not rescued by her gang, she'd have to be "broken" by the Dobermans and would then belong to them. If the gang was too weak to rescue her, this symbolic defeat had implications for their territorial delimitation ...'

I read this passage to Magadien and ask what he thinks. He instinctively goes into defensive mode. 'Well, not quite,' he replies. 'Remember that alcohol in a night club is a very dangerous thing. And remember also that women are snakes. You will eye a girl, offer her a drink, ask if she has a boyfriend. No, she'll say. Meanwhile, she does have a boyfriend, and he's the fucking king of the Mongrels, and all hell breaks loose.'

*

It would be no exaggeration to say that street gang life during Magadien's times was organised around the cinema. The Dobermans took their name from a French gangster film. The Sicilians took their inspiration from the *The Godfather*. Going into street battle, gangsters would shout out lines from *The Gladiators*.

Ever since the 1920s, cinema had been huge among the coloured population of the inner city, and was associated with a camp and ebullient street culture. 'On the pavement outside the famous Avalon cinema,' the historian Bill Nasson writes in an essay on District Six in the 1930s and '40s, 'there were often buskers who sang and danced in front of patrons, or other inventive street entertainers with performing animals … To promote *The Mark of Zorro*, released in 1940, one cinema had a large cut-out of a horse fixed to a wall of a neighbouring shop, and fitted its ushers with black eye masks and fake silver spurs.'

But out on the Cape Flats in the 1960s and '70s, cinema was about gangsterism and gangsterism was about cinema. In the course of researching this book, I spent a lot of time with a cop called Jeremy Vearey. He is a couple of years younger than Magadien, and grew up in Elsies River, about ten kilometres north-east of Hanover Park. He also spent much of his adolescence on the streets of the Cape Flats, knife in hand. He was a member of the famous Sicilian gang. 'There were two cinemas in Elsies River,' Vearey tells me. 'The Born Free Kids controlled the Monaco, and the Sicilians controlled the Panorama. Mr Makanam owned both of them. He was the largest cinema owner in the ghettos. He owned cinemas as far away as Paarl. He let people smoke dagga in his cinemas. He knew that the gangsters were a huge, captive audience and he wasn't interested in anyone else. He had three shows a day. The first would start at 10 am, 5c entry, a double feature. All the movies he showed were violent. Some were mafia films, some Kung Fu, others medieval stuff; but the common denominator was that people got killed and fucked up. If he had a particularly hot film, like a new Bruce Lee, or *The Godfather*, he knew he would have to show it to the BFKs and the Sicilians on the same day, otherwise one of his cinemas would be attacked. So he would show it at the Monaco at 10 am, and as soon as it was over, he'd get a runner to take it over to the Panorama.'

Vearey remembers that a group of priests approached Mr Makanam to talk to him about his choice of films. They told him that he was stoking violence among the youth of the Cape Flats. 'Mr Makanam was very receptive,' Vearey recalls. 'He said, "Hell, I would hate to be responsible for youth violence. Let's sit down and talk it through."'

Together, Mr Makanam and the priests bashed out a programme of films. Each had a moral message. 'He started showing films like *The Cross and the Switchblade*,' Vearey says. 'The protagonist was a guy called Nicky Cruz. He was a gangster who had a really miserable time being a gangster and decided to become a Christian. The film ends with him in church.

'So they showed us this film, and Jesus, I don't think anybody has misinterpreted a film as badly as we misinterpreted *The Cross and the Switchblade*. We didn't give a fuck about Cruz's conversion. We just switched off when that happened, left the cinema.'

I ask Magadien about the cinema in Hanover Park and he tells me it was in the northern sections of the ghetto, on Mongrels' turf. 'We'd all go together: all the Never Worry Bastards would trek up north and we'd arrive at the cinema just before ten in the morning, in time for the first show of the day. While we were inside, word would get around that we were there, and by the time we got out the Mongrels had surrounded the whole cinema. We would have to fight our way out of their turf.

'We went into the cinema with knives and dustbin lids, and when we walked out we would do battle like the gladiators. The fighting in the film was preparation for the fighting in the streets.'

I ask Magadien about his favourite films from his youth. He thinks hard before answering. 'Sidney Poitier,' he finally replies. '*To Sir with Love*. You see, it was about a coloured teacher who fell in love with a young white lady. At first, they didn't want to show it in the ghettos. They said that's not the sort of stuff coloured boys should be watching. So we said to ourselves, "Why didn't they want us to see it?" We were curious to see this dangerous film. It was my first experience of black and white.'

Of course, it wasn't his first experience of black and white. Away from the screen, in his real life, he was watching his mother give her maternal love to two white children. And the feelings this spectacle invoked had made him a virulent racist. He hated the Sampsons in particular, the entire white population in general. Even the 'pseudo-whites', the coloured middle class, with their domestic workers and their family cars, he hated with a vengeance. His identification with Sidney Poitier in *To Sir with Love* is almost certainly a retrospective memory. It is the product of a conciliation he has made with the world during the last three years. It is also the symptom of a peace he has made with himself.

Back in the mid-seventies, he must have watched *To Sir with Love* with ambivalence at best: a toxic mix of longing and envy. In the late 1970s, he took this mix with him into the thick of the most famous popular uprising in South African history.

7
CROSSING THE NEVER-NEVER LINE

The true circumstances of Magadien's recruitment into the 28s are lost forever. This is, in one sense at any rate, unsurprising. He was crossing the boundary between working-class South Africa – a world of poor record-keeping – into the prison gangs, an institution that keeps no records at all. And yet, in another sense, it is surprising, because even in the absence of records, there is Magadien's memory. With the exception of this period of his life – his recruitment into the 28s – his memory serves him remarkably well. From the earliest stages of his childhood, right up to the recent past, the veracity of his recollections is evidenced in their vividness, in their alertness to texture, to detail and to objects. And they are always confirmed, either by other people's memories, or by the traces he has left in state archives.

His own story of his recruitment into the 28s stands out in stark contrast to the rest. The very substance of his narration changes; his customary attention to the specific and the tangible gives way to a milky, ethereal form of story-telling; he is no longer in the realm of recall, but in that of personal myth.

His final year of school he places in 1975. Norman Sampson, who has been keeping close tabs on Gadija's son, notices that the boy is doing very well, well enough to continue studying once his secondary schooling is complete. He pushes Magadien. He gets him to enrol for a university entrance examination. He coaches him. Magadien writes the examination. He passes. Norman has dreams that Magadien will become an attorney, just like him. He enrols him in a law degree at Cape Town's coloured university – the University of the Western Cape (UWC) – and pays his fees.

Jump a year. We are now in late 1976. Magadien is settling in to what will become his home for the next two-and-a-half years: Victor Verster Prison in Paarl, the jail from which Nelson Mandela will be released in 1990. His life is littered with irony, but this one, surely, is the most biting of all: it was Norman Sampson who, with the noblest intentions, carved Magadien's path to the heart of the danger zone, a journey that has put him in prison.

In June 1976, just four months after Magadien began his studies at UWC, South Africa caught fire and exploded. It began on 16 June in Soweto, when 10 000 school students marched in protest against Afrikaans-medium instruction in their schools. The police opened fire. By the end of the day, 23 children were dead.

In the following days, the disturbances spread to Alexandra, north of Johannesburg, then to Durban. Within weeks, there were running battles between children and police across the country. After more than a decade of relative quiet, thousands upon thousands of black South Africans had risen up in rebellion against apartheid.

Cape Town remained quiet for a time. But that, perhaps, is only because UWC was closed for its mid-year vacation when the uprisings began. By late July, the students were back on campus, and they began to organise; the storm was on its way.

Magadien joined the rebellion. Along with other student activists, he went back to his high school to mobilise the students there. 'We said to the kids at Crystal High,' he tells me: "Listen, your education is up to shit. What you are taught in Standard 8, the whites are taught in Standard 6." It was such powerful propaganda that they were prepared to burn down their schools. We used Pink Floyd's song, *Another Brick in the Wall*, to mobilise. It worked. But some of the kids died. That was the saddest part.'

He also joined the street demonstrations outside UWC and in the centre of town. He rolls up the trousers of his prisoner's uniform to reveal a deep black scar on the back of his thigh. 'I still have a knock here,' he says, 'from a rubber bullet. I was there when some kids were killed at a demonstration in Belgravia. I was there on campus when the police invaded. I was there when hundreds of us went to the banks in the city with R2 each and said we all wanted to open separate accounts. We marched down Adderley Street and broke windows. I was there when we went to our communities and the kids burnt their school work. And then I was picked up by the police. The astonishing thing is that there was no charge, no trial. We were picked up under the Riot Act. Our cards said "detained". It was in Bellville South, we were out on the streets demonstrating. I think it might have been late July, maybe August. The police had blue vans then, if I remember right. It was so long ago, I can't remember what sort of police they were. I think they brought cops down from the Free State and the Transvaal. It was the prime minister who gave the order to kill the *Boesman*. I stumbled. Some of us were shot in the back, some in the front. One guy lost his eye that day. We were shoved in a van and taken to Victor Verster. I didn't leave again for more than two years.'

*

His memory has been toying with time. It is betrayed by the detail of his recollections. He says that when he went back to his high school to mobilise students, 'we used Pink Floyd's *Another Brick in the Wall*'. Yet the song was only released in 1979, three years after the uprisings. It was indeed used during anti-apartheid campaigns, but in 1980, during the city-wide school boycotts of that year.

There is also the question of his gang name, 'JR', which he was given during his first spell in prison. 'JR' is almost certainly a reference to JR Ewing, the character in *Dallas*, a television drama that was screened for the first time in South Africa in the latter half of 1978.

Examining the student admission record at UWC, I discovered that no Magadien Wentzel was registered there between 1976 and 1980. Nor is there any record of him having matriculated from Crystal High.

And yet, much of the story he tells about his journey to the 28s is undoubtedly culled from real recollections, recollections he has scooped up and rearranged to tell the story he tells.

'Norman Sampson sent him off to university,' Gadija told me when I met her. 'It was Norman's dream that Magadien would become an attorney like him. But he went to the college for only three months. Then he went to jail. It was because of the riots. He was involved with the students: burning tyres and throwing stones and God knows what. He went to Victor Verster. Norman tried to get him out, but it was the government, they were fighting the government, and nobody can get you out for that.'

'What year was that?' I asked her.

'You want dates?' she replied. 'I'm no good with dates.'

I have also interviewed two of the men who recruited

Magadien into the 28s at Victor Verster. They remember his recruitment well. By their lights, it happened exactly as he told it to me. They also recall that he was an educated man; indeed, that is what attracted their attention to him. Like Gadija, though, they too are 'no good with dates'. Nor do they remember whether he was a political detainee.

When Magadien and I discussed these matters, he was left feeling disconsolate. 'Who do I trust,' he asked me, 'my fucked-up memory or a fucked-up record system? I did so much violence to my name and my history that maybe my word should mean nothing. My head was in such a mess that half my life passed me by. But the records are just as violent to me. Sometimes they remember me, sometimes they forget me. They treat me like a thing that can be kicked around, not a human being. All I have is the way I remember things.'

I would imagine that Norman Sampson did send Magadien off to study. Perhaps it wasn't to UWC. Perhaps Gadija's employer despaired when he saw her son – obviously such a gifted boy – going to waste, wandering the Cape Flats without a matric. Perhaps he sent him off to college to finish his secondary schooling.

Family legend may well have fiddled with the memory of Magadien's studies, just as it did with the time he spent at Bonnytown. Gadija, perhaps, remembers him at university in order to tell herself that she managed, against all odds, to place the world at his feet, and that he turned his back. Magadien has perhaps come to think of himself as an erstwhile university student to tell himself that the world was indeed at his fingertips, and that he was unceremoniously thrown back into the ghettos.

I also imagine that Magadien did flirt briefly with anti-apartheid politics; he went to his old high school to mobilise students; he found himself in street demonstrations which were brutally dismembered by the police. But this, I would guess, happened in 1979, or perhaps in 1980, a tumultuous year in Cape Town's history, when students at dozens of schools boycotted classes, and when scores of them were thrown in jail without being charged. I believe that he was held at Victor Verster, not for two-and-a-half years, as he remembers, but for several months.

In any event, even if – indeed, perhaps because – Magadien's recollections have added to and subtracted from what happened, his account of this time is of great value. For it places him at the cusp between crime and politics, between childhood and adulthood, between being a coloured boy from Hanover Park and a black man under apartheid. These are indeed the central questions of his existence, and his memories of the manner in which they confronted him foreshadow how he was to live the rest of his life. It is unsurprising that he blurred them with the stuff of personal myth; they are about the fount of adulthood, the origin of everything to come. That he has fiddled with his own formative moment, placing it in June 1976, one of the most formative moments in recent South African history, is poignant and telling. For he is doing with his personal history precisely what a nation does with its own; it freezes a moment in time, paints it in bold and gaudy brush strokes, and uses it as a device to explain where it has come from and why it has turned out the way it has.

*

'I guess there are many ironies about those times,' Jakes Gerwel tells me in a telephonic interview. 'But the one that sticks in my mind is this: in late July 1976, the first student meeting at UWC convened in support of the Soweto school students was conducted in Afrikaans.'

The kids in Soweto had been marching against Afrikaans-medium instruction. But in Cape Town, that was obviously not an issue: Afrikaans was the mother tongue of coloured students. 'It didn't matter,' Gerwel continues. 'The thing is that coloured students discovered, for the first time, that they were black.'

Gerwel was a young lecturer at UWC at the time, fresh from his studies in Europe. He went on to become the university's rector. When the ANC was swept into power in April 1994, he was appointed director-general of the new presidency under Nelson Mandela, and thus became South Africa's most senior civil servant.

'People forget that 1976 was the triumph of the Black Consciousness movement,' Gerwel says, referring to the strain of anti-apartheid ideology attached to the name of the legendary Steve Biko, who argued that blacks had to retrieve their own dignity and self-respect before they could work alongside whites. 'Black Consciousness offered coloured youth an identity refuge. That's why the uprisings spread to Cape Town so quickly.'

'Were you surprised that coloured youth responded so well to an ideology that called them black?' I ask.

'I was both surprised and unsurprised,' he replies. 'I understood their longing for an identity. But I was amazed at just how militant they turned out to be.'

Magadien, when he joined the flanks of the political movement three or four years later, was militant, all right; I can just see him revelling in the destructive creativity of the crowd, watching the shop windows shatter with giddy ecstasy. But how did he feel about being black? The answer is complicated; his whole relationship with the political movement, as he remembers it now, was fraught and ambivalent, a cocktail of fascination and excitement mixed with suspicion and hostility – even paranoia.

When he speaks of his involvement in politics, he conjures two rival sets of the recollections; they jostle for control of the same sentence, the same words.

On the one hand, there is Magadien the activist, clean and true. 'There was a woman I knew on campus called Fatima Philips,' he tells me, 'and she was politically involved. She took me off to meetings. Everyone there was talking about how to overthrow the government. People stood up and said, "The way we study is not right. Our curriculum level isn't up to standard. There is a huge difference between [the white universities of] UCT and Stellenbosch and us. We are just here to become clerks and secretaries, not lawyers and doctors. We are being trained to be assistants." That is the sort of propaganda the student activists aimed at people.

'It worked. It made sense to everyone. After the uprisings nothing was the same in South Africa. The hatred was more intense. People were prepared to stand up. The only problem is that today, it is the black kids in Soweto who take the credit. Coloured kids died too, here in Cape Town. Maybe Soweto lost more kids, but every life is special.'

Then, in the same interview, a second Magadien steps in. He is angry and suspicious. He is not sure whether his enemy is the apartheid state or those who organised the rebellion against it.

'I met the famous Alan Boesak,' he tells me. 'He was a pastor at the time. He called a meeting here, a meeting there. He rallied us, told us to march. We said, "What about the riot police?" He told us not too worry about the riot police. Some kids were killed and I sat in jail.'

'Boesak betrayed you?' I asked.

'Not just him. There were a lot of people involved, people who are very esteemed today, in the very highest positions. I don't think I should mention their names; they have the power to destroy me now. Some of them called the cops on us. Some were in cahoots with the riot police. They sold us out. People died. I went to jail.'

'You were scared?'

'Very scared. I learned my lesson. When the uprisings started again in 1984, I kept well away. I didn't want to get killed by the police. And I didn't want to get stabbed in the back by my own comrades.'

It is clear that, more than twenty years later, Magadien is still scarred by the violence he witnessed. True, he has seen bucketfuls of blood in his time, but this was different. The choreography of a gang fight marks out a dance of equals; each participant is a wilful soldier, doing battle by volition, equipped with the same armoury as his opponent. A crowd of violent youth is another thing entirely. 'As soon as a man has surrendered himself to the crowd,' writes Elias Canetti, the great theorist of crowds, 'he ceases to fear its touch ... The man pressed against him is the same as himself. He feels him as he feels himself. Suddenly it is as though everything were happening in one and the same body.'

To watch this organism – which has emerged elusively, as if from nowhere – suddenly disintegrate into broken bodies and howls of pain, to experience the crowd's death via the sensations emanating from one's own being, is to feel an intensity of loneliness and fear unmatched by any other context. So it is hardly surprising that the ghosts of shattered crowds still haunt Magadien.

But why does he attach these traumatic memories to the theme of betrayal? Why is he convinced that the leaders of the uprisings made cannon fodder of its soldiers? Recall the geography of his adolescence. Hanover Park itself was divided into 16 rival territories; to walk to the station was to negotiate a path that skirted the homegrounds of foes. And beyond the boundary of the ghetto was the land of the perfume-shitters, the middle class of Lansdowne. Magadien's youthful identity consisted in one layer of chauvinism packed on another; the chauvinism of one small patch of Hanover Park, the chauvinism of class, and finally the chauvinism of race. He was a minority, within a minority, within a minority.

When Magadien flirted with politics, he brought with him a hatred of urbane coloureds that bordered on paranoia. To say that he was deeply suspicious of the literate, university-educated people who led the political movement is to understate things. These were the people for whom he had spent his life playing the *skollie*. Now they were telling him he was black. He did not trust the place from which this discourse spewed; it went against the grain.

Look at the texture of the uprisings themselves, and you will see that there was plenty to excite the imagination of the budding gangster, not just the activist. The activity on the street was not nearly as orderly and disciplined as is sometimes maintained. Much of it was unguided, youthful euphoria. Groups of kids stood on the bridges above the N2 and hurled stones at passing cars. Shop windows were smashed in the satellite towns of Bellville and Belgravia, and in the city centre itself. In what remained of District Six, cars were overturned with their occupants trapped inside.

When Magadien describes the scenes, you can make out the complex strands of his identity; the activist, celebrating the memory of white retreat, the haunted soul remembering the fallen figures who were once merged into a crowd, and the gangster who watched with glee as the world was turned upside down.

He rolls up the trousers of his prisoner's uniform to show me his scar once again. This time, it is no longer clear who put it there: the policeman who shot the rubber bullet, or the activists who put him in harm's way; the white men who bundled him into a police van and threw him into the cells of Victor Verster Prison, or the coloured perfume-shitters who coaxed him into the crowd. In any event, he was off to the 28s, the alter-ego of the treacherous activists of his imagination. It is the prison gangsters whom he would come to remember as his true brothers, as the real revolutionaries.

*

When the uprisings began, and the jails began filling with young people, the authorities at Victor Verster Prison divided political prisoners into two categories. Activist leaders were detained indefinitely under the Internal Security Act and isolated from the rest of the prison. The warders who brought them their food were carefully hand-picked. Their exercise time in the yard never coincided with common criminals.

'The closest I got to meeting a criminal inmate,' Johnny Issel, a leader of the uprisings who was detained at Victor Verster in late 1976, told me, 'was through the toilet bowl. We would empty the bowl and shout through the sewerage system. By that method, I struck up a friendship with a General in the 26s. I never saw his face; but I got to know his voice intimately.'

It was different for Magadien. Between 1977 and 1980, scores of rank-and-file demonstrators who had been picked up off the streets were thrown into the prison proper. Some were charged with public order violations, others detained without trial for several months. But all shared their space with the Number gangs.

'We were really shocked by what we saw, the way prisoners were treated,' Magadien tells me. 'They were treated like animals; they were people with lice in their hair. Their food was not up to standard. They had to sleep on these fucked-up mattresses with two thin blankets.

'At first, they came to us for advice. Among us political detainees there were educated people, and they knew we could be helpful to them. They would ask for help in writing letters, in briefing attorneys, in getting assistance from their families, in raising the issue of prison conditions.

'Meeting them was an eye-opener. I had never been interested in the Number before. Of course, I knew about them. Everybody in the ghettos knew about them. But all I had heard was the rumours – about how these guys hurt people, robbed people, sodomised people. I was shocked to see that they were as political as we were. They were fighting the apartheid prison system. That is what they were about, before anything else.'

The truth is that, culturally and socially, Magadien was far closer to the prisoners on the other side of the divide than to his fellow political detainees. They were from neighbourhoods like his; they had come of age in street gangs like his; they had broken into the homes and the factories of the Cape Flats, just as he had. And indeed, it was not long before Magadien was recognised, not just as a ghetto boy, but as the younger brother of Victor Mekka, a high-ranking 26.

'I got nosy, I got curious. Me and a colleague, another detainee – his name was Peter, Peter Philander, I think – we started chatting with this Germiston in the 28s. And he started telling us about the war between the Number and the *boere*, and I thought, "These are fighters, these are not people who will stab you in the back."'

The moment Magadien began to express curiosity, he was taunted. This corrupted Hanover Park boy, with one foot in the ghetto, the other in the university – he was ripe for ridicule. 'They sent this 28 to see me; his gang name was China Bok. He said, "So you want to join." I said, "Ja." He said, "You've got to be joking. You can only join if your heart is in the right place. You people are soft." He teased me quite a bit, and I didn't like it.

'Next time I saw him, I asked, "How do I show you that my heart is in the right place?" and he laughed again, and said he would go and consult, properly this time. The next day he came back. He said, "You know that to join the 28s, you have to stab a warder. Can you stab a warder?" I was already part of a gang, the Never Worry Bastards, and stabbing someone meant nothing to me. I said, "I'll kill a warder if you like," and he said, "Fuck, no – you can't kill a warder; if you do that we will kill you. We are going to give you a knife, with a very short blade, and you must get him below the shoulder, where there is just flesh, no organs."

'He looked at me very closely for a long time, and he said, "Do you understand? Do you understand what you're getting yourself into? The brave part is not the stabbing. It is what happens after that. Because they are going to beat the shit out of you. And if you cry out, just once, the stabbing means nothing; you have failed. And after they have fucked you up, they are going to put you in a dark cell, with not enough food, for a long time. And if you go mad in there, if you come out crying like a baby, the stabbing means nothing."'

We are sitting in Magadien's Pollsmoor cell when he recounts this story. He reaches over to his cabinet, picks up a toilet roll and breaks off a wad of paper. 'He taught me a trick, and it served me very well many times. When you are going to stab, you do this,' and he shoves the wad of paper into his mouth, tries to scream, and all that comes out is a muffled squeak.

'The only other detainee who knew what was being planned was Peter. He said to me, "For God's sake, don't do it. You are going to fuck up your life." I said, "Our lives are already fucked up. There are riot police out in the streets. When we go out, they will put us back. I don't want to be beholden to them. I have made my choice."

'I actually thought the whole thing was a joke. We were thoroughly searched every day. I thought there was no way they were going to get a knife to me. But they did it. I couldn't believe it. They said it would be Friday afternoon and it was; I picked up my tray of food outside the kitchen, and it was there, hidden away, this little knife, all wrapped up with bandages, with just the tip of the blade sticking out. I learned later that the Nyangi [a corruption of the word *nyanga* – 'diviner-herbalist'], the doctor, had wrapped the knife. That is one of his main functions, to determine the length of the blade.

'I was told I must stab as soon as I saw the knife. So I brushed past a white warder, and when I was just past him, and his back was to me, I grabbed the knife, dropped the tray and stabbed him in the back, beneath the shoulder. I don't know how the 28s got there in time. It was so quick. But suddenly there was a scuffle around me, I felt the knife being taken from my hand, and suddenly, it was gone. It was just me standing there in shock, with empty hands, and the warder standing there in shock; the knife was gone.'

'What was the warder's name?' I ask.

'I don't know. I didn't care.

'But they beat me, brother. They beat the shit out of me. By the time they had locked me in the one-ones – in a single cell – I had pimples all over my body. I was so swollen I looked like a body builder. But I did not cry out, not once.

'After a couple of days in the one-ones, I noticed things started happening. The cells around me were being filled with 28s. They went there deliberately to be with me. They would break rules – like shouting, or pretending to fight – so that they could come to the one-ones. And they started talking to me. At exercise time – all the one-ones exercised together – they began probing me.

'I didn't realise it at the time,' he tells me, 'but what they were doing was putting steel in my blood, giving me support to prepare for what was going to happen next. Because what happens when you stab a warder is very rough; if you're a new recruit, you need to know that your brothers are waiting for you on the other side.

'After some time in the one-ones, the authorities took me to what we call the X court, the internal court. The magistrate comes to the prison and there is a trial.

'In the X court, I said to them, "How could I have stabbed this warder? Where is the knife?" And they said: "Shut up. You stabbed him, finished and *klaar*." They sentenced me. I don't remember what the sentence was. That was the X court punishment. Then there was the warder punishment. They put me in segregation, I don't remember for how long, on a spare diet – no salt. You feel weaker every day, until you are floating. We call the one-ones *agter die berge* – behind the mountains – like where Po went to contemplate.'

Magadien says the 28s surrounded him in the one-ones in order to put steel in his blood. It seems to have worked. During the first days of segregation, before he had officially joined the 28s, he was behaving like a maniacal militant, quite literally inviting the violence of white warders.

'The first thing I did in segregation – I looked around for weapons. I broke off a piece of the toilet lid and spent the whole night chipping away at it, sharpening it. The next morning, when the warder came to open my cell, I stabbed him in the shoulder. Of course, the news immediately went to the 28s, and that's when I started getting my reputation.

'After that, they beat me up all over again, and sentenced me to more time in isolation. Again, I didn't cry. You learn soon: you learn to feel all the pain inside, and show nothing on the outside. For my second sentence, they put me in a straitjacket for a while, because I couldn't be trusted with freedom of movement. And when I came out of the straitjacket, they chained me to the bars of my cell. There was a warder named Mr Wells. He was in charge of the group of warders who came to take off the straitjacket and chain me up.

'He said to me: "*Jy gaan vrek hier*." "You will die like an animal here," and he spat in my face. I spat back in his face, completely defenceless, chained to the bars, and he told the warders to beat me up, which they did.

'A couple of days later, another warder, Mr van Wyk, came to see me. He was very different from Mr Wells. He sat down on a chair and spoke to me in a soft voice. He looked at me with a lot of concern in his face, and said, "This is not the way". I said: "Listen here, you can't tell me how to live my life. You are treating me like an animal; at least I have my own will."

'He shook his head. "There is no choice," he said. "This is our legacy, the white man's legacy. It will always be like this."

'I said, "You watch. We will win this battle."

'"No," he replied. "You will never win. We have all the guns, all the ammunition."

'"Maybe you have the guns," I said, "but we are *gatvol*."

'He shrugged. "What do you think you are trying to achieve?"

'"We will keep stabbing," I replied, "keep stabbing. Even you, with your soft voice, I will stab."

'Then he lost patience with me. "Ja, you will keep stabbing," he said, "but we will fuck you up so bad you won't walk out of here."

'It felt so good to talk like that: like it was worth the straitjacket and the chains.'

*

During exercise time, the others 28s – who had got themselves into the one-ones to put 'steel' in Magadien's blood – would speak to him. I ask Magadien what they said, and he gives a strange answer, one which, I suspect, is drawn half from myth, half from his actual experience. It is said that when a new member is being recruited into the 28s, the Glas (a colloquial and idiosyncratic word for 'binoculars') – a senior member, one of whose tasks is to conduct gang business in 'the bush', those parts of the prison where the 28s are not active – comes to the new recruit and confronts him with a riddle. How the newcomer responds determines whether he will be recruited, and, if he is, into which department of the gang.

'At exercise time, early on in my stay in the one-ones, the Glas, his name was Buttons, came to me and he said: "It is raining. You are standing under an umbrella. I say to you, 'I am getting wet; I may get sick.' What are you going to do?"

'I answered correctly. I said, "I will come out into the rain with you," which means, "I am prepared to live like you. We are brothers. We will live and die together."'

'And if you had invited him to share your umbrella?' I ask.

'That means I am inviting him into my bed. If I had given that answer, they would not have made me a 28; they would have made me a sex-son.

'I guess they'd already decided that if I was going to be recruited into the 28s, it would be into the silver line, not the gold line, because I had brains, and a good memory. What they were deciding through that riddle is whether I would be a sex-son, or a real silver. A sex-son is mixed with the probationers in the silver line, and to an outsider, he is just like a probationer. But actually, he is a sex object; the soldiers, the members of the gold line, sleep with him at night. He can't progress up the silver line. He is never told much about the history. He is not really a 28.'

'And a real probationer in the silver line ...'

'Nobody is allowed to sleep with him. He is groomed to be an officer in the camp one day, like I was.'

The 28s are divided into two parallel hierarchies. The one is called the silver or private line; controversially, some call it the line of *wyfies* – wives. The other is the gold line, also referred to as the line of soldiers. The 28s are shrouded by a dense fog of rumour and legend concerning their sexual practices. Recall the story of Nongoloza and Kilikijan: in particular, the great fight that ensued when the progenitor of the 27s found Nongoloza and the young bandit Magubane making love under a cow hide. Recall that the bandits never resolved their dispute about the permissibility of sex, that, instead, they splintered into rival groups, one which permitted sex – the 28s – and one which outlawed it – the 27s. Ask a 26 or a 27 about the relationship between the silver and the gold line, and he will tell you that the men of gold, the soldiers, are the real 28s, the silvers their concubines and whores.

Magadien sighs with well-rehearsed exasperation when I recount the other two camps' standard position on the gold and the silver line. He pulls up his shirt to reveal his stomach; a tattoo of an erect penis emerges from beneath the waist of his trousers, its head staring up at his belly-button. 'If I am a woman,' he says, 'what the fuck is this doing on my stomach? Do you think the 28s would have allowed me to walk around like this for 25 years?'

He explains his version of the relationship between the gold and the silver line. 'We think of ourselves as Zulus, because our father, Nongoloza, was a Zulu. Think of a Zulu kraal, of how it is organised. The soldiers are not in the heart of the kraal. They are at the outposts, guarding the centre. That is the gold line. At the heart of the kraal are its brains, its memory, its very soul. That's us: the silver line. We are the Number, the keeper of its rules, and its history. The soldiers are not the Number; they are its protector, its outer shield. When you recruit a soldier, you are not looking for a brain; you are looking for an aggressive maniac who acts before he thinks, someone who will put his life on the line instinctively, without asking questions.'

This is, I think to myself, precisely how Magadien behaved when he was recruited, but I keep my counsel.

'Nobody in the silver line is fucked,' he continues. 'It is the sex-sons who are fucked. They sleep next to the silver probationers. They look like they are silver probationers. But they are not. They never get close to the heart of the Number. And when I say they are fucked, I mean something very specific. You know when a young Zulu man meets a young Zulu woman, they are allowed to have sex before they are married, as long as it is not penetrative sex. It is the same between the sex-sons and the soldiers. They can only have thigh sex. When they sleep together, it is in the middle of the night, under a blanket. The Judge is entitled to lift that blanket during the night. If he finds that the two are not face-to-face, if the sex-son has his back to the soldier, if he is being fucked up the arse, there is hell to pay.'

In the months following this conversation with Magadien, when I got to know the hierarchies of the 28s better, I discovered that the silver line reveals traces of both rival accounts I had heard. At the top of the silver hierarchy is Nonzala, a symbolic position; Nonzala is the spirit of Magubane, the silver line's original forebear, and when silvers are recruited into the camp, they are told that he is their mother. At the top of the gold line is the spirit of Nongoloza, and newly recruited soldiers are told that he is their father.

But the top two positions in the silver line – the Mtshali and the Nyangi – tell an interesting tale. The Mtshali is entrusted with Rooiland's skin, and thus with the rules and the sacred history of the 28s. Indeed, he warehouses all the gang's accoutrements – its knives, it bayonets and its uniforms. He does so figuratively rather than literally. Rooiland's skin is, of course, imaginary, as are the uniforms. But what this means materially is that nobody steps into his new uniform, and thus his new rank, without the sanction of the silver line's leader; nor can soldiers arm themselves without his approval. And the Nyangi, although not himself a soldier, is the one who inspects and issues weapons to the combatants in the gold line. Any soldier who uses a knife that has not passed through the hands of the Nyangi has committed a crime. So the silver line is clearly a great deal more than a group of concubines; its leaders are the law-keepers in the 28s.

*

Magadien's recruitment in the silver line of the 28s was anomalous. A silver ought not to stab to join the 28s; that is reserved for a soldier, a gold line member. Indeed, a silver is barred from spilling blood until he has climbed far up the hierarchy.

In November 2003, I travelled to Paardeberg Prison outside Paarl to visit an inmate there: Buttons, who had been the Glas of the 28s at Victor Verster in the late 1970s, the one who had asked Magadien what he would do with his umbrella. I asked him why he had recruited 'JR' into the silver line.

'Because of his intelligence,' Buttons replied. 'He was busy with his studies. That was unusual for us. His schooling, his knowledge – we can use it. If I am a Glas and I see a *frans* with a brain, I must recruit him into the silver line. The gold line has no mercy – they just take a knife and stab.'

'But if he was being recruited into the silver line,' I asked, 'why did he have to stab?'

'Because the educated ones can be unreliable,' he replied. 'He had to show us we could depend on him, no matter what. Once we know he is with us, we take away his knife and use him for other purposes.'

*

When Magadien was released from the one-ones, he was taken to the communal cells where he was surrounded by 28s. His formal recruitment began in the same week.

South Africa's prison gangs are among the most ritualised structures you will ever find. Each day of the week is reserved for a carefully circumscribed set of functions. The tasks of weekdays – distributing rations, teaching, taking complaints – can all be performed within the confines of the cell. But Saturdays and Sundays are different. On these days, the central structures of the gangs in each section of each prison must meet. Saturday is the day of the wrongs, Sunday the day of the rights. (The gangs say, 'the *year* of the wrongs'. Everything about the metaphors of prison gang language is expansive. An overcrowded cell becomes a vast plain; a day becomes a year.) On Saturdays, the various judicial structures of the gang meet to pass sentence: an errant member is punished; a new recruit is scanned for illicit allegiances. On Sundays, newcomers are recruited; members are promoted; victories are celebrated.

On his first Saturday after his release from the one-ones, Magadien was placed in the centre of a cell and told to strip down to his underwear. The Glas, Buttons, circled him slowly, scrutinising his skin for *vuil papiere* – contaminated papers – the tattoos of other gangs. If the Glas had found the mark of the 26s or 27s on Magadien's body, negotiations with the rival gang would have begun. If he had found the mark of a prison gang the Number considers illicit – like the Big Five, whose aim is to spy on the Number on behalf of the warders, or the Air Force, whose aim is to escape from prison – Magadien would have been beaten and his recruitment halted.

On the Sunday – the year of the rights – his recruitment ceremony is performed. He is again placed in the centre of a cell, but this time several people surround him. The first to approach him is the Nyangi, the doctor. What happens next is metaphorical and is enacted in a simple process of physical mimicry. On the shoulders of the Nyangi's imaginary uniform are 12 pipes: six are gold, six silver. He tells Magadien to hold out his arms, palms upwards; he takes a gold pipe off his shoulder and slaps it on Magadien's right wrist, then a silver pipe on his left wrist. He checks Magadien's pulse and declares: *'Die man se pols klop twee keer per jaar'* – 'This man's pulse beats twice a year', which means that Magadien is being recruited into the silver line. If he had said three times a year, it would have meant the gold line. Then the Gwenza – a senior member of the silver line – places a handkerchief on the floor and slips a knife under it. He stands up and addresses Magadien:

'From today,' he says, 'you are no longer a *frans*. You are a 28. You will never swear at your brother. You will never hurt your brother. You will never do anything that reflects badly on the camp. And if you leave the camp, you will leave by your own blood.

'I am giving you your uniform. You have a white pair of sandals. Your socks are also white, stamped with the sign of 28, both inside and out. You have a white shirt, and white belt with silver buckles. You have a white tunic with two buttons, stamped with the sign of 28, inside and out. You wear a green tie. You have a white jacket, which also has two buttons, the first open, because you belong to the Number day and night, the second closed, for discipline. You wear a white beret with a silver badge, and on the badge a hammer and a handkerchief are engraved.'

Then the Magistrate comes forward, takes out his green and white stamps and gives Magadien's recruitment his approval. The Magistrate carries four imaginary stamps – white, green, red and black – signifying the four hooves of Rooiland. When a silver is recruited or promoted, he takes out his green and white stamps. When it is a gold, he takes out the green and the red, the red signifying blood. His black stamp is reserved for the death sentence.

Next, the Gwenza steps forward and takes out his imaginary white and green pens to inscribe Magadien's recruitment in the 28s' proverbial record book. Like the Magistrate with his stamps, the Gwenza has four pens, which signify Rooiland's legs.

Now, Magadien is marched out of the circle, and the formal recruitment ceremony is over. The 28s take the news of his recruitment to the 26s and 27s. They do so in the form of an exacting ritual.

Every night, the Glas and Draad of the 28s meet with the Glas and Draad of the 27s, and the Glas and Draad of the 26s, in a forum called the Valcross. Only the Glas is allowed to speak on the Valcross. The Draad – the 'wire' – must remain silent; he is the one who will report back to the 28s what happened on the Valcross. Hence his name; he 'wires' the gang to the rest of the prison, so that they can hear what happens everywhere. The two 28s on the Valcross are not allowed to speak directly to the 26s. They communicate through the 27s, who are the upholders of the law, and mediate between the other two gangs. At the Valcross meeting on the evening after Magadien's recruitment, the Glas 'bugles' his recruitment to the 27s, who, in turn, pass on the information to the 26s.

In the weeks to follow, Magadien will sleep alongside a different member of the 28s every night, and each will describe his uniform and his functions. The structure he is to join is called the four points of the twos ('two' is a reference to their pulse – it beats 'twice a year'); it is the lower tier of the silver line. He learns that one of its functions is that of a court; it deals with infractions committed by low-ranking silvers.

The five members of the twos are, from most junior to most senior, the Silver-Two, the Silver-One, the Goliat-Two, the Goliat-One and the Landdros. The Silver-Two tells Magadien that he is the one responsible for the security of every meeting of the twos.

When a junior member is to stand trial for a minor infraction, it is the Silver-Two who searches him for weapons, leads him into the circle, and then leaves the circle again in order to guard it. The Silver-Two is also responsible for the sex-sons; if a soldier forces a sex-son to have penetrative sex, the sex-son must report the incident to the Silver-Two.

The Silver-One is the intelligence officer of the twos. He tells the court what the culprit is accused of, and the circumstances of the case. The Goliat-Two is the keeper of the laws of the twos. He will determine the punishment at the conclusion of the case. The Goliat-One is the defence lawyer in the silvers' misdemeanours court; he will argue the accused's case. And finally, the Landdros, the most senior member of the twos, is the prosecutor.

It is not from the four points of the twos that Magadien learns their functions; it is senior members of the gold line whom he sleeps next to every night. They too, have their own 'sub-court' – to deal with the infractions of gold line members. Their court mirrors precisely the functions of the lower silver line court. So they explain to Magadien their own functions, and in so doing teach him the functions of the silver line court he will join. They also begin to teach him the history of Nongoloza and Kilikijan. But only a fragment of the history; he is still too junior to be told the whole story.

Finally, he is taken to a section of the gang called the Mambozas, or the Forties. The 28s here are senior, but inactive. They are either too old or too injured for active duty, or their position in the structure is already filled by someone else. For instance, the 28s cannot have two active Nyangis in one prison. If a second Nyangi is transferred to Victor Verster, he is dormant; he sleeps in the Forties.

The Mambozas begin to teach Magadien to *sabela* – to speak prison language – and it is a long, gruelling process. 'Your blackboard [teacher],' Magadien tells me, '*sabelas* with you day and night. Your first two months in the Number you are not allowed to receive visits, to read or write letters, or to read books. You must focus on the Number, and when you learn too slowly, the punishments are severe. If you cannot remember something you have been taught, you are stripped and stood under a cold shower until you "find the Number" – until you get it right.'

One of the last things Magadien learns about the structure of the 28s takes the form of a ghost story. There is a position in the silver line held by a man called Mtjoetjies; but he is dead, his place in the hierarchy is left empty.

'How did he die?' I ask.

'Back in the beginning,' Magadien tells me, 'when Nongoloza was imprisoned at The Point, he refused to learn English, or Afrikaans, or any language spoken by white men. He refused to look white men in the eye. But one of the 28s, Mtjoetjies, was fluent in English, and Nongoloza used him to negotiate with the *boere*. After a while, Nongoloza realised that he had made a mistake. "What does this man talk to the *boere* about? I cannot understand what he says; he may be betraying us." So Nongoloza killed him, as a precaution.

'And now, his position remains there, empty, as a reminder; that we do not negotiate with words, we negotiate with action, with violence. There have always been social workers in prison, you know. And they want to talk to you behind a closed door. If you do that, if you talk to an authority alone, one-to-one, you are severely punished.'

The expression on my face must have revealed my distaste, for Magadien gives me a sympathetic smile. 'The Number is only heavy at the beginning,' he says. 'Once you know everything, the Number is very light.'

*

Light, indeed. There is something unsettlingly ethereal about Magadien's recollections of his time in Victor Verster. It is not just that he has turned an unhappy place into a receptacle of blissful memories. It is, primarily, that the world he describes is entirely unpeopled; there are Nyangis, Mtshalis, Gwenzas and Silver-Twos, but there are no flesh-and-blood beings. I try, several times, to get him to describe the men behind the positions. 'What was your blackboard's name? What was he like? Who was the Silver-Two when you were a probationer?'

'It was a long time ago,' he replies. And that is all.

It is as if he has dissolved the concrete and the bars, the bad food, the bile that passes between men confined together, and abstracted from it a pure form, an idyll.

What sort of idyll? The way Magadien tells it, he was attracted to the gangs because they, and not the political activists, were the real freedom fighters. The *ndotas* were the ones prepared to stand side-by-side, shedding blood and having their own blood shed in turn.

Listening to Magadien's account of his recruitment, though, what struck me most was not the gangs' resistance to authority, but their dependence on it. This unsettling, double-edged relationship with warders begins with the recruitment ritual itself. To become a *ndota*, the initiate must be beaten publicly; he must then endure a spare diet in solitary confinement. *Ndoda* means 'man' in Zulu, but it is a stark, shorn version of a man who emerges from the initiation ritual. He must be flagellated and show stoicism; he must be starved and show no hunger. And it is the violence inflicted by warders that makes him a man. He is, thus, not a man as such, but an inmate-man; his initiation co-opts custodial punishment and uses it as its primary tool.

And what does the initiate do with his newfound status? Here, there is a silence in Magadien's story. He says nothing about the relationship between *ndotas* and *franse* – those prisoners who are not members of the Number gangs. He does not tell me, for instance, that the *frans* is someone who has been stripped of the jail equivalent of his juridical personhood. When he receives a parcel from a visitor, he must hand it over to the *ndotas* in his cell; they will decide how it is to be distributed. If he wants to conduct a commercial transaction – sell his watch, swap a t-shirt for a toothbrush – he must ask the permission of the *ndotas*. In exchange for allowing him to conduct a transaction, he must give the *ndotas* something in turn. When *ndotas* in a cell hold a meeting to discuss Number business, each *frans* must sit with his face to the wall and remain absolutely silent.

The relationship between *ndotas* and *franse* strikes me as a parody of the relationship between warders and prisoners. The *frans* is, quite literally, told when to shit and when to eat, when to stand and when to talk. He has no right to personal possessions, to any of the accoutrements around which a person forms his own quiddity and individuality. *Ndotas* resist prison authority to be sure, but only to mimic it.

I think of Magadien's childhood relationships with Quinton and with Gadija; of how he loathed Quinton's violence but courted it; of how he hated Gadija but felt compelled to make her hate him in turn. The gang's obsessive and symbiotic relationship with warders seems to have echoes in Magadien's past.

I begin sharing my thoughts with him about the gangs' strange relationship with their custodians. I have barely cleared my throat when he interrupts me.

'You're the boss,' he says. 'This is your book, not mine. Write what you like.'

He does not want to discuss the matter any further. He does not like me interrogating his memory of his recruitment into the 28s. Victor Verster must remain cleansed and abstract; it is not a place that permits questions.

I am left feeling puzzled. Magadien's relationship to this entire episode of his life is peculiar, out of character. His mythologising of the events leading up to his imprisonment; the weightless, sublime nature of the Victor Verster he remembers: these are out of sync with the texture of the rest of his memories, both about Cape Town and its jails. What is it about this period – the period in which he crossed the boundary between the world outside and the Number?

There are, I guess, many ways in which a middle-aged prison gangster might remember how his life of crime began. At one extreme, he may recall his early adult years as an empty period of drifting and aimlessness. The Number was simply the shore on which the currents dumped him. At the other extreme, he may remember his youthful self as a latter-day Ulysses, a character heavy with the political symbols of his time, his every decision a beacon in a grand and universal tale.

The story Magadien tells about his path to the 28s does indeed have all the hallmarks of a moral and political fable, rather than a slice of real life. And the structure of the fable is not unlike that of Nongoloza's story. Nongoloza was lured to the city by a promise – the promise of gold. Yet the prophets who beckoned him were false prophets; they were, in fact, leading him to his own death. It so happened that fate was kind to him; on his journey to the city he was intercepted by a good and wise man – Po – who stripped naked the false prophets and unveiled the trap they had set for him. Nongoloza was saved from those who had set out to betray him. He spent the rest of life avenging them – he slaughtered them mercilessly and stole the gold they had promised him. His life of crime is thus both a tale of personal redemption and a political philosophy; banditry, Nongoloza learns, is a form of personal flourishing and a righteous attack on injustice.

This is precisely the structure of the story Magadien tells about his path to the 28s. The city of gold that beckoned him was an escape from the ghettos, a university degree, the life of a lawyer, a place in the ranks of the anti-apartheid movement. He was promised that he too was going shit perfume. Like Nongoloza, he was being led into a trap. The false prophets who lured him were the perfume shitters themselves: the coloured elite and their ostensibly anti-apartheid politics. They led him, not to riches and freedom, but to apartheid's prison cells. And that is where he met his Po – the 28s, the true revolutionaries, who stripped bare all the lies.

It is no wonder that he has placed himself in June 1976, that iconic moment in the anti-apartheid struggle. For the point of his personal fable is to invert the meaning of that moment, to show that it is hollow. Joining the 28s, his fable illustrates to him, was not a drift from politics; on the contrary, it was a moment of political awakening, the place from which he could avenge those who had betrayed him: Gadija and Norman Sampson; the whites and perfume-shitters; the apartheid state and its ostensible enemies.

That is the personal fable through which he made his life meaningful, and the remainder of his story is about his failed attempt to live it, and his growing disenchantment with it. If his memories of his first spell in prison are sprinkled with magic, his recollections of jail in years to come will grow all too real, all too bitter. He will come to see the first two decades of his adult life as a wasted time, a time he might have spent living a fully human life.

8
TWO WOMEN AND A GIRL

Magadien was released from Victor Verster in early 1980, and in the months that followed he began to live the life for which he now curses himself. Back in the mid-1970s, when much of his existence had been confined to a few blocks of a Cape Flats ghetto, he had felt like 'a chicken in a coop'; he wanted to spread his wings. Now, after his release from Victor Verster, he did indeed begin to live the most expansive of lives, skating from one corner of greater Cape Town to the next. He had a home in the Strand, the coastal town where his mother grew up, a home in Hanover Park, with Annie, and a string of legitimate jobs in Cape Town's city centre. But in each of these lives he went by a different name, a different religious identity, a different family lineage. He had serious but troubled romantic relationships in two of these lives: with Colleen Finch in the Strand, and with Margie Smith – with whom he would soon have a child – on the Cape Flats. He would love them both for decades to come, but they would not know of each other's existence until the mid-1990s.

And there is something else most of the people in his life would not know for a long time. Of Magadien's many identities, one was now written on his body; there was a tattoo of a penis along the length of his stomach, a symbol of the 28s' celebration of sex; and on his left collar bone were the words 'Moliva Boy', the Moliva being the river into which the rock carrying half the laws of banditry was lost.

'I cannot count the times Margie and I slept in the same bed,' Magadien tells me, 'but she never saw one of my tattoos. When I took a bath, I would go alone and close the door. When we had sex with the light on, I would wear a t-shirt. I would take it off after we had said good-night. And when I got up in the middle of the night to go to the bathroom, I would put it back on, in case she woke up and turned on the light.'

Indeed, the political dimension of his affiliation to the 28s – expressed in the sorts of crimes he was about to commit – is less interesting than the personal dimension. He had joined the ranks of a movement which told him he was no longer coloured, but an honorary Zulu; that his family was no longer family but just a bunch of *franse* – uninitiated fools. It is as if he had found a piece of ground from which to express his alienation, a place from which he could trick the world that had tricked him in turn.

That is, perhaps, the most fruitful way to make sense of the life he chose to lead; this man drifting in and out of many worlds, leaving most of himself elsewhere, hiding his body from the women he chose to love. For years to come he would be, for those who peopled his life, the man who was not really there.

*

It was yet another fruitless attempt to save Magadien that took him to the Strand. By 1980 he had known for nearly a decade that Bapi – the elderly man in the Strand he had visited on weekends – was Gadija's father and thus his grandfather. But he had never been close to the old man. On his return to Hanover Park from Victor Verster, his education wasted and his prospects bleak, Annie, with Gadija's consent, decided that drastic action was required to set Magadien straight. She sent him to live with his grandfather, in the hope that the old man's religious ways would rub off on the errant youngster. Strange, the resources people find to set straight a life gone wrong; she had brought 'Darryl' up as a Christian. Now she was sending 'Magadien' off to be a good Muslim.

Rusthof, the coloured township in the Strand, is about forty kilometres east of Cape Town, just inland from the False Bay coastline. Behind it are Sir Lowry's Pass and the summits of the Hottentots Holland mountain range, a solid line of towering blue peaks. Yet the township itself is entirely flat. It is laid out in a symmetrical grid, some roads tarred, others sand, the houses one-room matchboxes, packed together in dense rows. There isn't a patch of grass in the township's public spaces; it is as if the place is forever a few days old, the soil just turned, the flora not yet planted. And with the mountain-peak colossi staring down the backs of the houses, comes weather. Ill-tempered clouds form before your eyes above the summits, bringing sudden rain, violent wind, and a thick mist that lingers throughout the day. The combination of the flat, arid township, the gigantic peaks and the wild energy of the weather, leaves one feeling small and exposed.

I ask Magadien what Bapi was like and he says he does not know. 'He was a silent man. He just used to nod at me and I knew: "Shit, it's time for mosque again." I'd put on my kufi, and go off with my cousins, following the sound of the call to prayer.'

I remembered that Magadien had celebrated his discovery that he was a Muslim. When we first discussed his experience of mosque, his description of the sounds and smells was deep and evocative, textured with that indefinable quality of the ancient, of a long line beginning before your own birth. But he is less enthusiastic this time.

'Ja, I liked mosque – but every fucking Friday, every day during Ramadan? You've got to be joking. Bapi would give me the nod, I'd wash, put on clean mosque clothes and leave the house like a good Muslim boy. A few blocks from the house, I'd look around, dart off into a side street and put on my jeans. Later, when everyone was coming home from mosque, I'd put my kufi and everything else back on and return home. My cousin would say to me, "I didn't see you at mosque." And I'd say, "No man, I saw you. I was sitting behind you."'

'And where had you been?'

'To see Colleen.'

Colleen Finch was Magadien's age. She, too, had enrolled at UWC after leaving school, but abandoned her studies after less than a year because her family could no longer afford to keep her there. She got a job at a local department store, sacrificing her prospects to put bread on her parents' table. Magadien had met her already, and become her lover, on trips he had taken to the Strand before his incarceration, and Colleen had been one of the few people from the outside to visit him in Victor Verster.

'I met her at a dance one Saturday night at the Strand,' he tells me. 'I was fascinated the moment I laid eyes on her. She was a tomboy, a woman-gangster. She wore Lee jeans and Grasshopper shoes, and she'd look men in the eye and tell them to fuck off. She once pulled a knife out on a man, and if she hadn't been held back she would have stabbed him without blinking.'

Colleen is dead now. She died of cancer in early 2002, a little more than a year before Magadien was released from Pollsmoor. When I go to Rusthof to visit the house in which she had lived and died, I find a photograph of her among a pile of old papers and mementos under the television set. She is sitting on a couch, in the very room where I now stand, her head thrown back in laughter. She is indeed the hard, gutsy woman Magadien describes: powerful shoulders, closely cropped hair, her face broad and lined. But there are traces of gentle mirth in her laughing face, and kindness in her eyes: she is immediately likeable.

'I loved Colleen in my own strange way,' he says, 'this woman who acted and talked like a man. In the Never Worry Bastards, the women on our turf were our possessions. Colleen would never be anyone's possession as long as she lived. She was a challenge. I wanted to see her walk like a woman and smile at me like a woman.

'She had one problem, though, and I was part of the problem. We were *the* couple in the Strand. There were always lots of girls and guys around us. Drugs were there in quantity, and any type of alcohol you could think of. She is the one woman I have been with who would go wild with me.

'We stayed at her mom's house on 9th Street. Sometimes, we spent summer days at the beach. But mostly I was on the run. She was the first to know I was a 28, because I confided in her. That was our relationship: we would get into big trouble together and we trusted each other with our lives.'

In the decades to come, it was Colleen Magadien would seek out whenever it was time to do business with stolen money and wares. In the late 1980s, when he took receipt of his employer's new bank cards, he drew thousands of rand from a bank telling machine, bought as many clothes as he could fit into the boot of his car, and went straight to the Strand to sell them. And in the mid-1990s, when he stole truckloads of glass from Mr Morris, he went to the Strand to set up a glass-fitting business.

All the while, Colleen knew nothing of the rest of his life. By the time he had stolen from Mr Morris, he was married to a woman in Manenberg and supported a family. Colleen was oblivious to this. By then, she herself had had a child by another man, and had lived another life.

And Magadien was, at times, cruel to her, as he was with all the women in his life. 'We had an up-and-down history,' he tells me, 'because half the time we were stuffed with drugs, and the other half I was in prison. Once, when I was in jail, she came to see me, and I was furious with her. She had had a daughter with another man and I was raging, I was jealous. I told her I wished her daughter dead. It was a crazy thing to say; I said it through anger. A couple of months later, the child actually got sick and died. And she blamed me. She said I had something to do with it: black magic stuff. I tried to convince her that I didn't go and see a witch-doctor, that I would never, ever, wish a child dead. I don't know if she ever believed me.'

So even Colleen, Magadien's soul mate, felt his estrangement and feared his darkness. When I think of this story, I imagine Magadien at the payphone in the corridor outside his cell, some time in 2002, telling the family members at the other end of the line that there has been a change in his life, a change so big he cannot begin to describe it. And I wonder what is going through their minds as they listen.

*

Although they were dirt poor when Gadija was a child, by the time Magadien got to the Strand his family there was relatively prosperous by the modest standards of the neighbourhood. 'My uncle had a job putting tiles on roofs,' Magadien tells me. 'One of my nephews worked at Deltatex, where they make towels. Everyone worked. I can't say they were poor. There were cakes and tarts in the kitchen, cheese in the fridge, lots of meat in the freezer.'

Shortly after he arrived in the Strand, his family got him a job, laying tiles with his uncle. 'We worked for a white woman who ran a business in the Strand,' he says. 'We called her Anna *Daktiles* – Anna Rooftiles.

'One day, I was fixing a roof at this very fancy house near Sir Lowry's Pass, with a beautiful view of the sea. I think the owner was German. He lived abroad; it was his holiday house.

'There were just two of us doing the work, me and this man who was almost totally deaf. You could smash a tile right in front of him, and if he didn't look up, he wouldn't know. He was working on the roof and I was in the ceiling. I needed to go to the toilet, so I climbed down into the house and wandered around, looking for the bathroom.

'On my way, I saw this piece of wall with glass in front of it, and behind the glass was a huge collection of guns. I went a bit nearer, because the house was empty, and the guy on the roof was deaf. There were German Lugers, Dirty Harry's guns, Davie Crockett's gun. Pistols. It was nice. Each gun was on a hook, and underneath each hook a brass plate, saying "Dirty Harry", or "Uzi – Israel", or "Luger, First World War". I opened up the glass cabinet, took one off its hook and examined it. I thought, shit, these things are in good working order. So I put it back, went to the toilet and then looked for a bag and put all the guns in it. There was also a collection of Krugerrands in the cabinet and I took those as well. And while I had been looking for the toilet, I saw other things: a camera with a zoom lens, a full jewellery box, foreign currency – I think dollars or pounds. You remember the postcards and stamps I showed you, and the half-cent coin I gave you? It was from this German that I got my habit of collecting.

'I left immediately with that bag. I couldn't go back to the Strand. The first place they would look was my grandfather's house.'

It would be the first of many times that Magadien was to steal on a whim and make a split-second decision to abandon a section of his life. A decade later, he was to leave the woman he had married eight days before, without saying goodbye, to avoid being caught for car theft.

'The police came to look for me in the Strand, but I was back in Hanover Park by then. I missed Colleen though, so I would sneak back on weekends, with a bank bag full of Mandrax tablets. I'd go and smoke with Colleen and my friends, in the shack lands. The shacks were like a mouse maze. The cops couldn't get in there. I felt safe.

'Then my nephew came along and smoked with us for a while, and then he disappeared. He had gone to tell my aunt I was there and she called the police. She sent him back to the shacks to keep me there until the police arrived. But by the time he got back, somebody had already told me what he had done. So he walked in and I took out a gun and cocked it and announced that I was going to kill the fucking bastard. Everyone screamed at me, begged me not to do it. Colleen stood in front of me, right in front of the barrel.

'And that was the end of my relationship with my Strand side of the family. I went back often, but to see Colleen; I avoided their house.'

'What did you do with the guns?' I ask.

'I'm the reason Hanover Park is so full of weapons,' he replies quietly, an impish smile on his face. 'I sold them to all different gangs. Anyone who had the money.'

*

Back in Hanover Park, he was 'Darryl' again, Annie's son, and a member of the Never Worry Bastards. But things had changed. The last time he had lived in Hanover Park, he had been a schoolboy; he went to Crystal High in the mornings, and when he came home there was lunch on the table, and later, dinner. He had thought nothing of earning a living; the thefts he had committed in Lansdowne and Epping had been recreation.

Now, he and his phalanx of peers in the Never Worry Bastards had finished school and were faced with the choice of how to live adult lives. The majority went clean: Stan Landman became a cabinet maker; Brian van Rooi, who had only flirted with the Never Worry Bastards, and who was later to marry Magadien's sister, Anne, enrolled for a trade and became a carpenter. Others, like Jack, shied away from formal employment and melted into the margins of the Cape Flats' criminal economy.

And so, with its members now in their early twenties, the Never Worry Bastards divided into two streams. For most, it was a soccer club in winter and a softball club in summer; sometimes, it was the occasion for a raucous turf battle. For a minority, it was a loosely-knit association of robbers and thieves. They were, really, little more than part-time scavengers. The great Cape Flats gangs of the 1980s – the Born Free Kids, the Cape Town Scorpions, and, later, the Americans and the Hard Livings – were just emerging. They were to be associated with entrepreneurs and extortionists who would come to control the Cape Flats' liquor market, its taxi industry and its burgeoning narcotics trade. But none of this touched Magadien's corner of Hanover Park. None of his peers would ever become more than small-time criminals.

Magadien lived in every one of these worlds: in the formal job market, in the softball and soccer teams, and in crime. On his return to Hanover Park, he got a job as a packer at a factory a few kilometres from his home. He has always found honest work with ease. He is remarkably industrious, skilled with his hands, and clever. Above all, he is charming and seductive; he wins confidence easily.

Yet he has never taken employment with the intention of keeping it. By the time he returned to Hanover Park, he was a child of Nongoloza. His white employers were ideological enemies of a sort, and his mission was not just to steal from them, but to belittle them.

'I wouldn't dignify it by saying it is political, this hatred of mine,' he tells me. 'I stole because I enjoyed it. It empowered me. Whenever I took something from a white man, and he didn't catch me, it would prove to me that he was stupid. Whites say they are the cleverest people, the bosses of the world. I always tried to prove that I was cleverer than them.'

He would, no doubt, have stolen at the factory where he worked if he had been given sufficient time, but the business went bankrupt a few months after he took up employment there, and he was retrenched. 'I can't even describe for you how bored I was there,' he tells me. 'It was utterly meaningless. If it had gone on much longer, I might have done something terrible.'

Less than a month after his retrenchment he was employed again, this time at a furniture store in the centre of Cape Town. He was a messenger and a delivery man, carting receipts, cheques and furniture around the city. I can imagine him there, doing what he does best: reinventing himself with a made-up history and a gentle disposition. It was not long before he got access to the company's cheque book.

'I tore three cheques out of the book,' Magadien tells me, 'and I cashed them one at a time. With the first, I bought two expensive watches. I kept one for myself and gave the other to a girl in Hanover Park who I wanted to sleep with. With the second cheque, I bought new sports clothes, a tracksuit. The third I used to rekit our soccer team. We were poor, you know, and our kit just wasn't up to scratch. So I bought goalkeeper gloves, a very good quality football, and other soccer stuff.'

'You didn't make a cent from any of these cheques,' I comment. 'You didn't sell any of the stuff you stole.'

'Ja,' he says, a little irritably, 'how can I make you understand? It wasn't about money, it wasn't about getting rich. It was about stealing things from whites and taking them to Hanover Park.

'After work one day,' he tells me, 'I didn't have enough money on me to get a train ticket home. I went to a pawn shop in Long Street to change something I had bought, so that I wouldn't have to walk out of Cape Town. When I went into the pawn shop, two cops came in after me and asked where I had got the thing I wanted to exchange. I don't remember what it was; it must have been something of value. I was carrying a tog-bag, which had a "Logans" logo on it, and they asked me if I had stolen the bag from Logans. That was my downfall; I had bought the bag with one of the stolen cheques. They took me to Logans, called the manager and traced the cheque back to my employer at the furniture shop, Mr Philips. He pressed charges straight away. They took me to the central police station, put me in the holding cells and told me I had one phone call. I called Gadija. "I'm in shit," I told her. "Get Norman Sampson."'

'You were unlucky,' I comment.

'I got caught because I was stupid,' he replies. 'Young, coloured, male, and I walk into a pawn shop with goods I'd bought with a stolen cheque. That's not unlucky; that's stupid. And all for a fucking train ticket.

'So Sampson came to my rescue,' he continues. 'This was in 1981. I was 21 years old. I should have gone to prison. But Sampson pulled strings, and instead I got six lashes, which really should be reserved for minors.'

He pauses and thinks, and his brow begins to crease. 'Maybe I should have gone to jail,' he says, 'because those lashes were terrible. All my family was in court; Anne and Annie were crying. And when sentence was passed, everyone left, and I had to stay behind. They took me down to the holding cells and administered the lashes. I was afraid, very afraid, because of the abuse I had suffered from Quinton, all the belts that had gone over my back. While I was standing at the gate outside the court, after the lashes, I thought, fuck this. On the bus, going home, I had to lean against a pole to stop myself falling over. Somebody even offered me a seat; I said no, I want to stand. That very night, I went out with Jack to housebreak and rob.'

*

By the time Magadien had received his six lashes, on 26 June 1981, he was a father. Margie Smith had given birth to Glynnis earlier in the year. It is difficult to unlock Magadien's feelings for Margie; an articulate man when he is speaking of his alienation and his loneliness, his feelings for the women in his life tie his tongue. He can talk endlessly of how much he sometimes pines for Margie, and of what a fool he was to lose her, but when it comes to describing his relationship with her, he is mute.

But the key to Margie, perhaps, is that she lived in Newfields. Newfields is just a stone's throw from Annie Mekka's house. It shares a border with Hanover Park, less than 1 500 metres from the outskirts of Never Worry Bastards territory. But to Magadien it was a respectable neighbourhood, the sort of place that made his blood boil, and which he would visit under the cover of darkness to burgle and steal. And that, in the first instance, is what Margie was: a taste of the unattainable, a woman above his station.

On an afternoon in February 2003, after a session with Magadien in his Pollsmoor cell, I drive out to the neighbourhoods of his teenage years and find the block of flats in Newfields where Margie lived. It appears as forlorn and neglected as Grace Court and Daphne Court, the blocks of Magadien's childhood; its residents are obviously very poor.

'No,' he says, when I tell him Margie must have been poor. 'Didn't you notice? There are no staircases on the outside. The stairs are on the inside; one family, two floors. To me, back then, it meant they were middle-class. We called them *sturvies* – people who shit perfume.

'I met her at her niece's 21st birthday party in Mitchells Plain,' he continues. 'I was there because Brian van Rooi, who married my sister, is a relative of hers. Margie's family is huge. They are based in Mitchells Plain, but they have family all over the place. When the family gets together for a party … Jesus, man, it's just people and more people.

'She is soft,' he says. 'She cries easily. She is sweet. She's a bit deaf in one ear, but that made me more attracted to her; it made her seem more vulnerable, more human. I loved her far more than Colleen. Colleen was something else – a tomboy, a gangster. She smoked drugs, she drank, she was like me. Margie didn't smoke or drink. She didn't even swear. That's the kind of girl I love, and I fuck up whenever I meet one.'

Magadien was destined to fuck up with Margie, at least as far as her family was concerned. 'Her sister and mother hated my guts. I would arrive at her house wearing boss-of-the-road trousers, a nice t-shirt to match and a pair of takkies. They just took one look at me, and I was bad news. They told me to my face I was a piece of shit and that they didn't want me near Margie.'

'What would you have to wear to make them comfortable?' I ask.

'Well, I would have had to have been someone else entirely, wouldn't I? The sort of boy who is born wearing a pair of chinos and a bowtie.'

By the time he met Margie, her family was, in fact, probably as poor as the Mekkas. Her father had died when she was young, leaving the family in financial difficulty. Indeed, her family's poverty had denied her an education; she left school in her mid-teens. When she brought Magadien home, his presence must have evoked the family's worst fears – a downward spiral into the bowels of the ghettos.

'Did you fulfil the Smiths' expectations?' I ask him.

'I did, ja. I treated Margie like shit. She had the hardest time of all my girlfriends. I was horribly abusive to her, even when she was pregnant with Glynnis. I would chase her, throw bricks at her, not to hurt her intentionally, but to scare her. I would hurt her verbally; I said terrible things to her. But she always came back. She was the only one who did that. She must have loved me so much. I have no idea why. Any other woman on this earth would have got a restraining order against me, or had me thrown in jail. Her family would have loved that.'

'When Glynnis was born,' Magadien tells me, 'Margie's family really didn't want me around. I'd knock on the front door, one of them would open up, and just pull a face, not even greet me. But there was nothing they could do. I was the dad, and I insisted on being there.

'Although to say I was there – for Margie and for Glynnis – would give the wrong impression. I never gave a fuck, actually. Annie helped to support Glynnis, but I never did. I was very proud of her, in my own stupid way. I'd go round to the house, carry her around for a while, and then get bored. I'd bring her little presents, but never anything valuable, and never money. I'd call her my princess, but when it came to supporting my princess, to actually being a father, I didn't give a shit.'

When Glynnis was three, Magadien went to jail for a long time, and while he was there, Margie finally abandoned him and got married.

'When I got out of jail and found out she was married, I was furious,' Magadien says. 'I would arrive at her house to visit and her husband would look at me with suspicious eyes. Everyone did. No one trusted me.

'And then I started stalking him. There was one week when he was too scared to go to work. Me and some others from the Never Worry Bastards would arrive at his bus stop at 6.30 in the morning and wait for him. So he just didn't go to work.

'And still, even after that, Margie would forgive me, because I was the father of her child, and because she had once loved me.'

When Magadien talks about Margie, I am reminded of his trip to the welfare office when he was 12 years old. Just as he had gone to the social workers to announce that he was a *skollie* in the making, so, too, he entered the Smiths' lives to confirm their worst fears of what a young man in boss-of-the-road trousers was capable of. The very soul of his relationship with Margie was a set-piece enactment of its failure.

And yet, his viciousness is so visibly tinged with envy and longing. He *did* want things to work with Margie, and he wanted to share in all she represented. He hated what he took to be a prosperous petit bourgeoisie because he suspected that there was happiness locked within the walls of their houses, a happiness he could only imagine via his increasingly idealised memories of what life had been like before Johnny Mekka died. His relationship with Margie was, among others things, a ritual of self-torture.

Tattooed on Magadien's chest are the names Margie and Glynnis. He put them there long after Margie had moved on, long after Glynnis had abandoned the hope of ever having a real father. No other living person's name appears on his body. That he put them there is testimony of his longing for the life he might have had. And yet the irony is striking. In the eyes of the Smiths, there is nothing more damning than a prison tattoo. It is the ultimate signature of the tainted. In writing their names on his body, he was affirming, not just his longing, but the impossibility of its fulfilment. It was the most *skollie*-ish way imaginable to fantasise about a life beyond *skollie*-hood.

*

After he was lashed for stealing cheques from his employer, Magadien drifted from one casual job to the next for more than a year. In February 1983 he found a job as a messenger again, this time at another downtown retail store. Two months into his employment, he took the company car home on a Friday afternoon without his boss's permission. On the Sunday morning he was arrested at Annie's house and charged with car theft.

Once more, Norman Sampson was there to negotiate with the prosecutor. The car theft charges were dropped and Magadien was charged with a lesser crime: 'use of a vehicle without the owner's permission' is how it reads on his conviction record. And under 'sentence': 'R100 or six months in jail'. Sampson paid the fine.

Two months later he was arrested again, for 'housebreaking with intent to steal', his prison record reads, 'and theft of a hair-dryer, football boots and a camera'. He has no recollection of the incident. I show him the citation on his conviction record. He frowns and peers at it. 'Must be true,' he says. Norman Sampson was there for him again. He was sentenced to six months in prison, conditionally suspended for three years.

Sampson protected Magadien from receiving a prison sentence, but he could not keep him out of jail entirely. After both of his arrests in 1983, he spent brief periods in the awaiting-trial section of Pollsmoor Prison. It was a frustrating time, a teasing encounter with a world that he wanted to know much more about.

Back in the early 1980s, the Number was not properly operative in the awaiting-trial sections of prisons. There were no recruitments and no promotions. The gangs considered it dangerous to begin a process of initiation that might end prematurely in the initiate's release. Gang business proper was reserved for sections housing sentenced inmates, where initiates were captive to the Number's universe.

'I was irritated on remand,' Magadien recalls. 'The Number was right there in front of me, but I couldn't touch it. I even thought of convincing the *ndotas* there to allow me to stab so I could go to the sentenced section. But I didn't; I knew I'd be back.'

He did not have to wait long. In early 1984, he was to commit a crime that would finally get him sentenced to serve time. This crime was more colourful than his last; it was stamped more forcefully with his personality and his sense of the world.

'Jack and I broke into a house one night,' Magadien tells me. 'I don't remember where it was: one of the "nice" neighbourhoods.

We found a whole policeman's uniform: the cap, shoes, belt, the entire thing. I kept all that stuff. About a month later, I put on the uniform and marched into a shebeen, screaming at everybody. I had brought about six Never Worry Bastards with me. The others came in behind me, and we took money, belts, watches, wine. It worked. So I did it again, but not a shebeen this time: at Athlone Station. I stopped somebody on the platform, asked to see identification, and while he was searching in his pockets, I'd attack him. That worked too, so I did it again the following afternoon, and that's how I was caught.

'Somebody went to the Athlone police and said that there's this cop at the train station beating people up. Two undercover detectives came to the station and they arrested me.'

'Nongoloza's enemies were white,' I say. 'Why did you prey on coloureds?'

'It's not just about robbing,' he replies. 'It's about power. And with that in mind, you sometimes have to turn to the coloureds; not just any coloureds, but the sort who reaped the same benefits as whites. There are plenty of fancy people getting on the train at Athlone Station, and I only targeted them.'

His narration has placed the image of an affluent coloured in his head, and he is off again, his mouth twisting with bitterness. 'We hated them as much as we hated whites. They still piss me off. The people from Honeyview, Surrey Estate. They speak English, not Afrikaans. They have servants in their kitchens. When their children turn 18 they get cars. We would do anything in our power: rob them, break into their cars, rob their children. When we caught them, we took their shoes, just to spite them. We'd make them take off their jeans, their shirts, their watches, their rings. Not even all of them had straight hair. Some of them were *kringkoppe* like me. And yet there were times I had to go to bed without anything to eat. Their dogs would eat better than us. It still pisses me off thinking about it. I have never had a heart for those people.'

He was sentenced to 13 months in prison. And his suspended sentence from the previous year – six months – was now enforced. On his conviction record, he is named Moegadiew Martin. He had begun to play with his name.

9
IN THE COUNTRYSIDE I: WHITE WARDERS

To head north out of Cape Town, you take the N7 freeway, the road the Flower Gang travelled on their journey to Niewoudtville. For the first 25 km or so, the landscape is flat and featureless, the horizon empty. Every now and again, you see evidence of the scramble to the metropolis that has consumed the last two generations of the rural poor: a city of brightly coloured matchbox houses, packed together in dense rows, despite the wide-open spaces around them; a teenage prostitute standing in the tramlines of the freeway, lifting the bottom of her mini-skirt as you drive by.

Soon, the dull scenes give way to an undulating, fertile landscape. You are in the farmland districts that fan out from the small rural centre of Malmesbury, a series of shallow valleys, more serene than beautiful, places of utter and pleasing stillness. At Malmesbury you turn right onto a quiet district road, and after 20 kilometres you find yourself in the hamlet of Riebeek-Kasteel. There is a small prison in the town; it is where Magadien was sent to in early June 1984 after he had been convicted for impersonating a policeman and for theft.

*

The tiny prisons that dotted the Western Cape hinterland were, in reality, stations for the distribution of cheap labour. The system Magadien got to know had been in place since the 1950s; farmers' district associations were permitted to build 'prison farm outstations' which were managed by the Department of Prisons. Farmers throughout the district could employ prisoners in proportion to their contribution to building the prison. The inmates themselves were paid nothing.

I ask Magadien what the work had been like at Riebeek-Kasteel.

'We worked on huge farms,' he tells me. 'Mainly, I worked at a place owned by the Marais brothers. They grew grapes, but most of the farms in the area grew wheat. I don't know if the Marais brothers had relatives in the prisons service, or what the connection was, but everything was about their farm. There was a big panic early one morning in the jail, with warders rushing around, gathering all the inmates together. "The Marais' harvest is rotting," they said. "You must all go and work there until it is done." And we worked and worked, right through the daylight hours.'

Magadien also recalls working for a tobacco farmer called Pieter Brink. 'He'd watch us working. If someone stopped for too long, or worked too slowly, or gave him uphill, then at lunch break Brink would drag him by his shirt, put him in a hole he had especially dug, and bury him up to his neck. Then Brink would put his lunch plate in front of his face and make him eat it like a dog, without his hands. Sometimes, he'd drive his Bedford over the hole first, leaving the mealiemeal caked in red dust. Then he'd force the prisoner to eat it.'

Compared to some other Western Cape prisons, Magadien had it quite easy at Riebeek-Kasteel. I spoke to a coloured warder, Pieter Loggenberg, who had been recruited into the prisons service in 1973. He is now a senior manager at Pollsmoor, but back in the early 1970s he was a lowly black man; his first posting was to the rural prison of Brandvlei, and among his tasks was the supervision of a team of prisoners who were building a dam.

'I didn't get to know any prisoners while I was at Brandvlei,' Loggenberg told me, 'because for us coloureds, interaction with them was strictly banned. "Don't get cosy with inmates" is how our white supervisor put it.

'But there are things about the construction of that dam that will stay with me forever,' he continued. 'The prisoners had to do their work in locked cages, surrounded by guards. Piles of stones were thrown into the cages, and their job was to break them into smaller pieces with heavy hammers.

'If the white supervisor decided that a prisoner had not broken enough stones that day, he could deny him food, just like that: "Right, no supper." I remember one case – I don't know where the inmate got a razor blade, but he sliced off a piece of his calf because he was so hungry; he wanted to eat it. Jesus, man, I couldn't finish a meal for weeks after that. And another prisoner sliced through his Achilles tendon so that he wouldn't have to go back and labour in the cage.

'They were treated like animals, so they started to behave as such. They killed each other with those hammers, paralysed one another, made one another brain damaged, just to get out of that environment. Because if you commit murder, you have to go to Pollsmoor for the duration of your trial, and they were so desperate to go to Pollsmoor, they did not even contemplate the fact that they would probably be hanged for what they had done in the cages; they were not thinking that far into the future.'

*

'They were also busy with building a dam behind the prison at Riebeek-Kasteel,' Magadien tells me. 'If I wasn't on the farm, I would be at the dam. One day, I was forced to do a really ridiculous job at the dam. They gave me a very heavy wheelbarrow, and I had to push it up the bank. The part that attaches the wheel to the barrow was crooked, so it couldn't walk straight. You push this heavy fucking thing up the bank and it goes in a circle and then falls over. Jesus, I struggled with it. So I got into an argument with this warder. I tried to reason with him. I tried to tell him no human being could push this wheelbarrow. He cut me off with a punch in the face. I staggered, got up, and went back to the wheelbarrow.

'Some of the guys in the 26s, 27s and 28s were working at the dam and they saw what happened. This put me in a predicament. I was now in danger in the Number. The warder had broken a rule; you do not hit a *ndota* for something like that. A *frans*, okay, he can smack a *frans* for refusing to push a barrow, but not a member of the 28s. So it was now my duty to stab him. If I didn't, I would be shaming the Number; I would be showing that a *boer* can smack a *ndota* and get away with it. If I did nothing, the Number would punish me, maybe hit me on the back of the head with a prison mug, which causes quite an injury, quite a gash.

'So we went off on our lunch break, and the 28s made a plan. When you leave the prison to work, you have a leather belt around your waist with a holster to carry your spoon. When we went for lunch, a sharpened spoon came down to me from the Nyangi. I put it in the belt. Watching me walk, you would not know it is a homemade knife. Only the rounded part sticks out; the sharpened handle is buried in the belt.

'We went back to work at the dam, and when I was close to the warder who had punched me and his back was turned to me, I stabbed him twice, one on each side. When I did that, the call went out from all the inmates at the dam. *"Nangampela!"* ("There it is indeed!" in Zulu.) *"Die Nommer is vol!"* ("The Number is complete!" in Afrikaans.) All the *ndotas* shouted and whistled – 26s, 27s and 28s.

'I was punished. They beat me up with their batons, all the way from the dam to the prison. By the time we got back inside, I could hardly see. They put me *agter die berge* for 15 days. I got food, but with no salt. No coffee, no bread, no porridge. Only putu. I would squeeze my daily putu ration into balls. When you get hungry during the day, you pop one. You make it last. Also, the Number managed to smuggle some salt to me. I would put the salt in water, and then dunk the putu ball into the salt water. You can feel your body strengthen minutes after you do that.

'When I came out, I was summoned by the Number. I had done everything right. I did not cry out when they beat me, and I was strong *agter die berge*. I sat down with the four points of the twos, then with the four points of the ones, and was given my new rank. Because when they punish you in the proper way for stabbing a *mapuza*, with beatings, solitary confinement and a spare diet, and if you handle it correctly, then you move up a rank. I moved from Silver-Two, to Silver-One – the second lowest rank in the private line.

'The Mtshali presented me with my new uniform and took back the old one. Then the Draad bugled the news to the other camps, the 26s and 27s, that this *ndota*, JR, had moved up a rank.

'After my promotion was bugled, I was sent to the Mambozas where I studied for two or three weeks for my new position. My main job as a Silver-One was this: when a probationer in the silver line has done wrong, I take out my silver handcuffs and I cuff him. Then I read him his rights. I take him to his case on a Saturday – the year of the wrongs. The case is heard by the four points of the twos – the Landdros, the Goliat-One, the Goliat-Two, and the Silver-One. I, the Silver-Two, am what is called the centre post. I search the accused for weapons, unlock his cuffs with my silver key, take him into the four points of the twos, and read out his file. Then I step out of the meeting and guard it. If anyone tries to disturb it, my duty is to stab him.'

*

'But that case,' Magadien continued, 'where I stabbed the warder at the dam, that is not a typical case for a rural prison. There was another stabbing while I was at Riebeek-Kasteel, and it was more typical.

'Once again, it was a question of a warder who had broken the rules. You see, there are two types of warder. The first type, we say about him that he keeps his office clean. He will order us around, but only to do things that we respect, like sweeping and cleaning. That is good. Everyone needs a clean prison, even the Number. He will respect us as human beings: he won't deny people meals; he will listen to complaints; he will tend to a sick inmate; he will not openly say that the Number can operate, but he will respect the dignity of the Number.

'A bad warder, he is one who thinks he can get away with treating a *ndota* like shit, and that is one thing he cannot do. Because if you allow that, then slowly but surely, the Number can no longer operate in that prison. What would happen if we could no longer meet on the year of the wrongs? We can't allow that to happen.

'So, there was this warder called Malan. Jesus, he was *verkramp*. He would come up behind you and smack you on the ears, for nothing, no provocation. Malan and a soldier from the 28s called Cups had a quarrel. I don't remember what it was about. I think it was about clothes. He was responsible for issuing clothes. He was stingy. Some of us were walking around with holes in our trousers so big it was like not wearing trousers at all. It was undignified. He treated Cups like shit, in front of the other *ndotas*, told him to go fuck himself, or something like that. Later, the Glas of the 28s came to Cups and said, "Why does that *mapuza* start with you like that all the time?"

'He didn't have to say what he really meant; it was obvious. He was saying three things: one, you are losing your dignity; two, the Number needs to make this man afraid; and three, if you stab him, you will be doing a duty and will get promoted. So, the order came down to Cups: "*Skiet hom, so dat hy jou respek*" – "Shoot him, so that he respects you."

'Cups was given a knife that had been inspected by the Nyangi, and when he went to stab, he was accompanied by the Glas and the Draad. Their function depends on whether the stabber does his job. If he stabs, they make the knife disappear. If he chickens out, they do his job for him and they punish him; they stab the warder and the *ndota*. So Cups walked up to Malan and stabbed him just like that. He was talking to another inmate; his back was turned to Cups. The Glas and Draad were with him and the knife disappeared.

'This is the point at which the case becomes a typical rural prison incident. They beat the shit out of Cups and put him *agter die berge*, like what happened to me. But they did something else as well. Although they could not find the knife, they knew it was Cups. And because they knew it was Cups, they knew it was the 28s. They know that nobody stabs without being dutied to do so.

'They called the local farmers' association to tell them that a white man had been stabbed. And all the farmers from the district arrived in their jeeps and bakkies. They came with pickaxes, knobkerries, sticks – anything they could find. Then, the warders assembled every single inmate in that prison in the courtyard. They surrounded us and then the warders would separate us. *Franse* here, 26s there, 28s there. Then they would force the *franse* to take off their clothes, so they could search for tattoos. If they see that a 28 member has pretended to be a *frans*, they put him in the right group. Once that is done, they put the *franse* in the cells. Then the 26s. It is just the 28s left in the courtyard, and the farmers are all around us with their weapons. A warder shouts, "Up!" and all hell breaks loose. They break bones – kneecaps, legs, collar bones. Because they know it was the whole camp that made the decision to stab, so the whole camp must suffer.'

'Didn't you fight back?' I asked.

'No. The rule was that you never provoke. If you provoke, if you fight back in a situation like that, they will kill you. It was all tactical. Sometimes it was necessary to retreat, for the sake of the survival of the Number.'

*

What struck me, as I listened to Magadien, was not so much the brutality of the relationship between warders and inmates, as the delicate filigree of unwritten rules and corresponding tactics. Recall my conversation with Andrew Bosch, the Pollsmoor warder with whom I had stood outside the prison kitchen, watching the food teams come to collect lunch. He had said that his job was to keep the sections 'mainly closed but a little bit open'. He was telling me that the prison is a much safer place when the Number is not cramped too much. He was, in others words, intelligent enough to read the unwritten rules and to detect their invisible boundaries; he is the sort of warder who 'keeps his office clean'. Malan, by contrast, who appeared unable to decipher the subtleties of his relationship with inmates, learned the hard way.

'It was a bit like a game,' Magadien tells me. 'The question is: who's afraid of whom at the end of the day? We chose warders we needed to fear us, and we stabbed them. Sure, they fuck us up afterwards, but put yourself in the shoes of the individual warder, the one who has been stabbed. You go away for a while on sick leave, maybe a little longer on stress leave; but then you are back. When you walk in the yard, with all the prisoners around you, you are worried. When you walk alone down the corridor, or into a cell, your heart is beating fast. Maybe, in the front of your mind, you think these people stabbed you just because they are animals. But at the back of your mind, you know why you were stabbed. You do not shout; you do not scream; you do not clip a prisoner on the back of the ear. You are afraid.

'You remember I told you that when I became Silver-Two, and my job was to guard the four points of the twos on the year of the wrongs, I was instructed to stab anybody who disturbed the meeting? Why do you think the Number was allowed to meet twice a week – the year of the wrongs on Saturdays, and the year of the rights on Sundays? Why do you think the warders never broke those meetings up? Because they knew. Maybe they didn't know the details. They didn't know that JR is a Silver-Two and his job is to stab me if I interrupt that bunch of inmates. But they sensed the atmosphere; they knew that, for their own safety, there are places they must not go.'

Inmates, too, knew that there was a threshold they must not cross. When an inmate was dutied to stab, it was a sacred imperative that the Nyangi determine the length of the blade; it ought never to be long enough to kill. And the stabber was also issued with a strict instruction to strike the flesh on either side of the spine, never a vital organ. When the gang was collectively punished for a stabbing, their own self-imposed rule stipulated that they do not fight back. They knew that injuring a warder critically or fatally, or resisting ritualised punishment, would invite a deadly response.

On the few occasions that a *ndota* did die, the gang suffered acute trauma. In a later sentence, which Magadien served a couple of years after his time at Riebeek-Kasteel, three of his cell-mates were hanged for murder. On the day of the hangings, every 28 in the prison shaved his head. For the following month, they walked the passages of the prison in absolute silence, their heads bowed and their hands crossed at their waists, a symbol of inaction. Members only spoke with one another in their cells, after lockup, and only in hushed tones. And they banned all gang activity – promotions, punishments, all decisions. The 26s and the 27s understood that Nongoloza's gang would not be sending representatives to the Valcross; they observed the 28s' abstention with due respect. Only once the month was up, and the stubble had began to appear on their heads, did they begin to speak again, and to thaw the rituals they had frozen.

*

So, the violence was ritualised, formulaic. But what function did it serve? Why did the gangs need it? A simple answer is that violence manufactured men, *ndotas*, but what lean versions of men they were. The figure who emerges from the initiation rituals – having been beaten, taken *agter die berge*, subjected to a saltless diet – is, really, a distilled version of a man, the sort of man a second-rate philosopher cobbles together. He consists of a few hard, shorn virtues, and nothing else. One is solidarity, but a solidarity of a very particular ilk; the recruit is to be robbed of a part of his own physical integrity for the sake of the gang. His sacrifice is visceral and highly personal; he feels it on his body. A second is stoicism. It is critical that the recruit show indifference to his pain. He must not cry out when beaten. He must emerge from isolation unscathed. This is, perhaps, the starkest and most striking of the virtues the initiation fosters; the recruit must demonstrate the ability to amputate, or at very least to stunt, vital needs, feelings and responses.

And what do these men do with their newfound manhood? They become, in essence, a mirror to their custodians. 'We are what you are. You are an army, we are an army. Where you have a head of prison, we will have a Judge. Where you have a head of section, we will have a General. Whatever you do to us, we will do to you in turn.' Far from resisting authority, they are locked onto it like a deer in the highlights; their aim is to mimic it eternally.

If their goal is indeed to transcend their status as inmates and become an army just like their custodians, they are betrayed by their own rituals. For a *ndota* is beaten into manhood. To transcend his status as an inmate, he must be punished as an inmate is punished. He is never quite a man; he is an inmate man. And he must be meticulous in restraining his own violence, lest the real army – the custodians – annihilate him completely.

It is a precarious balance to maintain. The gangs took care to avoid death, to be sure, but the threshold of violence they were prepared to tolerate was very high indeed: broken kneecaps and collar bones. And, in the aftermath of a ritual beating, they did not receive due medical attention.

'We never trusted prison doctors,' Magadien tells me. 'For one, they were white. And they were also *mapuza*, the enemy. We called them *perdedokters*, "horse doctors". There were a lot of inmates who stumbled round the prisons with broken bones; a lot of people who were stuck in the Mambozas the rest of their lives because they were too fucked up to be active.'

Was it worth it? How did the damaged limbs weigh up against the importance of having warders like Malan running scared? Two years after Magadien was released from Riebeek-Kasteel, and he began to serve a sentence at Victor Verster, the 28s in that prison buckled under the violence that was meted out against them. They turned on themselves; the gold and the silver lines went to war, and when the fight was over, they tore up the gang's most sacred rules.

*

And what of white warders? How did they understand their presence in this invisible matrix of rules and prohibitions? What did they think of the Number?

I interviewed several white men who had served in Western Cape prisons during the height of apartheid. The one who stands out, for me, is Mr Smit. I was somewhat duplicitous with him when we met. I had sought him out, and I did so because his name kept cropping up; several veteran inmates had told me about him, and they had said that he was a truly terrible man. So, when we met, he did not know that I knew things he would never tell me. I have changed his name and cannot tell you in which prisons he worked, in order to protect his identity.

Mr Smit is a man of enormous presence. He has a voice that hoists every syllable into the empty spaces of the room. His eyes, while small and pale blue, are fiercely engaged; he locks them onto yours as he speaks, and neither blinks nor looks away. You sit there listening with rapt concentration and the whole room fills up with Mr Smit; he is the owner of his encounters, and of the places which host them.

'Things were tough in the old days,' he tells me. 'Very tough. Today, if an inmate stabs another inmate, you transfer him to another prison, and you also transfer the one who is meant to retaliate. Problem solved. There was none of that in those days. After a stabbing, everyone had to stay, and you had to deal with it.'

'So how did you deal with it?'

'It was lose-lose. There was no getting it right.

'In normal circumstances, when nobody had been stabbed, I kept the gangsters in mixed cells: 26s with 28s. If you do that, they keep an eye on each other. They have these very formal procedures. For a 28 to stab a 26, the *kring* of the 28s, the highest structure, has to meet to authorise it. If they are all together, if the 26s are in the very same room, the *kring* can't meet to discuss stabbing a 26. The only possible time it can meet is during exercise time. So you have to watch them like a hawk while they are in the yard. If you see a group of prisoners gathering together in a corner, and if they are all 28s, you rush over and break it up.'

It is interesting that Mr Smit chooses to describe things this way. Everything I have learned from inmates tells me that they would not have tolerated the sort of warder he has chosen to remember himself as being. The golden rule is that a warder who disrupts the rudimentary workings of the Number must be stabbed; he must learn that there are things he cannot do.

I am also struck by his understanding of the gangs. They are like dogs fighting eternally over a carcass; Mr Smit is the one who douses them with buckets of cold water.

'When someone is stabbed,' Mr Smit continues, 'you have to change everything. The gangs cannot be together; they will kill each other. So the mixed cells go, and you replace them with pure cells: some cells all 28s, the other all 26s. And you must make sure that they are never in the yard at the same time. They must, literally, never see each other.

'But that is not a solution either, because you must ask the question: why did we have mixed cells in the first place? And the answer is that pure cells are dangerous. When it is left by itself, the gang develops its power: every day, more power. After a week of pure cells, things have reached such a level, you worry that something is going to break, that all hell will break loose. So it is a lose-lose situation. You are damned either way.'

There is something new in Mr Smit's talk about pure cells, something almost mystical.

'How do you recognise a 26 or a 28?' I ask. 'Can you tell the moment he steps into a prison?'

'Ja. You can tell immediately. Don't ask me why. It's not something I can explain. It comes with years of experience. You can see it as soon as you make eye-contact.'

'What do you see in a 26's eyes?'

'Like I say, it's not something I can explain.'

'What,' I ask, trying to formulate the same question from a different angle, 'do you understand to be the main differences between the three gangs?'

'The 28s are difficult,' he replies. 'They're just aggression, pure aggression. You can make an agreement with a 28, look him in the eyes. And the next day, he will stab you. There's no use trying to reason with him.

'The 26s and 27s – that's a different story. The 27s are a very disciplined group. Inmates fear them, but I don't. There's something rigorous about them. Something straightforward. You can deal with them. And the 26s – you can deal with them too. They are not wild monsters, like the 28s. They are basically crooks. They are out to make as much money as they can. They are con-artists. So there is something rational about them. You know what it is they want.'

'Have you ever been stabbed?'

'I have been stabbed, ja,' he replies, and as he begins to tell the story, his baritone drops a tone deeper and his eyes lock onto mine more intensely, as if this conversation in particular is one he must own.

'I was in the wrong place at the wrong time. I was walking through the prison with a warder called Heunis. Heunis had no experience of the gangs. He didn't understand them. We were walking, and we saw this group of inmates running. They were 26s. It could only mean one thing. There were 28s behind them, attacking them. Now, you have to think fast in a situation like this. You must either get out the way and let them fight, or you must lock doors very quickly, so the attackers are separated from the ones who are fleeing.

'Heunis made a mess of things. He panicked. And he found himself right in the middle of the 28s and the 26s. So I went in to save him. There was a scuffle. Everything was flying around. I got stabbed in the side. Like I say, I was in the wrong place at the wrong time.'

'Who stabbed you?'

'A 28.'

'Was he promoted for stabbing you?'

'I think so.'

As I said earlier, my interview with Mr Smit was somewhat unfair. Among other things, I had already heard a rival account of the day he was stabbed. One of my informants was a 28 called Humphrey: he had been an inmate in the same section of the same prison at that time. The 28s, Humphrey told me, had been planning to stab Mr Smit for a long while. Their pursuit of the 26s was staged; it was meant to coincide with Mr Smit's presence at the scene; he was meant to be stabbed during the commotion.

'Why?' I asked.

'Because Smit was a 26,' he replied.

'What are you talking about?'

'In his section of the prison, there would be mixed cells, ja. But for him, mixed meant two dozen 26s, half a dozen 28s. Our people were this weak minority. He was close to this 26 General called One Touch. They made a deal – you let us do our thing, you can do your thing.'

'Meaning?'

'A few things. First, the 26s ran his section. If they beat the shit out of a *frans* or a 28 during the night, you don't go running to Mr Smit. He will laugh in your face. But other things too – more serious things. Together with Mr Smit, the 26s tried to destroy the 28s. Say, for instance, somebody in the gold line of the 28s got a promotion. That night, the warders would fetch him from his cell, and throw him into One Touch's cell. And the 26s would spend the whole night raping him. Next morning, he would be taken back to his cell, and the 28s did not want to look at him, did not want to go near him. A 28 soldier who has been raped has lost his manhood. He is fuck-all. So One Touch and Smit, together they robbed the 28s of their soldiers by making them women.'

It was not just Humphrey. Several people spoke to me about Mr Smit, and their testimonies were all much the same – that he forged an alliance with a 26 General, that they ran the prison together, that the substance of their alliance was the decimation of the 28s.

Listening to Mr Smit, I wondered what the story he was offering might tell me about the story he was hiding. It is possible that he accrued some perverse delight from the game he played. He might have marvelled at the ease with which he was able to set these mindless beasts against one another; and the inequality of the battle, an inequality he himself had staged, may have tickled him. But I suspect not. I suspect that his conduct was born, not from a megalomaniacal impulse, but from fear and from knowledge.

Mr Smit is not as stupid as the hapless Malan of Riebeek-Kasteel. He understood the rules of engagement. But he also understood, I would imagine, that playing by the rules was not a safe bet, that it still left one's position precarious. For one could give the gangs their requisite space, one could treat *ndotas* with the dignity they believed was owed to them, and one could still be stabbed. He understood the gangs, and not without reason, as impenetrable and mysterious beasts whose inner logic he would never unlock. Playing by the rules left too much to chance. It was better to break the rules, to make one section of the prison home turf, to carve out a piece of territory in which he was indispensable. And if people got hurt as a result, then so be it. This was, after all, a world of all against all.

What intrigued me, though, was how the alliance began, how Mr Smit reached across the divide.

He did, in fact, in the most oblique and unsatisfying way, tell me something of what I wanted: an idealised, somewhat fantastical account of his relationship with the 26 General named One Touch.

'How much do you know about the history of the gangs,' I asked, 'about Nongoloza, Kilikijan and Grey?'

'I know it all,' he replied. 'A General in the 26s wrote a whole book about it, and gave it to me.'

'That's insane,' I said. 'He could have been killed for that.'

'He trusted me. With everything. With his life.'

'How did you earn that trust? What happened between you?'

'It is difficult to say. There was not one encounter. It was an accumulation of things, over time.'

'But perhaps,' I suggested, 'there is one particular moment that stands out.'

'Ja, there is one thing, come to think of it. One afternoon, I was on the rugby field. There was a group of inmates on the field, and he was among them. I got an urgent call to go back to the office. As I was leaving, I went up to him, handed him my wallet, and told him to keep it for me until I came back.

'When I got back, about two hours later, he was standing there, with my wallet in his hand, looking shocked. I could see in his face – he couldn't believe I'd trusted him with my money. I mean, he was a bloody 26! He gave it back to me without saying a word. But after that, everything was different with him. He trusted me completely, because I had trusted him.'

I left Mr Smit feeling disturbed and unsatisfied. Not knowing whether the story of the wallet was true gnawed at me. Was it the poverty of Mr Smit's imagination I had just witnessed, or was it the horrible pathos of the place where he had spent his working life – a place where two men agree to enter into a terrible alliance over the safekeeping of a wallet?

10

IN THE COUNTRYSIDE II: A WHITE FARMER

Magadien was released on 3 March 1985, less than a week before his 25th birthday. He was finished with Riebeek-Kasteel. But he was not finished with the countryside, nor with the white farmers who owned it.

His conviction record states that he was 'released on parole until 18 June 1985', but it was an odd sort of parole. He was driven across the Western Cape hinterland and received into the custody of an orange farmer named Serfontein, on whose farm he would be obliged to work for the following three-and-a-half months.

'There were three of us,' Magadien recalls. 'They did not say where they were taking us. They put us into the back of a windowless van, and the trip took many hours, so we knew that we were travelling far.'

The journey must have been much shorter than Magadien remembers. Serfontein's farm is just outside the town of Clanwilliam, about 150 km north of Riebeek-Kasteel; it is lush, citrus-growing country.

Magadien was angered by his unexpected fate. 'Riebeek-Kasteel had made me tired of white farmers,' he tells me. 'We were just there to give them free labour, and we were treated like slaves. If a guy made a mistake in the vineyards, the farmer beat the hell out of him. We would complain when we got back to the prison that night, but the warders weren't interested: the farmer was always right.

'I'd had it up to here with whites,' he says, prodding his forehead with straightened fingers. 'And now it was more of the same.'

It turned out, in fact, that Magadien enjoyed the work itself. 'We spent the days in the orange and naartjie groves,' he says, 'and we planted mealies and potatoes. We also laid down a system of drip pipes. I assembled the system. I could read the plans. It was the sort of work that gives one pleasure. And the farm itself was nice. There were cows, sheep, pigs, and there was the open air.'

But that is all Magadien liked. 'There was a house on the farm allocated to us three parolees,' he tells me. 'We had to chop wood for the stove. We had to make our own food. After a while, Serfontein told us he needed the house for something else, and he moved us to a corrugated-iron shack. It had no stove, no facilities at all. Winter was coming. We could not even bake our own bread. We had to buy everything we ate. Serfontein paid us almost nothing. So we had to use what little we had saved to buy food and cigarettes. Out in the orange groves, my head would be swimming by late afternoon. I was hungry.'

Magadien's recollections of Serfontein are sparse. He has stripped away everything, leaving only his raw anger. But one can imagine their relationship. When Magadien arrived, Serfontein would have been informed that the thin one with the pointy chin, JR, was a young 28 rising through the ranks, that he had stabbed a warder during his last sentence. Serfontein must have glared at his new charge with hostility, and Magadien would have returned the venom.

'I didn't fear him,' Magadien says. 'And he couldn't cope with that. I could see it in his eyes. And I liked that. I was a proud 28; I wasn't going to be fucked around.'

There was a Saturday morning ritual on Serfontein's farm, something white farmers are wont to call a perk. At ten o'clock, his workers would file into the back of his bakkie and he would take them to town. His farm was too far from Clanwilliam to walk, and so the Saturday morning expedition was necessary for his workers – to buy cigarettes, alcohol and provisions, to circulate among the people of the district.

But the three parolees were not permitted to go to town on Saturday mornings. Why, Magadien does not know. Perhaps Serfontein believed that convicts ought not to wander too far. Or maybe, Magadien speculates bitterly, Serfontein resented the fact that Magadien did not, at the time, drink alcohol.

'Those farmers liked to see coloureds drunk and fucked up,' he tells me. 'They encouraged it. Maybe that I was sober and alert pissed him off.'

In any event, the inability to get to town weighed heavily on the three parolees. Without access to a shop, they relied on others for basic necessities, and the ones returning from town would sell goods to the convicts at a small profit. They could not afford to stay on the farm seven days a week.

One Saturday morning at ten o'clock, Magadien walked up to the window of Serfontein's bakkie and stared coldly at the white man.

'We need to go to town,' he said.

'*Jy bly hier*,' Serfontein muttered. 'You are staying here.'

'If you do not take us to town,' Magadien replied, 'we will be gone when you get back.'

Serfontein, or the Serfontein of Magadien's memory at any rate, was in a predicament. The convict was challenging him publicly, in front of his workers, in front of the very people for whom the demonstration of his control was of paramount importance. He said nothing, and the three parolees joined the other workers at the back of the bakkie. Serfontein started his car and drove to town.

The following day, a Sunday, Magadien was summoned to the farmhouse. There were several men standing around a braai. There were women seated around a table on the veranda. There was the smell of meat being cooked, and of beer. Afterwards, Magadien would remember the setting as a makeshift amphitheatre, an audience assembled around a stage.

Serfontein motioned Magadien to come to him. 'Closer,' he said. 'Stand right next to me.' Magadien felt a blow to his stomach, he felt himself fall. '*Kom ons wys wat maak ons met hierdie hotnot*,' he heard Serfontein saying. 'Let's show you what we do with this *hotnot*.' A pair of strong hands grabbed the back of his neck; the farmer pulled a rubber tyre tube over his head.

'He suffocated me until I thought I was going to die. Then he pulled the tube off my head, let me breathe a bit, then put it back over my face. When he was finished, I vomited on his lawn. He laughed, and I heard others laugh too. I couldn't get up. I lay there in front of them for a long time, and they laughed until they got bored and started talking amongst themselves about other things.

'I have hated water ever since then; it reminds me of not being able to breathe. In the bath, when I lower my head into the water, and it comes around my ears, I panic.'

On 18 June, when Magadien's parole came to an end, Serfontein dropped him in Clanwilliam's main street. He had very little money by then, not enough to get a train ticket back to Cape Town, and Serfontein offered him nothing. He spent his last cents on a bus ride to Graafwater, a tiny coloured hamlet midway between Clanwilliam and Lambert's Bay. He spent the night wandering the dirt streets of the village, and at the first light of day began eyeing the people who were emerging from their homes.

'I put my pride in my pocket and became a beggar for a day,' he tells me. 'I spoke to the small coloured community there and they helped me. They sent round a hat and collected enough money for a ticket to Cape Town. If I had not done that I would have become a stroller in Clanwilliam.'

Stroller: the word is perhaps best translated as hobo or drifter, but it means much more than that. It is not simply about falling off the edge, about getting lost forever. It is also associated with an image of the pre-colonial past, a denigrating conception of a particular strand of coloured heritage imbibed from whites. It is tied up with the idea that the Khoi-Khoi people, the earliest inhabitants of the Western Cape, drifted through the region without culture or history, until they were captured by the whites and were put to work. The origin of this myth is an 1809 Cape colonial law; it stipulated that any Hottentot found travelling without a permit be considered a vagabond and put to work.

*

The memory of Serfontein sat with Magadien. He has still not shaken it off; it crops up in our conversations again and again. Two years after the night he wandered the streets of Graafwater, he stole a car in Cape Town and drove north. He did not stop until he got to the gate of Serfontein's farm.

'I went back to kill him,' Magadien says. 'I had thought about killing him every day for the past two years. The distance from Cape Town was a problem. How to do it was a problem. But I went back just to see whether it was possible.

'It never materialised. It was quite a distance from the farm to the highway, and there was the question of escape routes. There was only one exit point in the whole district. If the police were alerted, I would have driven straight into them. In fact, I would have had to drive right past the police station in Clanwilliam. And the farmers at that time were organised into commandos, and were in radio contact with one another. They could have cornered off the area easily. If the farmers had caught me, they would have killed me on sight. I thought, I must get more guys. Plan it properly. But it never materialised. I went to prison again. And now we are living in a democracy.'

'What are your thoughts about Serfontein now?' I ask.

'They say let bygones be bygones,' he replies. 'I am a changed person. I am no longer someone who drives across the Western Cape to kill someone. But I must be honest with you: I still dream about killing him. And when I am doubting my change, during those bad times when I am not sure whether change is real, I do this mental exercise. I say to myself, why would it be wrong to kill Serfontein? And when I have come to the answer, I am on solid ground again.

'But I think one day I want to face him. I want him to admit he was wrong. I thought of phoning him, but maybe he would say that he doesn't remember me. And then what do I do? So maybe I will never face him.'

*

I have come to think of the Serfontein episode as the centrepiece of that period in Magadien's life. It is not a moment of dramatic rupture but a question of subtle re-ordering. In the middle of one of our discussions about Serfontein, Magadien, without invitation, suddenly began talking of Nongoloza, but not in the way he ordinarily spoke of the old bandit; he himself, now, was a latter-day Nongoloza.

'The moment I heard that man's story,' he told me, 'I understood it. I understood it as my own story. What happened in Clanwilliam made it even clearer. Nongoloza and Rabie. Me and Serfontein. Nongoloza was defined by his hatred of whites. And so was I. Don't get me wrong. I am not making myself into a hero. I am not saying I *was* Nongoloza, the king: just that I was inspired by his life.'

For the first time in a long time, the future he imagined for himself took the form of a coherent narrative. On the outside, he would be a fraudster and thief, taking from whites and *sturvies* the things that had never rightly belonged to them. But he would not be a street gangster: he would be a loner. The growing street gangs of the Cape Flats, which would soon become empires commanding the loyalty of thousands, held nothing for him. They were mere corruptions, disfigured shadows of a true brotherhood. His image of himself on the outside was that of a detached and solitary figure, walking through a world of the uninitiated. His family were *franse*, dull, stupid beings with whom he might eat and under whose roofs he might sleep, but that was all.

The real world was behind the bars, in the prisons. He began to believe that the story of Nongoloza, as told by one generation of inmates to the next, was quite literally true, that a young Zulu migrant did indeed meet a sage called Po in 1812, and that there were gold mines in Delagoa Bay at that time. He began to believe that this was the true history of South Africa, the only one that counted, that the things he had learned at school were lies.

He arrived back in Cape Town in late June 1985, on the eve of the most tumultuous period in the city's history. During the second half of that year, 'Cape Town and the Cape Peninsula produced something close to insurrection,' the historian, Bill Nasson, has written. 'Parts of the region were in open rebellion.' Unlike in the late 1970s, Magadien would have no truck with the political movement. He had nothing for it but scorn. Instead, he would negotiate his way through this upside-down world as he believed a bandit like Nongoloza might have done – as an opportunist and a deceiver, living off the confusion and the fear.

11
URBAN REBELLION, ROBBEN ISLAND

As in 1976, the nationwide uprisings of the mid-1980s arrived late in Cape Town. They began on 3 September 1984 in a cluster of townships in the Vaal Triangle, about an hour's drive south of Johannesburg. 'All day long,' the political historian Tom Lodge has written, 'angry mobs roamed the streets, burning businesses, government buildings, and cars; throwing stones; battling with the police; and killing several municipal councillors. The longest and most widespread period of sustained black protest against white rule in South Africa's history had begun.'

The story begins a year earlier, when South Africa's president, PW Botha, invited white South Africans to vote in a referendum to approve a new and reformed political dispensation. Coloureds and Indians would be provided representation in central government, but in their own separate chambers of parliament; the heartland of legislation-writing would remain in the white chamber. The new 'tricameral' legislature would exclude the African majority entirely; they would be granted greater local representation in segregated municipal governments.

It was, in retrospect, the beginning of the end of white rule. To give blacks the freedom to elect representatives to government structures entailed, inevitably, giving apartheid's opponents the space to rally against these new structures. As so often happens when an authoritarian state attempts reform, its enemies grab at the new slivers of political freedom and take possession of the coming era. To reform an unjust system is to wander onto the discursive terrain of one's foes, to enter a world of ideas in which one has already lost. The liberation movement could not have dreamed up a better platform from which to mobilise the population against apartheid – they are giving us sham structures through which to participate in our own oppression; let us tear these structures down.

At their height, the uprisings exuded the confidence of a people who believed they were about to take power. A tiny minority of coloureds and Indians went to the polls to elect representatives to the new tricameral parliament. In African townships across the country, local government buildings were burned to the ground. Students boycotted school classes en masse and spent their days gathering on the streets. Some would mass at taxi ranks and search the bags of township residents returning from the city, to see if they had violated consumer boycotts and bought food from white-owned retail chains. Even in remote rural towns, consumer boycotts brought white retailers to ruin.

Giddy with their initial successes, leaders of the United Democratic Front (UDF), the body that had been created in response to Botha's reforms, and whose thinly veiled allegiance was to the exiled ANC, declared that the country was being rendered ungovernable. The grassroots UDF structures that were forming across the country – civic organisations, street committees, school students' bodies – were hailed as 'organs of people's power', embryos of the new society, growing amidst the debris of the old.

The uprisings were, in fact, crushed during the course of 1986. Thousands of leaders of these grassroots institutions – whose supposed capacity to govern had always been more a glimpse of a fantastical future than a reality – found themselves detained indefinitely in jails across the country. But crushing the uprisings sapped the apartheid state of its moral and political substance. It became a pariah internationally. At home, intellectuals in the heart of the Afrikaner establishment grew increasingly estranged from their own government. The National Party could probably have kept on governing for years, nihilistically, aimlessly, with no thought for the wellbeing of future generations. In the end, it threw in the towel and unbanned South Africa's exiled liberation movements in February 1990, less than four years after it had quelled the uprisings.

The conflagration took its time to reach Cape Town. It was only in August 1985, nearly a year after the Vaal Triangle went up in flames, that state institutions on the Cape Flats came under serious attack. Ironically, from Magadien's perspective, the catalyst was an attempted march from Athlone Stadium to Pollsmoor Prison on August 28, led by the charismatic cleric, Alan Boesak, to call for the release of political prisoners. The police met would-be marchers on the streets of the Cape Flats that morning and attacked them with birdshot, rubber bullets, batons and tear gas. The march never happened, but the clashes on the streets went on for days. By the end of the month, 28 people had been killed. Cape Town exploded. A week later, the government had closed down 500 coloured schools and colleges. The UDF called for a two-day general strike. Much of the city came to a standstill.

*

By early September 1995, Magadien had been back in Cape Town a little more than three months. He was living with Gadija and her second husband, Victor Tommy, in Heideveld. It was several years since Denise Sampson had thrown Gadija out of her house in the southern suburbs, leaving Stephen to face adulthood without his beloved Miriam.

Relations between Magadien and his mother and foster-father were icy. Victor, although poor himself, was from a wealthy family; his siblings were professionals who had emigrated to Australia and the United States. Magadien held him in contempt for his background, and, by proxy, Gadija too.

'You are trying to marry above yourself,' she remembers him scowling. 'You're kidding yourself. You are still a servant girl from the Strand.'

Watching the anti-apartheid rebellion from the vantage point of Gadija's house, Magadien might have been expected to join the fray. On the Flats, the institutions of the white state he had claimed as his enemy were in flames. On the fringes of the uprisings, things were tantalisingly anarchic. Cars on the N2, the motorway that runs through the Flats, were being stoned from overhead bridges. Retail stores, factory premises and warehouses were occasionally attacked by mobs.

Magadien did not join. For one, memories of the violence of the late 1970s were still fresh in his mind, and still haunted him. He had seen the spectacle of the crowd and experienced its terrifying dissolution; he did not want to go through that again. Also, the core leaders of the uprisings were, as sociologist Jeremy Seekings has commented, 'thoroughly urban, well educated [and] upwardly mobile'. They were the sort of coloureds Magadien scorned as much as he did whites. The prospect of them, of all people, leading him onto the streets, and into danger, was unthinkable. From the vantage point of the universe he now inhabited, that of Nongoloza, both sides of the fight were his enemies.

And yet, while he felt estranged from what was happening around him, he was as alert to his context as ever. Reading job advertisements in the daily newspapers, he saw that the private security industry was desperate for recruits. Schools and businesses across the city were clamouring for armed guards in droves; they did not want to leave their premises vulnerable at night. He began investigating discreetly.

'Security firms were so anxious to hire,' he recalls, 'that they had stopped running regular security checks on new employees. They took your fingerprints, and sent them away to be checked against the police's data bank, but that took a long time. Until the prints came back, they would not know who you are.'

Late in 1985 he walked into the headquarters of one of the larger security firms in town, and consented to the taking of his fingerprints.

'I gave them a false identity document, with my picture carefully pasted, that I had picked up a few weeks earlier. My name was "Clive Makhene". I knew that I had six months. That's how long it would take before they found out that I was "Darryl Wentzel", "Magadien Wentzel" and "Moegadiew Martin", and that I had been convicted under each of those names. I had half a year to steal as much as I could.'

To begin with, the work was, in fact, deadly boring. Magadien was issued with a pump-action shotgun, but during the first months of his employment it lay idle night after night as he sat and stared at the empty city.

'Me and two other guards had to look after a tavern in Belgrave Road,' he tells me. 'We sat there doing nothing every night. There was an office we had access to, and there was a telephone in the office. The other two would spend the whole night on the phone talking to their girlfriends. I kept pestering them. I said I also wanted a girlfriend to phone, that I wanted somebody's phone number. Eventually, one of them gave me his girlfriend's sister's phone number. Her name was Natalie. She lived in Manenberg.

'We spent hours and hours on the phone, every night for over a week. She told me she had been raped a few years before and that she had a child from the rape. We spoke about that a lot. Eventually

I said to her, "Listen, this is ridiculous; we have to meet." So I saw her for the first time early one morning, shortly after the end of night shift. We had sex for the first time on our second or third date.'

As with most of the women in Magadien's life, he has next to nothing to say about his relationship with her. He was beginning to smoke a lot of Mandrax, every time his shift ended, and he and Natalie would smoke together. At least half of his wage, he says, he spent on drugs. He often mentions the fact that she was raped. It seems to have touched him deeply, but he cannot say why.

*

Soon, the work at the security company grew more interesting, from a thief's perspective at any rate. Shortly after his time at the tavern on Belgrave Road ended, Magadien was assigned to guard a white primary school in one of the fashionable inner-city suburbs at the foot of Table Mountain. He spent each night alone in the deserted building, and passed his time picking at the locks on closed doors.

'First, I got access to the kitchen. So I made myself big meals every night. Then I got access to the offices. I stole a television set and a video machine one night, and a box of money that was being collected for Christmas celebrations the next night. They never suspected me. It never crossed their minds that the man guarding the building might be the one who should be guarded.'

After the assignment at the school, Magadien was put on emergency standby. He was to spend his nights at the security company's headquarters, waiting for a call to be sent out into Cape Town.

'One night, a jewellery store was broken into and I was instructed to go there. I stood the whole night next to the broken window. My job was to guard the place until the police took over the crime scene in the morning. By the time they arrived, my bag was full of jewellery. I greeted them politely and went home.'

It was not long, though, before Magadien was sent to guard buildings at the epicentre of the uprisings: first, a hostel for construction workers in the African township of Guguletu, then a hospital in the township of Langa. He encountered trouble there, and he did not like it.

'One night, there was an attack on the hostel,' he tells me. 'People were throwing stones and petrol bombs. We had to take cover, and then we had to fight them off. My shotgun had two rounds of birdshot in it. I used them both. Things were very tense. It took ages for the police to arrive. I was angry after that. I thought to myself, "What the fuck are you doing, nearly getting yourself killed?"'

'So you became a *boer*,' I quip. 'You defended white property against blacks.'

He does not see the humour. 'No,' he says, 'I was not a *boer*. I was there to steal. It just so happens that I did something useful while I was there.'

'Did something useful.' It is a revealing slip, one he probably would not have defended had I pushed the point. He is saying, in essence, that taking part in the quelling of a black rebellion against the apartheid state was 'something useful', a good deed he performed incidentally. How does this tally with everything else he thought about himself and the world at that time?

The gangsters of the mid-1980s did indeed have a mixed, often contradictory understanding of the events unfolding around them. They felt, on the one hand, a natural affinity with the cadres of the uprisings, since they were both breaking the laws of the white regime. Tony Ehrenreich, who is now a prominent trade unionist, told me of the role street gangsters had played in a school students' march in Elsies River in 1980.

'We, the protesting students, marched down the street, towards the police,' he recalled. 'Suddenly, this group of gangsters came up from behind the police and started throwing stones at them. Partly, they were doing it because they liked trouble. But they also sympathised with us; we had a common enemy.'

Yet there was also a strain of gangster discourse that echoed the things the apartheid state said: that activists were communist agitators, that they were leading ordinary people to the devil. You can see why this was so. A career criminal may be breaking the law of the whites, and his identity may well be that of a rebel or a bandit, but the prospect of real political change holds a great deal of uncertainty for him. A successful drug merchant or an illegal shebeener, for instance, would not greet the legalisation of the Cape Flats liquor market with glee. Nor would he like to watch the drug users in his market become clean-cut activists or the willing citizens of a new order. He has, in fact, become somewhat dependent on the injustices that have sentenced him to a life in the ghetto.

And what of a lone fraudster like Magadien? He has no horizons; he steals from whites. The life he imagines is one in which apartheid goes on forever.

And, finally, what of the prison gangs, the world Magadien had chosen as his surrogate home? They, he says, were the real comrades; unlike the upwardly mobile opportunists who orchestrated the uprisings, they were the ones who faced down the apartheid state in their daily lives, and paid for their bravery with their blood.

But the gangs were, of course, hooked into an eternal relationship with their captors. Their very soul required the violence meted out against them for its nourishment. Victory, for them, was to get thicker blankets, a bed, permission to wear a watch. Like the lone fraudster, they too had no horizons.

The turn to crime, even to self-styled banditry, is among the most conservative responses to autocracy imaginable. It has nowhere to go. Its imagination is entirely consumed by the present.

So, Magadien's slip is not that surprising. By guarding the buildings from which he stole, he was, in an unhappy and muddled sort of way, acting as sentry to the only world he could imagine.

*

Nonetheless, it was not a role he was prepared to play for long. The incident at the hostel in Guguletu had frightened him; his purpose in becoming a security guard was, after all, to steal, not to die.

He left his job by getting caught for fraud, arrested and thrown in jail. It is a peculiar thing to say, I know. I'm sure he did not consciously decide to go prison. It is not as simple as that. But he was caught out in such a foolish manner; he found a cheque book in a building he was guarding in downtown Cape Town; he stole a cheque a day for the following week; he used each cheque within hours of stealing it. The trail he left behind him furnished alarm bells and a siren. He has never been a stupid man. This was a stupid thing to do – for somebody who wished to remain free at any rate.

If he had simply resigned from his job at the security company, where was he to go? To live off his mother, the sight of whom he resented? To another temporary job, acquired with a stolen identity document, where he would commit another fraud? The world behind the bars beckoned.

I put this to him, and he responds with some excitement. 'You are,' he replies, 'the first *frans* I have met who understands that a *ndota* must go back to prison. Remember, whenever you are discharged from prison, there is something to collect. There's something waiting for me that's mine. My rank. It's there in your subconscious. My family didn't realise it. I had to get back to prison. I had to go. So I could go further and further. It was like a driving force.'

*

The sentence Magadien served for stealing the cheques began in April 1986 and ended in March the following year. It was not what he had expected. The words 'gangster', '28' and 'violent' were now written into the front of his prison file in bright red ink. He was treated accordingly; he was shunted from prison to prison during the first months of his incarceration. Eventually, in the dying months of 1986, he was taken to Robben Island, a place gangsters referred to as 'the sticks'.

Robben Island, which lies in the middle of Table Bay, about eight kilometres from the mainland, is famous for its maximum security prison, now a museum, where Nelson Mandela and the other Rivonia trialists served the bulk of their sentences. But among Cape Town's criminals, it was famous for something else. Not the maximum security prison, where Mandela was kept, but the medium security prison at the other end of the island; it was the place where prison life as inmates knew it was suspended.

The island is flat and stark and eternally loud; the noise of wind and ocean never ceases. Magadien's account of his time there is like a dispatch from another world.

'At Robben Island,' he says, 'there was one phrase: "Everything dies in the sea." Nothing that happens reaches Cape Town. You know that if you stab a white warder at that place you die. Who wants to die like that? We knew that. The warders knew that. That's why they sent us there. There were lots of 28s and 26s there who had once caused trouble at Pollsmoor.

'It was a shit prison. There was no fresh water. They had to ship it from the mainland. The water stood in two tanks in the courtyard.

It was too precious to clean yourself with; if you wanted to wash, you washed in the sea. And the work they made us do was ridiculous. If you look out to sea from Robben Island, the surface of the water is covered with heavy seaweed like bamboo shoots. You must clean them off the beach every day. Each day the sea brings thousands of that stuff. We also had to pick up penguin shit. There was a company that paid the prisons department for collecting it.

'But it became a nice place if you behaved, and you did behave because you didn't want to die. After a while there, you find this restfulness creeping up on you. The food was good. It was the only prison where they didn't have enough water to drown it. And it was also the only prison where you could take a little piece of fishing line and fish. We made the harbour a little bit bigger. We caught fish and cooked it there and then, right by the sea.

'The warders there were very corrupt. They'd choose two or three inmates, give us wetsuits and take us into the water to dive for crayfish and abalone. Then they'd sell it on the side to line their own pockets. And you know what? When they took us diving they gave us knives. Each inmate would get his own knife, fucking hardened gangsters. That's how we knew the island's rules: "Ja, you can stab me to death, but you'll go nowhere."'

It is an odd story, isn't it? The gangsters' fears were surely unfounded. Apartheid was a callous system, but its prisons were not concentration camps, not even the jail in the middle of the sea. If an inmate were to vanish from the face of the earth, his family would ask questions. The prisons service would have to provide answers. On murder, at any rate, there were accounts.

But gangsters believed that if they stabbed, they would die. And their perceptions shaped prison life. The Number became a shallow echo of its usual self. There was no recruitment and there were no promotions. Nobody was hauled before inmate courts and no one was punished. 28s would get together and talk, but idly. For Magadien, it was wasted time, time he could have spent at a maximum security prison.

Robben Island was, in a way, an incidental control experiment. If the relationship between gangsters and warders is indeed framed by a structure of implicit rules, what happens when one side throws the proverbial rule book away? What happens when warders announce – wordlessly, by the gesture of giving inmates knives – that Number ritual is punishable by death. The gangs evaporate. They become ghosts, living their frail afterlife on memories of what they did when they were flesh-and-blood beings. Indeed, the gangs' own metaphors described things this way: 'In maximum, the Number is *vleis-en-bloed*, "flesh-and-blood". Robben Island is *die stokkies*, "the sticks" – limbo.'

It is testimony to the massive gulf that lies between the camps of a totalitarian state, where people can indeed 'disappear' with little fuss – as the inmates at Robben Island thought might happen to them – and the brutal jails of a merely authoritarian state, which is still held to account. There were no gangs in Auschwitz – a world where camp guards killed at will. However much the veterans of the Numbers may talk of the Holocaust they witnessed under white rule, the apartheid prison was no concentration camp.

Yet there is, of course, another way of throwing away the rules. What if warders refused to meet violence with violence? What if stabbing a warder would earn one, not a beating and a heroic period *agter die berge*, but a further conviction in a civilian court? Would the Number become a ghost in these circumstances? Some of post-apartheid South Africa's prisons, which emerged less than a decade after Magadien's incarceration at Robben Island, were to constitute another control experiment.

*

When he was released from Robben Island in early 1987, Magadien slipped easily into the contours of a schizophrenic life. His first port of call was not his mother's house in Heideveld, nor the Hanover Park streets where he had spent his adolescence, but Manenberg: he was looking for Natalie, the woman he had courted on the telephone a year earlier.

She was pleased to see him: she took him in. Within days of his release, he had moved into her home, which she shared with a brother and an assortment of extended family. On Saturday mornings, he would walk the five or six kilometres from Manenberg to Hanover Park, where he took his place in Lags Eleven, the beloved football team he and his fellow Never Worries had started in the mid-1970s.

I am not sure what he felt for Natalie. But it was only a matter of weeks before another woman distracted him.

'Natalie had a brother called Peter,' Magadien recalls. 'One day he said to me, "I've seen you play soccer in the streets. You're good. Why don't you come and play for our club in the Sunday league?" I told him I already belonged to a club in Hanover Park, where I played on Saturdays, and that if I was caught playing Sunday league for another club, the soccer board might ban me for life. He said, no, this league was very informal; there would be no officials.

'So I played, and you won't believe it, the very first game I played I met Faranaaz, the woman who was to become my wife. I played number five, sweeper. I played well; I cleared two certain goals off the line. The crowd started shouting, "Number Five! Number Five."

'After the game, a few girls gathered around me. They wanted to be with the one who had stood out. One of them was Faranaaz. I asked her for a cigarette, and we chatted. Her father came over and I was introduced to him. He's a Mandrax smoker, Mr Benjamin. He invited me back to their house to smoke a pipe in the yard. Then I stayed for dinner. Afterwards, the family watched videos. I sat next to Faranaaz and held her hand.

'I never went to Natalie's house ever again. I didn't even tell her I was leaving. After that Sunday, I started spending more time in Hanover Park. But whenever I went to Manenberg, I went straight to the Benjamins' house. It became a big problem. When Natalie heard I was there, she would come to the corner and make a hell of a noise. On Sundays, when I played soccer, Natalie and Faranaaz would both be there. It was quite difficult for me.

'Soon after I met Faranaaz, I was told that Mrs Benjamin, Faranaaz's mom, had practically brought Natalie up, that she had once been like a daughter in the household. I felt like a villain.'

Faranaaz is now among his most bitter enemies. I ask him what he saw in her then. His answer is more than unsatisfying: it comes, quite literally, from an afternoon soap opera.

'How can I explain it? The other day, on *The Bold and the Beautiful*, they were talking about soul mates. They also spoke about it in *Generations*. It was like that. Something just clicked. Not just on my side: on hers too. Something just said, this is the one.'

Magadien's inability to capture his relationships with women in words is unsettling. During the countless hours we spent together in his Pollsmoor cell, he was acutely alive to the meaning of my body language, and to moods and thoughts revealed by subtle changes in my tone of voice. There was no deficit of emotional intelligence, nor of empathy. But about his romances there is this impenetrable wall: an inability to say anything.

When I gave Magadien the first 150 draft pages of this book to read, the part that moved him most was his own account of the cruelty he had meted out to Margie, Glynnis's mother. The previous night, he told me, when he read that passage, he had put the manuscript aside and stared at the ceiling for hours.

I was a little puzzled. 'I was only quoting you back to yourself,' I said. 'What was new?'

'I started thinking about what I've done to Margie,' he replied. 'I think maybe I've fucked her up – inside her head, I mean. I think, maybe, for all these years she has been carrying pain wherever she goes, that maybe she's never felt safe with another man – because of me.'

*

'What did you do for a living during that time when you met Faranaaz?' I ask.

'I wasn't working for the first while,' he replies, 'but then I got a job at a security company again. It was a small company that guarded factories and businesses. I don't know if you've seen the road works camps in Kraaifontein. All their equipment is there, welders, machines, the places where their trucks fold up. I was guarding that complex.

'And then this thing happened. Do you know where the Capetonian Hotel is, in Adderley Street where the custom house is? On the corner is a branch of Nedbank. Inside, there's a square. There is a glass building opposite. After the job in Kraaifontein, I guarded that building. One night, when I was there alone, I found all the company's cars, car keys and petrol cards. I took a single-cam Nissan XL 600 to the Strand for the night. I was going to take it back the next morning. Because of my smoking and drinking and drugs, I overslept. If I went to work, everybody would have been there; they would know that I had taken the bakkie. So I thought, fuck it, I'm not going back.'

I laugh.

'Don't,' he says. 'I'm serious.

'I kept the bakkie. It had a petrol card so I didn't need to worry about petrol. That is the car I took to Clanwilliam, to Serfontein's place. I woke up one morning and I had been dreaming about it. I thought, fuck it, I am going there. I just got in the car and drove.

'I also had a hired car, a Citi Golf, hired at Avis in Stellenbosch. A friend of mine had hired the car for the weekend. He was a soldier on weekend leave. On the Sunday, he was so drunk he couldn't take it back. He asked me to. I didn't; I kept it as a back-up car.

'I was caught through stupidity again. I sold the bakkie in the black location in the Strand. The bakkie wasn't legal. It had no registration, no third party disc, only temporary registration. I sold the bakkie for R1 500: R500 up front, the rest in two instalments. About two weeks after I got rid of the bakkie, I went into the location to pick up the second R500 instalment. I didn't know that the guy I had sold it to had been caught in a police roadblock. The police made a deal with him – help us catch the guy who sold it to you, and charges against you will be dropped. So I walked into a trap. The police were waiting for me. If I hadn't gone back for that R1 000, I would have been scot free. But I had a drug problem by then, and I was not earning a wage. They sentenced me to four-and-a-half years.'

*

Something else happened during Magadien's time at the Strand in 1987, something I only discovered later. He left an unborn daughter there; he would only meet her in the early 1990s, after he had served his sentence. Her name is Noes.

Her mother was not Colleen, but someone else, a woman Magadien speaks very little of: Nikki Cupido. She was killed in 1991, beaten to death by her lover. Noes was three years old at the time. Much later, Magadien's life would be consumed with the task of making up to her, of saving her.

12
THE WAR OF THE 28S

I have been telling you Magadien's story as he told it to me. On the outside, he is a figure of eternal estrangement, stalking the periphery of several worlds. He presents himself, fleetingly, in the homes of his family, only to remind himself that he does not belong with them. He seduces women, befriends their families, becomes a needed man, then silently slips away. He seeks employment among whites, and remains long enough to steal from them. And then he retreats, vanishing into the depths of Nongoloza's world.

It is a double vanishing. He disappears from his family and his lovers, but he disappears from me too, the man to whom he has decided to tell his life story. For Magadien does not exist in the place his narrative takes me. Nor does any other human being. The prison world conjured by his tongue is stylised and clean, a theatre of abstractions. There is violence there, to be sure, but it is idealised violence, animated by a logic so crisp it appears more a description of a chess game than a world inhabited by human beings. There is sex, too, but it occurs within codes so laden with metaphor that the bodies and desire are almost incidental.

It is unsettling to listen to a man tell his story thus, especially since we are sitting in a cell in Pollsmoor Prison. Around us are the fetid smells of poor food, the stale sweat of the men who pass us in the corridor, the eternal relay of curses and insults that batter the prison walls. There are times when I want to stop him and command him to listen: '*This* is jail,' I want to tell him, 'not the world in your head. Tell me about the place we can hear and smell around us.'

But I don't say what is on my mind. I have decided, since the beginning, that I must not break down doors he has chosen to keep locked. The places he conceals from both me and himself, he should visit only with a counsellor or a therapist. A journalist has no business there.

*

It turns out, though, that since the very beginning there have been things he has wanted to share, things about his experience in prison. But he has had to tell me in his own carefully chosen way; the demons must only emerge when the time is ripe.

We have been moving through his life chronologically, starting with his childhood in District Six. He has told me that we must work this way, that certain things cannot be severed from their contexts. Throughout, our conversations have been menaced by the unspoken. Every 26 and 27 I have interviewed has told me that the 28s are sexual predators. Everyone has said that the silver line is a posse of concubines, their sole function to service the desires of the warriors in the gold line. These rumours have entered our conversations often. Sometimes, Magadien has dismissed them as lies. Other times, he has told me to be patient: 'I will get there, I will explain everything to you, but only when the time is right.'

We have reached 1987 in Magadien's narrative. The year 1987, it turns out, is the time of truth-telling.

*

While writing this book, I come across the following comment in Gore Vidal's memoir, *Palimpsest*. 'It was my experience, as a soldier,' Vidal comments dryly of his sexual adventures in the US Army during World War II, 'that just about everyone, either actively or passively, was available under the right circumstances. Certainly, things were pretty open in the Pacific Islands, where on one, no doubt mythical, island an entire marine division paired off … Perfectly "normal" young men,' Vidal continues, 'placed outside the usual round of family and work, will run riot with each other.'

You do not need to have stepped inside a South African prison to know that Vidal's comment speaks to the predicaments of South African prisoners; that for the past century, generations of inmates – placed outside the usual round of family and work – have indeed been running riot with one another. You can tell just by listening to the mythical story of Nongoloza and Kilikijan.

Recall how Magubane, a minor figure at the beginning of the narrative, hijacks the entire tale and takes it places it was never meant to go. It began as a salutary story about the initiation of a group of anti-colonial rebels: they became bandits to defend themselves and their people from the whites' gold mines. Yet, no sooner has the band formed, than it splits acrimoniously over whether it is permitted for Nongoloza to sleep with Magubane. From now on, the heart of the story is no longer about fighting whites: it is consumed by the question of sex.

The quarrel can never be resolved: that much is built into the structure of the story. There was a man who knew right from wrong in this matter – Po – but he is dead. There was a document of founding principles, but half of it has been washed down the river. This is, perhaps, a begrudging acknowledgment that the problem is both fundamental to prison life and irresolvable, that it will never go away.

What haunts the gangs most, it seems, is not so much the sex itself, but an ambiguity that comes with the sex – the inmate who is both a bandit and a passive sexual partner: Magubane. He is the intolerable, unthinkable figure.

Each gang deals with him in its own way. The 26s and 27s say that they have prohibited sex entirely, that they have banished Magubane from their camp. Magubane lives, they say, in the silver line of the 28s. Silver line officers are called *ndotas*, men, but they are in fact concubines to the gold line, to the soldiers. How can an inmate be both a man – a bandit – and a wife, they ask.

The 28s deny this vociferously. They say that *ndotas* cannot have sex with one another, and that silver and gold line officers are all *ndotas*. Rather, they argue, gold officers are permitted to have sex, but not with fellow-28s; they have sex with 'sex-sons'. A sex-son is a *frans* who lives among the 28s and sleeps alongside probationers in the silver line. But he is not a *ndota*. He will never be initiated. He will never learn about the Nongoloza myth, nor about the rules and lore of the 28s. He is, they say, a sort of a prostitute. He is too weak to survive in jail on his own strength, so he turns to the 28s for protection, and in exchange he gives them sex.

But even this, sex between a 28 *ndota* and a sex-son, is highly ritualised and meticulously clothed in meaning. The 28s consider themselves the children of Nongoloza, and as such they see themselves as Zulus – in war, in justice, and in sex. In regard to sex, the relationship between a *ndota* and his sex-son is understood as the relationship between a young, unmarried Zulu warrior and a Zulu maiden.

Most 28s in the Western Cape are coloured men. They have made themselves into Zulus for the purpose of having sex with other men. Zuluness – a culture which many of them think of with superstitious distaste when they are on the outside – is embraced in prison because its strangeness helps them to elide the ambiguity of what they are doing. In jail, they are Zulu men; they are having sex with Zulu maidens, with girls, through the thighs, the way they imagine Nongoloza and his forebears did. The line distinguishing men from women, the active from the passive partner, is drawn repeatedly, obsessively. To be the active partner one must be a gold line *ndota.* In other words, one has to stab; one has to be beaten to a pulp without crying out; one has to sit in a dank cell for weeks and eat a saltless diet; one has to emerge from *agter die berge* strong. To be a woman, one must be nothing: a being who can never join the Number; who must walk barefoot and never leave the cell without permission; who must not conduct business in the public world of the prison. And as a reminder that things are not really so, that she is indeed a man, she must never be penetrated; there can be no real consummation.

So the 28s claim that they too have gotten rid of Magubane, the figure who is both a woman and a bandit. They have done so by drawing and redrawing the line between *ndotas* and sex-sons, making sure that the distinction can never be blurred.

But there is a problem with this story. For where does it leave the silver line? They are called *ndotas,* but they do not have to take blood. They are men, but they do not have the right to invite anyone into their beds. And at the head of the silver line is the ancestor of Magubane; and they call him their mother. The silver line officers, it appears, are the dangerous ones; they flirt with banishing the carefully erected distinction between bandits and women. No wonder they are the subject of so many rumours among the 26s and 27s.

When I ask Magadien and other silver line officers to define their role in the 28s, I am told that they are the gang's brain, its intellect, and therefore its core. They are the keepers of Rooiland's hide, and thus the interpreters of 28 law. They are the ones who must approve a declaration of war, and who must give their assent to the manufacture of weapons and determine the length of blades. They are, by this reckoning, a kind of a sexless council of wise ones.

This dangerous ambiguity that characterises the silver line – their simultaneous status as men, women and eunuchs – would play itself out in a frenzy of violence during Magadien's 1987 prison sentence, leaving his relationship with the 28s forever scarred.

*

In early May 1987, Magadien was convicted of car theft and sentenced to serve four-and-a-half years in prison. He said he had been unlucky, that if he had not ventured into the Strand's African township to collect his money, he would have walked free. But a part of him had also yearned for jail; he wanted to fetch his rank, to take up a position he had been waiting for since before his Robben Island sentence.

Things began quite well. He began serving his sentence at Pollsmoor Prison, and while he was there he got the promotion he had been waiting for; he was now a Landdros – which means 'magistrate' in Afrikaans – in the silver line of the 28s, his first step out of the junior ranks, into the heart of the Number itself.

The function of the Landdros actually has little to do with the meaning of its name. He is the bridge between the junior forum of the silver line – the four points of the twos, which tries junior silver line members for minor infractions – and the corps of senior silver line officers. He remains in the four points of the twos, where he acts as prosecutor, but he also acts as the liaison between the junior ranks and the officers. As such, he sits in all the gang's forums, roaming up and down the hierarchy of the 28s, catching glimpses of all of its workings.

'I was over the moon,' Magadien recalls. 'I had been waiting to become Landdros ever since before my Robben Island sentence.

'As things turned out, I was robbed. I was made a Landdros at Pollsmoor, but after a couple of months, before I could play my role there, I was transferred to Victor Verster. And at Victor Verster, all hell broke loose. The silver and gold lines went to war. It all started on a Wednesday, the Landdros's day.

*

'Wednesday,' Magadien tells me, 'is the year of the complaints. It is the year when anyone who has grievances must tell the Number. When I arrived at Victor Verster in 1987, I was Landdros. This made Wednesday an important day for me; I was the one who took grievances in the junior ranks of the silver line to the officers. A probationer's complaint goes to the Silver-Two, and he takes it to the Silver-One, then up to the Goliat-Two, then Goliat-One, then to me, the Landdros. I take it to the officers.

'The complaints kept coming, more and more; probationers came and said that junior gold line soldiers would capture them in the courtyard, or on their way down the corridor, or during exercise time, and rape them. Each time it was a different place, but it was always where people move round the prison. There were three rapes in two weeks.'

'It came as a surprise?' I asked. 'There was no tension before?'

'There was plenty of tension before. We did see it coming. You see, there is this rule in the 28s: soldiers must be lean and spare. They must be hungry, they must never relax. Like I told you, some of us saw their job as the job of animals. They weren't allowed certain things. Their clothes must be ... how can I say? When the silver line is dressed, you'll look at them and say wow – these boys belong to a group, they dress carefully, they are beautiful. The gold line is the opposite. When you look at them, it's like they've taken their clothes straight out of the laundry basket.

'They were not allowed to eat meat – they could only have the bones. They weren't allowed to eat eggs – they had to give their eggs to the silver line. No sugar in their porridge; they must have bitter porridge. No sugar in their coffee. They got sick and tired of the way they were treated. They wanted our life.

'How can I explain to you? You have twenty, thirty guys living together in one fucking room. There is this thing called the Number which says these inmates must have a spare diet, and those must eat well. Thirty guys living together in one cell: after a while, the Number stops making sense. All you think is – these cunts are getting my eggs, I'm hungry, this place is fucked-up enough even if I could keep my eggs. So the Number no longer brings people together. Its rules make people turn on each other.'

The story, in fact, is somewhat more complex than that; it is not just that 'the Number stopped making sense' – there was a more specific cause.

When Magadien began telling me this story, I started looking for veteran 28s in the gold line who had been interned at Victor Verster during 1987. I found three. Two walked out of the room the moment they discovered what it was I wanted to discuss. The third, a man called Ishmael, who had not seen the inside of a prison since 1989, and for whom the question of gold line dignity was a dim memory, a foreign feeling from another lifetime, spoke eagerly.

'Ja,' he told me, 'it's true that soldiers were raping silver probationers, and that that's why the silver line went to war with us. But that wasn't the first cause of the war. The first cause was panic in the gold line. It all started with the hanging of the three Pollsmoor inmates in 1986. All three were gold line 28s. They were hanged for a murder that happened in their cell in the early hours of the morning. The Number was shocked. It never recovered from its shock. We mourned for a month, and then tried to carry on as normal, but things weren't normal any more. Throughout 1987, the talk was that the gold line must stop stabbing; *ndotas* cannot keep dying like this. Enough is enough.

'But that created its own problems. What do soldiers do? We stab. So if we decide to stop stabbing, there is no space for soldiers any more. The silver line becomes the Number. We couldn't have that. We tried to take over the Number before the silver line could do it. So we started demanding that it is time for soldiers to eat meat again, and have sugar in our coffee. And went further than that. We not only wanted to eat again; we wanted the silver line to stop eating. We took away their food, their cigarettes, even their soap and their toilet paper. We didn't want them to be able to wipe their arses. And then they fought back.'

'You've left out the rapes,' I said. 'Why did you start raping silver probationers?'

He smiled at me mischievously. 'A retirement perk,' he said. 'For years, we had been the ones taking the beatings, getting our heads split open and our legs broken, while the silvers sat on their fat arses and stuffed their faces with food. Now we were retiring from battle and we wanted perks from the cunts who had grown fat all these years.'

*

I went back to Magadien and asked him to continue his story: 'You said that as Landdros, you started receiving complaints from the silver line probationers that they were being raped, and that the rapes were a kind of punishment and revenge. What did you do?'

'At first, we didn't think it would lead to war,' he replied. 'The culprits were junior gold line members, not officers. We thought, let's take this thing to the gold officers, as we should, and see if they call the Twelve Points – the highest structure in the gang – to punish the offenders.

'So we did that. We approached the Jim Crow; he is the gold line officer who interfaces with the two-times in the silver line. His name was Macomic. We told him, and he agreed that the soldiers were destroying the Number, that they must be disciplined. So he took it to the other officers in the gold line. But when he got there, there was an argument. They told him to let the soldiers rape the probationers. He said no, it is wrong. And the Colonel in the gold line, his gang name was John Lazarus, stabbed Macomic. And that was it. That was war. There was no use calling the Twelve Points. The whole gold line was now against us. They had become our enemies.

'So we went to Holland, to the 27s. We told them what was going to happen. We said, "*Daar's bots in ons kamp*", "There's warfare in our camp". They said: "We just want to see: we don't want to be involved." We said: "Fine. We don't want you involved. It's an internal thing."

'We spent a week gathering knives. The silver line was preparing to become an army for the first time. We planned over meals, sitting at our own table, separate from the gold line.

'One morning at breakfast, we said "Up!" and we attacked them. And after that, every morning, every morning, every morning. Some of us were taken *agter die berge*, some of us were transferred to other prisons. And that's how it spread. The news arrived at every other prison in the Western Cape: the gold and silver lines are at war in Victor Verster. The war went to every prison. Because the issues there were the same: soldiers raping privates, the question of meat and eggs.

'We destroyed them. People say the silver line is a bunch of softies, but we were fighting for our dignity: we had the will. We fucked them up. People on our side got fucked up too. But it was much worse on their side. There were prisons where every soldier in the officer corps was in the hospital wing. They were scared to walk down a corridor, scared to go to sleep at night. In Victor Verster, it took less than a month. They said: "Okay, what do you want?"'

I went back to Ishmael and asked him why the silver line won the war. 'Was it because they were better fighters?' I asked.

He laughed. 'They won the war because the 27s told the 26s to join in on their side,' he said. One of Kilikijan's jobs is to protect Magubane from Nongoloza. Remember, Magubane was Kilikijan's soldier before Nongoloza took him away. Kilikijan must defend all his soldiers, past and present.

*

'You said the gold line threw in the towel and asked you what you wanted,' I said to Magadien at our next meeting. 'What did you want?'

He bowed his head and spoke to the floor. His voice was quiet and grave. 'This is why I've waited to tell you this until now,' he replied, 'because I want to answer some of the questions you have been very eager to ask, about the rumours you have heard about the 28s.

'We closed down the gold line. The silver line took control and stood in all the gold positions – Judge, General, Colonel. Not one gold officer was allowed to work. That was one of our biggest mistakes. Because that's when the corruption started. Since 1987, you don't walk to the Number, you come with the train.'

The expression on his face told me he had just made a stinging confession. I looked at him queryingly.

He smiled. 'In all the hours we have spent together, I have never told you about the long road?'

I shook my head, and he sighed with exasperation. He began the story of the long road, listlessly, unhappily.

'The long road is the way a new recruit came into the Number before 1987. It goes like this:

'"I told my mother and my father I was leaving to find work. I walked into a dark forest. I rolled and I rolled deeper into the forest. I came across someone and he was chopping wood. He asked me who I am, what I want, and so on and so on."'

Magadien interrupted his story. 'You don't know it yet, but the man chopping wood is the Glas. He is recruiting new 28s. When he chops, splinters of wood fly up. They are the new recruits.'

I nodded and gestured for him to continue.

'"When he stopped chopping his wood and asked who I am, I told him my name is Magadien Wentzel. I am looking for work. He took out a bag. He said, 'Don't be frightened by why you see in the bag. I am not going to kill you.' He took out an assegai and a knobkerrie. 'Which do you want to work with? Do you want light work or heavy work?' he asked. I told him the knobkerrie. It means I have chosen to join the silver line. I will not be a soldier. I ask him what else is in his bag. 'Grass,' he replied. 'It is your mother and father. Leave it with me. Where you are going to now, you can never leave. You will never see your parents again. From now on, your mother is Magubane. Your father is Nongoloza.' He tells me to walk further along the dust road. I come to a gate. I open it and step inside ..."

'That's enough,' Magadien said. 'I can't go any further. But I have told you what you need to know. The point is, you enter the Number on the silver side with a knobkerrie. A soldier, though, a member of the gold line, enters with the assegai. That means he must use a knife to enter the Number; he has to stab. Note that nobody must have sex to join the 28s, not silvers and not soldiers.

'Now I must tell you about coming to the Number with the train; the way things have been done since 1987.

'You arrive at the train station outside your home on a Friday evening. You see a dark cloud on the dusk horizon, the western horizon. You buy yourself a train ticket. It can be first class, second class or third class. The train leaves the station. It goes on, and on, and on, through the countryside. Eventually, it comes to the end of the line. You get off. You hear a voice. "Everyone seeking work, follow me." It is Saturday night. You are issued with a mug and a spoon. The next day, you are given a pick and taken to the mines. You spend the morning working. Somebody comes up to you and asks if you are satisfied with mine work. You say, no, it is heavy work. He points you in the right direction. "Take this road. Where it goes, there is good work." You walk until you get to a cross-roads. There is a man waiting there. He asks you who you are, what you want. You say you are looking for a job. He takes you to a guava tree.'

Magadien interrupted himself again. 'I'm not going to tell you what happens under the guava tree. It is too complicated. There are too many symbols. You will ask millions of questions, and you will drive me mad. Let's just say that after the guava tree, he takes you into a cave. He has sex with you. You wash yourself in the river. Then you arrive at the gate. The same gate you arrive at when you walk the long road to the Number. The man who takes you into the cave is an officer in the 28s; to join the 28s, an officer must have sex with you.'

I regurgitated his story aloud. 'The old way, soldiers came by stabbing, silvers without stabbing. The new way, there are no soldiers, the gold line is closed. Nobody takes blood. Everyone comes in by being fucked.'

He nodded gravely. 'The silvers won the war. We closed the gold line. Well, not closed as such. You still have people sitting as Generals and Judges, so that the Number can function. But they are not *vleis-en-bloed* soldiers. They have not stabbed to take their positions. They are just there "for the minute", as we say in the Number. There are no real soldiers any more. No bloodline.

'We did the most stupid, corrupt, fucked-up thing. We declared war on them for raping our junior members. And when we won the war, we raped in turn. We said, you can only join the Number if an officer fucks you. And we made up this bullshit story of coming to the Number by the train. And all the sex-sons were absorbed into the Number. Their boyfriends in the officer corps made them *ndotas*.

'And now the Number is treacherous. Many who have been recruited since 1987 have been fucked. They will never admit it. They will stab you if you suggest it. So everyone whispers about the 28s, behind our backs. No one says what he thinks to our faces.

'We lived the lives of animals in prison. And so we became animals. It's hard to explain to you about boredom in prison. We tattooed each other until there was no more space on our bodies. Maybe for a year, maybe for two years, you sit with the same fucking guys in the same room. You've heard their life stories; you're fucking bored. You go mad.'

I saw now why he had to tell me the story chronologically. And I recalled our first meeting, when he reprimanded me for being a journalist: my profession spreads lies about sex in the 28s, he told me. I recalled all the times he had cursed somebody for claiming that the 28s rape. He had been defending the 28s of his memory; he was fighting a rearguard action in the name of a spectre.

The history of the 28s in his head appeared to me as an entirely private history. He had organised his understanding of the past in a way that allowed him to cope with his own disenchantment. There were two 28 gangs in his memory: the abstract gang of pure bandits who floated through a world of myth; and the horribly concrete world of men locked together in a room, a place of madness. 1987 was the dividing line; the mythical bandits lived before then, the corrupt men after. To his mind, the Number disappeared 16 years ago.

*

What exactly happened in 1987 that upset Magadien so? Beneath his account of that time, there is obviously a more personal story, one that he will not share. So I try to think about the things he has told me at a more abstract level.

It seems to me that the entire ensemble of Number gang rituals was erected to defend prisoners from two awful fates: becoming boys, and becoming women. Prisoners are turned into boys by their relationship with their custodians. They are told when to eat, when to sleep, when to wash and when to brush their teeth. Their personal possessions are constantly searched; when they return from court, they are stripped naked and their very bodies are searched. Imprisonment is the most infantilising experience imaginable.

The initiation ritual – the stabbing, the beatings, the solitary confinement – is about the making of men, *ndotas*. It is not just that the initiate must display a range of hard male virtues in order to succeed. It is what is done with those virtues – how those virtues are used to resist infantilisation. What better way to retrieve the adulthood prison has stolen than to borrow the agency of one's custodians? Instead of holding up an image of inmates to prison warders, the gangs hold up a mirror. 'We are what you are. You are an army, we are an army. Where you have a head of prison, we will have a Judge. Where you have a head of section, we will have a General. Whatever you do to us, we will do to you in turn.'

The creation of men through violence plays another, equally important function – it allows homophobic men to rationalise sex behind bars. The relationship between inmates who have become *ndotas* and those who have not is gendered; they are men and women. The line separating them is drawn emphatically, obsessively, as if any confusion will strip the world of all meaning.

But there is, of course, a heavy price to pay for the making of men who are not boys or women. *Ndotas* are beaten senseless, starved and battered. There are a host of rituals designed to ensure that the pain never becomes insufferable, like the decree that violence committed against warders is never fatal, and the rule that when a *ndota* is being punished by warders, he does not fight back and thus provoke a lethal response.

What happened in Magadien's 1987, it seems, is that the price became too high. The threshold of tolerable pain was crossed. The soldiers rebelled against being soldiers. And the moment they put down their arms – the moment the manufacturing of men ceased – so the line dividing men from women was erased. The entire edifice of 28 myth was a careful, painstaking attempt to separate *ndotas* from women. Now it fell apart. With the new form of initiation – 'coming to the Number with the train' – women and *ndotas* became indistinguishable.

I put these thoughts to Magadien, and he tells me he wants to spend the night thinking it over. When we meet the following morning, he is animated. He tells me his head is full of ideas, that he wants me to sit down, shut up and listen, that if I interrupt, his ideas will disappear.

'You tell me the silver line confuses you,' he says. 'You say we are men, but not men; women but not women; and also these wise beings with no sex. You say we are everything and nothing. The whole night, I've been thinking of a story to tell you that will explain why I am so proud of the silver line, what it is we represented before 1987. So here is a story for you.'

He begins speaking, and I recognise the story immediately; it has been told to me by other silver line 28s. But now, in this context, it carries a new meaning. It is a beguilingly sexual story. It concerns the silver line's role in the passing of a death sentence on a 28.

'There is only one structure in the 28s that can sentence a member to death,' Magadien tells me. 'It is called the Twelve Points; it consists of six gold line members and six silver line members. When the Twelve Points meets to decide a case, the Judge, the most senior officer in the gold line, is the first to speak: he argues for a conviction. The Mtshali, the most senior member of the silver line, stands up against him and argues for an acquittal. Then the forum debates the two positions. The Judge ends the discussion by announcing the verdict. Then he suggests a sentence. If the sentence is death, the Mtshali stands up straight away and begins an argument in mitigation. The second most severe sentence in the 28s is a "band", gang rape. The Mtshali will generally argue that the death sentence be commuted to a "band".

'Then everyone votes, except for the General and the Mtshali. If five vote for death and five for a lesser sentence, the Mtshali casts his deciding vote and the accused's life is saved. The Judge accepts that his recommended sentence has been overruled. If the ones who vote for death are in the majority, the Mtshali shows his protest by refusing to vote at all.'

At this point – once the accused has been sentenced to death by a majority vote – the Goliat-One – the lowest-ranking silver line member of the Twelve Points – steps in to save his life. He strips off all his clothes and runs naked round the edge of the Twelve Points; as he does so, he lets out a scream, in the most plaintive and haunting voice he can muster, pleading for mercy.

'The Goliat-One,' Magadien tells me, 'is called The Man of the Light, the one who shines a light into the darkness of the 28s. To sentence somebody to death is a deed of blackness. The Number must ask itself: "How did we get ourselves into this position? Have we become lost in the darkness?" Hearing the cry of the Goliat-One brings us back to the light. And if that does not work, if the hearts of the Twelve Points are not stirred by the Goliat-One, then the accused must be executed.'

He stops speaking and stares at me intently.

'You say the silver line isn't male or female,' he continues. 'You are right. We are not the male sex or the female sex. We are sex itself. Life itself. We celebrate sex. We celebrate life. Our job is to *defend* life.'

13
VINCENT

Listening to Number gang members' accounts of what happened in 1987, I was continually frustrated by the opacity of their stories, by the gaps in their memories, by the fact that each had co-opted what had happened into his own private narrative. I wished I had been there myself: a fly on the wall. So I looked for the next best thing: a person who had been right inside the gangs at that time, but who understood the world, not as a gangster does, but as I do.

It was a somewhat dimwitted desire. A fly on the wall, a fly with a human brain, would have understood little of the war unfolding before its eyes. It was, after all, a Number gang war; only understanding the passions that animated it could make it intelligible. To understand what had really happened required that I step, however fleetingly, into the skin of a prison gangster – into Magadien's skin.

I did, nonetheless, find the person I was looking for, a man who had been in the heart of Number gang territory in the late 1980s, and who had watched as an observer does. His name is Vincent Shabangu. He does not possess the final word on 1987: he was as puzzled and traumatised by what he witnessed as I would have been. But my misguided quest did not prove futile. The things I learned from him were invaluable.

Shabangu is a social worker. We meet at his place of work, Boystown, a home for juveniles who have begun to flirt with lawlessness, an institution whose mission is to save its charges from entering the criminal justice system proper, before it is too late.

The journey to my appointment with Shabangu suggests that he is fighting an uphill battle. Boystown is about forty kilometres from Cape Town. You head east along the N2 freeway for about thirty kilometres, then follow a series of quiet country roads. Out on those roads, apparently in the middle of nowhere, I see a teenaged girl standing in the tramlines, looking idle and bored. As I pass her, she suddenly stands erect, looks me straight in the eye, and lifts her skirt. A few kilometres on, another girl in the tramlines, another silent solicitation. The journey to Shabangu, it seems, is paved with his charges – with fallen children.

Shabangu is a social worker, not just by profession, but by vocation. He exudes earnestness, a desire to mend. He insists that the interview can wait a while, that we begin with a brief tour of Boystown; 'I am my work,' he seems to be telling me. 'By introducing you to Boystown, I am introducing you to me.' I soon discover that this consuming activism – this need to fix broken things – is precisely what shaped his extraordinary experience of prison.

He is a little younger than Magadien, and he tells me he was born in the Strand, the son of an African father and a coloured mother. I ask him whether he ever knew the Wentzels of the Strand.

'The ones in the music business?' he asks.

'No. I think one was a roof tiler.'

'Oh, the Muslim Wentzels. The builders, the tilers. We had little contact with them. They were from a close-knit community, religious people. They woke up at five every morning and did what they needed to do. Those were the days our fathers and grandfathers used to go out to work every day. Not just sitting on the corner, in the shebeens, drunk every day. You wonder where they get the money to drink. You wonder about crime.'

Shabangu's face is broad and pockmarked. It is also open and declarative; throughout our conversation, he looks at me square-on, never taking his eyes from mine. He wants his story to wash over me.

His family was forced to move from the Strand shortly after the 1976 uprisings, he tells me. 'The area we were in was classified as white,' he explains. 'My father was a very proud person. He would not live in someone else's back yard.'

So the Shabangus moved to Macassar, which, three centuries earlier, had hosted a small settlement of exiled Malay aristocrats and holy men. It is also the site of the oldest kramat in the Western Cape. But the Shabangus are not Muslim, and, for them, Macassar was a dumping ground for people removed from their homes because of the colour of their skins.

In the early 1980s, on the eve of Cape Town's insurrectionary moment, Shabangu enrolled at UWC to study social work. He joined the Black Consciousness Movement and became a serious and earnest activist. In 1985, during his final year of study, he found himself in the furnace of the uprisings. In September of that year, he was picked up off the streets during a demonstration and charged with public violence. He was convicted in 1986 and sentenced to five years in prison. He appealed. The sentence was amended to three years, half of which was suspended. On 20 January 1987 he was taken to Pollsmoor and thrown into C Section, which was controlled by the 26s and 27s at that time.

'I believe that making us activists into criminals was a brutal political strategy,' he tells me. 'The regime said to itself: "Why send these political activists to Robben Island? They will get a revolutionary education there. Rather put them in the inland jails, where the gangs are." It was like – the gangs will sort you out in prison.'

So Shabangu was thrown into the heart of prison gang land. He was petrified; he believed that he had been taken there to be destroyed – psychologically, physically, he did not know which.

'We were taken to C Section. It was immediately clear that the 26s ran the place, not the warders. When I arrived in my cell, I was sent to a corner and told to wait. Then one of them came up to me and asked me in their jail slang who I am.'

That is the first test to determine whether a new cell-mate is a *frans* or a *ndota*. A *frans* cannot fake an answer to the question 'Who are you?' The proper reply is so codified, so thoroughly soaked in the story of Nongoloza, no outsider can imitate it.

'"My name is Vincent," I replied.

'He looked at me for a long time, saying nothing. He was clearly puzzled. Then he went to talk to his people. He came back and said, "You are a first time."

'"Yes," I replied.

'He asked to see my prison card. It said I had been convicted of public violence.

'"What does that mean?" he asked.

'I said: "Listen: I am a political activist. It is unfortunate that I have ended up with you people. I should be on the Island. But I'm here. And this is who I am."

'He went back to consult with his people and they spoke for a long time. It seemed as if my answer was a good one. It was like I was put on a pedestal, put to one side as a curious case. He came back and said to me, "You will sleep with us," and they gave me new blankets.

'One guy who arrived on the same day as me had told them he was a 26. But I could see immediately that there was something wrong. He was also told to sit to one side. Later, they came back to me and said, "That guy – do you know him?" I said no.

'"Listen," they said to me. "He claimed he is a 26, but he isn't. Tonight, we are going to beat him up, but tomorrow morning, you haven't seen anything. You haven't heard anything."

'At around midnight, all hell broke loose. They used soap in a sock, and metal mugs. He was badly beaten up. The Colonel came round the next morning, asked the guy what happened. He said he had slipped. But you could see he didn't slip. The Colonel smiled and walked away.

'That's when I realised that this is a community all by itself. It has absolute power. You close your eyes, you turn your back; what's happening must happen behind you. There is no safe haven. One guy wanted to opt out of the 26s: he asked to be put in isolation. I don't know if the cooks were in on the conspiracy, but he suffered from food poisoning the next week. It is like the mafia: there is nowhere you can be kept safe, no prison in the country.

'I think that what saved me is that I engaged with them. I disagreed with them openly. There were things they said that made me worried about their state of mind, and I said so. One guy told me that there used to be no toilet paper. "We fought for it," he said. "We won it." I asked what they did. He said, "No, we stabbed one another."

'"How on earth can you kill one another for soap and toilet paper?" I replied. "Isn't it because of the guys who sit on Robben Island? They had the Geneva Convention behind them. And then the international law they raised moved to the inland prisons. Are you sure it is because of what you guys have done?"

'They listened to that. You could see some of them were really thinking about it. You could see them thinking: "We stabbed Jonny the other day, and nothing happened." I said, "Look at your meat. Look how little you get. If you killed 80 prisoners, do you think your food would increase? No, your sentence would increase. The meat would stay the same."

'I took a chance. I disagreed with them every time they did something I thought was crazy. I said, "I know I am small, and you are big, but I want to ask you, how can you beat this guy you call a *frans* for not polishing your shoes? Ask him nicely. Polish *his* shoes. You break his fingers, he can't polish your shoes."

'They listened. They respected me. They were struggling with how to understand who I was. We were watching each other's moves like a game of chess. When news came in, I was the first to read the newspaper, straight after the General. They started asking me questions. "I have a mother here, a brother there – can't you find out how to contact them?" Or: "I have this case, is there something you can do? Are there channels to a good lawyer?"

'It got to the point when they allowed me to walk freely around the section. I was the only non-gangster who could go wherever he wanted without asking permission. And I still went on challenging them. I said, "Why can't the other *franse* walk around? It is unfair. I am a *frans* like them. They deserve the same rights as me."

They were curious about me because I was as serious about fighting for prisoners' rights as they were. My perspective confused them. They came to me one Friday evening and they said: "You are so clever. Don't you want to join the 26s?" I said: "It sounds interesting. But what must I do to join? I don't want to go through these funny things. I want to join as second in command, in command of your law section. I want to run your court, because it is not run properly." They said: "You can't do that." But then they left me alone – I was this special *frans*.'

There were other political activists with Shabangu in Pollsmoor. Many were not as successful as he in holding onto their dignity.

'There was a guy in Pollsmoor called Michael Lukas,' Shabangu tells me. 'He was charged with murdering a bus driver or an inspector during the uprisings. He had said that he was 15 when he committed the act; a juvenile cannot be hanged. They put him in a gang cell. The gangsters made him comfortable. They are not stupid; they are like psychologists. They know what buttons to press. They come and brag about their own deeds. If you are not awake, you tell them things in return, and they just keep silent. Michael admitted to his cell mates he was 19 when he committed the murder. One of the guys in his cell testified against him and he got the death sentence.

'You see, the gangsters thought us activists were pieces of shit.

They didn't respect people who did not obey their rules. So they were quite happy to work with the security police against us. They were easily co-opted.'

Shabangu saw other activists lose their dignity in more subtle ways, ways that were of special interest to me.

'After a few months in C Section with the 26s,' he tells me, 'I got permission to study. I enrolled for a law course. They moved me into isolation, so that I could study in peace. I was kept in the section where people are held before they go to Pretoria to be hanged. There was a little chair in the corridor for the warder.

'In isolation, I met two other guys who had been convicted of public violence. One was called Arthur. I was moved to isolation on a Friday afternoon, he was moved on the same Friday night. It seemed that something terrible had happened to him before he was moved to isolation. He cried all weekend. He was really frightened. I coached him; I told him that if he keeps to his faith, he'd be okay.

'Unfortunately, I soon discovered, he had been drawn in. He had become a *wyfie* to feel safe.'

'A *wyfie* in C Section?' I asked. 'A 26's *wyfie*?'

'Yip. Even though they said they did not have *wyfies*. Even though they claimed that only the 28s have sex. They all had *wyfies*. Let me tell you how I found out about Arthur. The General in C Section decided that there were certain weekends when Arthur must go to his cell to watch movies. One Sunday, a warder came round to fetch Arthur, and I said I also wanted to go and watch a movie. Why shouldn't I be allowed to go too? When I went, I saw they were making Arthur a special bed next to the General's bed. It was so strange to see. They were making preparations for the General to have sex with him. And it wasn't just Arthur. Two other activists also became *wyfies* to 26s. If you are not strong, if you are not well prepared, they corrupt your mind, get into your mind.'

'But the 26s and 27s hate the 28s,' I say. 'And they hate them because the 28s have sex.'

'Yes,' he says with excitement. 'They claim they are not having sex with the guys. They don't call them *wyfies*. *I* do. They claim they are protecting the young guys from the 28s. They say, "Look at that *ndota* from the 28s; his eyes are all over you. You need me to protect you from him." They even said to me, right at the beginning,

"Don't mix with 28s. If they get a chance, they will rape you." But that is exactly what the 26s were doing. They have the young ones with them. They are having sex with them.

'And let me tell you something interesting. For a one-week period, just before I was put into isolation to study, I was taken to E Section, the 28 section of the prison. What was happening in the 28 section was different. There was a different atmosphere. There was sex happening there too, but you didn't feel frightened at night. You would go to sleep in your little corner and know you were safe. Not in C Section, not with the 26s. There, things were unpredictable; they could decide to do things in the middle of the night.

'I told the 28s. I said, "On C Section, the 26s say the youngsters have to be protected against you." They laughed. They said: "The 26s are hypocrites: the youngsters need to be protected against *them*, not us."'

*

Shabangu has traces of the missionary about him. He was not content with having preserved his own dignity, nor with the modus vivendi he had negotiated with the *ndotas*. Their political confusion tormented him; he wanted to take the whole century-long tradition of prison gangsterism by the scruff of the neck and drag it out into the light.

Some time in 1988, he was transferred from Pollsmoor to the countryside prison of Helderstroom. Once again, he was placed in isolation, so that he could study. He struck up a friendship with the inmate in the cell next to his: a man called Brian Sibiya, an African, and a General in the 28s.

It was fortuitous that he met Sibiya when he did. The General had been sentenced to death for rape a few years earlier, had gone to Pretoria where he sat on death row for 18 months. Shortly before he was due to be hanged, he was given a last-minute reprieve; his sentence was commuted to 25 years' imprisonment, and he was taken back to the Western Cape to serve his time there.

Sitting on death row day in and day out, thinking of the rope that awaited him, Sibiya reflected on his life with a degree of anxiety and depth that would have been unavailable in other circumstances. By the time his sentence was commuted and he had arrived back in the Cape, the Number seemed foreign to him, a place in which he no longer quite belonged.

'I spoke to Brian for hours on end,' Shabangu tells me. 'He said, "Listen, Vincent, I nearly lost my life, because I thought that what I believed in was right. It is *not* right. Things must change. People must be told the truth: you can join the Number if you want to, that's fine, but you must know what is waiting for you; you must know what really happens there."

'Brian told me that it had not always been like this. Before the Number had been corrupted, you were not allowed to have sex with somebody. You were not allowed to rape people. The Number was civilised. They debated, rather than fought. Their aim was to fight for better prison conditions, not to kill and violate one another. The problems arose, he told me, when the coloureds took over the Number. When Africans were in control, the gangs stuck by their original rules.'

Listening to Shabangu recount Brian's testimony, I feel déjà vu. It is like listening to Magadien all over again. I wonder, as I sit with Shabangu, how many countless men are walking the streets of the Western Cape, each with his own wonder-land account of what the Number was really like when he joined.

Sibiya's stories seduced Shabangu. He thought he had discovered a redeemable tradition buried beneath the confusion; he believed it might be possible to clean away the dross and resurrect the Number of Sibiya's memories.

'I told Brian I wanted to call a big seminar of all the gangs. I mean all the gangs, even the Airforce and the Big Fives. I wanted to discuss everything. Who is Nongoloza? Who is Grey? Where does it all come from? How did the 28s begin? So many things. I wanted to see exactly where everyone fits in. And where do the prison authorities fit in? Who created whom? Do they have a finger in every pie? Who is controlling whom? I thought that if everything could be dissected, everything laid bare, we could see where things went wrong and why.

'I knew it would be difficult. I hadn't taken blood or been through the ranks. They would ask what I was going to do with all this information.

'I told Brian about the seminar I was proposing and he sent the message down the ranks. He said it would be arranged that someone would be put in isolation next to me. They sent a 26 called

Richard. We spoke for a long time. He sent messages back down the ranks and finally got back to me with a decision.

'"I believe that what you want to do is good," he said, "but the time isn't right; there is too much squabbling among the gangs."'

'It may have endangered you?' I ask.

'Exactly. He said he trusts me, but others might think I'm a plant. Something happens, and then it is blamed on me. People talk to one another about secret things, a warder overhears, and the next day there is a raid. I get blamed because I was there, and I am the outsider. The rumours go round and then there is an order to kill me.'

So Shabangu's wildly ambitious project failed; when he was released from prison in 1990, he left the Number much as he had found it.

But there was a moment of profound happiness during his incarceration, a personal rather than a public moment. It was an encounter that seemed to have been touched by magic, an exchange that, by rights, should only take place in a wistful dream. It happened before his transfer to Helderstroom, while he was still at Pollsmoor.

'There was this dog handler at Pollsmoor,' Shabangu tells me. 'A white guy. I think his name was Rossouw. I told him one day that I and two comrades I was with wanted to meet Nelson Mandela. I said I wanted him to arrange it.'

It was a crazy request. Mandela and his fellow Rivonia trialists were kept in isolation. A carefully screened handful of warders were the only people permitted to speak to him. Orchestrating a meeting between Mandela and an inmate designated a common criminal was a dismissible offence.

'A few days later, Rossouw came to me and said that me and my comrades must go and wait at the entrance to Mandela's exercise yard. We went. We waited a long time. Rossouw arrived out of the blue, opened the courtyard door for us, and locked it behind us. And there was Mandela, alone in the courtyard.

'I introduced myself. And he said, "I'm Nelson." Not Mandela. Not Mr Mandela. Just Nelson. He asked why I was here and I told him. He told us never to stop believing that we would be free one day. He said maybe not in his lifetime, but definitely in our lifetimes. He told us we were young, that the doors would open for us, for our future. He said that no matter how hard things got in prison, no matter what they told us, we must always remember that what we are doing is right.

'It was just 15 minutes; it was enough. Here was this man who had been locked up for so many years, who believed he was going to die in prison, and he still had this serenity, this confidence. I floated back to my cell. I knew I could survive anything.'

*

'Tell me about Rossouw,' I ask. 'Why did he risk his job for you?'

'I don't know. He never really said much to us. But he would do things. He would give us a copy of the newspaper to read without anyone else knowing. Like he knew that our sanity rested on knowing what was happening outside. He never asked for anything in return – not even a conversation.'

*

I meet Magadien in his cell the day after my visit to Boystown, and Shabangu's story is still swirling around in my head. I recount the entire interview and he listens in silence.

He is only interested in one aspect of the story.

'Why do you need to hear it from an outsider?' he asks reproachfully. 'Why do you not believe me when I say it?'

'What?'

'That the 26s have *wyfies*; that those who spread rumours of sex and rape and sodomy in the 28s are doing it for only one reason: to take attention away from themselves.'

I say nothing.

'Let me tell you about a part of the Nongoloza story you have not heard before,' he continues. 'Remember that Kilikijan comes back to the cave and finds Nongoloza having sex with Magubane. They fight with their sabres; afterwards, the two camps go their separate ways. Magubane goes with Nongoloza, with the 28s, not with Kilikijan. Many years later, when the 28s and the 27s meet again at the Point Prison, when they discover Grey spinning his coin, Magubane is no longer with Nongoloza.

'Now I want to ask you, what happened to Magubane?'

There is anger in his voice. He has about him the disposition of a disgruntled preacher. I tell him I don't know what happened to Magubane.

'There are different versions,' he continues. 'Some say he informed for the whites against the 28s, that Nongoloza found out he had been betrayed, and that Magubane had to flee for his life. Others say that Magubane used tricks and cons to steal money from the 28s, and that when he had stolen enough money, he disappeared.

'Now let me ask you another question. Grey, the head of the 26s, the one Nongoloza and Kilikijan found in The Point, what does he do?'

'He tricks and cons to steal money from people,' I say.

'Ja, my friend, ja. Now let me tell you a secret. There are some who say that Grey *is* Magubane, that the man they found conning and tricking in The Point, the one who started the 26s, is the one Nongoloza had sex with. Nobody says this version in front of a 26. A 26 who respects himself will kill you if you say it to his face. But people say it behind the 26s' backs.'

'It seems nobody can get rid of Magubane,' I say. 'The 26s and 27s say he lives in the 28s. For the first few months you and I knew each other, you kept denying he was in the 28s. But actually, he is everywhere.'

Magadien nods. 'Ja,' he says. 'That's why the fighting gets so vicious.'

14
MAGADIEN AND NONGOLOZA

Early December 2002. Magadien and I are still new to one another; it is our third interview. We are both excited by the person who has just entered our respective lives: the prisoner has found a stranger who arrives faithfully every morning and listens to him with rapt attention for hours on end; the journalist has stumbled upon a subject who talks freely, who shows no signs that he will ever tire of talking. But our enthusiasm is checked by mutual doubts. Why is the prisoner talking so freely to a man he does not know? What is the journalist going to do with these confessions? What, precisely, is happening during these long morning hours?

I have been asking several inmates to talk to me about Nongoloza's story. Magadien offers some advice. 'Be careful about dates. People get very confused. Remember that 1812 was the year that Nongoloza and Kilikijan met the old seer. It was in 1824 that they fought over Magubane, and 1836 when they met up again in the Point Prison. Those are the three important years in our history.'

I am surprised by the significance he places in the dates. I assume everyone knows that there were no mines in South Africa in 1812, that *ndotas* understand the Nongoloza story as an allegory.

'I am not sure about these dates,' I say. 'Gold was only discovered in 1886.'

'They never said a gold mine,' he replies.

'Diamonds were only discovered in the 1860s.'

'What about coal?' he asks.

*

I leave his cell with an unpleasant feeling in the pit of my stomach. From the beginning, I have been carrying in my head that glib and unworkable maxim that journalists like to sprout: 'Don't change what you see. Leave life as it would have been had you never arrived on the scene.' I have always known that this maxim would be useless for the relationship Magadien and I are establishing. You do not sit with a man month in and month out, inviting him to explore the most tender parts of his soul, and expect that your relationship with him will leave him unchanged. But this has come as a surprise. I did not expect to intrude so early, and by utter accident. What is at stake in his belief that the Nongoloza myth is true? How important is it to his understanding of his past and the preservation of his dignity? I cannot let this question of dates pass; the historical Nongoloza will be there in the book.

*

The following morning, a Friday morning – our fourth interview. I tell Magadien there is an historian called Charles van Onselen, that he has written a biography of Nongoloza.

'This Van Onselen,' Magadien asks, 'is he a white man?'

I tell him that in 1912 Nongoloza told the story of his life to a white warder and that the story was transcribed and then lodged in the Director of Prisons Annual Report, that it was one of Van Onselen's primary sources. I take a copy of Nongoloza's statement out of my bag, together with a copy of Van Onselen's book, and hand it to him.

He takes it, gets on his hands and knees, and files it among the carefully ordered papers under his bed. He sits down again and waits for me to proceed.

Nongoloza was born in 1867, I tell him, on a white man's farm; he worked for two white farmers before disappearing to Johannesburg to skirt an unjust debt; he learned the art of highway robbery from four white employers who lived in Turfontein. I get as far as 1912, when Nongoloza disavows the Ninevites and agrees to become a warder.

He has been listening expressionlessly. Now he interrupts me. 'Let me tell you something. I have heard your story now. Number one, I want you to remember one thing – that is Van Onselen's story. He is a white man. There are a lot of white men in his story. In our story, there are no whites. In his story, there is no Kilikijan, no Grey, no Magubane, no wise man. It can't be true. In our story,

Nongoloza refuses to read or write. He refuses to learn English or Afrikaans. He refuses to look a white man in the eye. Now you tell me he worked for white farmers, then learned crime from white men, then wrote his story for white men. In our camp, there was a guy who spoke to the whites. His name was Mtjoetjies. Nongoloza killed him because we did not trust him speaking to whites. That's why his post lies empty. We do not negotiate with whites because Nongoloza didn't.

'And how did we come to two hundred years ago, Van Onselen to a hundred years ago? I don't understand. There is the black man's story and the white man's story. Go to any prison in this country, you will hear the black man's story – exactly the same in every prison. You go there with Van Onselen's story, they will kill you. Serious. How can you say Nongoloza spoke to a white man?

'You can go and ask Mr Jansen,' he says, appealing now to an entirely different genre of authority. 'When he took me to Ladismith to talk to the community, people came to him after my speech and asked if what I said was true. He said, "Ja, it's all true."'

*

Saturday and Sunday pass, and we do not see each other. We have arranged to meet on Monday morning at ten o'clock.

I am forbidden to walk through the interior of the prison alone. To get to my meeting with Magadien, I must wait at the entrance for a warder and ask him to accompany me. Monday mornings are slow. There are few people about. It is 10.25 by the time I get to his cell.

I find him sitting on his bed, playing anxiously with his fingers.

'Sorry I'm late,' I say. 'I couldn't find anyone to take me here.'

'Either you must say it's not your fault,' he snaps, 'or you must say you are sorry. You can't say both.'

He checks himself as he issues his reproach. By the time he has finished speaking, he has a chastened grin on his face. There is an awkward silence.

'I write poems,' he says finally. 'There was this woman who came to see me, a white woman, some sort of NGO person. She took every poem I had ever written – I had been collecting them for years. She was supposed to bind them for me. She vanished off the face of the earth.

'She was a divorcée. She had to support her children. I supported her through her crisis. Then she met another guy. We weren't in love or anything. I was just helping her. She vanished with my poems.'

'What were they about?'

'In 1999, a tornado destroyed our house in Manenberg. For a whole week, I didn't know whether my sons were alive or dead. The telephones were down. And I was safely behind these solid walls. It nearly drove me mad. I wrote about that.

'There were poems about my dad, about love, about my heart; poems about my change, about the people who helped me through my change. She was meant to put them in a spiral binding.

'I've lost a lot of trust. I've had bad experiences.'

It is clear to both of us that he is talking about me too; he wants to erase the things he has just implied. 'You are the only one so far, you are not like the others. You are comfortable in my presence. There are no warders with us: you sit alone with me. With the others, they think I am a threat to them. With you, I can be myself. I can joke with you, I can be serious with you. You ask questions, I ask questions. We both educate ourselves. It inspires me; I've never experienced it before.'

He is expressing a hope, rather than a statement of fact, and the ambiguity of what he has said sits with me. I have brought him Nongoloza's 1912 statement. In doing so, am I taking something away from him, something akin to poetry? Or am I helping to deliver him from a world he wishes to leave behind?

'I'll try not to anger you again,' I say, 'with a white man's stories about Nongoloza.'

'No, no, no,' he protests. 'It fascinated me. You came with this story about Nongoloza, about what the white man thought about Nongoloza. He is meant to be a historian, but he came with his own perceptions. We are not historians: we are members of the camp. We were prepared to die for that history. If I am willing to die, I should know the history. I can't die for Van Onselen's version. We hated the white people. I don't think Nongoloza would be remembered and revered around prisoners if this white man is right. You are an intelligent guy; you can think for yourself. How can millions of people have been prepared to sacrifice their lives for that history? If I go into the courtyard now and tell people Nongoloza was involved with whites, I'll be stabbed. I can prove it to you. I can go and do it right now.'

'Do you not think,' I ask, 'that there can be a difference between a man's real life and his life as an idea? The Number's version might not be strictly true, but it is there to inspire. It is there for what it says about South Africa.'

'There are old guys,' he replies, 'some of them can't see straight, some of them are blind, some are crippled. But they all have the same version of the story. I've been to many prisons in my life, experienced lots of different cultures – Xhosa, Tswana, Sotho. They all have the same version. So I can't understand the white man's version.

'Let me tell you something about white historians. The Rastafarians say Jesus wore dreadlocks. The whites say no, he had straight brown hair, like a white man. Then I come and ask my questions. I ask, "Did any of these historians see Jesus?" No. "At that time, did they have shampoo, did they have combs and brushes?" No. How could he comb his hair? When a white man washes his hair and doesn't comb it, it knots and bundles. The Rastafarians are right. Van Onselen is like the preachers; it's like he's trying to say that Nongoloza had straight brown hair.'

I begin speaking about something, but he interrupts me. He is not finished.

'Van Onselen is fucking with something very fucking important. You look at Shaka's history, you look at Piet Retief, at Jan van Riebeeck. This is history people believe. It is like a power. People are prepared to die for their stories.'

*

For the remainder of the week, we do not talk about Van Onselen; we become absorbed in other things – his childhood in District Six, the Mekkas, the Sampsons. He makes just one oblique reference to the documents I have given him; he asks if he can borrow a highlighter. 'To underline the parts that are important,' he tells me.

Then I leave Cape Town and go back to my home in Johannesburg. I return three weeks later, and our daily ritual resumes. I arrive at 10 o'clock every weekday morning; we talk until noon. A week goes by, and again neither of us mentions Nongoloza's 1912 statement.

By now, I have heard about a dozen inmate accounts of Nongoloza's story, including Magadien's. I ask him if we can revisit a couple of things, a few places in the narrative I find confusing.

'We can do that if you want,' he replies, 'but after reading that 1912 statement, and Van Onselen, I am not sure what is the truth. That statement from the archive makes sense to me. It is Nongoloza. I've spoken to a lot of guys, shown it to a few guys. They don't feel great about it. But I'd be stupid to deny it. Facts are facts.

'So ja, I will do what you ask and tell you more about Nongoloza and Kilikijan. But you must know it doesn't make me happy to talk about it, because it's not the truth.'

'Why is it so important that it is literally true?' I ask. 'Everybody tells stories about their own history that aren't literally true, but it doesn't make those stories valueless. You joined the 28s because you believed in what they stood for, because it made sense in the context of your life, in the context of the South Africa you grew up in. Why must the Nongoloza story be exactly true?'

He bows his head into his chest and sighs deeply. When he begins to speak there is anger in his voice.

'It means fuck all to you,' he says. 'For you, this is just a bunch of prisoners telling interesting stories. Let me tell you a little secret. You came with those documents, and I put them under my bed. I left them there for nearly a month. You know why? You know why I buried them there? Because I was scared. I was scared to see what they said.

'How can I make you understand? For 25 years, I dedicated my life to the Number. I treated my family like shit. I hurt people. I made babies and then fucked off, leaving their mothers to take care of them. I have children who barely know what I look like. I took a shot at my own mother, for fuck's sake.

'And what for? Because I believed in this fucking story. I believed in it enough to destroy my life.

'And now you come with your documents. They say that what thousands and thousands of prisoners have staked their lives for is a stupid joke. We have all been idiots. Nongoloza became a fucking warder.

'So you ask why it is so important that the story is true. You shouldn't need to ask. You should know.'

*

I leave the prison that day feeling hollow and unhappy. In writing this book, I have used the words 'I' and 'me'. 'I say to Magadien ...' 'Magadien tells me ...' As if we are equals. We are not. The relationship between a journalist and his subject is never a relationship between equals. The 'I' in the pages of the book the journalist pens is not a flesh-and-blood being with a soul to be bared and a heart to be scorched. He is a cipher, an abstraction; he is a pair of eyes that sees all. The subject, on the other hand, the 'Magadien', he is the one with bared soul and scorched heart. The 'I' is capable of doing him violence.

'This is not what you expected,' I say to Magadien a few days later.

'What do you mean?'

'Why were you so keen to have a book written about your life? When we met, it was like you had been waiting for years for me to come along. And when do I arrive, it's not what you thought. I make you into a fool. I bring these documents that make you feel like an idiot.'

He sighs deeply and shakes his head. 'No,' he says. 'It is now that you are making me a fool. Not a fool, but a little baby. You are the one who came here with stupid ideas. You thought you could get me to tell my story without causing me pain. Are you mad? How can I talk to you about my life without feeling pain? I wait for ten o'clock, and I think, "Jesus, what is he going to ask me now? Is he going to ask me something, something important, and I will have forgotten?"

'You know what conclusion I came to last night? I told myself, if I hadn't been so fucking angry all the time, if I hadn't been such a rude, negative bastard for 25 years, I would have been more observant, I would actually remember my life. Even a lot of inmates here remember me from the old days, and only after we start talking, I begin to remember. I feel I am losing something. I am afraid. The more my memory goes, the more my life goes.

'So, ja, every time you come into this cell, I am scared, scared to find that I haven't been there for most of my life, scared that you will have discovered something about me I can't afford to remember. But you know what? I'm a guy who speaks his mind. If I didn't want it, I would have thrown you out long ago. I would have said: "Jonny, it's been great, you're a great guy, but this is fucking me up. We must stop. Thanks for your time."

'I need my memory back. I need to remember. I even need to know about the real Nongoloza. That's why I haven't told you to fuck off.'

'The things you say you need from me, you need from a counsellor or a therapist, not a writer. I …'

'I have seen a lot of counsellors and therapists. I saw a therapist from the University of Cape Town. It was good. He said any time I think I need therapy, I must phone him. I haven't phoned him. With you, I have gone further. I say and think things with you that I can't with counsellors. I have chosen you because you are good for me. Can you understand that? I have chosen you.'

'I'm writing a book, for fuck's sake. I am sharing your pain with the world.'

'You are treating me like a fool again,' he says. 'You know what? I want to write a book about my life, but I can't. I can't because it's too fucking painful. I need you here. I need you to take me to the man I used to be. I can't get there myself. And the result is that it's your book, not mine. That is the price I am paying. If I was writing this book, it would be so fucking different from your book, people would read them both and think this isn't even the same human being who's being written about.'

'I'm not sure you know what you're saying. Only when you've read it in black and white will you know what it means for someone to write a book about you.'

'Do me a favour. Shut up and write your book. Stop saying Magadien this, and Magadien that. It's giving me a headache. Just write the fucking book. Do it from your heart. Make it true to how you have experienced me. Do that, and I will be proud of you.'

I shut up. The subject had dusted off his most eloquent words and shut the 'I' up. But he had, of course, told the 'I' precisely what every 'I' wants to hear. He had assuaged my bad conscience, had given me licence to scorch his heart and open his soul. The victory was mine, not his, and it left me feeling no less anxious than before.

*

'When I went back to Johannesburg after my last visit,' I tell him a few days later, 'I imagined you sitting here in your cell reading Nongoloza's 1912 statement, and I wondered whether you were struck by the similarities between your change and Nongoloza's change. It seems that Nongoloza had his own Mr Jansen.'

'I noticed,' he replies. 'I thought about it, and then after a while, I didn't want to think about it any more.'

In truth, it is not possible to know precisely what prompted Nongoloza to pour his life story into a white warder's notebook in 1912, nor why he subsequently turned on the Ninevites and joined the prisons service. It is not just that the documentation is scant; it is also suspect. A bandit king spilling his confessions to his captor – the very spectacle is pregnant with the concealed and the unspoken. There can be little doubt that the complexity of his motives lies buried between the lines of his confession.

Yet if Nongoloza did indeed have his own Mr Jansen, it was the figure of Jacob de Villiers Roos, a Renaissance man with an extraordinary breadth of erudition and interests, who was appointed Director of Prisons in the Transvaal in 1908. Roos was 39 when he began his term at the helm of the prisons service. By then, he had established his name as a journalist, a cultural historian and a leading attorney. He had been a correspondent covering the Anglo-Boer War of 1899-1902 for Reuters; had collaborated with Gustav Preller, an early Afrikaner nationalist whose project was to transform Afrikaans from a parochial dialect into a written language; and had established himself as a respected scholar of early Dutch settlements in the Cape.

In his new role as Director of Prisons, Roos embarked on a campaign of penal reform, and the changes he shepherded were to affect Nongoloza's experience of prison profoundly. The previous prison administration had tried to beat the bandit king into submission; between July 1900 and September 1904, he received 160 lashes. Under Roos, the lashes stopped. In 1910, Nongoloza was placed in isolation. Roos hand-picked a white warder with fluent Zulu – a certain Warder Paskin – to take sole charge of Nongoloza.

Who knows precisely what happened between the bandit and the warder in the quiet of Nongoloza's cell? 'Making skilful use of [Paskin's] linguistic gifts,' Charles van Onselen speculates, 'Roos gradually proceeded to replace isolation with enquiry, deprivation with dialogue and lashing with listening … Nongoloza, accustomed to fighting on the more familiar terrain of vengeance and violence, lost his footing on the softer ground of sympathy and then, on 27 December 1912, collapsed completely.' He called on Paskin to translate a statement to Roos, the statement that lay unread under Magadien's bed for nearly a month.

'You say that as I was responsible for the organisation which spread my name throughout South Africa, I must say how the organisation should be broken up,' Nongoloza said near the beginning of his statement. 'I do not know. The former [pre-Roos] administration tried to do it by harshness and failed. We were lashed and starved and still the Nineveh flourished. We swore to maintain it at all costs. We even passed a sentence of death on the former director of prisons and had he come among us in the yards he most certainly would have died. But the new law and the new administration have made me change my heart. Many times I have had murder in my heart and wanted to spring at the officer with a knife, but that is past.'

And then, Van Onselen tells us, 'in a classic switch familiar to observers of human behaviour in total institutions, Nongoloza indicated his willingness to work as a warder for the new prison administration.'

Magadien would have to be blind not to see his own image in Nongoloza's story. He too was 'lashed and starved' year in and year out, and his identification with the 28s only grew stronger. And then, out of nowhere, came the gentle head warder, Johnny Jansen, who banished the batons and attack dogs from his prison, and seduced Magadien with his humanity. The veteran 28, who believed he had become a man long ago by stabbing, was flung back into boyhood, and knelt gratefully at the feet of his new father.

There is something else about Nongoloza's statement that must have struck Magadien. 'The attraction of the Nineveh organisation to the natives is that they have tasted the benefits of combination in theft and robbery,' the bandit dictated to Warder Paskin. 'With no work they succeed when out of prison in a short time amassing quite a lot in the proceeds of robbery. Of course, they are ignorant and have not yet learned the lesson which I have. Here was I with bags of money, the proceeds of the robbery of my gang, and today getting old in prison, when I might have had a wife with growing sons and cattle for my old age in Zululand.'

Magadien, too, was entering middle age when he met Johnny Jansen, and the nihilism of his life was eating at him. It was Jansen who unearthed Magadien's buried yearning for 'a wife with growing sons and cattle for my old age' – his desire to retrieve his family. Presumably, like Magadien, Nongoloza also dreamed of retrieving his name – Mzuzephi Mathebula.

So I ask Magadien if Nongoloza reminds him of himself; he says he thought about it, and then after a while, didn't want to think about it any more. Why not?

'I am just an ordinary member of the 28s,' he says. 'Nongoloza was the founder, the king. If I turn my back on the camp it is one thing. But if the founder betrayed us right at the very beginning, we are bullshit, just a laughing stock.'

Perhaps it is Magadien's residual loyalty to the 28s that makes Nongoloza's betrayal unthinkable. But I suspect there is something else behind the uneasiness with which he greets the prospect of identifying with the founder, an uneasiness that would have grown as he read the final chapters of Van Onselen's book.

If Nongoloza did indeed harbour a dream of growing old with a wife, children and cattle, he failed miserably. After working with the prison authorities for three years, he announced his desire to retire to a peaceful old age. The government duly bought him a small plot of land in Swaziland. This tranquillity lasted six years; in 1923, out of the blue, Nongoloza expressed a desire to return to the Witwatersrand. He was given a job as an orderly at Weskoppies Mental Hospital in Pretoria. His return to the metropolis proved a disaster. He habitually stole vegetables from the mental hospital's garden and bartered them for dagga and alcohol; in the Pretoria township of Marabastad, he robbed workers of their wages at the side of the road.

Eager to humour and protect their most famous convert, the authorities sent him away from trouble to the sticks – to a remote diamond mine in the Free State – where he served as a compound policeman. After two years there, he was convicted of raping a young woman and found himself back in prison.

Thus Nongoloza's life went until he was well into his seventies – an irascible old security guard with his nightwatchman's knobkerrie and his ill-temper, drifting from one lowly job to another, barking out instructions to his superiors as if he was still king of the underworld. Just as his name was becoming legend in every prison in the country, he died an anonymous death in Pretoria in 1948, having spent the last two years of his life wandering the streets of Marabastad.

'When nobody came forward to claim the body,' Van Onselen tells us, 'the state arranged for a normal pauper's funeral ... [He] was buried in shared grave number 1438, in Native Section D of Pretoria's Rebecca Street Cemetery.'

Magadien and I do not discuss the final chapters of Nongoloza's life, but they must weigh heavily on him. Is his own path from the 28s to end like this? His greatest dread is that he long ago lost the resources to retrieve his family and his name. Beyond the 28s, he fears, there is a lonely death and a pauper's burial.

15
MARRIED LIFE

Shortly before midnight on 9 December 1988, Nelson Mandela was taken from Pollsmoor Prison, where he had spent the preceding four years, driven to the quiet Boland town of Paarl, and ushered into the grounds of Victor Verster Prison, where Magadien and 1 500 other inmates lay sleeping. 'We drove across [the prison's] entire length,' Mandela recalls in his autobiography, 'and then along a winding dirt road through a rather wild, wooded area at the rear of the property. At the end of the road we came to an isolated one-storey whitewashed cottage set behind a concrete wall and shaded by tall fir trees.' Mandela was to spend the following 14 months in that cottage, which was furnished with a chef, a swimming pool and a collection of fine Western Cape wines, before he was released into freedom before an audience of a billion television viewers.

A few weeks earlier, Magadien had been among a team of prisoners who renovated the cottage and slapped on its new coat of paint. It was only in early 1989, when the government announced that Mandela had been moved from Pollsmoor to Victor Verster, that he and his fellow inmates discovered that they had been preparing the final prison home of South Africa's most famous son.

Magadien tells me none of this. I discovered it incidentally, when interviewing a 28 who had shared a cell with him at that time. That he served his Victor Verster sentence during one of the most momentous periods in South African history – the beginnings of the transition to democracy – seems to have passed him by. He was, instead, distracted by the somewhat arcane matter of the war between the gold and silver lines of 28s, and by the gang's scandalous new initiation ritual: the making of bandit-recruits into women.

By the time Mandela was released in February 1990, Magadien had been transferred to the small, countryside prison of Allendale. I try to draw out his recollections of that day, but he is reluctant.

'Most of the warders were sent to Victor Verster on the morning Mandela was released,' he recalls, 'and with the prison understaffed, we were locked in our cells the whole day. When the staff came back in the evening, the coloured warders were very excited. They started telling us everything that happened, in every detail. It was weird. It was like there was this bond between coloured warders and coloured inmates – as if to say, "On this day, we share something, because we have the same colour skin." So, ja, in retrospect something special was happening, but at the time, we didn't make a hype of it. We weren't a part of it. It was still not the end of apartheid.'

It is hard to believe that Magadien's indifference to Mandela's release was representative of prisoners in general. Vincent Shabangu, for instance, was serving his final months in Helderstroom Prison at the time, and he vividly remembers the heady euphoria and messianic expectations of the inmates around him.

'A few days before Mandela was released,' Shabangu told me, 'the prisoners at Helderstroom began preparing for their own release. They literally thought that when the old man walks free, the prison doors would fall down. The authorities called me and pleaded that I speak to the gangs and explain to them that they were staying inside. They were worried that there would be riots the day after Mandela's release.

'I went to the gangs and I explained to them: "Remember, you didn't commit the same crime Mandela did." They started shouting me down. They said we are all here because of apartheid. I said, "Ja, but he committed crimes against the state, you against other human beings. There's where the difference is. Once you make peace with that, you will realise that your time to be released will come." They moaned and groaned and said it was all bullshit.'

Magadien was released from Allendale in September 1990, seven months after Mandela walked out of Victor Verster. By then, the leaders of the African National Congress had come home after nearly thirty years in exile, and negotiations for a democratic dispensation were under way. It was a magical time. The repressive machinery of the apartheid state was locked away, for the moment, and the violence that was almost to derail the transition had not yet erupted. It was a brief, unrepeatable period of delight.

'When you got out of jail,' I ask Magadien, 'was the outside world different at all?'

'Maybe for others,' he replies caustically. 'Although there was a moment after I was released when I thought, apartheid is dying, now is the time to start over again. But what had changed, really? If I had tried to get a job with my own ID document, people would have turned me away. I was still a criminal. I still had to live a lie. So I did what I had always done: I got a false ID and looked for work, with the intention of stealing again.'

If history was passing Magadien by it is, in part, because the war of the 28s at Victor Verster had rattled him. He was 30 years old now. During the course of his twenties he had entered and re-entered the gates of the Western Cape's prisons with relish, thoroughly seduced by the brotherhood behind the bars. Now, after what he had seen at Victor Verster, he felt the first dull jab of disenchantment. For the first time in his life, he began, inchoately, to imagine himself somewhere in the future. The children he had sired barely knew him. His mother was a stranger long turned hostile. The 28s, he dimly feared, were not a family in which one invests one's middle age. He thought often of the day Serfontein had dumped him penniless in the backwater town of Graafwater, when he had imagined the rest of his days wandering the streets as a stroller.

*

The ten months he was to spend on the outside were crazy, unhinged and horribly unhappy. They began, on the first night of his freedom, with a new woman.

Her name was Elizabeth Booysen. She was a seasonal contract worker on Paarl's wine farms who supported her parents and siblings by picking grapes during the harvesting season. Magadien had met her a few months earlier, in the vineyards, during his incarceration.

'While I was at Allendale Prison,' he tells me, 'a whole team of us was taken to Koelenhof Prison in Paarl. They were closing the prison down and we went there to clear it out. While we were there, there was panic among the farmers in the area. It was harvest time and they did not have enough labour. They had always used Koelenhof inmates to pick their grapes, and now the prison was gone. They complained that their grapes were rotting. So drafts of us were sent to the farms. That's where I met her. She was a seasonal worker in the vineyards.

'At first, the women in the fields were afraid of us inmates. So we coaxed them, relaxed them, and finally they would have lunch with us every day. I behaved like a gentleman with her. Because I was a criminal and a 28, she expected that I would want to go into the fields with her to have sex. I could see her weighing it up in her mind – whether to have sex with me in this way. "No," I said to her. "If we ever make love, it must be under the sheets, at home." She was charmed. She never expected a prison gangster to treat her like that.'

When the grapes were harvested, Magadien went back to Allendale Prison. A week after his return, he was informed that he had a visitor. He went into the reception room and found Elizabeth sitting alone at a table, cradling a bunch of grapes she had brought for him. They sat and talked and ate grapes. It was not unlike many of his previous seductions – long, measured periods of patient courting – longer, in fact, than the relationships that were to ensue.

When he was released in September 1990, he found her waiting for him at the prison gate. She took him to her home in a poverty-stricken township near Kraaifontein, on the north-eastern outskirts of Cape Town.

'She did everything properly,' Magadien recalls. 'She introduced me to her parents in a very dignified way.'

But the meeting did not go well.

'Her parents were drinkers. The whole family drank heavily. She was the only sober one among them. She was the breadwinner. Everyone else sat around at home and shouted at each other. So her parents hated me from the minute they laid eyes on me. They were worried that I was going to take her away, and that they would be left without income. They wanted to throw me out the house, but they couldn't.'

He spent the night with Elizabeth in her room, the only bedroom in the Booysen home. The rest of the family slept in the lounge, and outside in the yard.

'While I was sleeping next to their daughter,' he says, 'her parents were dreaming of putting knives in my back.'

The following morning Magadien did what he always does the

day after he is released from prison; he caught a train to Cape Town and went to visit his mother, his foster-mother, his sister Anne, and his foster-brother John.

'I always visit everyone the day after I am released, just to see that everyone is still alive, and to tell them that I am still alive. I don't want to ever find out by accident that my mother is dead. They were always pleased to see me, always welcomed me with open arms, especially Annie and Anne. What confused them is why I always went back to prison again. They would say: "We are here for you. Settle down. Behave yourself. There's no reason to go back." They didn't understand why I had to go back to prison. I didn't understand myself. I could have started living a normal life any time, with Annie and Anne supporting me. I just didn't have the head for it. So I nodded and smiled, and I was pleased to see them, but only for a few hours. Then I left.'

Not everyone was pleased to see him. Gadija was nonplussed when her son arrived at her doorstep. She greeted him coolly and offered him a cup of tea. An hour later, he told her he had to get going; she barely managed to conceal her relief.

That night, he returned to Elizabeth in Kraaifontein. He had not gone to Manenberg to see Faranaaz, nor to Mitchells Plain to see his daughter Glynnis, nor to the Strand to see Noes.

He stayed with Elizabeth in her poisonous, overcrowded household for three months. 'Some of the time she supported me, even though she couldn't afford to. For the rest, I got a casual job making bricks at a place on the Cape Flats. The project was run by Nicro [a social support organisation for ex-convicts]. So I didn't need a false ID. In fact, being an ex-convict was a stipulation of the job. When that job finished, I packed my bags and left.'

'Why?' I ask.

He shrugs. 'At the bricklaying place, there was a shed with this old cupboard. I looked through it and found an old ID book. So I thought to myself: "Here we go. I'm on the road again." I had an ID-size picture taken of myself, stuck it in the ID book, put it in my pocket and left Elizabeth to look for a job. I don't even remember the name in that ID book; I've been through so many.'

'You abandoned Elizabeth, just like that?'

He shrugs again. 'What was I going to do in a poverty-stricken household in the middle of nowhere? There was no work there, nothing for me to do. It wasn't a match made in heaven.'

So Magadien left Kraaifontein with his stolen ID book to look for a job. He went back to the Cape Flats, but not to his mother and her husband Victor in Heideveld, nor to Annie and Quinton in Hanover Park; he went to Faranaaz in Manenberg, and, in a moment of absent-mindedness, he married her.

'It kind of happened by accident,' he explains. 'When I arrived at the Benjamins' doorstep, Faranaaz wasn't pleased to see me. I had been out of prison more than three months, and instead of going to her and Johaah, I went to this other woman in Kraaifontein. Now I suddenly wanted to be with her.'

By now, Faranaaz had two sons: Johaah, who was five; and Jumat, who was a few months old. Johaah's father was dead; Jumat's father had recently been jailed for murder.

'I said to Faranaaz: "You are my woman. And you are bringing up two boys without a man. They need a father. If they are under my roof, I will love them as my own."'

It is a promise he would keep, but only many years later.

'She could have told me to go away and never come back. But that's something she never did, no matter how much of a bastard I was. She really wanted me, badly. She'd put herself through serious punishment to keep me. So I moved in, and instead of throwing me out, she sulked. She nearly drove me mad with her sulking. I started getting pissed off with her. I had an affair with her niece who lived just down the road. Word got out around Manenberg: "This *poes* is living with a woman, but fucking her niece." She was humiliated. She threw things at me and swore at me. But still, she didn't throw me out. Instead, she said: "There's only one way to fix this. Marry me."

'It felt right. At least it felt right the afternoon she said it to me. I liked the idea of being a father to her children. I smoked buttons with her father in the yard. Her family adored me: why, I don't know, because I was behaving like a *poes* with their daughter. So I said: "Fine: you want me to marry you, I will marry you."'

The night before the wedding, he drove to the Strand to see Colleen. 'That's how the marriage started. I was unfaithful to her a few hours before the wedding. I had only been out of prison a few months, and already I'd slept with three different women in three different parts of Cape Town. Marriage? What the fuck did I think I was doing?'

And that's how Magadien's lifelong entanglement with Faranaaz began. When he met Johnny Jansen eight years later and took the dramatic decision to renounce the 28s and gather a family around him, Faranaaz was nominally his wife. Among the chaotic web of entanglements that constituted his life, she happened to be the most recent; she was there – the woman he had married in a fit of wildness. In 1998, in the visitor's room at Pollsmoor Prison, he tried to explain to her that he needed to spend the rest of his life with her and her sons, that his sanity depended on it. Like every other member of his family to whom he tried to explain what Jansen had done to him, she stared at him in disbelief.

*

It pleased Magadien that he was marrying as a Muslim man, to a Muslim woman. 'The wedding was at the Benjamins' house in Manenberg,' he tells me. 'The ceremony was at the mosque across the street. There were a lot of people there, a big wedding for a poor family. My in-laws were delighted. They loved me from the moment Faranaaz's father brought me home after that soccer game on the field opposite their house. In their eyes I could do no wrong. There was only one person who was not there. A few weeks before the wedding I went to see my mother with Faranaaz. I got them to chat, to relax with each other. And then I invited her to the wedding. I told her I knew we'd been through shit, but this was my wedding.

'She didn't come.

'And then I fucked off. A week after the wedding I disappeared. And I didn't come back for four years.'

*

By the time he and Faranaaz married, Magadien had used the identity document he found at the brickworks to get a job. He was, of all things, a travelling salesman.

'It was me and two other guys. We sold everything, everywhere. Glasses, plates, duvets, sheets – everything for housewives. We sold the merchandise out of a catalogue. Every day, we'd spend the whole fucking day on the road, going into suburbs and knocking on doors to talk to housewives. We went everywhere, from rich white areas to the Cape Flats townships, out into the small towns in the Boland. I was quite good at it. I don't remember the name of the company we worked for. But when we arrived back at the office, they were very happy with us. I could sell the whole fucking catalogue in a week.

'One day, about a week after I married Faranaaz, we were out in Stellenbosch. The two guys I was with were drinkers. Whenever we made a few sales, they would find a pub wherever we were and drink. I wasn't drinking at that time. I'd just married a Muslim and was living in a Muslim household. So I stayed in the car and listened to music. Sitting there in the car, I got very pissed off. I thought to myself: "What the fuck are you doing walking door to door every day, selling duvets out of a catalogue? Are you fucking crazy?" I started the car and drove off, and I didn't come back.

'First I went to visit an old girlfriend in Stellenbosch. Then I drove to Kraaifontein to say hi to Elizabeth. By evening I was driving into the Strand, on my way to Colleen. As I entered the Strand I realised what I was doing and why. I wasn't just running away from my job as a travelling salesman. I was running away from Faranaaz. You see, I had a stolen car now, and I couldn't go back to Manenberg.'

*

Looking through the car's cubby hole outside Colleen's house that night, he found an identity document. It belonged to his boss, or his former boss at any rate; his name was William Steenkamp.

'I had plenty of IDs by then, but this one was perfect. It had endorsements for a driver's licence and a gun licence. And Steenkamp was white, ja, but it isn't impossible for a coloured to be called William Steenkamp. So when I looked for my next job I did it with this ID. And that's how I got stuck with this fucking name. I was charged as Steenkamp in my last sentence. So every day here in Pollsmoor it's "William this and William that." It's not me. It's just a reminder that I fucked up my life.'

At the time, though, it was extremely useful. A few days after settling in with Colleen, he went out to look for a job. 'William Steenkamp' worked wonders; by evening, he was employed again.

He was a security guard once more, this time at a company called Armour Guard. His longest experience as a private guard, during the uprisings of the mid-1980s, had not, you will recall, been a happy one. Overcome by boredom and listlessness, he had stolen a cheque book and used it flagrantly and carelessly, as if he willed capture and a return to jail. Why did he decide to go through it all again in 1991, especially since getting caught once more and returning to the 28s was a prospect he now greeted with ambivalence? At the age of 31, his life, it seems, had reached a cul de sac. He was retracing paths he knew from experience led nowhere. Perhaps this is why he had taken the strange and wilful decision to marry Faranaaz; perhaps it was a fitful trial run. It was not long before he would realise, quite consciously, that if he was going to negotiate his way into middle age at all, it would have to be in the form of a very different kind of life.

In any event, he was now an old hand at defrauding his employers; even if the life was beginning to haunt him, he played it like a master this time round.

One of his first assignments was to guard a construction site in Bellville South, a few kilometres from the UWC campus. His job was to stand in front of the skeleton of what was going to become a warehouse from mid-afternoon until midnight. The manager of the construction site was a white man by the name of Mr Perel.

One afternoon, manna fell from heaven. Magadien was alone, at the entrance to the warehouse, and a courier arrived with new credit and debit cards for Mr Perel, complete with secret pin numbers. Magadien immediately took receipt of the cards and signed for them in the assistant manager's name.

'Jesus, I drained that guy,' he recalls. 'I bought clothes, a tape recorder, gold rings, a watch for every day. Mr Perel reported his card stolen, and I re-opened it. By then, I had his home address, his ID number, his date of birth and his passport number. I phoned the bank and told them I was Mr Perel and that the card hadn't been stolen after all. It was just a question of putting on a white accent. The bank was incredibly stupid. It took a long time in those days to replace stolen credit cards, so I had a good two weeks while Mr Perel thought his new cards were being processed. All that time, I was still working at the warehouse, on time every day, so it was not obvious to anybody that I was the guilty party.

'I got to work. I went to all the wholesale stores on the N2. I bought running shoes in bulk – Nikes, Hightechs, all the best brands – sports clothes as well, and started selling them for next to nothing in the Strand. I did 215 transactions on that card in 12 days. When Mr Perel's credit account ran out, I transferred money from his savings account.

'I'm not sure if I would have gotten caught if I hadn't have chosen the wrong business partners. There were these two guys in Colleen's street in the Strand. One of them was called Jake Williams. They were unemployed; they stood on the corner every day doing nothing. Every time I walked past them on my way to work I thought to myself, these lazy cunts could be making money for me.

'So I said to them: "Listen here. There is no food shop in this part of the township. And I have lots of money. If we start selling food here, we'll make a killing." So I took them to the Checkers warehouse to buy stock, to the Pick 'n Pay warehouse to buy stock, and we started a nice little food shop. They ran it. So I could go out every day, to go to work at the construction site, to sells sports shoes, and my little investment would be ticking over.

'They became greedy and sold me out. They didn't like sharing the profits with me. It didn't seem to dawn on them that without me there'd be no fucking merchandise. We went to Checkers to buy stock. I went in; they waited in the car. While I was inside, they went to a payphone and called the store manager. They told him: "Listen, someone is about to buy a shitload of food from you with a stolen credit card. Here's the credit card number." When I got to the till I was arrested. In the mean time, they disappeared with the car and all the goods in the car. The car was full; we had just come from Pick 'n Pay. I was charged with fraud.

'When the cops got hold of the credit card record later that day, their eyes nearly popped out of their heads; 215 transactions in 12 days. A whole lot of very serious people came to visit me in prison; a detective from the organised crime unit, another detective who they flew down from Pretoria. They said to me: "This is a lot of stuff. You didn't do this on your own. This is organised crime."

'They wanted to talk organised crime, I thought, fine, I'll talk the same language. I said, "Ja, I work for these big fuckers, and the bosses sold me out outside the Checkers warehouse." So, they said to me: "We'll make a deal with you. If you give us the names of the syndicate bosses, we'll make sure you're only charged for some of this stuff." I said, "Jesus, are you mad! They'll kill me. Do you think you can protect me from these people?"

'They kept coming back and demanding that I tell them who I

work for, and I kept telling them I would never do that. They said: "Fine, we are going to charge you for all 215 cases." I said: "No, I didn't do all this stuff myself. I am a poor man." So they gave me a list of all the cases and told me to point out which ones were me. I decided on 20. It seemed a nice figure. So we went down the list. I said: "Ja, I did this one, no not that one, not that one." I miscounted. It came to 21. I was sentenced to six-and-a-half years.'

16
A FUCKING MALAY

If history had passed Magadien by during his last spell in prison, it all caught up with him this time. He was in jail from 1991 to 1995, a period that coincided almost exactly with the brief and tumultuous interregnum between apartheid and democracy. It is a myth that being locked up in a cell insulates one from momentous events on the outside. On the contrary, total institutions like jails have a manic intensity that the diffuseness of ordinary life does not possess. Currents that filter in from the outside become hurricanes, turning the world upside down. During the four years Magadien spent inside, South Africa experienced the bloodiest prison riots in its history; he watched the people who had run the prisons for 40 years stumble and panic in the face of change; he witnessed the century-long institution of prison gangs sizing up the strange happenings around it, perplexed about its place in the new era.

In the tiny world of prison, where one shares every minute of one's life and every inch of one's space with a handful of strangers, everything political is transmogrified into the personal. One confronts societal change in the form of one's relationship with this warder, that gangster. Magadien's experience of the transition possessed a quiddity no history book will ever capture. By the time he was released, he had been shorn of most of the things he had taken for granted. For the first time in his life, he had to think in order to be.

*

His sentence began somewhat eccentrically, with an experience he had never in his life contemplated. After a few days in Pollsmoor, he and several dozen Western Cape prisoners were driven north, through the Karoo and across the Orange River, into the Free State province. They would spend the next month in Goedemoed Prison. He does not remember now why they were taken there, nor why the stay at Goedemoed was so short. In any event, it was the first time he had crossed the boundaries of the Western Cape, his first experience of a part of the world where there are no coloureds – only whites and Africans.

There had always been a small minority of Africans in the Number gangs of the Western Cape, but never enough to leave a significant legacy. For the most part, the 28s of the Western Cape were coloured men who had been inducted into a faux-Zulu cult. When they were initiated, they were informed that Nongoloza, their king and father, was a Zulu, and that from now on, they were Zulu too. Their emblem was a Zulu shield made from Rooiland's hide. They were told that when they had sex, they were young Zulu warriors taking part in an eternally premarital romp with their virgin Zulu brides. They knew that, back at the very beginning, Nongoloza had drunk poison and relished it, a tantalising allusion to some dimly imagined black magic which they too now possessed. They had, in essence, clothed themselves in exotica, in third-hand notions of a foreign and mystical culture.

Now, they walked into Goedemoed Prison and the 28s who ran the place were genuine Africans – the real thing. They were in for the shock of their lives.

'Let me tell you a secret I've never told anybody,' Magadien says to me. 'When I arrived there they *sabelaed* me – talked to me in prison language – I said ja, ja, but I didn't understand a fucking thing. But they understood every word we spoke. There was no Afrikaans in their *sabela*. It was three-quarters Zulu.'

Magadien's fears cut deep. Arriving at a strange prison is a delicate time for a *ndota*. Locked in a communal cell with a group of people he has never met, he is asked a simple question: 'Who are you?' How he replies determines his fate. If he is a 28, he must *sabela* a reply that he is Nongoloza, that he works by night. If the questioner is a 27, he will respond by declaring that he is Kilikijan, that he works by day. The two then run through the motions of a formulaic and well-rehearsed exchange, together describing the early history of Nongoloza and Kilikijan. The new arrival must use the right words and the right metaphors; everything hinges on his mastery of prison language. When Kilikijan is satisfied that the new man is a genuine child of Nongoloza, he delivers him to the

Draad of the 28s, who asks him the same question: 'Who are you?' Now that he is in his own camp, the new arrival must describe each rank in the 28s. 'The Glas blows his bugle, the Nyangi throws his pipes, the General sits with his back to the four points of one times …' He must describe every rank except his own; he identifies himself by his omission.

Magadien stumbled nervously through his identification ritual, feigning recognition of the words addressed to him. As he did so, he saw himself for the first time through the eyes of an African prison gangster; he was a traveller who had wandered in from some remote outpost in the colonies, bringing with him his half-baked, bastardised ways.

'I was okay. I pretended to understand, and I described the rank structure properly, and they accepted me. But there was someone else among us, another 28, who told them he was an Inspector. They didn't believe him. They told him he would have to prove his rank by stabbing a warder. It was all done the proper way. The Nyangi gave him the knife, and the Glas and Draad went with him, one on either side. When they reached the warder, he hesitated; he did not want to stab. So they took the knife and stabbed him. That's the proper way; it's what happens when you are dutied and you fail.

'Fortunately, it was not necessary for me to be active. My position at that point was Magistrate; I had been promoted from Landdros during the war at Victor Verster. There was already a Magistrate active in the 28s at Goedemoed, and you can't have two active Magistrates in one place. I was sent to the Forties, the Mambozas – the place where inactive *ndotas* sit when there is no work for them. We sat around and smoked dagga and *sabelaed* a bit, and talked. Usually, being in the Forties is a relaxing time. But I was not relaxed. I was on edge the whole time.'

He soon discovered something else about the 28s of the Free State. 'There had been no war between the gold and silver lines. The blood line was still open. They still had a Judge [the head of the gold line]. They still did things the proper way. I saw now that that terrible, corrupt war we had fought was a Western Cape thing, a coloured thing. Across the border, the 28s were still pure. They had never heard of this war that had changed all our lives, that had made us throw away the oldest and purest traditions.

'I was uncomfortable. I felt foreign. But I was also full of respect. The Number was real here.'

Although he does not say it to me in so many words, an old and painful story of self-denigration lies beneath his account of Goedemoed. Countless times, I have been told by Western Cape *ndotas* that the coloureds have tarnished the legacy of Nongoloza, that they have neither the depth nor the maturity to preserve the heritage bequeathed to them.

'Coloureds abused the power the Number gave them,' a veteran 27 told me. 'My people are ill-disciplined because we are mixed, because we have no past. We do not have things like clan loyalty.'

'The Zulus have their King Shaka,' another veteran *ndota* told me. 'The Swazis have their king. The Afrikaners have Jan van Riebeeck. What do we have? We don't even have our own language. So the Number was given to us, and we made it into a coloured thing. We fucked it up. Nongoloza must be turning in his grave. "Why did you give me to these fucking *hotnots* to look after? Look what they've done to me."'

Coloured men went into the Number dragging their cursed heritage behind them, an idea of themselves as a history-less people. The Number was meant to be an escape from that, an immersion in the sacredness of a real and tangible past. Seeing themselves through the eyes of African *ndotas*, they felt themselves to be frauds, leeching on a rich vein of other people's meanings, other people's histories.

It was not long before Magadien and his Western Cape peers descended into a state of ethnic paranoia.

'While we were at Goedemoed,' he tells me, 'something terrible happened to one of us. He was a *laaitie*, 18 years old, maybe, a *frans*. He was *hardegat*, a pure Capetonian. He got poisoned. It was horrible. Nobody knows exactly what happened to him. He became blue, his head swelled like a soccer ball, and then he died. It was black magic poison. I didn't see his dead body, but people who saw it say they vomited. He looked like some reptile. They say the blacks captured him and took his head. They dry it in the sun, make powder out of it and put it in their food.

'That prison, I don't want to see it again. I don't want it in my dreams. I don't want to think about it.'

The irony is pretty stark. He walked into Goedemoed a 28,

inheritor of an indigenous anti-colonial legacy. He left a deracinated man who had wandered into the warrens of savages.

On returning to Cape Town, he was relieved to be in the realm of the familiar again. But he had been robbed of some deep-seated illusions; he felt the heavy weight of his coloured skin like never before. It was somewhat serendipitous, as if his experience at Goedemoed was a preparation for the next significant encounter in his life; less than a month after returning to the Western Cape, he was to meet an unusual young coloured warder by the name of Basil Coetzee. Coetzee's project was to make coloured men feel proud: more than proud – superior.

*

Magadien spent a short time at Pollsmoor again and was then transferred to Paardeberg, another of the Western Cape's rural prisons. It sits at the edge of a postcard-pretty Boland valley: acres of green vineyard and whitewashed Cape Dutch farmhouses. On the road to the prison, you pass a faux-Huguenot B&B.

When Magadien arrived at Paardeberg early in 1992, he found strewn about him the debris of a recent war between the 26s and the 28s.

'They had taken the taps off the basins, broken tables and chairs. The place was a mess. A lot of *ndotas* were in hospital.

'The commanding officer of the 28s at Paardeberg at the time was an old friend of mine. His name is Paul. He had started all the shit. He started telling me why he had declared war against the 26s, but I lost concentration before he was finished. There were all these wars, people got their heads cut open, and a few months later, nobody remembered what it was about. It made me feel sick. I wasn't interested.

'The authorities didn't know that, though. My file said I was a *hardegat* 28, so they thought I'd fuel the war. They put me in the concrete cells in the Further Charges section, even though I wasn't on trial at the time, probably to keep me away from the main section of the prison. I was fine with that. I wanted some time to myself.

'But I wasn't there for long. There was a warder, Basil Coetzee. He took me out of Further Charges and made me recreation officer. That's when I started to calm down. He calmed me down. He was the first to do it. I have great respect for him.

'He actually calmed the whole fucking prison down. He took the highest-ranking 28, me, and the highest ranking 26, Gerald Moses, and he made us run the prison together. We kept the Number open, but there were no stabbings, complete quiet between us and the 26s for over a year. It was like he had performed a miracle. Looking back, I'd say that Coetzee was the beginning of my change, although I didn't know it then.'

Basil Coetzee is a stubborn, prickly man. He is living testimony to the fact that a person's looks often belie his character. His long, gently lined face appears preternaturally serene; when you begin conversing with him you realise that what you took for serenity is in fact the dogged stubbornness of a scorching contrarian. When I interviewed him in early 2003, he took issue with the terms of every question I put to him. Talking to him was like pulling teeth. He would stare accusingly at me, with that clear-eyed, indignant expression reserved for the self-righteous.

If and when he reads this book, the terminology I have used will blow his fuse. 'Why do you call the prisoners at Goedemoed Africans?' he would ask me sharply. 'We, the Khoi-Khoi, are the oldest people of southern Africa. Isn't it convenient that everyone seems to have forgotten that? And how dare you call us coloured. Coloured doesn't exist. It was invented by Europeans to make us forget where we come from. It is the greatest violence that has ever been done to us.'

Coetzee's mission at Paardeberg was breathtakingly ambitious and somewhat eccentric, but he executed it with genius. His task was to coax the gangsters in his charge into breaking with the ethos of the Number and to retrieve their lost ethnic pedigree. He wanted them to embrace the most maligned and ridiculed branch of coloured South Africans' heritage, to trace their ancestry to the Khoi-Khoi – the herders and pastoralists who had occupied the Western Cape peninsula when the Dutch established themselves there in the seventeenth century.

To understand the ambition of his project, you need only look a coloured prison gangster in the eye and call him a *hotnot*, the most offensive piece of racial invective one can hurl at a coloured person. It is a belittling mutilation of 'Hottentot' – a word first used in 1652 by Jan van Riebeeck to describe the Khoi-Khoi; it means 'stutterer' or 'stammerer', depicting a people so primitive they are incapable of human speech.

Seventeenth- and eighteenth-century European naturalists did not regard the Khoi-Khoi as part of humankind; they were, instead, beastlike creatures, stranded somewhere between apes and people. The early Dutch colony of the Cape, in turn, did not consider them juridical persons. They were tried, not by the Dutch colonial judiciary, but by their own leaders. It was also illegal to enslave them. The bulk of the colony's manual labour was imported via the transoceanic slave trade; between the mid-seventeenth and early nineteenth centuries, thousands upon thousands of slaves were imported from Mozambique, West Africa, Madagascar, India and Indonesia, adding innumerable layers to the Western Cape's polyglot heritage.

Yet, despite the law, early settlers on the periphery of the Cape colony enslaved the Khoi-Khoi anyway. 'By the sheer weight of their numbers, their horses and guns,' writes the historian Robert Shell, 'the burghers [of the Cape colony] first dispossessed, then enserfed and absorbed the Khoi-Khoi people into their households.' By the early nineteenth century, the Khoi-Khoi no longer existed as a distinctive people; they had been melted into the pot of Western Cape slavery, along with the descendants of the human chattels who had been imported from around the world.

In coloured working-class culture today, the word Khoi-Khoi provokes laughter and derision. 'When we learned about the Khoi-Khoi at school,' Magadien tells me, 'we called them *Strandlopers.' Strandloper* – another Western Cape word laden with a thousand connotations. It literally means 'beach walker', conjuring an image of a rootless people wandering the peninsula's coastline without aim. In the twentieth century, it found its way into James Joyce's novel, *Finnegans Wake*: 'keepy little Kevin ... child of a strandlooper ...' – child of a vagrant.

It connotes something else too: slavery and bastardisation. The early colonists picked the vagrant women off the beach, the story goes, put them in their kitchens as slaves, and fucked them like beasts to produce bastards. 'Khoi-Khoi' conjures a being twice cursed; what derelict heritage he did have was robbed from him by miscegenation – he is a half-breed, a person without pedigree.

So Basil Coetzee, a middle-ranking, coloured recreation officer at a prison still run by whites, walked into gangsters' lives with the news that they were not coloureds, but Khoi-Khoi, and that they ought to be proud of it. His tools were rugby and soccer balls, musical instruments and the beauty of human voices. He wanted the inmates to perform and sing their way back to their rightful heritage.

It was an awesome task, but a noble one, for the substance of his anger was right. Coloureds should indeed be able to boast the oldest civilisational heritage in South Africa. That coloured 28s can only place themselves in history by inventing a faux-Zulu past is ironic and disturbing. That Magadien walked into a Free State prison and felt himself to be a cipher is symptomatic of a social tragedy. For all that Africans talk of colonialism having torn them from their roots, it is only the coloured minority of the Western Cape that suffers collective amnesia; where their past used to be, there is only insult.

*

I asked Coetzee if he remembered his first encounter with Magadien.

'Steenkamp was what people would call a pig,' he replied. 'He was a very active gangster. To be pounced on and beaten up by warders meant nothing to him. He was rude, he was provocative. Whenever things went wrong, he was there.'

'Yet you persisted with him.'

'He was no fool,' Coetzee said. 'He knew very well the consequences of gangsterism. It was like he was willingly jumping into a fire, willingly burning himself to death. I thought to myself,' Coetzee continued, adopting a plaintive, mournful tone, 'where had his intelligence gone? When had it been removed, his capacity to process information? Because he had all the information. He knew what he was doing to himself.

'So, like with the other gang leaders, I asked myself: "Is this Steenkamp I see, the outer Steenkamp he presents to me and the world, who spits at everything he encounters, is this the only Steenkamp? Or can I delve in and find a receptive, intelligent Steenkamp on the inside?" It's not so difficult to find a man's soul. It's just that the Department of Prisons didn't know how to get there, didn't want to get there.'

'How did you find his soul?'

'I identified the top gang leaders, particularly two men, Steenkamp and this big 26, and I called them into my office. I didn't say to them, "Right, you are Khoi-Khoi and you forgot that, but I'm going to make you proud of it." I didn't say, "I have a vision of these sports teams and choirs, and you are going to run them." No, I chatted with them about their lives. I asked them,' and here Coetzee returned to his plaintive, searching voice, '"Who were you before you were a gangster, before you ended up in prison? Where's your mom? Where's your family?" I refused to address them as prison gangsters. I didn't want to know about their rank. I wanted to draw out the things they had lost, their humanity.

'I'd talk to them person to person, not warder to prisoner. They had never experienced that before. Then, after I had met with them a few times, I would tell them my vision, that I wanted them to manage and play in sports teams, and to sing in choirs, that there would be gangsters and non-gangsters in these groups, and that everyone would be equal. "Do you think you could fit into this?" At first, they told me I was mad, that no non-gangster would ever be equal to them. So I asked them: "How are you different? How are you not like them?"

'Then I'd take them and a whole lot of inmates out to the sports field and I would not carry a gun; fifty or sixty inmates with one unarmed warder: it was unheard of. And nothing ever happened to me. I was showing them my humanity. I was asking them to show me theirs in turn.'

'How long did it take to bring Steenkamp round?' I asked.

'He was not responsive at first. That came as we went along. Particularly after the success I had with the prison choirs, that affected them a lot. We took part in a competition at Drakenstein and we won some prizes.

'The authorities were at first not keen on the choir, so I funded it myself, my mother and myself. The choir went to all the prisons in the region where they performed in competitions for trophies. I said there is no way they will go into a performance in prison dress. I bought the materials for their outfits, not the clothes, the materials. They had to make the clothes – bowties and so forth. I taught them church music, choir music, but also light Afrikaans music. I brought them the instruments and taught them how to play – soprano and alto recorders, violins: I brought all these things to prison. One of them taught me how to play the guitar. They practised once a week for months, but every day in the weeks before a competition.'

'And that's what brought Steenkamp round,' I asked, 'the success of the choir?'

'Yes. He flourished in the choir. He embraced it.'

*

Coetzee is right. It was the choir that brought Magadien round, but not quite, by Magadien's lights, in the way Coetzee suggests. The story is more interesting than that.

'He raised the question of the choir a bit later,' Magadien tells me, 'after I had been taken out of Further Charges, after I was involved in the soccer team. He called me into his office and told me he wanted me to join his Khoi-Khoi choir. I said, "Fuck off. I'm not a Khoi-Khoi. I'm a fucking Malay. I'm a Muslim." And I walked out of his office.

'It just so happened that this conversation happened during Ramadan. All the Muslims who were fasting were put in one cell. I got everyone in the cell together, and I said: "We are a small group. We get on well. They say it is our right to practise religion. I'm going to write to the head of the prison." I wrote to him and I said: "You have Christian groups, you have this Khoi-Khoi group singing church music. We want a Malay choir." He said: "Let's try it out. What do you need?"

'One of the guys in the Ramadan cell was a member of a Malay choir on the outside. The head allowed him to phone one of his fellow choir members. They were about to perform at a Malay choir competition in the Good Hope Centre. They taped their performances and sent us the cassettes. We listened. We rewound again and again and wrote down the words. We rewound again and listened for how all the individual instruments fit in. We rewound again and listened for the rhythm. Then we phoned the outside again for instruments, for the materials for choir uniforms. We practised and practised and practised.

'When the head of the prison heard us sing, he was amazed. He said: "This is going to be our prison choir." There were lots of problems with the other choir, Coetzee's Khoi-Khoi one. We represented Paardeberg at the prison choirs competition. And when some warders from Allendale Prison came to visit, we entertained them. They were so impressed, they invited us to a warder function where the warders make music. We played together, warders and inmates, until well into the night.

'Once, some people came to Paardeberg in a bus and we were asked to play for them. We didn't know until after we had performed that they were a real Malay choir. They were stunned. We had perfected their songs by listening to a bad cassette recording.'

*

Malay. It's no wonder Basil Coetzee chose to omit this part of the story.

When Magadien told Coetzee to fuck off and stormed out of his office, his gesture was laden with a story long enough to fill a book. He was telling Coetzee that there wasn't a drop of *hotnot* blood in his veins, that his earliest known ancestors were slaves imported from Indonesia in the late seventeenth century, that they were proud and skilled craftspeople, that they had built with their hands the spectacular national monuments that mark Cape Town's city centre.

How did Magadien come to imbibe this story? Like most heritages, his is largely invented. But that is not what is interesting about it. The interest lies in why it was invented at all, why the last three centuries of Cape Town's history have offered this, of all imagined pasts, for Magadien to understand himself by.

It is a quirk of history that of all the races, languages and peoples imported to the Western Cape on the back of the transoceanic slave trade, 'Malay' is the only identity that survived; the rest are forgotten. As Robert Shell points out: 'By 1660, all the major language groups of the world, African (Bantu and Khoisan), Indo-European, and Malayo-Polynesian were represented in the wind-swept peninsula near the southernmost tip of Africa. South Africans began their colonial era with one of the most polyglot populations in the world, a dramatic reunion of all the main branches of humankind …

'Arriving in the typical small, often quite isolated, Cape slave-owning homestead,' Shell writes of the late seventeenth century, 'the uprooted slave was abruptly thrust into a foreign domestic milieu. There was a less than negligible chance of encountering someone of the same kin group, and a slender chance of encountering persons who spoke the same language, ate familiar food, or who even looked familiar.'

By the 1760s, a hundred years after the institution of slavery in the Western Cape, the majority of slaves were local-born. The languages their forebears brought with them were dying; instead, they spoke a creole language – a hybrid of Portuguese, Malay and Dutch. They were fast losing their identities as Mozambican, West African, Madagascan: they were slaves, their histories dissolving behind them.

There was one exception, and it only became an exception later, on the cusp of the abolition of slavery. From the late eighteenth century, slaves and ex-slaves began converting to Islam in large numbers. In 1790, less than 10% of Cape Town's population were Muslim or Malay (the terms became largely synonymous in the Western Cape). Fifty years later the number had swelled to one-third of the population.

What had happened in the interim was a confluence of two historical accidents. Laws passed in the late eighteenth and early nineteenth centuries made it illegal for slave owners to sell Christian slaves, and obliged them to provide a rudimentary education to the children of Christian slaves. The result is that owners actively discouraged conversion to Christianity. WW Bird, a Cape colonial official, commented in 1822 that whenever one asked a slave why he had become a Muslim, the answer was: 'Some religion he must have and he is not allowed to turn Christian.'

Islam was not just 'some religion'; it had an attractive history in Cape Town. Not all the Malayo-Polynesian Muslims who came to the Cape in the late 1600s were slaves. In April 1694, 49 political exiles from the Dutch East Indies arrived at Table Bay. Some were members of a Javanese aristocracy who had rebelled against Dutch rule. Others were holy men and imams. They brought with them a muscular anti-colonial politics and a strong religious heritage. They were banished to the farm of Zandvlei, current-day Macassar, where they established a small but lasting Muslim tradition.

A hundred years later, it was the legacy left by these men that welcomed slaves into the Muslim fold. Given its history in the Western Cape, conversion to Islam was a seductive prospect; it was, perhaps, the only tradition available to slaves and ex-slaves that offered access to a heritage that could claim to be antique, autonomous and proud.

'Being Malay' also offered access to another historical legacy. From the first days of Cape slavery, the colonists divided their slaves into a host of racial stereotypes. 'The Negro,' Bird wrote in 1822, 'who is the least valuable, was brought from Madagascar and Mozambique. These slaves are chiefly hewers and carriers of wood and drawers of water ... and also employed by the boers and others as the hardiest labourers of the field ... The Malay slaves are coachmen, tailors, painters, shoemakers, carpenters and fishermen. In fact, they usually engaged in every thing where what is called cleverness is required.'

To be Malay then, also made available the prospect of placing oneself in a long lineage of craftspeople, to claim that it was one's ancestors who built Cape Town.

So that, in a word, is what was going on when Magadien told Coetzee to fuck off. He had been brought up by the Christian Mekkas; his father, he believed then, was either a coloured Christian or a white man. But it was from Gadija, the mother he despised, that he drew succour. It was only through her that he could claim an ancestry, not among *strandlopers* and *hotnots*, but among the proud heirs to an ancient culture.

He was, though, acutely aware that he was *choosing* a heritage, and he knew why he was doing so.

'Every human being wants to belong somewhere,' he tells me. 'That's why you have people sleeping on the roads and under the bridges. Because they do not belong somewhere. It is the most painful experience a human being can have. Look at the young prostitutes at the side of the road. Why do they sell their bodies? Because they don't belong. They feel they belong to the guy who pimps them.

'I thought I belonged to the 28s. But then you reach an age and you look at other people and other families, and you think: "Jesus, where I am is scary. I am nowhere."'

*

Basil Coetzee must have been furious as he watched the formation of the Malay choir. It was, after all, 'the-not-the-Khoi-Khoi choir'; it was laced with the denigration and slander he was trying to destroy. Had he been just a stubborn puritan, he would have washed his hands of it.

But he was much smarter than that. Instead, he worked with it, and he infused its management and organisation with all the principles he held dear. These principles may seem banal and workaday from the outside, but in the context of a prison run by gangs, they were revolutionary.

'I only had two principles,' Coetzee tells me. 'First, that the inmates manage their own teams and choirs. And second, that they manage them collectively. Nobody is the permanent coordinator, the permanent manager. It all rotates. You understand how difficult that is for gangsters? They come from the most militaristic hierarchy in the world.'

'In the sports teams,' Magadien recalls, 'I, a 28, was in charge of soccer, and Gerald, a 26, was in charge of rugby. But in the choir, we were gangsters and non-gangsters mixed together. And the one who knew most about Malay choir music, the one who brought the cassettes from the outside, he was a *frans*. He was the natural choice for choir leader. But how the fuck can you be ordered around by a *frans*? How can a *frans* tell a *ndota* he is playing his instrument all wrong and he must do it like this? Where I come from, a *frans* dies for that.'

Coetzee recalls that Magadien came to him one day in a fit of exasperation. 'He was desperate. He said to me: "I am a Number. How can I work with you? How can I work with *franse*?" I said: "I don't want the Number to work with me. I want you to work with me. The Number is your business."'

I doubt that Magadien and Coetzee had unalloyed affection for each other. Coetzee must have infuriated Magadien with his Khoi-Khoi claptrap, his self-righteousness, his insistence that one could only enter his seductive world if one left one's Number rank at the door.

But he took Coetzee's offer, as did many of the other *ndotas* who joined choirs and sports teams. For more than a year at Paardeberg, the Number went into hibernation. As at Robben Island six years earlier, *ndotas* still went through the motions of running a gang. But it was just a gesture; there were no promotions and no stabbings, no battles for turf. At Robben Island, it had been done with the threat of murder. Coetzee had done it, flighty as it may sound, with footballs and music.

*

Coetzee left Paardeberg in late 1992. His wife had a job in Cape Town, and the daily commute from Paarl was exhausting her. So the Coetzees packed up their home and moved back to the city.

Basil asked for a transfer and was appointed recreation officer at Pollsmoor's Medium B Prison. He was deeply unhappy there.

'At Medium B,' he says distastefully, 'recreation was reserved for the section of the prison that was predominantly white. Even lower-class whites weren't allowed recreation because the other whites were ashamed of them. So I gave it up and did other work. Paardeberg was my time. That's when I worked directly with my people. There were no white prisoners there. I was bringing our people back to what they were before missionaries and Westerners got us to hate ourselves. I wanted to free our people, to decolonise them.'

Eighteen months after Coetzee left Paardeberg, on the eve of South Africa's first democratic elections, the prison's inmates quite literally tried to free themselves; they set fire to their cells, thinking that the prison walls would crumble around them. It was a far cry from Coetzee's violins and rugby balls.

*

The Paardeberg inmates were, in fact, caught up in nationwide prison rebellion, the largest and deadliest wave of jail disturbances in South Africa's history. Between March and June 1994 (the elections were held on 27 April), there was unrest at 53 prisons across the country. Together, these prisons housed more than three-quarters of the country's jail population. In every case bar six, inmates attempted to burn the prison down. By the time the rebellion was subdued at the end of June, 37 prisoners had been killed and 750 hurt. No warder died, but 145 were injured.

In the narrowest of terms, the disturbances were fuelled by two issues. First, black prisoners assumed it their right to vote in South Africa's first democratic elections. Yet an election law drafted in 1993, and promulgated with the ANC's blessing, excluded many sentenced prisoners from voting. The majority of *ndotas* found that they would remain disenfranchised, as they were under apartheid. For a group that quite credulously regarded itself as the oldest anti-colonial army in the country, this was more than a slap in the face: it was a sign that the transition to democracy was passing power from one enemy to another. Shortly before the elections, the law was amended to exclude from voting only prisoners convicted of murder, rape and robbery with aggravating circumstances.

Ndotas greeted the amendment not as a victory but as an empty compromise.

Second, ever since the ANC was unbanned in 1990, word had spread through South African prisons that the new government would, on coming to power, announce a general amnesty, or, at very least, a generous remission of sentence for all prisoners. Throughout the early 1990s, political prisoners on both left and right were released from prison. There was a great deal of bartering between political parties over the issue, with the result that the line between common criminals and political prisoners was drawn and redrawn. *Ndotas* watched with horror as right-wing extremists who had committed terrible crimes walked free. As one *ndota* put it to me: 'The ANC came home and started preaching high words of forgiveness and reconciliation. But they meant forgiveness for their own people and for right-wing murderers. We are the ones who fought the *boere* in prison; but as far as the ANC was concerned, we could rot in hell.'

After months of rumour, expectation, announcements and retraction of announcements, the new ANC government finally declared on 10 June 1994 that there would be a six-month remission for all prisoners. The gangs were enraged. They regarded the remission as nominal, a hollow gesture.

To make matters worse, in March – the apartheid government's second-last month in office – the prisons department implemented a dramatic change in release policy. Under the old release regime, first-time offenders could expect to be released unconditionally after serving two-thirds of their sentence; repeat offenders could look forward to a one-quarter remission. Now, under the new regime, the date of release was to be determined by a mind-bogglingly bureaucratic procedure; prisoners would be awarded 'credits' by a prisons service Institutional Committee for a host of dimly defined categories of good and constructive behaviour.

'The bastards who run the prisons hate us,' a lifer at Pollsmoor told me. 'They are sadists. Now, the new regime gave them the power to decide when we would be free. It gave them another lever to torment us and drive us insane. It was hard to stomach one month before the beginning of democracy.'

When the new policy was announced, scores of prisoners had their release dates 'taken away'. The date of their freedom, which they thought had been set in stone, would be determined by the 'credits' they accumulated, and by the predominantly white apartheid functionaries who sat on the Institutional Committees.

*

Those, strictly speaking, were the issues, but in themselves they tell only part of the story. The disturbances were as much about the prison itself; they were the culmination of a strange, haunting mutation in the relationship between inmates and warders that had been growing with ominous quiet throughout the early 1990s.

For the sake of simple story-telling, the beginning of this change can be dated. On the evening of 6 November 1989, a group of coloured and African policemen and prison warders held a press conference in Cape Town. They announced that they were forming a trade and civil rights union – the Police and Prisons Civil Rights Union (Popcru). Johnny Jansen was among them.

'I arrived at work the next day,' Jansen tells me, 'picked up the daily newspaper, and there we were on the front page. I felt a cold shiver go down my spine. I put the newspaper in my desk drawer and closed it. I had this childish thought: if I hide my copy of the newspaper, maybe the *boere* will never find out what we had done.'

It was indeed a bracingly provocative action. The prisons service was a para-military organisation, one in which orders were obeyed without question. And if its members were considered combatants, coloured and African members were regarded as second-class soldiers, one up on the scale from the criminals they guarded.

Forming Popcru was a declaration of mutiny. Its leaders made it plain from the start that they were more than a trade union: in its inaugural statement, the organisation denounced the treatment of black inmates and swore to fight for the civil rights of those behind bars. It promised to attack the principles on which prisons were run.

The prisons service responded in kind. A 1990 amendment to the Prisons Act banned strike action and made it illegal for a warder to join a trade union without the permission of the Commissioner of Prisons. Popcru members were ostracised; all were refused promotion as a matter of course, and many were demoted. At Pollsmoor, Jansen and others were suspended during the course of 1990. For the first couple of years of its existence, Popcru was forced, to all intents and purposes, to operate underground.

This was the broader context when Basil Coetzee brought his violins and soprano recorders into Paardeberg. The Prisons Service, which only a few years earlier had appeared to inmates as a seamless block of authoritarian control, was split into racial factions. An intimation of disorder drifted through the prisons.

Inmates sensed something else, too. Aside from the revolt they were facing internally, the white men who ran the prisons service surveyed the heady, anticipatory mood in the world outside, and felt the chill of uncertainty. They could only guess at what the ANC envisaged for the prisons service; at first, they were not even certain they would keep their jobs. In 1991, in anticipation of things to come, the Department of Prisons changed its name to the Department of Correctional Services; this was less a programme for the future than a signature of fear. And, between 1992 and 1993, solitary confinement, dietary punishments and corporal punishment were abolished. Yet, for many years, these new regulations would be practised in the breach.

A fragrance of Bastille was in the air, and prisoners smelt it. 'It was all a shaky business after Mandela was released,' Magadien recalls. 'The whites weren't sure how to run the prison. Coloured warders who had been as meek as mice started coming to the fore. The whites were scared about the future. There were things going on. Nobody could describe what they were, but you could feel it. You could feel it was big.'

The world behind bars is delicate, its stability precarious. A small group of armed officials, vastly outnumbered by the hostile men they keep captive, must schedule, monitor and oversee every minute of every inmate's waking life. It is by its nature a fragile universe. You saw from Magadien's early experiences of prison that the relationship between the Number and its keepers was taut and dangerous. Each side had to absorb the meaning of a fine web of rules. A whiff of uncertainty, a momentary breach, and the tight filigree could snap apart.

'And then it happened,' Magadien recalls. 'In April, just before the election, a whole section of a prison in the Western Cape was burnt to the ground. The prisoners from that section were transferred to jails all over the region, including to Paardeberg. That's how it spread. They came with their story that they had burnt down their prison. People said, if they can do it, we can. These walls are here today. Tomorrow, we can make them disappear. The strategy was to raze every prison to the ground so they would have nowhere to keep us. We would simply walk free.'

What had happened, perhaps, is that things usually concealed were stripped naked. The men of the Number saw, for the first time in their lives, that the authority warders wielded was as much symbolic as physical, as much about the cumulative history of wielding power as about the actual presence of batons, dogs and guns. Setting alight the very buildings that imprisoned them was, perhaps, a frenzied, manic and ultimately metaphorical enactment of this realisation.

'Of all the means of destruction,' writes Elias Canetti, the theorist of crowds, 'the most impressive is *fire* ... It destroys irrevocably; nothing after a fire is as it was before.'

*

In the early months of 1994, an extraordinary debate took place among the inmates at Paardeberg. At issue was the question of what the coming of democracy meant for the future of the Number. In Magadien's recollection, the participants were divided between those who had participated in Basil Coetzee's sports teams and choirs, and those who hadn't.

'We were in a minority,' Magadien tells me. 'There were senior *ndotas* among us, but we were few in number. We said that out of respect for all those who had died and been injured over the years, let's bring our secret history out into the open. I suggested the idea of putting a plaque in the courtyards of all the prisons of the Western Cape. On the plaque there would be the story of Nongoloza and Kilikijan, the story of how we fought the *boere*, and the honest story about how we sometimes became stupid and killed one another. There was no such thing as a Truth Commission yet, but what I was suggesting was something like that. We said we must take our whole history out to show the world – the good, the bad and the ugly – and then leave it there on the plaques and move on to something more positive.

'The majority told us we were traitors, that they would stab us if we did that. How was it possible to explain to them what was happening in our heads? It would have come out funny. How could we have said: "We have been singing, and this singing has shown us something about ourselves. We have learned that we want to become ordinary people again, surrounded by our families, with proper names and bank accounts, with a history of our people in our minds, a knowledge of where we came from and what we are leaving for the future."'

'What was the majority saying?' I ask.

'The majority said we were mad. They said: "The *boers* are fleeing. The blacks are taking over the prison. There will be more corruption. We can rule these prisons after apartheid. Blacks will go for money. We can get fucking rich selling dagga and buttons in this place." And that was their experience of black warders; they could be bought off more easily, not because they were more corrupt, but because they hated the whites as much as we did.

'We would never have won the debate, I know, but the ANC really came and fucked things up for us. No amnesty, no votes. How can you keep arguing that the Number must close down when this is what the people who are going to govern the country are doing to you?'

*

When news arrived in April that prisons across the country were burning, the 26s and 28s at Paardeberg convened a joint meeting. The overwhelming majority wanted to set their mattresses alight and burn down their cells. Magadien's minority argued fervently against it.

'Eventually, they said: "This is the decision of the Number. If you oppose it, you will be stabbed." We said: "Fine, stab us." They tried to go through with it. A 28 was dutied to stab me, and a 26 was dutied to stab Gerald Moses, the head of the 26s. The 28s didn't have the heart to stab me. The 26s tried to stab Gerald; they couldn't get to him, so they stabbed another 26 who supported us.

'Let me tell you a secret, something I've never shared. After they threatened to stab me, I felt good. Sometimes you want to be part of something big, something that really moves you as a human being. And the thought of making a sacrifice for that, the thought of having your blood spilled for something that really means something – it is a good feeling.'

Early one evening, less than a week before the election, three cells at Paardeberg Prison begun to burn.

'Two of the cells had a normal, thin ceiling,' Magadien tells me. 'The fire burned the ceiling away and the inmates could get out of their cells. But one cell, cell 16, it doesn't have a normal ceiling. There is concrete above your head, and concrete doesn't burn. Set that cell alight, and you are setting yourself alight.

'You know what? The inmates in cell 16 knew that; they knew that if the warders did not unlock the door, they would be burned alive. But they lit the fire anyway.'

The inmates of cell 16 had, in fact, forced the warders into a chilling transaction: 'Open our cells and we will overpower you and escape from prison, or let us burn to death.'

'They had lots of time to open cell 16,' Magadien says, 'but they didn't do it. They were scared. They were waiting for reinforcements, for a SWAT team to come onto the roof with their sniper rifles. They waited and waited and watched the cell burn. By the time the SWAT team arrived, three 26 members were dead.

'The irony is that the authorities said in their press release that they were killed by 28s. It is propaganda; they were saying – these people want to vote, but look what they do to each other.

'But everyone at the prison knew what had really happened. After those deaths, the coloured warders refused to work with the head of the prison. He had to be transferred; he was chased away.'

'You weren't in one of the cells that burned?' I ask.

'No. You see, our room was the choir room. We kept lots of things there. We had musical instruments, sports equipment. It took us more than a year to build up that stuff, so we weren't going to burn it. There were 30 of us in that room. 28s, 26s, *franse*. The decision was unanimous: 30 against zero.'

Abstaining from revolt in order to preserve soprano recorders and choir uniforms: this is the signature of the man Magadien would try to become.

17

TOKKIE

Great portents seldom wear their meanings on their sleeves; they slip into one's life in the guise of the innocuous. It is only much later, when the world has already been turned upside down, that one thinks back and remembers the first signs.

In Magadien's case, it was a workaday exchange among convicts in a prison van. In hindsight, it contained in embryo everything the Number would become after apartheid.

It was late 1991, more than two years before the prisons were set on fire, and a few days before Magadien met Basil Coetzee. He was being transported from Pollsmoor to Paardeberg to serve the remainder of his sentence for 21 counts of credit card fraud. The van was packed with inmates, most of them *ndotas*. Among them was a stranger, a diminutive man, no more than 5ft 4, who carried himself with the swagger of a seasoned gangster.

As with all strangers, he was asked a simple question: 'Who are you?' He replied that he was a soldier in the blood line of the 28s, and as he did so, the *ndotas* in the van eyed one another knowingly; his *sabela* was broken and scant, his knowledge of the metaphors bitty and incomplete. He was no 28; he hadn't even been to prison.

'I took one look at him,' Magadien tells me, 'and I saw his future. When you say you're a 28 and you're bullshitting, one of two things happen. Either you are beaten up, or you are strung along. *Ndotas* come to you and say: "You know *mos*, because I am senior to you, you have to do this and that for me. Because I'm senior to you, you must take off your pants so I can fuck you in the arse." They were going to make him a prostitute.'

When they arrived at Paardeberg, Magadien took the stranger aside. His name was Vernon Jonkers, his nickname Tokkie – a description of his dwarfishness.

'Where were you recruited into the 28s?' Magadien asked.

'In Hawston,' Tokkie replied – a small fishing town some hundred kilometres east of Cape Town.

'But there is no prison in Hawston.'

'I wasn't recruited in prison. I was recruited by the Rooidakkies.' This was a major Western Cape street gang that was soon to be absorbed into the region's largest supergang, the Firm.

'Tell me exactly how they recruited you.'

'I was ordered to do a hit, to shoot somebody. They said that to join the gold line of the 28s, you have to take blood. Once I'd done the hit, I would be a 28.'

Magadien reeled. He had never heard anything as crazy in his life.

*

The underworld has scant institutional memory. Nobody remembers for certain how it started – how the supergangs on the outside began donning the garments of the Number. Everyone has his own anecdotal account.

In mid-2003, I interviewed an inmate by the name of Howard Jacobs. He was from the Cape Flats township of Athlone, home base of the Americans. In the late 1980s and early 1990s, Howard had been a senior lieutenant to Jackie Lonti, the charismatic leader who had grown the Americans from a minor street gang into a regional superpower.

'I'm not good with dates,' he told me, 'but some time back then, in the 1980s, Jackie spent a while in jail. When he came out, he brought the Number out onto the street. To deal now, you had to know prison gangs.

'I remember once, a few days after Jackie was released, there was someone dealing in buttons in Athlone who Jackie didn't trust. He said it was time to get rid of him. But he didn't say it like that. He said: "No, that guy is a *frans*; he can't work with money." He called this guy to his house and said to him: *"Hei, wie is jy?"* "Hey, who are you?" – just like in prison.

'It was strange when I heard that. On the one hand, it was new – nobody had ever said that on the street before. On the other hand, it felt like it was old, like we had always thought that way; only now, Jackie had put the right words to it.'

By the late 1990s, it was close to pervasive. The Firm was calling itself the 28s, and the Americans the 26s. They recruited new members with paraphernalia borrowed from the Number gangs, and they ran their turf with the rules *ndotas* use to run their prison cells. After 70 years behind bars, the Number had spilled onto the streets.

Ever since the early 1970s, the street gangs of the Cape Flats have been extorting protection money from neighbourhood shops, demanding a cut of liquor distributors' profits, taking transit fees from the taxis that drive through their turf, maiming those who dare to sell anything without their permission. But now, beginning in the 1990s, street gangs began using prison as a metaphor to understand their relationship with those upon whom they preyed. The street gangsters are the *ndotas*; the taverners, liquor distributors and taxi drivers from whom they extort are the *franse*. Like the *franse* behind bars, they too must rent the air they breathe.

For much of the twentieth century, inmates imagined the jails that housed them as the open plains of the nineteenth century highveld and the forests of early Natal. Joining the 28s, for instance, was described as a Homeric journey through a wooded wilderness. Now, in the 1990s, the youths of Cape Town's ghettos began to imagine their neighbourhoods as prisons, each piece of turf a massive jail cell of the initiated, every taxi owner a *frans* to be milked.

The street gangs had finally 'stolen' prison: they had turned the institutions that punish them into founts of inspiration.

It is not just the supergangs. The inspiration of prison has permeated the most parochial street corners. In 2002, in Mitchells Plain, I met a 21-year-old man who had joined a gang unheard of outside his neighbourhood – the Jolly Killers. I asked him to do a piece of research work for me and he agreed on condition that I pay a third of his fee in advance. A week later, I phoned him to ask how the work was going.

'I'm not going to do it,' he replied. 'I'm a 26. My work is to con you out of your money.'

'You're a fool,' I said. 'It wasn't much work and if you'd done it you would have earned a whole lot more.'

He laughed patronisingly. 'You don't understand. I'm a 26. That's my ethos.'

'Who made you a 26?' I asked.

'The leader of the Jolly Killers went to jail and became a big 26,' he replied. 'When he got out, he recruited us all.'

*

Why, after so many years, did it happen when it did – in the late 1980s and early 1990s? One can only speculate, but the answer is surely rooted in the fact that the character of Cape Town's underground economy had begun to change substantially by the late 1980s. The major gangs of the previous decade – the Born Free Kids, the Mongrels, the Scorpions – all had a regional presence in the Western Cape, but they were, in reality, little more than regional affiliations of local groups. Gang leaders made money, but not that much money. They controlled turf, but not that much turf. The typical gang leader would control a few dozen blocks of a ghetto. He would run its Mandrax and marijuana trade, much of its liquor trade, extort protection money from its shopkeepers, control its commercial sex industry, buy and sell stolen electronic equipment. He was not much different from Pang DK, the local gangster of Magadien's teenage years.

The gang leaders who came of age in the late 1980s did so in a very different world. The rapid insertion of South Africa into global markets brought new drugs into the country – like crack, heroin and club drugs – new merchants, and, above all, new markets. An impressively innovative network of West Africans took over inner-city prostitution and used it to create a brand-new crack market, one that, significantly, cut across class and racial lines. Also, the emerging rave scene in South Africa brought with it a host of new club drugs, bringing scores of middle-class youths into the drug market.

The traditional street gangs of the Western Cape found not only that drug consumption was growing rapidly, but that a sizeable proportion of the emerging drug market was located outside their traditional turf. With the prospect that their own clients would desert them for new drugs and new players, they knew they had to expand quickly or risk being swallowed.

The major gangs scrambled to consolidate their traditional constituencies and to lay down new turf throughout the Western Cape – from the inner-city suburbs of Cape Town, to the coastal villages both east and west of the Cape Peninsula, to the rural towns of the Western Cape hinterland.

It was a time of great risk and uncertainty for Cape Flats gang leaders, but a time of great reward for those who succeeded. The late 1980s saw the emergence, for the first time in the history of the

Western Cape underworld, of stinking rich Cape Flats men, millionaires many times over: people like Colin Stansfield, who cut his teeth in the Scorpions and scaled the ranks of the 28s; Jackie 'Lonti', a 26, leader of the Americans before his assassination in 2000, and the man reputed to have brought crack cocaine to the Cape Flats.

Men like these were the first in the history of Western Cape crime who needed to build and maintain province-wide allegiances. They required the allegiance, not only of foot soldiers, merchants and street dealers, but above all, of consumers. A large portion of Western Cape drug consumers had always bought their drugs according to their gang allegiance. Now, the allegiance would have to be to a large, abstract, province-wide entity. In other words, the imagination of consumers became a vital resource on which to work.

What better set of tools with which to reshape the imagination of marginalised young men than the iconography of the prison? For decades, rumours, tales, slivers of narrative about the Number gangs had been trickling onto the streets. Prison Generals walked out of jail demigods. The words 28, 27 and 26 had long been sprinkled with magic. The real question is why Number lore had not taken hold on the streets earlier. Indeed, the way some interviewees describe it, the introduction of Number lore on the streets seemed organic, natural: it captured the imagination immediately.

*

Back in 1991 at Paardeberg, before all of this had happened, Magadien thought it an ominous wind that brought Tokkie Jonkers into his life. He himself had always observed the *ndotas'* most sacrosanct rule: never take the Number outside. Since his first spell in jail, he had committed most of his crimes alone. And when an ex-convict in Hanover Park or Heideveld greeted him with a 28 salute and began to *sabela*, he would chat politely for a while and walk on. The secrecy of the Number was sacred for him. For many years, it had been the screen that sheltered him from his family, his lovers, his life.

He didn't in his wildest imaginings think that Tokkie represented the future of the 28s. By the time he returned to jail in 1998, politics in prison had become an appendage of street gang politics on the outside; they were barely recognisable.

Listening to Tokkie's story, Magadien took pity. He thought the small man the victim of a ghastly trick; he shuddered to think of the unhappy nights that awaited him. 'I protected him. When others wanted to make him into a target, into their prostitute, I said no, I will teach him the real way. We spent hours and hours together. I taught him to *sabela* until he was fluent. I taught him the history and the ranks. After a few months, he could walk anywhere in the prison and behave like a 28 should behave. I saved him from being a *frans*. We became close. You sit with somebody explaining everything to him, you teach him a new language and listen patiently while he makes mistakes, and you start to feel like he is a son or a younger brother.'

It was, in fact, the most meaningful relationship Magadien had established in many a year: one of simple empathy.

Through Tokkie, other people entered Magadien's life. A 28 called Wayne, who was soon to become a leader of the Firm and one of the most powerful crime bosses in Cape Town, came to visit Tokkie from time to time. Magadien would go along to the visiting room to meet with him. At the end of one his visits, Wayne wrote his phone number down on a piece of paper and handed it to Magadien.

'When you get out,' he said, 'call me. I'll have work for you.'

It was an invitation to the heart of Cape Town's underworld.

'I kept this paper with me for the next two years,' Magadien says: 'This invitation to hell. If I'd known then that Tokkie's work in the Firm was going to lead to his death, I would have killed Wayne with my bare hands there and then.'

18
DOUBLE-CROSSING MR MORRIS

I visit Robin and Helen Morris at their home on a Sunday afternoon in early March 2003. They live in one of the north-eastern neighbourhoods of middle-class Cape Town, not far from the railway line that divides the suburbs from the ghettos.

There is a class of living room that appears to have chosen its occupants, long before they moved in and furnished, long before they even coupled and settled down. It is pleasant and homely, but also somewhat formal, vaguely reminiscent of the Afrikaans *voorhuis* – the room in which the priest was received for Sunday tea. The room is more the bearer of an idea than of any particular taste – the idea that there is a family here, that they go to church and that the children are brought up well.

The Morrises once owned a glass-cutting business in downtown Cape Town. Robin is telling me of a day in August 1996 when he employed a man called William Steenkamp as a driver. Steenkamp was charming, Robin recalls. He was warm. Above all, he was very clever.

'We like to foster a generous relationship with our employees,' he tells me, while Helen nods in vigorous agreement. 'Not because we want to be rewarded some day for treating people who are not white well, but because that is our nature. You don't want resentment and unhappiness around your business. It's not a pleasant way to live. So I nurtured people. If they had problems, they came to me. If they wanted a piece of glass to sell on the side, I'd give it to them. At Christmas, Helen and I would give the staff presents. We simply treated people as people.'

Two teenagers walk into the lounge, a girl and a boy. She wears jeans and a simple t-shirt. Robin introduces her to me as his daughter. She stands very erect and greets me with studied courtesy. The boy is on tenterhooks. He greets Robin and Helen with excessive enthusiasm, his voice lilting into a clumsy combination of diffidence and strained casualness. Robin smiles back at him regally.

The teenagers leave and Robin grins at me. 'My daughter's little friend,' he says. '*My* little friend.' He smiles to himself unconvincingly. 'He's a good boy.'

I nod politely and smile back at him. 'What were your first impressions of William?' I ask.

'He took to us immediately,' Robin replies. 'He was extremely charming, extremely engaging. And his work ethic was extraordinary. He might have been a driver, but it wasn't long before he could cut glass and glaze. It wasn't long before he could be sent out on a job alone, and one would have complete faith in him.

'He had business sense, too. He watched how things were done. He had a brain for the way things worked. I sensed it wouldn't take much for him to understand my business as well as I did.

'I not only trusted him, I liked him very much. He would take the company bakkie home every night and at weekends. He smashed it up once or twice, but that's how things go. Once, I gave him the bakkie for three weeks over his Christmas leave. I didn't worry about it for a moment.'

Indeed, the white bakkie with the 'City Glass' insignia pasted on the door was a venerable institution in 'William's' life. Every morning before work, he would pick up Gareth, a co-worker who lived in Bonteheuwel, and Farieda, City Glass's manager, who lived in Mitchells Plain. In the evenings he would take them home, sometimes stopping at his own house to show his children and his in-laws off to Farieda.

'Mr Morris understood that taking taxis or the train is dangerous,' Magadien told me a few weeks before I met the Morrises. 'Especially on Fridays when the robbers know that people's pockets are full of wages. The bakkie was for us too, for our safety and comfort.'

Robin excuses himself and disappears into his study. He returns a moment later with a black stationery holder.

'William gave this to me,' he says, 'for Christmas. And when he got married, my wife and I gave him a dinner set and a few days off work. I wouldn't say he was my friend – he was an employee. But we cared for each other.

'In retrospect,' he continues, 'there were signs. But I didn't notice them at the time. My staff warned me. They said he had a tattoo of something on his stomach, that that meant he had done bad things. They said I was stupid to trust him. I brushed it off. I judge people by their character, not by what is on their stomach.

'And there was an incident once – two of my cheques were stolen. They were signed and cashed, for about R2 000. I demanded the money back. I told the bank only my wife and I were authorised to cash cheques, so it was their fault, not ours. They sent me a copy of the ID of the person who cashed the cheque. The name was strange, but the picture looked like William. But the expression on his face – it looked like he came out of a concentration camp.

'I thought to myself: it looks like him, but it can't possibly be. I mean, he came to my house. He was with my wife. I would send him to the bank with a lot of money. I trusted him.

'And then it happened. We arrived back at the shop one day and a guy came rushing out. He said one of my guys had broken into his house. He was caught in the act, got into a City Glass bakkie and sped away. I said that's impossible – William and Peter are out on a job in Camp's Bay with the bakkie. To cut a long story short, I was proved wrong.

'What happened was, William and Peter were out at Camp's Bay. William drove back to town to get some extra glass or putty, leaving Peter on the job. While he was driving back, something must have snapped.

'He never came back. One day went, then two, then three. We had to phone the police to report the stolen bakkie. Then, traces of him started cropping up. We got an excited call from Africa Glass in Blackheath. We never used the guy. He was too far away. We just had him as backup. He thanked us for bringing our account to him – someone in a City Glass bakkie had bought R26 000 worth of glass from him.

'I don't know how William did it. He didn't have our order book. It must have been his charm and his cleverness.

'About a week later, we got a call from a glass outfit in the Strand. They were angry. They wanted to know why we were meddling on their turf. We said, "We don't do your area. What are you talking about?" He said there's a City Glass bakkie driving around here, doing business. That's when the police got properly involved. They found the place in the Strand William used to store his glass. He wasn't there. He was gone.

'Then, suddenly, about three weeks after he had disappeared, we got a call from the police: the bakkie had been spotted somewhere way out east.'

'Robin was away,' Helen interrupts. 'Farieda's husband and I drove out to get it. There it was, undamaged, parked nicely in a parking lot, the keys in the ignition. He seems to have left it for us. A few days later he was arrested at his house.'

The Morrises are religious Christians: not of the original sin variety; they believe in eternal redemption.

'The day he was convicted in court,' Robin says, 'I looked at his face and I saw the pain there. Whatever went through his head on that awful day in Camps Bay was causing him immense suffering, immense confusion. I thought, if it was in my power, I should say to the magistrate – just scrap it; he has suffered enough. He got six years. My heart dropped.

'I was devastated by what he did to us. Truly devastated. But you know what? I don't have my own business any more. We've had our own trouble, there was a sword over our own heads. But if it was in my power, and he came to me after he is released, I would employ him all over again. Because he is a good man. Whatever his past, whatever he did, he is a good man.'

They ask me many questions about William: when he is getting out of jail, what he plans to do. In the end, all three of us agree that going straight after a life of crime is near impossible, that the prospect of getting a straight job under one's real name is remote, that one must either lie or steal to get by. The conversation is forlorn and depressing.

'Is he Muslim or Christian?' Helen asks. I had mentioned earlier that his real name was Magadien Wentzel. 'His name sounds Muslim.'

'It's complicated,' I reply, and I begin to tell them about Gadija and Annie Mekka and about how 'William' is Christian and Muslim – and neither.

'Difficult,' Helen says. 'Very difficult. I work in a Christian bookshop. We get a lot of requests from prison. Tell him he should drop me a line. I'll send him a book. It might reaffirm his faith. So he knows there is a god.'

She pauses and corrects herself: 'Not *a* god, but *the* God – our Lord and Saviour Jesus Christ … He can address the letter to me.'

*

About a month earlier, Magadien and I had sat in his Pollsmoor cell talking about the Morrises.

'I was brought here to serve this sentence because of what I did to Mr Morris,' he tells me. He swallows hard, stares at his hands for a while. 'I loved them, you know, Mr and Mrs Morris. But a piece of me always held back. I would do stupid things to hurt him. I would smash the bakkie on purpose and then blame it on someone else. I would break his glass …

'A couple of years ago, I phoned Farieda. She said there was a new boss now; the Morrises went bankrupt. I walked back to my cell in a daze. I put my head on the pillow and cried. You see, I knew it was because of me, because of the glass I stole from him. I had destroyed him. He offered me love and I spat on him and destroyed him.

'I don't know how to express my remorse to them. I've got no illusion they'll forgive me. But I need to tell him the whole story, my whole story, why I did it, why it wasn't his fault, why I wormed my way into his life to harm him. The guilt will never go away. Those people at City Glass, I phone them every month to see how they are doing, because they lost Mr Morris as a boss, and I think, maybe one day when I phone, the place will have closed down and their families will be starving.'

'Maybe you're wrong,' I say. 'Maybe his business problems have nothing to do with you.'

'I don't know. I don't know. That's how I feel, you understand? Nobody told me what the real circumstances were. That makes me …

'When I get out, I want to work and save and try to pay him back. I know it will take me a long time. If he's not there I can pay back his children. This is one debt I need to repay.' His voice falters; he doesn't trust himself to continue. He lowers his head and begins speaking to his navel. 'As you can see, it's breaking me up.'

There is a long silence. He stares at his stomach. His breathing becomes laboured and his body shudders quietly. When he looks up, his cheeks are wet.

He smiles at me. 'Thank God you're going back to Joburg tonight. Tomorrow, there'll be no one to remind me that I cried.'

*

Magadien walked out of Paardeberg Prison on 2 January 1996, seven months before he met and began working for the Morrises. His head was swimming with Basil Coetzee, Malay choirs, a vision of the Number's secret history written up on public monuments. He tried to put this all together and decide what it meant for how he was to live his life. He had vague, half-formed notions of fatherhood and of being a son; he wrote to the parole board and told them he wanted to live in Manenberg or Heideveld – the world of Annie and Gadija, Faranaaz and Johaah. At the beginning of his prison sentence, Faranaaz had sent word that she had gone to an imam and was granted a divorce. Gadija hadn't visited him once during his sentence. The world he dimly imagined he might inhabit – a world of mothers and wives – was, in fact, unpeopled.

In any event, the parole board rejected his application; he was instructed to live in the Strand. A bitter irony of having lived the life of a chameleon – a bunch of faceless bureaucrats, sifting through a biography that had been reduced to a slim dossier, determined which of Magadien's lives was really his. They may as well have closed their eyes and stabbed the page blindly with their pens.

The Strand was a disaster. Colleen had a new boyfriend. When he heard that Magadien was back in town, he went to look for him, put a knife to his throat, and told him that if tried to take Colleen back he would die. Magadien leered at him, told him he was a useless *frans*, eased the knife out of his hand, and chased him through the streets of Rusthof.

Jake Williams, the one-time business partner who had shopped Magadien to the police outside the Checkers warehouse, had, in the intervening period, become a wealthy drug merchant.

'He had spent the past four years worrying that I was going to kill him when I got out of jail,' Magadien recalls. 'He spent four years preparing to stay alive. You should have seen the house he built for himself in Rusthof: huge fences, a surveillance camera – just to keep me out of his house. He had even got some idiot to make him a 28, because he had heard that a brother does not kill a brother.

'Jesus, it was a bad start to life on the outside. You can go through a whole spiritual transformation on the inside, you can imagine a brand-new life. You pay your debt, go back to your life with the best intentions, I mean *the best* fucking intentions, and some cunt from the old days wants to kill you because of something that happened so long ago you can barely remember it. You have to run and hide. You have to start a new life. It's like you have to start a new fucking memory. That's why I'm like a chameleon: different names, different lives. I can adapt myself to anything.'

Magadien left the Strand in despair, breaking his parole restrictions. He had been out of jail just a few days, and he was an outlaw again.

A week earlier, as he awaited his release from prison, he had imagined going to Heideveld and Manenberg to gather up the debris of his family. Now, Heideveld was a distinctly bad idea; his parole officer would almost certainly find him there, and throw him back in prison. He went to Hout Bay, which is a good seventy kilometres from the Strand, at the top of Cape Town's peninsula, to look for Tokkie Jonkers.

*

Hout Bay's steep shelves command a magisterial view of the Atlantic Ocean; you look out and the peninsula's coastline stretches for miles beneath your feet. Behind the bay, the hill slopes are carpeted in thick, pristine fynbos. Indigenous forest climbs up the bay's southern arm. It is home to some of the most coveted real estate in Cape Town.

A quirk of history has left a poor coloured community there. Its forbears had lived beneath the southern slopes of the bay for generations. When the architects of the Group Areas Act got to work in the mid-1960s, there was a great deal of bickering among whites about what to do with them. Property developers eyed their land. But the fishing companies that launched their boats from Hout Bay harbour railed against the prospect of their entire labour force disappearing into the hinterland of the Cape Flats. A compromise was reached. The coloureds were moved a few kilometres – to a 30-degree cliff face that towers over the northern flank of the harbour.

It is the strangest of sights; you drive up the steep harbour road, the sea dropping further and further beneath you, and instead of ocean-view mansions, you enter a world of stone-façade tenement blocks, washing hanging from the windows, unemployed men loafing on the streets. Behind the tenement blocks, a jumble of wooden shacks crawls up the slopes, each shack on its own pair of stilts. Up in the tenement flats, the living rooms are tiny, floored with cheap floral tiles and crammed with three generations of family: outside the window, mile upon mile of brilliant blue sea.

The Jonkers are fishing people. Tokkie's parents were both born on the other side of the bay. His father and grandfather worked for the fishing companies, his mother in a fish-processing factory. They cannot remember, nor have they been told of, a time when the Jonkers lived elsewhere.

When Magadien arrived in their lives, they welcomed him like a long-lost son. Tokkie had been released a year before Magadien. When he got home, he told his family of the man who had saved him from the degradations of prison life. They had travelled all the way to Paardeberg to thank him – a costly trip for a poor family. They had told him that, should he come to them once he was free, they would treat him as one of their own.

Tokkie was his mom's precious boy; in her eyes, Magadien rode into Hout Bay on a noble stallion, a halo around his head, his armour glittering with righteousness.

The relationship between gangsters and their mothers is an unsettling one. So many middle-aged Cape Town women tell you that the source of the trouble is there, never here: in that adjacent block, in that neighbouring ghetto; that's where the evil ones live. Her own son can do no wrong. The gun she once found under his bed has vanished from her memory. The money he brings home to fill an empty cooking pot she receives gratefully; it comes from nowhere.

'Tokkie was a good boy,' Grace Jonkers tells me wistfully when I visit her, a large portrait of her dead son smiling down at us from the living room wall.

Tokkie was not a good boy. Before his mother's eyes, he was vanishing into the darkness of a world from which he would never return.

*

Shortly after Magadien moved to Hout Bay, there was an offer from the Firm: Magadien and Tokkie were to be given a house in Betty's Bay, a beautiful seaside hamlet some eighty kilometres east of Cape Town. They were each to be given a gun, and a ready supply of Mandrax and crack; they were to establish a drug outpost in the provinces.

It was 1996. The Firm had just begun moving into the fishing villages east of False Bay. There was a thriving poaching industry along the abalone belt that stretches from Betty's Bay in the west, all the way to Gansbaai in the east. South African Cape abalone fetch staggering prices in the fish markets of Hong Kong and Taiwan. Small-town schoolteachers, general traders and labourers who lived on the abalone belt were sending unemployed teenagers into the sea and getting rich overnight.

It was too good an opportunity for the Firm to pass up. They built gaudy, double-storey face-bricks in the fishing villages' coloured townships, and sent dozens of soldiers from the Cape Flats, each armed to the teeth, to live in them. Their plan was to make the abalone belt their turf, to extract a healthy protection fee from anyone who entered the sea illegally. By the late 1990s, they were making a fortune.

Tokkie and Magadien were to join the first stage of the Firm's expansion to the fishing villages and resort towns. While other of the Firm's men took the poaching industry by force, Tokkie and Magadien were to sell drugs quietly – a modest position on the flanks of the Firm's growing business.

Magadien politely declined. 'I wasn't going to go and live in a rich white village to sell drugs,' he tells me. 'It's not my terrain. I can't read it. My birthday was less than two months away. I didn't want to spend it in prison. Besides, you must be careful what you accept from the likes of the Firm. Nothing that comes from a street gang comes for free. There is always payback, and it is always ugly.'

Magadien did not decline everything he was offered, though: he said no to the house, but he took the gun – 'for my own protection,' he says, 'Cape Town is not a safe place' – and he took the offer of a steady Mandrax supply.

'That's different,' he explains. 'I wasn't given the drugs, I bought them. It was a supply for my own business rather than an arm of the Firm's business. There are no strings attached. When you stop buying, you stop buying; nobody asks questions.'

He and Tokkie moved into one of the stilted shacks on the slope – about fifty metres from the tenement block where Tokkie's parents lived. They never kept their Mandrax in their own shack; they seldom laid hands on it themselves. Instead, they threaded an elaborate chain of transactions through the shacks that surrounded their own, giving their neighbours a cut of their proceeds in exchange for the danger they were deflecting from themselves.

'An undercover cop could have come to the shacks and bought our buttons every day for a week,' Magadien tells me. 'He still wouldn't have known that the business was ours. He just would have seen these two unemployed guys in a shack doing fuck-all.

'Our business grew fast. All the rich white guys from the Hout Bay mansions came to buy our drugs. So did the people on the boats when they got home in the evenings. With our profits, we'd buy crayfish from the poachers for next to nothing. With the crayfish money we'd buy wine and beer and sell it from the shacks. We started making money, more money than I'd made for years.'

He lasted six months in Hout Bay. By July he had packed up and left. By August, he was standing outside an employment office on the Cape Flats looking for a lowly labourer's job.

'You were earning good money,' I say to him. 'You were your own boss. Why did you give it all up in order to beg a white man for a job, to get bossed around and earn peanuts?'

'In the evenings,' he replies, 'I would sit at the entrance to my shack watching people coming home from work. I envied them. I was bored out of my mind. I would just sit the whole day smoking, fucking girls, listening to people nag, listening to family quarrels, to unemployed people tormented by boredom and taking their problems out on each other. I felt like a housewife.

'Maybe you don't know what it feels like to do nothing for days, weeks, months. It feels terrible. Tokkie drank all day. I smoked buttons. I was smoking up my own merchandise. It was frightening. I would wake up in the middle of the night sweating and panicking; I had been dreaming of my future.'

Grace Jonkers, her memory steeped in maternal imaginings, remembers things a little differently.

'Darryl would have stayed here forever if I hadn't have thrown him out,' she tells me. (Whenever Magadien found himself in a Christian household, he would introduce himself as 'Darryl'.) 'I said to him: "Darryl, we love you very much, you are like my son, but that is why you must go. You are in your late thirties. You have a divorced wife there in the Flats who you must take back. You have kids you do not see, a mother who is forgetting what you look like. I watch you sitting in your shack all day, and I can't stand to see it. I am chasing you away; you can't stay here any more."'

Magadien sits next to Grace as she tells me her story. He looks at his hands, dons the pose of a chided boy. '*Ja ma,*' he says. '*Wat ma sê is die waarheid.*' 'Yes ma, what ma says is the truth.'

Magadien cashed in about R3 000 from the business. He bought himself a pair of Caterpillar shoes, a good pair of dungarees, a couple of pairs of Levi jeans. When he arrived in Heideveld, he looked like a rich man.

Tokkie accepted the Firm's offer. He went to live in Betty's Bay. Magadien dusted off an old proverb and gave it to his friend. 'Live by the sword, die by the sword,' he said.

Tokkie's younger brother, Liam, had just been retrenched; he had been working for the municipality, mending broken manholes and filling in potholes on the roads of the peninsula. He moved into the shack in Hout Bay, and Magadien gave him a crash course in running the business.

He would never see either of them again. In early 1999, Tokkie and Liam were shot to death outside a drug outpost in Atlantis. Tokkie was about to be charged with murder along with high-ranking members of the Firm; his bosses got wind that the prosecution wanted him to turn state witness. Liam just happened to be in the car.

The Jonkers lost both their sons in one night.

*

I am not sure whether Magadien returned to the Cape Flats in order to become a husband, a father and an industrious labourer. He knew that his life in Hout Bay was slowly torturing him to death. And the days when he pined to go back to prison and take his rank in the 28s were long gone; the Number for him now was a disfigured shadow of the fantastical world it had once been. But he didn't have the resources to imagine a sane future. He put one foot in front of the other, not daring to think more than a few weeks ahead. When the good life came, it landed in his lap, unexpected, barely real – an unlikely gift from Robin Morris.

He did not go back to Faranaaz at first. When he left Hout Bay, he went to Heideveld, knocked on Gadija's door and asked if he could stay. He was wearing good clothes and had money in his pocket. He said he would pay his way.

'What do you do when your son appears from nowhere and says he is back?' Gadija tells me. 'Your heart wants to trust him, even though your head knows you shouldn't. So you let him in, and when you get home at night, you don't check to see that your money is still under the mattress because he is, after all, your son.'

He went to a labour recruitment office in the Cape Flats.

'There were queues and queues and queues. Everyone wanted a job. I stood for hours. I came back the next day and stood for hours again. My money was running low. I was panicking.'

On his third day in the queue, a coloured man came up to him, introduced himself as Stephen, and told him he worked for a glass outfit in the centre of town. He said that the company driver was away for a few weeks and that they were looking for a temporary replacement.

Magadien thanked his guardian angel and took William Steenkamp out of his pocket, driver's licence and all. That afternoon, Stephen introduced him to Robin Morris.

'He was just the boss at first, another white boss, no different from all the ones before. First time I met him I was wondering whether I would stay long enough to rip him off. He said he needed me for a week or two, that it was only temporary. I said okay.

'But then something happened. Mr Morris didn't know prison inmates. You know, the *boere* work inmates very hard. You learn how to work like no other human being on earth. So you come out, you work for a white man, and he is amazed at how much you get through in a day, at how quick you learn. Mr Morris sits there and watches this – how the new guy is so productive, while the old guy works shit. So first he says to me, another week, then another month. But he can't stand to see me go. So, actually, it becomes a full-time job.'

At first, Magadien did what he had always done. Keeping his honest face and donning his solicitous manner, he took in the terrain: how the cash register worked, where the cheques were kept, who looked after the order book, the procedures the Morrises adopted with their suppliers.

After a couple of months, he started taking chances. He stole into the office at the back of the workshop and took two cheques, then cashed them using the identity book of Magadien Wentzel; he slipped the City Glass order book in his pocket and bought a drill.

The credulous Mr Morris stared at the photocopied mug shot the bank had taken from Magadien's identity document. It was William, but a William from a foreign world, gaunt and wild-eyed. He stared at the photograph and refused to believe it – there was no place in the soul of his industrious, gregarious new worker for these cruel eyes; he put it in the wastepaper basket and expelled the incident from his mind.

Whenever Magadien has gotten away with fraud, it has been in this way. He does not run; he stays where he is, as garrulous and competent as ever. He steals behind the screen of the normal. He has always understood the power of this mask; his photograph stares his victim in the face – it is William, but it cannot possibly be William.

And then things began to change. What was it? How does a man who has spent his life mastering the art of duplicity, investing trust in his foe without ever leaving an ounce of his soul behind – how does such a man begin to love his white boss, to feel the tug of reciprocity? Perhaps it began with the wheels – with the City Glass bakkie.

I don't mean the bakkie itself, of course – I mean the idea of the bakkie, the meanings the Morrises invested in it. For one, it signified trust; Magadien took it home every night, every weekend. It was taken for granted that he would bring it back; he was a man in whom one could put one's faith.

But that is not enough. He had always wooed trust and then betrayed it; that was his way, the most powerful weapon in his arsenal. And indeed, he abused the Morrises' bakkie at first, wilfully, his only benefit the satisfaction of breaking trust and getting away with it.

There was something else about the bakkie and the things it signified – family. Farieda, the Morrises' manager, lived with her husband and children in Mitchells Plain; Gareth and Peter, City Glass's most experienced glazers, were raising their own families on the Cape Flats. Magadien was given the bakkie because, in the Morrises' eyes, breadwinners must be sheltered from the predators that stalk the trains and taxis. Breadwinners arrive home safely to their children at night – intact, fit to provide. In Magadien's twice-daily ritual – ferrying City Glass's workforce from their homes to their livelihoods, and from their livelihoods back to those they clothed and fed, he was, in a sense, a caretaker – a bodyguard to the most sacrosanct institution of the Morrises' universe.

The idea was utterly seductive. Ever since his encounter with Basil Coetzee, the envy he had long coveted towards fathers and children became an open desire, an aspiration. He had just never imagined how he might make the journey from here to there – from the life of a drifting criminal to that of a family man. And now, here he was, guiding families like a tender shepherd across the badlands of his childhood.

He savoured it. He began to play the part himself. Driving Farieda home to Mitchells Plain in the evenings, he would take a long detour through the north of the Flats and stop outside the Benjamins' house in Manenberg. He would call for Johaah, and the shy, eleven-year-old boy would peer into the bakkie and greet Farieda tentatively.

'This is my son,' Magadien would announce with pride. 'Look at his nose, his chin. He is his father's child.'

Even Jumat, Faranaaz's seven-year-old son, whose father was alive and well, Magadien called his son.

'My baby,' he said to Farieda. 'My youngest.'

On entering Mitchells Plain, Magadien would take one more detour – to Margie's house, to show Farieda his daughter Glynnis.

'When I think back on it now,' he tells me, 'I feel like an idiot. I had never been there for Glynnis, I had never offered her consistency, never even contributed a cent to her upbringing. And there I was behaving like I was a normal father with a daughter.

'I did some stupid things, pretending to be a father. Glynnis was about fourteen. There was this boy who came to her house. I gave him a hard time. I joked with him. I said, "Behave with my daughter otherwise I'll come and terrorise you at night." I had no idea how to be a father; I thought that is something fathers said. Looking back now, I have an image in my mind of Glynnis's face as I gave this boy a hard time. There was real fear on her face. She was scared of this monster who would come into her life from nowhere and threaten people.'

He was performing for Farieda, and clumsily at that; after

dropping her at home, he would return to his room in Gadija's house, not to Johaah or Glynnis. But the drama was not entirely expedient, not entirely unreal. Ferrying Farieda to his imaginary family, he was accosted by an emotion he had not felt in ages – guilt. He would show Farieda his children, knowing full well that they were fatherless children, and the realisation would come to him as a shaft of physical pain.

'They were inheriting my childhood,' he tells me. 'That's the only thing I had ever given them – my own fuckedupness. I pictured Johaah growing up to be an adult like me. I saw him in a prison cell, with *ndotas* surrounding him, and one of them asking him: "Who are you?" The thought made me break out in a cold sweat. What the fuck was I doing to my children?'

He began to circle cautiously around the people who might become his family. Every evening after work, he started dropping by the Benjamins' place in Manenberg – without Farieda, without an audience. He would sit alone with Johaah, sometimes in silence, sometimes asking tentative questions, observing the boy he had claimed as his son.

*

Faranaaz noticed these things – the bakkie, the steady job, the money in his pocket, his newfound flirtation with fatherhood. When Magadien came round to visit Johaah and Jumat, she would hover cautiously in the background, watching.

'Johaah asked me to come back,' he says. 'One evening, I went to Manenberg after work to visit the kids. At about eight, Faranaaz's father and I went to the yard to smoke a pipe. We chatted, smoked another, then another. It grew late, I was in no state to go home, so I spent the night.

'The next morning, the kids came to me with a cup of coffee. Johaah said: "You should be sleeping here every night."

'I was still half asleep. I still hadn't recovered from the pipes I'd smoked with Mr Benjamin. I said to him: "No, your mother and I can't live under one roof. It won't work." Faranaaz and I had hardly said anything to each other up to that point. I came to visit the kids, not her, and we avoided each other.

'He stood there for a long time saying nothing. Then he walked off.

'About a week later, I was there at the house again, watching TV with the boys. I sent Johaah out to buy cigarettes for me, gave him a little extra for a chocolate. While he was gone, Faranaaz came into the room. She said: "You know what? It can't go on like this. It's not good for the children. For their sake, let's reconcile."

'"That's what you say now," I replied. "What about tomorrow?"

'And then she said something to me that put goose bumps on my skin. She said: "I have something to tell you. I never divorced you. I lied to you. I never went to the imam. You are still my husband."

'I can't find words for how angry I was. You know *mos*, I have a history of people lying to me about who my family is. It took 12 years before they told me who my mother was. I still don't know who my father is. Now this woman tells me she is actually my wife, that I'd been wandering around this fucking city not knowing I was a married man.

'I swallowed my anger. I didn't show it to her. Instead, I said: "Fine, for the kids' sake we will get back together. But this time we do it my way. No imams. We must marry all over again, this time in front of a magistrate. You're not going to pull this one on me again."

'So I married in bad faith all over again. I married her at the very moment I trusted her least. And as for her, how could she trust me after the way I had fucked her around in the past? I told myself I was doing it for the kids, that that was the sacrifice I was making to be a proper father.

'In fact, at that very moment, I had just begun to glimpse what love might actually be. Just a glimpse. In the street where my mother lives in Heideveld, there was a 17-year-girl called Lenza. I had become close to her mom and her stepdad: Beaty and Mario. She was a wonderful girl. We never slept together. I never touched her at all. But she had this gentleness – I hadn't known a woman like that since Margie, Glynnis's mother. I imagined myself together with her, and I saw that with her there could be no drugs, no drinking, no shouting. You couldn't do anything like that in front of her. Being with her meant being decent, being faithful.

'I ran away from that, from the image of what a man and a woman might be like together. I ran because she was 17 and I was 37, because I was close to her parents and they would have thought I was stealing their baby, because the idea of being in a happy relationship with a woman was so frightening.

'It's a strange thing – I was going back to my wife and my boys, something I had never been able to do; but still, I was running away from being normal. Faranaaz and me were never going to be normal.'

*

Magadien announced to the Morrises that he was getting married. They were delighted. They bought him a wedding present – a six-piece dinner set; they gave him three weeks off work and advised him to take his new wife on honeymoon. It was mid-December: the business was winding down for the holidays; they told him to take the bakkie. It was a wonderfully generous gesture.

'Simple affection,' Magadien says. 'These two white people – they just wanted me to be happy. They wanted nothing in exchange.'

He and Faranaaz had a quiet ceremony this time, in a magistrate's office downtown. He took the leave the Morrises had offered him – he slept late in the mornings, took Johaah to soccer practice, sat in the yard with his father-in-law and smoked drugs. But the truth is that he missed his job. He loved the daily ritual of ferrying his City Glass colleagues to and from work. He loved lunch hour; the entire workforce would descend on a halaal curry restaurant across the road from City Glass; they would order take-outs and eat on the street under Table Mountain. He missed the work itself. Formally, he was still the company driver. He would take Peter or Gareth, the glazers with whom he partnered, to addresses in the City Bowl and in the upmarket suburbs on the Atlantic seaboard. Peter would assess the job and send him back to the workshop for putty, glass and silicone. But in reality his job description was beginning to blur; he had learned to cut glass as well as anyone, to fit windows with expert ease. By the time he married Faranaaz, he could comfortably exchange jobs with anyone at City Glass.

He held onto one vice. He was smoking Mandrax every day: not as much as he did during the empty hours at Hout Bay, but still every day. And he did so at the Morrises' expense. Driving alone through the City Bowl to fetch glass and putty for Peter, he was often approached by a driver in the traffic and asked to fix a window. Back at the workshop, he would slip an extra sheet of glass onto his load and do the private job on the way back to Peter. He charged R50 or R60 for each job.

But this was a mere residue from another time, it seemed. The truth is that his life had undergone a breathtaking transformation. In mid-1996, he had been a parole-breaker and a drug pusher, living in a shack with an assassin. Eighteen months later, he was a married man, living under the same roof as his wife and children, going to an honest job each morning and loving it. This sort of thing does not happen to a veteran prison gangster and a serial recidivist. What happened to Magadien was one in a million. It was too good to be true.

Too good because it was not, in fact, true. He had always revelled in his multiple lives, his countless names. They had been his primary defence against the world – against commitment to his lovers, against the betrayals of his family, against the white men for whom he worked.

Now, for the first time, they began to eat at him.

'Who was William Steenkamp?' he asks me. 'If William Steenkamp was real, he would have a history, a family, a lineage going back a long time. Every time I went to work, I had to hide my real history. From the day I started working at City Glass to the day I ran away, I wore a long-sleeved shirt to work. No matter that the temperature was 35 degrees, I would sweat away all day in my long-sleeved shirt. I know this is a strange way of thinking of it, but I was protecting Mr and Mrs Morris from JR the 28, from Magadien Wentzel. JR was a man with tattoos going up his arm; if you can read tattoos, that shows you that a senior member of the most notorious gang in the country is coming to your workshop every day. I couldn't bring JR to City Glass. I had to wear long sleeves.'

When I meet Farieda in February 2003, City Glass has a new owner and a new name. But she is still there, sitting in the reception, and Gareth and Peter are still cutting glass at the back. I ask her if she remembers that William always wore long sleeves.

The question puzzles her. She frowns. 'It was company policy that William wear long sleeves,' she says. 'We didn't want to scare clients with his tattoos. You can't have a gangster working in your lounge!'

When I talk to the Morrises, they are the ones who raise the question of his sleeves. It is three months before Magadien's release.

We are talking about his chances of living a clean life when he is on the outside.

'Maybe you can take this as a thought to him,' Robin says to me. 'Maybe he can get a skin graft – take some skin from his legs and graft it onto his arms – to remove the tattoos.'

'He has thought of that,' I reply. 'But he does not want to run away from his past. He believes he can only live a clean life when he embraces his ...'

'I can understand that,' Robin interrupts. 'But then he mustn't be ashamed to roll up his sleeves.'

The sleeves have taken on a life of their own; everyone has their own private story about them. But the point is that everyone knew – William has prison tattoos and he hides them with his sleeves. His history was an open secret: he brought it into City Glass every day, written onto his body and into his eccentric relation to his body. It was a bit like the identity photograph from the bank that had stared back into Robin's face: there was another William; he brought traces of it to work every time he stepped through the door. Everyone chose to look the other way.

If the 'William Steenkamp' in his pocket was haunting his work, it was making life at home even more intolerable.

'When I'd been working a while, I started saving some money,' he tells me. 'The question was what to do with it. Do I open an account in the name of Magadien Wentzel? Or William Steenkamp? We opened an account in my wife's name. What sort of family man can't open a bank account? He doesn't exist.

'Then the phone would ring at home, Johaah would answer and it would be Farieda. She wants to speak to William. How do you explain to your son who William is? How do you explain to him that although he is your son, you have a stranger's name and he will not carry your legacy?

'Do you understand what it means not to have a name?' he asks me for the third or fourth time in the months since we met. 'You are lucky. You can take it for granted that you are Jonny Steinberg. You've never even had to think about what it means. It means you are a Jew, that your grandparents came to South Africa in x year, that your father was born in y year. That you know your name means you will never have to sleep in a gutter or wander the streets like a stroller. You belong.

'Basil Coetzee taught me that every human being has to belong. My whole life, I had been drifting towards nothing. He taught me that to be a human being, I had to go back to my people, my family, to my name. Here I was, a few years after Coetzee, with a wife and children and a job. But I still had no name. I had nothing to give my son for when after I was dead. I didn't even have a bank account.

'If I had died in 1998, who would they have buried? William Steenkamp? There is no William Steenkamp. He is a name in a stolen ID book. They would have been burying nobody.'

*

On the last Wednesday in May 1998, Gareth and William went to an address in Camps Bay to fit a set of windows. Gareth sent William back to the workshop for silicone and putty.

Less than a kilometre from the workshop, in the inner-city suburb of Tamboerskloof, he pulled up at a traffic light.

'A guy jumped out of his car and knocked on my window. He asked if I could put a piece of glass in his window at his flat. I asked his address; it was just round the corner. I said fine, and he gave me R60.

'I went back to the office and took a piece of glass. On my way back to Camp's Bay, I stopped at the address he had given me. I saw the broken window from the front door. It wasn't even necessary to ring the bell. I just started fixing it from the outside.

'Suddenly, the front door opens and this white guy comes out, puts a gun to my head and starts screaming at me, telling me I am trying to break into his flat, that he is going to shoot me.

'I tried to reason with him. I said: "Listen. Calm down. Look at my overalls. I am from City Glass. I am holding a piece of glass. I have putty in my hands. If I wanted to rob your place, would I have brought a piece of glass? Would I make such a noise? If I wanted to break into your flat, I would have gone inside."

'I tried to remember the name of the man who had asked me to do the job. I realised he never told me. I tried to remember the car he was driving; I couldn't remember.

'This guy wasn't listening to me anyway. He just kept shouting back at me, telling me he was going to shoot me.

'I was a 28. He was white. It was ridiculous. I said: "If you want to shoot me, shoot me. But I am leaving now." I walked away.'

'Why did you do what you did next?' I ask

'To this day, I cannot tell you. I got into the bakkie, drove straight to a friend in Bonteheuwel. I said: "Listen here: I need to smoke a pipe with you." We smoked and we smoked. And I just went berserk.'

'That morning, when you got to work, you had no intention of stealing the bakkie?'

'No. I did what I always did. I picked up the guys in the morning, arrived at work, set out for the day's jobs.'

'So that morning, as far as you were concerned, you were going to work for Mr Morris for another five years?'

'Ja. I was happy in my job. I never had a problem with anyone.'

'And by that evening, you were a fugitive.'

'Ja. I couldn't go home to Manenberg. The police would have found me. I went to the Strand, to Colleen. I didn't sleep for a second that night. I thought to myself: "Ja, you are William Steenkamp. You were never anyone else. William Steenkamp is a liar who enters people's lives to destroy them. He is someone who can't go home to his wife and kid because the police are waiting there for him." I thought to myself: "Ja, this morning you woke up with the illusion that you were a husband and a father with a steady job. You weren't: you were William Steenkamp. This is what William Steenkamp does."'

The next morning he took the bakkie for a long drive, watched the petrol gauge drop, and realised that he had no money to fill his tank. By the time he drove back into the Strand, there was sweat on his forehead and his hands were shaking: he hadn't had a pipe in 16 hours.

'All I could think of was the next pipe. I needed money. So I did the William Steenkamp thing. Less than a week after I'd run away, I went to a supplier in Blackheath with my City Glass bakkie and bought a huge amount of glass. There was this guy in Rusthof who fixed broken windows and I became his supplier.

'Then the police raided his place and I knew they were catching up with me. I was relieved. I thought – thank God; it will be over soon.'

'You wanted to get caught?'

'That's what I wanted, yes.'

'You wanted to go back to jail, like the other times?'

'No, I didn't want to go back to jail. I just wanted it all to stop. I wanted the nightmare to end. I went to a guy I knew who made false teeth. I've had no front teeth since I was 17. I got him to make me a pair with "28" written on each one. I paid him with my last money and then I drove around all day, watching the world. Then I parked the bakkie at the side of the road, cleaned it, and left the key in the ignition. Then I went to visit my wife at her work. I said to her: "Faranaaz, I've fucked up again. I'm going back to prison. I want to spend my last days with you and the kids." So we went home, and a few days later the cops came for me.

'The night before they came for me, I was lying in bed with Faranaaz and I said to her: "It never lasts long, does it? I marry you and then I go away. I don't know what you're going to do with the rest of your life, but I think you should leave me."'

*

A year later, shortly after he had been sentenced to six years for his crimes against the Morrises, he made the call to Farieda: the one where she told him that Robin and Helen had lost their business, that they had gone bankrupt.

He walked back to his cell and the image in his head was of this once-proud white family sitting on the streets, squatting in the home of a kind relative, begging for money so that the kids could stay in school. He knew immediately – with the certainty that comes to the superstitious and the paranoid – that it was all his doing; he was the one who had destroyed them. For four years, he sat with this certainty. Out there, the white suburbs of Cape Town were strewn with the catastrophe William Steenkamp had left in his wake. He never bothered to find out whether it was true: he needed to be responsible for a tragedy.

When I met the Morrises, I told them of Magadien's fantasy, of how it had reduced him to tears. At first they said nothing: they were reluctant to discuss their affairs with a stranger. But as we spoke, the thought of Magadien's torment brewed in the back of Robin's mind; he couldn't let it go. Shortly before the end of the interview, he said: 'Tell William, tell him that it is true we have had troubles. But tell him also that I never lost a cent as a result of what he did. You see, everything he stole, he stole without an order book, without an authorised signature. The supplier was at fault. We didn't pay a cent for that glass.'

I saw Magadien the next day and delivered Robin's message. He nodded expressionlessly for a long time. 'That's good news,' he finally murmured. 'Good news.'

He was relieved, to be sure, and it is possible that my own imagination interpreted too much. But I think a part of him resented me for the news I had brought him. I had robbed him of his cruellest punishment.

19
POLLSMOOR

Pollsmoor Admission Centre, June 1998. In the past seven years, the last of apartheid's old legislators and the first of democracy's new ones had, between them, rubbed out the apartheid prison with their government-issue erasers and built a new one with their pens. In the statute books, the jails Magadien knew in the 1970s and 80s had vanished. Solitary confinement had been abolished; the weeks of saltless diet were gone; corporal punishment had been outlawed. The coordinates of Nongoloza's world were no more. From now on, according to the statutes, when a Number gang initiate stabbed he could no longer expect to face the battering, stoical path to manhood *ndotas* had travelled for a century; he would get his day in court instead.

The prisons services' military rank structure had been replaced with the regular civilian hierarchy of the new civil service: no more colonels and brigadiers, only directors and deputy directors. Most important of all, perhaps, the rule of law had entered the prisons. The decisions of prison administrators were subject to judicial review. South Africa was now governed by a constitution with a bill of rights, one of which protected human beings from cruel and unusual punishment, while another gave prisoners the right to conditions of detention consistent with human dignity. In theory, a prisoner could take his custodians to court.

Even the name of Pollsmoor's most infamous prison had changed. It was no longer Pollsmoor Maximum Security Prison, but Pollsmoor Admission Centre, a somewhat Orwellian interpretation of the fact that three-quarters of its inmates were awaiting trial.

That's how Pollsmoor looked on paper. The actual prison Magadien walked into in June 1998 was unhinged. 'It was a war zone,' he tells me, 'except that in a war, there are two sides. Here, it was everyone against everyone else. There wasn't a single day that went by when someone wasn't stabbed or fucked up.'

He is not exaggerating. Between January 1995 and December 1997, there were 336 recorded assaults by warders on inmates, an average of one every three days. During the same period, the prison's books record more than four hundred assaults on inmates by inmates. And those are only the incidents which found their way into the official record. Pollsmoor Admission Centre was probably the most violent place in Cape Town.

I spoke to a European government official who had visited the prison in 1997. 'It felt like a war zone,' she told me. 'I'd walk down a corridor surrounded by warders carrying batons and tear gas canisters, and when we passed a group of prisoners, they'd tense up like wild dogs with their hair standing up and their fangs bared.'

Prisons are notorious for handling political change badly: but in Pollsmoor, the foundations had collapsed. In the nine years since Johnny Jansen and his colleagues had formed an oppositional trade union, Popcru, white and coloured warders had fought an exhausting war of attrition. The white men who had for their entire working lives run a docile and compliant military hierarchy were confronted by blocs of staff in more or less open rebellion. In their representations to parliament and the correctional services ministry, they begged that the service's military structure be preserved, lest they lose control completely. New South Africa-speak of rehabilitation and the rights of prisoners filled them with the fear of God. Persistent talk of affirmative action convinced them that no white prisons official would ever be promoted again, that their careers were shot.

Popcru itself, which had begun life talking of civil rights and prison reform, had long begun to lose sight of its original goals. Its eyes were on the prize now – on power and salaries. Some of its members jostled for position. There were scraps and fights, caucuses and conspiracies; the fault-lines were increasingly racial – coloureds versus Africans.

The fabric that holds a prison together is fragile and taut. So many of the rules are unwritten, barely understood by the protagonists themselves. Everything hinges on predictability: both warders and inmates must know the habits of the other side instinctively. When the old system crumbles, there is an interregnum: old rules die and new rules have yet to replace them. In Pollsmoor, the gangs pushed their confused and bickering custodians to the periphery and began to run the prison themselves.

'We were purely in defence mode,' a staff member who had been at Pollsmoor in the mid-1990s told me. 'The gangs could run the prisons as far we were concerned, as long as they didn't touch one of us. So we patrolled with dogs, we had batons on our hips. Our only concern was that they know that if they touch us they will bleed.'

Magadien's most vivid memory of warders during his first months in Pollsmoor was of 'the hit squad'. 'It wasn't us who called it the hit squad,' he told me, 'it was the warders themselves. It was a special task team whose job was to fuck up gangsters. There were seven or eight of them. And they were coloureds, my friend, coloureds. Their job was to make other coloureds bleed. Everyone who caused trouble was taken to D1 and before he was admitted they beat the shit out of him. One 27, they broke his jaw. But then the gangsters would retaliate. For every *ndota* fucked up, there was havoc.

'In fact, the warders were not running the prison. They were too afraid. They were too scared even to take us into the yard for exercise. We exercised once a month. There was no sport, no recreation – they were afraid of giving us the freedom to move around. So we sat there in our sections, day in and day out. And the sections were packed. Pollsmoor was maybe 150% full. We lived on top of each other, in the heat and the cold. The Number ran the sections. And Jesus, the Number was fucked up. I can't begin to describe it.'

*

From Magadien's vantage point, the Number was fucked up. Yet in the long view, something more interesting had happened: the Number had returned to the street after an 80-year absence. It was no longer just a prison phenomenon: it had begun to organise the collective imagination of Cape Town's underworld. After a century behind bars, Nongoloza was out now; and he had become a robber baron.

Six years had passed since Tokkie Jonkers had arrived in Magadien's life, announcing that he had been recruited into the gold line of the 28s by a street gang. In the intervening period, the masters of Cape Town's criminal economy had captured the world of the Number and made it their own. In the mid-1990s, as the street gangs struggled over new drugs and new turf, war had erupted between the Americans and the Firm; the battleground stretched across and beyond the Cape Flats, as far afield as the quiet fishing villages on the Cape Agulhas coastline. Big money had taken the war to the hinterland; but it was the symbolic power of Nongoloza that had recruited soldiers and wooed consumers everywhere. The world was full of new, half-baked 26s and 28s; they had been initiated on the streets.

The prisons were filling with young men who called themselves *ndotas*, but they had not stabbed when they joined, they had not been beaten in front of their fellow inmates, and they had not gone *agter die berge*. Their knowledge of the Nongoloza myth was scrappy and disjointed. They could not *sabela* fluently, and their understanding of the Number's rituals was laughable. To veteran *ndotas* like Magadien, the world had been unmoored. 'When I was recruited,' he told me, 'and I was taught the story of Nongoloza, part of the story said that a great shadow would fall over the Number in years to come, and that the evil would come from within. This was it. There was no Number in Pollsmoor any more, only little boys playing games.'

As the drug barons and their lieutenants started spending time in jail, they brought the new Number gangs of the streets with them. In 1996 Jackie Lonti, leader of the Americans, who had made his millions bringing crack cocaine to the Western Cape, was interned at Pollsmoor. In prison, he was just a middle-ranking member of the 26s, subject to Number gang discipline. Outside, he was a god. Many of his enemies were in the Pollsmoor cells around him. Outside, they were senior members of the Firm. Inside, many were rank-and-file 28s, people whom he was obliged by Number gang lore to respect on the Valcross, to share his money with, to fight alongside against prison warders. The new Number of the street stood face-to-face with the old Number of the prison.

Lonti's first week at Pollsmoor has become the stuff of legend. 'Jackie sent out an order to all 26s in Pollsmoor,' an American and 26 member told me. 'He instructed us to raise the Star-Spangled Banner in our cells, and to declare war against the 28s. You must understand that what he did was so wrong according to our tradition that he should have been sentenced to death for it. First, he told us as 26s to raise the flag of the Americans, a *vuil papier*, a flag of the fourth camp. That alone is punishable by death. Second, he declared war against the 28s when the issue that sparked the war was an issue from the outside, not from the four corners. That alone is punishable by death; you do not bring the outside into prison. Finally, he was not a General. He did not call a meeting of the Twelve Points. Only they can declare war against the 28s, and only in consultation with the 27s. That, especially, is punishable by death.

'But he was Jackie, and Jackie meant more than anything else. So we raised our American flags in our cells and we went to war with the 28s. Something like that had never happened before. After that, the Number was never the same again.'

But the gods of the supergangs on the outside, men like Lonti, were seldom in Pollsmoor Admission Centre for long. Unlike their disciples, they were rich men with high-calibre legal teams; they were soon out on bail. When they left, they took their authority with them, leaving the debris of a confused and battered inmate tradition behind them. Inmate life was characterised by one crisis of authority after another.

'A big dealer from, say, the Firm, would arrive in Pollsmoor,' Magadien tells me. 'Using his money and power from the streets, he would claim that he is a 28 General, that he must run the prison. Many of his soldiers from the outside would be here in prison with him, and he would recruit them all into the 28s, not in the proper way, but in his own ignorant way. A group of old *ndotas* would say, "No, you are not a General, and these people you are recruiting are not 28s. When did you ever stab someone? When have you been *agter die berge*? Who taught you the history of Nongoloza?" And he would reply: "Fine, you want stabbing, you'll get stabbing." And he would instruct his followers to stab the old *ndotas* who were opposing him. He would say to them: "If you stab a Colonel, you will get his position. If you stab a Magistrate, you will become a Magistrate."

'It was anarchy. Whenever somebody wanted power, he would suddenly grab hold of an old tradition – like stabbing – and say, "Okay, now I am legitimate." They were all pretenders, all a bunch of monkeys. I felt like I had been sentenced to spend time in a zoo.'

They were all pretenders, but not all were monkeys. By the time Magadien arrived at Pollsmoor, the greatest pretender of all, Doggy

Dog, had been in the prison for more than a year. He had used the power conferred on him by the Niewoudtville murders to recruit more than a dozen Americans into the 27s, while he himself was slowly disintegrating in his struggle with his demons.

The Doggy Dog story is the apotheosis of the world Pollsmoor had become in the late 1990s. He had done the impossible – re-established the 27s, of all gangs – and in the wrong way; his recruits did not stab when they joined, they did not embark on the long, painstaking learning of gang lore a new 27 ought to acquire. And yet he had given them authority. He had done so by placing his own ghastly story at the heart of the Nongoloza myth, contriving, quite artfully, to retrieve a golden strand of the old tradition.

And yet, in the end, Dog was as transient as the other pretenders. By the time I arrived at Pollsmoor in October 2002, nobody spoke of him any more. Some of those he had recruited into the 27s were still there, but the magic dust he had sprinkled on them had lost its power long ago. 'They are not real 27s,' I was told. 'They wouldn't know Kilikijan from a *strandloper*.' The prison stumbled from one crisis of authority to the next. Its collective memory was never more than a few months old.

One way of expressing what was happening at Pollsmoor is this: ever since Western Cape gangsters starting becoming multi-millionaires, Nongoloza had been split in two. Out in the world, he was the bandit turned robber baron; he had used his outlawry to build an empire, and he had become the hero of the region's criminal classes. Inside, he was still the stoical old figure who strives to re-establish the order of things in the upside-down world behind bars; through his painstakingly ritualised acts of violence, he holds up the dam wall between men and children, and between men and women. Western Cape inmates could not have both Nongolozas, but they could give either of them up. They tried to piece together a composite Nongoloza – bits of one, scraps of the other – but the composite figure could not stand on his own two feet.

*

In Pollsmoor in 1998, Magadien became a crusty, foul-tempered conservative. Like the old Tory who believes that the reservoirs of value all lie in the past, he set about attempting to retrieve a world that had long vanished.

'When I arrived, the 28s were very excited,' he tells me. 'I was known as a Magistrate *vleis-en-bloed*, the real McCoy, a *ndota* from the old days. They told me I must take up my position immediately.

'I said: "Fuck you. I'd stab you before I work with you. This is not the Number. This is a joke."

'I was housed on D Floor. Mr Jansen had just separated gangsters from *franse* in the awaiting-trial part of the prison and the gangsters were on D Floor. I walked around D Floor looking for *vleis-en-bloed* 28s, people who had been recruited the proper way in the old days. On that whole fucking floor, I found four of them. The highest-ranking was a man called Fred, a *Mabalang* in the gold line. I walked into his cell and started shouting at him. "How long have you been here? What the fuck have you being doing with yourself? Look at what is happening around you."'

Fred eyed Magadien with wonder. Here was Rip Van Winkle, fresh from the 1980s, behaving as if the world had not moved. Besides, Fred was selling drugs for the Firm in Pollsmoor. He was quite content with the new order.

Magadien harangued him nonetheless, and he finally conceded on one matter. Of all the half-baked nonsense ruining Pollsmoor Admission Centre, it was the recruitment of new initiates that angered Magadien most. One of the sacred rules of the old Number is that one does not recruit in the awaiting-trial section of prisons. The learning that goes with recruitment stretches out over months. If the new initiate is found not guilty in court, he goes into the world a half-*ndota*; his knowledge is partial and thus dangerous.

Magadien got Fred to agree that they would end recruitment on D Floor. The two old-timers commanded a great deal of authority. Their knowledge of the lore, the legends and ranks was vast. They could spin webs of history around their opponents. They worked through Doggy Dog, the most powerful gangster on D Floor, and got him to agree. No recruitment, no promotion. And that meant no ritual stabbing. One could only stab if one was wronged. And one only knew if one had been wronged if the gang's leadership said you had been. Magadien became the informal head of the 28s on D Floor. Dog was head of the 27s. An old-timer by the name of Alfred was dragged out of the 26s. It was agreed that nobody would be stabbed on D Floor without their consent. They would run the section as an awaiting-trial section is meant to be run – as *die stokkies*, the sticks – the Number in limbo.

'I stayed up late every night,' Magadien recalls, 'teaching these little Firm boys the Number. I didn't have the power to say they didn't belong to the 28s. I did the next best thing. I educated them.'

Magadien was using a plaster to staunch a gunshot wound. He didn't understand that Western Cape prisons had changed forever. Nonetheless, his quixotic exercise calmed him. His betrayal of the Morrises had left him a wreck. He needed broken things to fix. In Pollsmoor, he didn't have to search hard.

On an August morning in 1998, less than two months after his arrest, he decided to quit Mandrax. 'I had been watching Dog smoke himself out of his mind,' he tells me. 'I had been watching the whole fucking prison smoke itself out of its mind. I was feeling calm, like I'd risen above the jail and was watching its madness from far away. I thought, "Enough. It's time to stop now. If it wasn't for smoking drugs, I'd never have gone to fix that window in Tamboerskloof. I'd be living with Faranaaz and the kids and working for the Morrises."

'It showed me I have the will to do whatever I want to. It's all will power. It's in the mind.'

He has not touched Mandrax since. But, despite his conviction that it's all a matter of will, he has paid a price. A week after his decision to quit, his stomach rebelled against him. He couldn't eat more than a few morsels of food at a time. The smell of boiled prison fare made him nauseous; when the trolleys arrived from the kitchen at 7 am, he would go to the toilet bowl and wait for the retching to begin. For the duration of his imprisonment he lived mainly on bread and fruit, the latter brought to him from the outside by warders. He has always been a thin man, but when I met him he was skeletal; he weighed 54 kilograms.

I spoke to a psychiatrist who had worked in the field of addiction for many years. I asked him whether it was common for a former Mandrax addict to lose his appetite for food.

'No,' he said. 'It's puzzling. It is common for somebody to lose his appetite for a week or two, not four years. It can't be physiological. His giving up of buttons must be associated with severe psychological trauma.'

I was left with a disturbing image of Magadien in my mind: a frantic person scurrying around the prison, seeing broken things wherever he looked, attempting hopelessly to fix them: a bit like the neurotic housewife driven to insanity because her home is never clean.

In any event, this agonised displacement, if that is what it was, was not to last. He would soon meet Johnny Jansen and would begin to make a vocation of fixing himself. It was to be as frenzied as his attempt to fix the Number.

*

In early January 1999, Johnny Jansen, who had been head of Pollsmoor Admission Centre for about eighteen months, received an instruction from head office in Pretoria to remove televisions from his prison. South Africa was convulsed by its latest spasm of populist panic. It was said that the country's jails were not cruel enough, that criminals had it too easy in prison. Unfathomably, the issue that caught the imagination this time was television sets. 'Our prisons are not hotels,' the Minister of Agriculture and Land Affairs, of all people, blurted out at a press conference.

By mid-January, the televisions were gone and the jail was on the brink of rebellion. Pollsmoor was a place where inmates spent 15 hours of each day idle, locked up in their communal cells. Television was more than entertainment; it was an escape from the crushingly incessant presence of people, a conduit to the universe, and a fount of imagination in a monotonous world. Being denied television was only a rung down from being forbidden food.

Magadien was in his element. Finally, there was real Number business to be done. This, after all, is what the Number was for: to win space, to reclaim rights. He sits erect as he tells the story; he gesticulates regally.

'Alfred and I went to the Valcross to challenge the 27s,' he says. 'We said: "Our privileges were taken away for reasons we don't understand. What are you going to do about it?" They said, "What can we do about it?" So I told them: "I'm going to write a 'request' saying that if they don't give us our TVs back, we are going to stab warders, starting on our section. If they want a bloodbath, they'll get one."

'I wrote the letter and all three of us signed it – me, Dog and Alfred. We sent it through. It went to Jansen's desk, and boom!

They locked all the doors, including the outside doors, and the warders downed tools and toyi-toyied in the foyer. They said: "No, we can't work like this. We want danger money."'

He smiles with satisfaction. 'Actually, I did something good for the warders; they did get danger money.

'So they called the three of us in – our names were on the letter. We walked into Mr Jansen's office and every officer in the prison was there, including Mr Basil Coetzee, who had been transferred to Pollsmoor. As we walked in, I saw him whisper in Mr Jansen's ear and I knew he was talking about me.

'"So," Mr Jansen said: "What's this?"

'The most amazing thing happened. He started with the 26.

'"Do you represent the 26s?"

'"Ja."

'"Do you know anything about this?"

'"No."

'"Then you can go and stand outside."

'Same with Doggy Dog. He denied it, and was sent to stand outside.

'Then he said to me, "Do you know about this?"

'I said: "Ja, I wrote it. And I mean it." I said, "Listen here. You can transfer me: the warders will still be stabbed in this prison. I'll see to it. And the prison you send me to – I'll stab a warder there and they will send me back because they do not want this prison's scum."

'Then they all started talking: "Why are you so aggressive? Why can't you communicate like a civilised human being? This television thing – we received the fax from Pretoria; it was out of our hands. You know that. Are you fucking mad?"

'They called in a psychologist to evaluate me, a young white woman. She got me to write an essay on why I am aggressive, on what I think about prison. And she made an evaluation. She said I'm not crazy, I'm just very angry.'

*

I recount Magadien's telling of the television story to Johnny Jansen. We are sitting in his living room. His house is on Pollsmoor premises. Outside, six orange-overalled inmates are weeding his garden.

Jansen's presence is enormously authoritative. He is heavy, his gestures slow. He stares at me a long time and then his eyes begin to dance with gentle mischief.

'I was quite excited by Steenkamp's performance at that meeting. It confirmed what I already knew about him: I thought, shit, this *is* somebody I can work with.

'You see, Steenkamp was a prominent 28 gang leader. He was definitely one of the worst. You can't imagine what he looked like. He had a wild afro, a beard, his skin was dark, dirty. Obviously he did drugs on a daily basis. He was a terrible figure.

'And he was a very difficult customer. When we got together, he was always challenging what I was saying, was negative about what I was saying. But that attracted me to him. Because there was something about him. Gangsters live in a very emotional culture. You feel and then you do. Steenkamp was different. He could think. He could be rational much more than the others. I could talk to him.

'So I thought to myself, "Here is a man to focus on. He is a top leader. He has influence. If I get through to him, I will go a long way." So I listened to him in that meeting shouting about how he was going to stab warders and I smiled to myself.'

Perhaps Jansen is shy about telling me what he really saw in 'Steenkamp'. Or perhaps he does not have the vocabulary to express his emotional intelligence. Maybe he did not in fact understand what he was doing. But it was not just that Magadien was rational. Magadien was seeking a father, a larger-than-life man who would save him. And Jansen was a needy giant, the sort who spawns adoring sons. The connection was not only between two men who share a common rationality: it was also in the ethereal realm of emotion.

*

Jansen had taken charge of Pollsmoor Admission Centre during the course of 1997. He had been assigned to manage an inferno. The gangs controlled Pollsmoor's corridors openly and brazenly. His own staff were armed to the teeth and patrolled the prison with their hands clenched round their batons.

But that was only the start of his problems. About two years earlier, in 1995, a man called Stephen Conradie, who, like Jansen, had been a founder member of Popcru, was appointed Pollsmoor Area Commissioner, over the heads of several white men who had coveted the job for years. The following year, he was replaced by another coloured man, Freddie Engelbrecht. Engelbrecht was responsible for all five prisons in the Pollsmoor complex: the five prison heads reported to him. For the old guard that ran Pollsmoor, the enemy had now come to power; the coloured rebel had become the boss.

'From the moment I stepped into my office,' Engelbrecht told the Jali Commission of Inquiry into Prison Corruption in December 2002, 'I was confronted by passive-aggressive behaviour, especially from whites. I was assistant-secretary of Popcru, you see, the enemy. I would say that the prisons have to be run differently. We do not just incarcerate; we rehabilitate. They would say to me: "We've tried that. It doesn't work." Everything I did, there was resistance, automatically. After two months, I became a dictator: "You will do it, otherwise you must go."

'So they went. The first person to leave was the chairperson of the institutional committee, on medical pension. Two months later, one of the heads of prison, Mr Roelofse, also went on medical pension. At the end of April 1997, another head of prison. September 1997, two more heads of prison, and the head of personnel a month later. The chair of the parole board left at the end of November. The head of finance left the following year.

'All in all, 40 senior staff cleared out: 23 on medical pension, 14 severance packages, and the remaining three resigned with 48 hours' notice.'

Jansen took over Pollsmoor Admission Centre in the wake of a mass exodus. He had no experience of running a prison, let alone the most anarchic in the province, and nor did anyone around him. He was a novice among novices, charged with managing more than three hundred staff members and over three thousand prisoners.

He came armed with two attributes that were to hand him an unlikely victory. The first was an intuitive intelligence. The second was brazen confidence, which was cultivated by what I can only call his evangelical naivety.

His strength was his powerful identification with the men behind the bars. He was a massively proud man, an old-style patriarch, and the most profound experience of his two decades as a coloured warder in the apartheid prisons service had been his own humiliation. At the Jali Commission, he told the packed gallery the story he had told me when we first met: how he had been hauled into the head of prison's office, where the entire senior staff of the prison stood waiting for him; how they had called him a liar and told him to go back to his parents to bring him up properly; how they had chuckled and sneered.

'That day,' Jansen told the Jali Commission, 'I felt I could commit murder. I was so humiliated, I felt I could kill.'

So he believed that he knew why the men in his charge had murdered and raped; their psyches had been mangled by the collective humiliation of apartheid. 'I don't think the solution to crime is so complicated,' he told me. 'Human beings are supposed to be simple. They didn't become what they are by choice, but by their circumstances. If you expose them to different ways of doing things, it is like giving a child a new toy.'

It was all charmingly romantic. Human beings are naturally good: apartheid had deformed their souls. Jansen himself had almost succumbed to the cancer of racial humiliation; he had wanted to kill. But he was better now, a fully-fledged human being, and he was going to shepherd his flock back to goodness: one victim of apartheid taking the rest by the hand.

By the time Magadien got to Pollsmoor Admission Centre, Jansen was just at the beginning of his work. He had walked into a war between inmates and warders, and he began by disarming the one side he could – his own staff. He quite literally disarmed them: he cleared the prison of batons, dogs and tear gas. Warders were made to understand, for the first time, that the prohibition on violence was for real, that they would be dismissed for assaulting prisoners. He held workshops for his staff, telling them that they needed to replace violence with dialogue. They stared back at him like he was mad; many believed he was preparing them for slaughter.

So, he had to lead by example. He would walk alone through D Floor, where he had housed the gangsters in the awaiting-trial section, step into a packed cell, sit down on a bed and begin talking.

'At first, we took him for a joke,' Magadien tells me. 'He would come to our cells and talk about the community, our children, the environment, about how apartheid had fucked us all up, even himself. We just listened and said nothing. When he walked out, we would laugh: *"Hierdie man praat kak. Hy dink ons is moegoes."* "This man talks shit. He thinks we're idiots." We saw him as a foolish, arrogant show-off. We were his prize. He wanted to show the world that he could control the Number. It was a matter of honour that he should fail.'

But Jansen had a few tricks up his sleeve. His most powerful tool was the shocking state of his prison: no exercise, no sport, just a seamless succession of days locked indoors. He had a carrot with which to feed the gangs: a tolerable life behind bars.

He got D Floor to elect a committee of 20 representatives. They were duly elected, gang leaders all of them, which is what he wanted. He listed 20 portfolios – food, health, sanitation, sports, recreation, and so forth – and asked the inmate committee to appoint a person to each portfolio. Magadien was made chairperson of the committee. Jansen called the head of the hospital and the kitchen administrator, and instructed them to sit in on a meeting with the committee.

'In the middle of that meeting,' Magadien tells me, 'Mr Jansen introduced the kitchen administrator to the inmate in charge of the food portfolio. He said to the administrator: "This man is going to come to you with problems about the food. I want you to talk reasonably. His requests will be reasonable. Take them seriously." The kitchen administrator nearly fell off his chair. Mr Jansen was telling him to take instructions from an inmate.'

Jansen enjoyed these grand, polemical gestures, but the things he had in mind went well beyond the art of performance. He was, in essence, establishing the terms of a pact. The running of the prison bureaucracy would lose its dictatorial arbitrariness; all aspects of prison life would be administered in consultation with inmates. He was prepared to open up the prison; there would be cricket, soccer and gym – treasures for the inmates of a place like Pollsmoor. Activities would be run by inmates themselves – by the portfolio heads. But they had to play by Jansen's rules. He was offering them slivers of freedom in exchange for de-escalation. The moment the gangs used their newfound freedoms malevolently, he would close down the space he had opened.

It is difficult to overemphasise the eccentricity of his proposition. For decades, warders and inmates had regarded one another as the soldiers of opposing armies. The only channels of communication had been those of espionage and betrayal. Now, Jansen was building a new relationship, and its centrepiece was a bargain, and thus mutual trust. The moment one side betrayed trust, it was all over. If Jansen had been unable to rein in the arbitrary actions of his staff, the *ndotas* would have laughed in his face. If they had used the freedoms of the new regime to stab, the new regime would have ended abruptly.

*

Magadien was a sucker for Jansen's bargain. It fired his imagination at once. He read it, not as a strategy to tame the prison, but as a personal epiphany, an idea powerful enough to redeem his whole life. In retrospect, it is easy to see why.

He was fresh from his experience with the Morrises. He had tried to build a new life around them and had failed. Like Jansen, they had given him their trust. And yet the demiurge inside him – a creature of destructiveness he could neither control nor understand – had smashed his relationship with them to pieces. Part of the problem was his secrets. The very name he presented to them – William Steenkamp – was a deceit. He came to work every day literally shrouding the history that was written on his body. The being he brought to City Glass was, by definition, a cheat.

When he met Jansen, and imbibed what the prison head was up to, he quickly came to see the episode with the Morrises as a faulty trial run, a test for which he had been ill-equipped. Jansen was also offering his trust. And the terms of Magadien's relationship with Jansen were not dissimilar from that with the Morrises: a white employer and his coloured labourer, a prison head and his charges – both were marked with traces of paternalism. Only this time, there were no secrets. Magadien *was* a criminal. 'William Steenkamp' was not his name, but the alias of a criminal, the alias of Magadien Darryl Wentzel, serial fraudster and prison gang leader. It was in the open.

Not only was it in the open, it is what the whole story was about. Jansen offered another test of trust, but the offer itself came clothed in a rich narrative. The narrative was a Christian one about redeeming a wretched past; a political one about resurrecting a human being out of the deformed soul apartheid had created. It was a narrative that not only embraced the fact that Magadien was a criminal: it placed his criminality in a grand story, made the path from criminality a political and religious odyssey. The language Jansen spoke gripped him as fiercely as the language of Nongoloza had once done. And in some senses, the two languages were the same; both composed grand narratives about South Africa's past and a path to its future; both placed Magadien himself at the heart of the story; both gave him the power of comprehension, the power to look back at his personal history and make sense of it.

When I ask Magadien why he embraced Jansen so quickly and so wholly, he frowns at me, not bothering to conceal his disappointment at my incomprehension.

'To you it seems quick,' he says. 'To me, it seems like it was very slow, a whole lifetime. I had been trying to change for years. There was Basil Coetzee with his stuff about the Khoi-Khoi, and that failed. There was the Morrises, and that ended in disaster. Until I met Mr Jansen, I never understood why it always ended in disaster. I had been waiting for him almost for ever.'

He embraced, not just Jansen's bargain, but Jansen the flesh-and-blood man. On the inmate committee, he fought for all his worth against spoilers and obstructionists. 'Many times, people on that committee suggested that we derail it,' he told me. 'I'd snap at them: "What the fuck do you want instead? Dogs and batons? A fucking circus?" People would taunt me. "You're Jansen's little boy. You're fucking up the Number." When they said that, I'd already won. I knew more about the Number than the rest of them combined. I'd talk them into a corner.'

For Jansen, Magadien was too good to be true. 'It's unbelievable that a person can change physically and emotionally the way he has,' Jansen tells me. 'The Steenkamp I met and the Steenkamp today; it's close to a miracle.'

They courted each other. Magadien spilled out his life story, and Jansen was wholly absorbed. He was Magadien's listener. They always obeyed the strict protocol of the relationship between warder and prisoner. Indeed, the substance of their relationship was paternalistic. Magadien referred to him as 'Mr Jansen', always, even when Jansen was not around. When we met, he spoke of Jansen only in the most reverential terms. And Jansen addressed Magadien as 'Steenkamp': the prisoner was his charge, his convert.

But the paternalistic and the paternal sometimes live at close quarters. 'I knew Mr Jansen was for real,' Magadien tells me, 'when he gave me his home phone number. He said: "If there is a problem, a crisis, phone: I will come."

'A little while later, he actually invited a couple of us round to his house. It was an honour to be there. I met his family. I adore his wife. I adore his children. They are like my family. I think of him as a father.'

From Magadien's side, the relationship was indeed filial, and it became so much too quickly; there would be trouble in years to come.

*

There was to be another seminal influence on Magadien at that time, and it came in the form of two *'sturvies'* – Joanna Flanders Thomas and Michelene Benson. They were young, middle-class professionals, and they were coloured – precisely the sort of people Magadien had always regarded with primordial loathing.

In January 1998, Pollsmoor's management approached a non-governmental organisation, the Centre for Conflict Resolution (CCR), and requested its assistance in running conflict resolution workshops for warders and inmates. These were heady days at Pollsmoor. Its young coloured managers wanted to reinvent the prison; they were searching hungrily for ideas. So Flanders Thomas and Benson, both from CCR, came to Pollsmoor.

The work they were to accomplish would change the prison profoundly, at least for a while. Jansen was excited by their presence and used them liberally. During their first 18 months at Pollsmoor, they established, among other things, a workshop with warders, in an endeavour to unstitch the coarse and violent practices apartheid had bequeathed to the prison. In their second year, Flanders Thomas spent many of her days on D Floor, talking to Number gang leaders like Magadien. By September 1999, she had assisted in establishing a twice-weekly workshop among gang leaders on D Floor, a workshop that was to open a door for Magadien to a new language and a new conception of himself.

Joanna and Magadien both remember their first encounter vividly; their respective accounts are identical. It was a mid-December morning, 1998, in the courtyard, which was full of prisoners. Magadien watched Joanna walk across the open space, approached her, and introduced himself.

'So, you want to change inmates,' he said.

She began to reply and he cut her off, his lip curling with sarcasm.

'You know nothing about prison.'

Again, she tried to say something and he interrupted.

'You have nothing to say to me. You know nothing. Go and book yourself into the women's prison for a month and then come and talk to me about prison.'

They saw one another often during the following months, but Magadien was cool and wary. Their next significant encounter was in August 1999.

'I was walking along a corridor on D Floor,' Joanna tells me, 'and I saw his face. He was in one of the communal cells, staring out the window into the corridor.

'"What's the matter?" I asked him.

'He told me something terrible had happened, that he thought his family was dead. His face was grey. He was in a lot of pain.

'Manenberg had been hit by a huge tornado a few days earlier. He told me he had tried to phone his family, but that the lines were dead. He was sitting in Pollsmoor not knowing if they were dead or alive. He kept telling me he knew something horrible had happened to them: he knew their house had been hit.

'I asked him for their address and went to Manenberg that afternoon. He was right; their house had been seriously hit, worse than any of the others on their street. There was a field across the road from the house, and there were lots of people squatting on the field who had been made homeless by the tornado. I went there and asked for the Benjamins, and they were all there; they were all safe.

'I went to my sister-in-law and we organised some clothes and groceries for them, and the next day I went back to Pollsmoor and told him everything. He was so relieved; I've never seen someone so relieved.'

During the nine-month period in 2002 and 2003 when Magadien and I spoke every day in his cell, the tornado cropped up in his conversation time and again. The manner in which he spoke of it brought to mind his paranoid fantasy about the Morrises. He believed, you will recall, that he had bankrupted them and ruined their lives and those of their children; that the evil inside him had brought a decent family to its knees. His nightmares about the tornado were of the same ilk, but more dramatic, their image of devastation wilder and more horrifying. He believed, instinctively, in his gut, that his own wrongdoing had torn the Benjamins' house down.

'I couldn't cope when I heard the news,' he told me. 'I was going out of my mind. I had images of the house falling on my son's head. I was driving myself mad. I thought maybe God was punishing me for the things I had done. I asked myself: why does this happen now, right at the time that I am getting ready to really be a proper family man? Is that why God is taking away my family now – is he telling me I've already done too much harm?

'When Joanna came and told me they were all right, I cried. She comforted me. I was crying in front of this woman I had shouted at in the courtyard.'

So that is the context in which Magadien became close to Joanna – in the wake of a natural catastrophe that he had read as a personal message. His fantasies about the violent consequences of his destructiveness were not new – there had been the Morrises. But what was new, I think, was the stark religious dimension; he met Joanna among the frightening symbols and codes of what he took to be a divine warning.

*

The workshop with gang leaders on D Floor that Joanna had spent months of painstaking work establishing began in September 1999, shortly after the Manenberg tornado. It met twice a week. There were 18 inmates in the workshop, most of them Number gang leaders and members of the inmate committee Jansen had established. The workshop had four legs. The first was called 'Introduction to Human Dynamics' and was modelled on a body of work which Joanna had recently studied. She had been trained by two of the pioneers in the field, the American and British psychologists Sandra Seagal and David Horne. The publisher's blurb on the dust cover of their book, *Human Dynamics: A New Framework for Understanding People and Realizing the Potential of Our Organizations*, says that Seagal and Horne 'introduce a developmental system that demystifies the complexities of how we interact with one another ... a powerful framework for understanding the distinct ways in which we process information, learn, develop, communicate, relate to one another, manifest stress, and maintain well-being'.

It was, to say the least, a foreign language for men who had grown up on the streets of the Cape Flats. I asked one of the inmate participants at the workshop what he had learned from the Human Dynamics course. 'Basically,' he said, 'that if we understand each other and ourselves better, we'll be less inclined to fuck each other up.'

The second course was called 'Creative and Constructive Approaches to Conflict', the third 'Action Learning for Development'. The fourth was a course on trauma debriefing and was run by a clinical psychologist, Stephen van Houten. The focus of the course was how to debrief oneself in the absence of a therapist. In a report he wrote after the completion of the course, Van Houten commented that 'for some participants, there had previously not even been a link between their traumatic childhoods and the crime in which they had become involved. This linking of trauma and crime catapulted participants into new views of crime, themselves and each other. It was the first time ever for some prisoners that they were able to verbalise their traumatic childhoods and/or their crimes.'

That, indeed, is much of what the workshops were about for Magadien. At the age of 39 he learned a foreign language, a language of self. It opened the door to an entirely new universe. The idea that one can make of one's life a project, an internal and inward-gazing project, that one can retrieve the most intimate of one's memories, work on them, shape them into a single narrative of meaning – this was radically foreign, and a revelation. It was foreign, not only in the sense that the language of self is largely a bourgeois language, a million miles from the way a man of the ghettos thinks about himself. It was quite literally spoken in a different language: the workshops were largely conducted in English. Until his 1998 sentence, Magadien's command of English had been adequate, but pragmatic. After the workshops, he not only became fluent in English: it came to constitute a significant part of his internal dialogue; many of his most intimate thoughts he could only think in English. And so everything about his new experience smacked of revelation, of a radical rupture, just as certain Christians describe the sudden presence of God in one's life. The result is that there were discrete worlds in his head – the

Number, his family, the English-speaking world of Change with a capital C – each with its own morality, its own stories, its own language. This was to cause some trauma in time to come; there were moments when he was to feel ominously schizophrenic.

During the workshops he also met Michelene Benson, and she became his counsellor. He spent hour after hour with her, reconstructing his past, rediscovering memories that had long vanished, expressing the violent anger towards Gadija he had harboured since he discovered that she was his mother. These were probably his most intimate moments at Pollsmoor; the sessions with Benson were also conducted in English.

This was the Magadien I met in October 2002. He was trying out his new language and his new self on me. He spoke English when talking about his past, his emotions, himself. Many of the words and concepts he used were unknown to him when he had come to Pollsmoor four years earlier. Talking about his dead friend, Tokkie Jonkers, for instance, he once said to me: 'I need closure. I need to go to his grave. I need to work though all the feelings of revenge I have and put them in Tokkie's grave.' He was speaking a discourse in which the jargon of psychology casually slips in and out of conversation. I wondered, if I had met him a few years earlier, how he would have spoken about Tokkie.

Journeying with him back to his past, I felt we were two outsiders looking into the world of a stranger. The tools he used to think about his history were not available to him when he lived it. There is a sense in which he was re-inventing his past when he spoke to me, using his new knowledge to write a history of himself.

*

This period in Pollsmoor brought something else to Magadien's life. In early 2000, at the request of inmates and warders, Joanna began to arrange Sunday church services inside the prison. At one of these services, which was packed with more than 250 inmates, Magadien got up and denounced the gangs in the name of Jesus. Today he remembers it as one of the bravest actions he has ever taken.

About eight years earlier, at Paardeberg, he had announced to Basil Coetzee with ferocious pride that he was a Muslim. Indeed, ever since he had discovered that Gadija was his mother, he had grasped and then coveted his Muslim name, 'Magadien', as an aggressive act of reclamation. Now, in 2000, the epiphanic changes he had experienced became attached in his mind to Christianity. But he was by no means an instant convert. His two religious identities were to spar with one another until well after his release. He was to discover during his first harsh months of freedom that the identity one forges is more a pragmatic choice, an attempt to make the best of what comes one's way, than a search for truth.

*

Aside from a new language and thoughts about a new religion, Joanna brought something else to Magadien's life: the prospect of doing battle for a cause, and with that, the possibility of personal sacrifice, indeed of martyrdom.

Jansen's experiment at Pollsmoor Admission Centre was astoundingly successful. In 1999 there were 11 recorded assaults on inmates by inmates, down from 78 in 1995. Recorded assaults by warders on inmates were down to three. The prison truly was a different place. An outsider who visited the prison regularly between 1997 and 2000 told me: 'It was extraordinary to see the prison change before my eyes. In 1997, you walked through the corridors with armed guards. The tension was so severe you felt the goose bumps rise on your skin. By 1999, you walked freely through the prison, talking to inmates casually. The food was the same, the overcrowding was the same, but the atmosphere was that of a different planet.'

Joanna's workshops, though, caused trouble. About two-thirds of the way through her course, a rumour circulated the prison that the 26s had dutied somebody to stab her. The impulse to hurt Joanna probably had little to do with the content of her workshops. More than anything else, I think, it was an expression of the state of perpetual and aimless envy in which prison gangs reside. Joanna was threatening simply because her workshops were there – they were strange and new, they were drawing excitement; they had to be destroyed.

In 2002, I interviewed one of the men who had taken the decision to stab Joanna. 'What were these *ndotas* discussing behind their closed door?' he asked me rhetorically. 'Were they telling her our secrets? You don't do that. You don't take *ndotas* into a room and lock the door.'

'When they threatened to kill Joanna,' Magadien tells me, 'I thought, right, now my life is on the line. Me and a couple of other people from the workshop went to the 26s and said: "Okay, you want to stab her, you stab us first. And if you get to her, we'll pick up her blood."

'I walked out of there feeling better than I had ever felt in my life. All these years, I had been prepared to die for Nongoloza, for somebody I did not see once. Why can't I be prepared to die for something I see every day, something that is good for me, my family and its future? Why can't I die for a future? People like Mandela, Martin Luther King, why not for them?

'What I realised then, for the first time, is I had given myself an opportunity to die as somebody, not just as another 28. I thought to myself, if I had died before 1999, I would have died a gangster, a scum, a low life, a nobody. But if I was killed fighting against scum, for the future ... It would be one hell of a funeral. The whole fucking prisons service would be there. Politicians would be there. My children could visit my grave in the future and say to themselves: "Ja, our dad died for something we can be proud of."'

This was flighty stuff – fantasies of death, of martyrdom, of a kind of state funeral. It was, to my mind, the first fleeting manifestation of the underbelly of his dramatic conversion; to mix a struggle for the future with sweet dreams of death is to reveal, to my untrained eye at any rate, traces of exhaustion, and of depression.

To be sure, the Joanna incident dissipated quickly, and Magadien's belief that his life was in danger was probably a little fanciful. But there were times when he did go to the brink, flirting quite brazenly with mortal danger. In December 2001, for instance, he joined a fledging Pollsmoor-based anti-rape organisation called Friends Against Abuse. Seven of the founder members were inmates, Magadien the only *ndota* among them. The organisation monitored incoming prisoners, identified those who had never been to jail before, and housed them in their own cells; the idea was to shelter them from predators during their most vulnerable time – their first weeks in prison. They were joined in their cells by inmates who had identified themselves as rape survivors. Prisoners were trained as lay-counsellors to counsel rape survivors.

If Joanna was threatened with violence simply because of drifting currents of envy, Friends Against Abuse came under attack for more specific reasons. The terms of its existence constituted a provocative challenge to the Number. First, it had always been understood that while warders controlled the prison between seven in the morning and four in the afternoon, the Number controlled the cells after lockup. The prison's daily cycle was its signature; power changed hands during the course of the day – that's how things were. Friends Against Abuse messed with the cycle; it created 'cells of sanctuary', and thus dared to interfere with the way the prison was run after lockup.

There was something else too. The moment Friends was formed, Magadien was accused of instigating a campaign to reveal the Number's secrets. It was not a spurious accusation. Forming the organisation was, in essence, an announcement that Magubane was to be dragged into the daylight. For a century, the Number had hidden him with neurotic fastidiousness, disguised him with such pained and elaborate care. Friends wanted to let out the secret, to announce that he was everywhere. It was not just an attack on the Number, but on its rawest, most dangerous spot.

'A few days after the formation of Friends was announced,' Magadien tells me, 'we were threatened with our lives. I knew that was going to happen, and I knew that it was serious. I had thought about it a lot; there was only one way to deal with it.

'I asked permission for a public address system to be set up in the courtyard, and I was given permission to address every inmate on D Floor. I talked as one *ndota* talks to others. I said I knew there were fathers in the audience, and that I knew they were worried what would happen when their sons came to prison. I asked them what they would do to the man who raped their son. I said in that address: "I don't say what you are doing is wrong, but I want to warn you about the dangers. There is this thing called HIV. It's not right for men to come out of prison with a disease that will kill their families." I said I had no problem with sex in prison, but to force someone, or to get them to carry a poke of dagga up their arse, is wrong. "We say we are *ndotas,* wise men of the prison. Let us act as wise men, show the generations to come how to be responsible." After my speech, I introduced everyone in Friends to D Floor. I made the *ndotas* look them in the eye and shake their hands.'

During the nine months I spent at Pollsmoor, Magadien's account of the speech he had given in the courtyard was the only time an inmate mentioned HIV to me. In 2001, the year Magadien gave his courtyard speech, 1 169 people serving prison sentences died of natural causes in South Africa. Six years previously, the number had been 186. There was sickness and death all around, and it was new, but inmates refused to speak about it. For all the Number gangs' talk of fearlessness in the face of mortal danger, the presence of death in their midst left them mute.

*

By now, Magadien was a minor celebrity at Pollsmoor. William Steenkamp was wheeled out for all visitors. Pollsmoor was doing well, beyond the wildest expectations, and the change managers wanted to show off their good work. They invited all and sundry to the prison.

'My life was at its most interesting then,' Magadien tells me. 'My whole life, the only time I'd ever been out of the Western Cape was in the back of a prison van. Now, people from all over the place were coming. In my little cell, I was seeing different pieces of the world – NGO people from all over the world, government delegations.'

He searches through one of the bags that live below his bed in his Pollsmoor cell and emerges with an electronic address book – a gift from one of his many visitors.

'There are people from everywhere in here,' he tells me. 'You could throw me onto another continent, and I would probably be able to find someone I know who lives nearby.'

If the world came to Pollsmoor and met Magadien, by late 2002 he was being booked out of Pollsmoor to meet the world. Jansen was relentlessly energetic at this time. He had recently co-founded a modest community-based organisation called Ukukhanya Kwemini Association (Uka). Ukukhanya Kwemini means 'a brighter day'. 'I've always believed the problem doesn't come from the prison,' he explained to me. 'There is a factory that manufactures gangsters out there. Look at recidivism. People are coming and going, coming and going. There must be a problem on the outside. More and more, I think, if we want to solve the problem of gangsters, we must start with the families. I started feeling that my work was a little hollow, like I was warehousing people who were going to come back. I had to do work on the outside as well.'

In October 2002, Jansen booked Magadien out of Pollsmoor and they drove for three hours into the Klein Karoo to the small town of Ladismith. There, they met several other members of the Uka board of directors. That night, Magadien addressed a packed Ladismith community hall. The following day he spoke at the local school's morning assembly. The way he tells it, he was the town's hero for a day.

'I spoke straight to their hearts. To the kids I described the horrors of prison. I told them prison does not make you a man, it fucks you up and rapes you and then throws you out. I said that no human being who cares for himself will want to go to prison. To the parents, I said how I had fucked up the task of bringing up my own kids. I said that in some homes, you have three generations sitting around smoking drugs together. I said we had to rebuild some sanity in our communities.

'They all crowded round me after my speech in the town hall. A woman came up to me and hugged me and burst into tears. She explained that her son was in prison.

'It was one of the greatest moments of my life. The Uka delegation all had dinner in a restaurant that night. I was served by a waiter for the first time in my life. I ordered chicken livers for starters. It was my first taste of food outside the prison since 1998. I savoured every mouthful. I felt I could learn to eat properly again.

'I looked round the restaurant, and looked at myself eating in the restaurant. I thought to myself: "I am somebody now. I am a decent human being, someone a waiter takes an order from."

'I laughed at myself. I thought: "I have dignity now. And getting it was so simple. A bunch of people just showed me they cared about me and that made me into a human being." I thought to myself, "I can do the same. I can go back to Manenberg and I will know how to treat the fucked-up people, the people who scream and shout and hate the world. I will know how to treat them because I am fresh from where they are; I have been there."'

Magadien's next speaking tour was to a school in Manenberg. 'I wasn't told which school,' he tells me, 'just that it was in Manenberg. When we got close, I saw we were headed to Johaah and Jumat's school. I felt butterflies in my stomach. I was going to be addressing my sons. What happened in the next hour shocked me so badly it is a miracle I was able to see the speech through.

'We went to the principal's office and he started saying how there was this new gang at the school, the Diamond Gang, and it was terrorising all the kids. I asked who started this gang and he said it was the Benjamin boys. My whole body went cold. I started sweating. Someone asked me what was wrong and I just started crying, in front of everyone. I said: "Forgive me: those boys are my sons. I am responsible for what is happening."'

'That's a bit harsh,' I comment.

'Ja, the principal also tried to tell me that I must not blame myself. But it is not harsh; it is the most profound truth. Because everything Mr Jansen had said was coming true. He said that however you live, your children will follow in your footsteps. As I closed my eyes I saw my children going to prison, and I couldn't allow it. I had this frightening thought that my change had come too late, that I had already fucked up the next generation. When I addressed the school, I emphasised the Diamond Gang. My voice was shaking but I spoke with more conviction than I'd ever done. Afterwards, I had a one-on-one with my kids and they started to cry. I said I'm not going to beat you but you must stop this and never go back to it again. It was a huge lesson for me. When I was a child, people didn't talk to me, they beat me. Now, I was talking to them as one adult does to another. I was trying to give them the space to make their own decisions, even though I was desperate. I was trying to be a real father for the first time, and it seemed like everything depended on it.'

By the time he spoke at Jumat and Johaah's school in Manenberg, he was less than a year away from his freedom. Jansen had plans for him. He was going to try to raise money for a salary. If things worked out, Magadien was to work for Uka from the day of his release. He would be a professional change agent, moving from school to school, from community hall to community hall. He began dreaming. Every day I visited him in his cell, he would regale me with another of his plans.

'I want to create a festival atmosphere in Manenberg,' he told me once. 'I want to create an establishment the likes of which has never been seen before. One of Manenberg's many problems is the lack of entertainment. People are stuck in the ghetto with no money to get out and the only place to go to is a shebeen. I want to set up something that will take people away from the shebeens, a place that only serves beer and cider, no hard liquor and no drugs. It will be somewhere you take the whole family. A cheap meal, a playroom for young kids, video games for older kids, extra maths and science teachers for the kids to go to in the afternoons. I'll get a sponsor to provide cricket equipment and I will form a team. I will be their coach. They will learn to take pride in the game. There will be outings – to the beach, to Kirstenbosch Gardens, to climb Table Mountain, to hike through the wonders of nature. When Manenberg kids think Cape Town, they think slums. We have a beautiful city. The kids must see it. They must see the world.'

He was drunk on his dreams. He sat there in his cell and imagined that he was going to heal the Cape Flats single-handedly. He was a crusader, a knight; there were enemies in the world he was imagining.

'The street gangs will try to destroy my work,' he told me. 'Only an old *ndota* has the power to steal kids from them. Only someone who has been to hell can teach the young not to go there. The gangs will see me as their enemy. They will try to stop me. Maybe they will. Maybe I have a 50/50 chance of dying. I don't care. I can no longer live my life any other way.'

Once again, the romantic tones in which he casts his own death jolt me. 'Nonsense,' I tell him weakly, half-heartedly. 'Martyrs are sick people and fairy tale characters. Healthy people are afraid to die.'

He is not listening. 'Imagine my family at the funeral,' he says. 'When they see the head of the prison at my grave, and the provincial fucking commissioner of police, their eyes will pop out of their heads.'

20
DREAMING

That was the public face of Magadien during his last months in prison. It was heartfelt, but it was mixed with bravado. His private world had been allotted its own physical space. When he was convicted for his crimes against the Morrises in 1999, and had to move from D Floor and into the section of the prison for sentenced inmates, Jansen had given him his own cell, a source of much bitterness. He was locked in that room 15 hours a day, away from the important visitors and the community halls, alone with himself.

The most emblematic object in his cell was a bible Joanna had given him. A Christian bible – and yet he had added two inscriptions: 'Magadien,' his Muslim name; and JR, his gang name – as if to alert visitors that things were not as simple as they seemed. The Change with a capital C he had undergone over the past four years had not excised his past – how on earth can a human being be reborn? He was an onion, truly, each layer quite discrete and intact. During our two-hour sessions every morning, he would dart from one identity to the next, each clothed in its own language, its own account of the past, its own sense of the order of things.

For the duration of my visit to Pollsmoor, I had a regular routine. Between seven and ten in the morning, I would shadow a warder as he moved through the prison. Watching his work from over his shoulder, I would try, unsuccessfully at first, to decipher the impenetrable politics of the prison. I would then go to Magadien's cell, tell him what I had seen, and ask him to interpret.

On those occasions, he was the old *ndota* once more, railing against the young generation for the damage it was inflicting on the Number, defending its purity for all his worth. Once, for instance, during my daily excursions through the prison, I watched a prominent 26 on D Floor, Gerald, walk hand-in-hand down the corridor with his lover, Benjamin. Gerald was enormous, about 6ft 3, his face contentedly blank. Benjamin was about nineteen, boyishly slim and ostentatiously camp. Like most gay men in prison, he was, by necessity, inveterately tactical.

'*Frans* dick is useless to me,' he told me with bland honesty. '*Ndota* dick is my passport to being okay.'

On the outside, he had worked as an upmarket rent boy; he had brought fragments of his clients' world with him into Pollsmoor: a novel by Jean Genet, an expensive Trissot pen. As I passed them on the corridor, Benjamin looked up at Gerald's face, and his eyelashes quite literally fluttered. His pretence was so extravagantly mercenary that I giggled. He raised an eyebrow when he heard me laugh, then winked at me over Gerald's shoulder, as if we were sharing a joke at a stupid man's expense. Gerald was oblivious. He was showing off his prize like a gaudy jewel, slipping his hand down the back of Benjamin's trousers with tacky exhibitionism, licking his ear lavishly.

I reported what I had seen to Magadien. 'Seems like the 26s have abandoned their prohibition on sex,' I commented. 'Gerald struts down the corridor parading Benjamin like a badge of honour.'

'*Kak!*' Magadien sneered. 'The 26s have abandoned nothing. Wait until Gerald is sentenced and has to go to B Floor. The Number is pure among the sentenced prisoners. They will fuck him up for having sex in prison.

'Do me a favour. Come here tomorrow at seven in the morning; there will be eight prisoners from D Floor waiting to be transferred to B Floor. You must come and see the fear in their eyes. They know that when they get to the other side, they will be punished for the nonsense they got up to on remand.'

A few weeks later, the 27s on B Floor – the part of the prison where Magadien insisted the Number was still pure – recruited three new members. There were plans for the recruits to stab, but somebody warned a warder and the three initiates were quickly removed from the floor.

'You know what happened there?' Magadien asked me rhetorically. 'They whispered in the warders' ears because if they had allowed the stabbings they would have been transferred to Brandvlei or Helderstroom. And in those prisons, the Number is still pure. They would have been punished for recruiting 27s in the wrong way.'

In Magadien's head, the pure Number was always just around the next corner – in B section, in Brandvlei, in Helderstroom. And if we had visited those prisons together, he would have insisted it was somewhere else, up in the Free State perhaps, where the coloureds had not corrupted it.

The uncomfortable discussion we had about whether the story of Nongoloza and Kilikijan was literally true happened just months before his release, long after he had turned his back on the 28s and embraced the world of Johnny Jansen and Joanna Flanders Thomas. Nongoloza's tale was so deeply sedimented in his mind, it seemed, that no amount of Change would ever remove it. In a carefully fenced corner of his universe, Nongoloza's story would always be synonymous with South Africa's, his initiation into the 28s a privileged rendezvous with truth.

And so, when he raged bitterly against what the Number had become, it was not always clear whether he was seeing the 28s as he had at that Sunday church service in 2000 – as an earthly embodiment of the devil's work – or through the eyes of his *ndota* self – as a once-glorious organisation that had been corrupted. There were times, I am sure, when he did not know himself.

Then there was 'Magadien', a Muslim inscription on his Christian bible. Being Muslim was not something he had inherited, but a victory he had earned. He had grown up in a Christian household; both the Mekkas and his neighbours in District Six and Hanover Park had called him Darryl; until he was 12, he went to church on Sundays. It was only once he learned Gadija was his mother that he understood why the word 'Magadien' was written on his birth certificate; he grabbed it and celebrated it with bitter defiance. It carried a barbed message to his mother: you tried to deny me my heritage, and I am taking it back.

So, writing 'Magadien' on a Christian bible was a coherent and rational gesture in the logic of his internal world. Insisting that he was Muslim was, among other things, an aggressive reclamation, a sign of his unfinished business with his mother. His newfound Christianity did not reach deep enough to excise the roots of his Muslim identity. He would have to be both; he would have to be a Muslim-Christian.

Then, there was the question of his family. As with his religious identity, this was something he had to mould with his own hands, something he had to choose from the chaotic strands of his life.

There was his mother, Gadija, and his foster-mother, Annie Mekka. Between the children these two women had spawned, he had a sister, Anne, and seven half-siblings and foster-siblings, some of whom he had not seen in decades. He had a 15-year-old daughter in the Strand, Noes, of whom he had not heard since the mid-1990s. Then there was Glynnis, the daughter he had with Margie. She was 21 now, and lived in Mitchells Plain. She had long resigned herself to being fatherless.

And then there was the Benjamin household in Manenberg. His in-laws were there, and they had always been fond of him. Faranaaz was there, his wife of five years now; but their marriage had been treacherous to say the least. And there were Faranaaz's children, Jumat and Johaah; they were not of Magadien's blood, but he proudly called them his sons.

He was ambitious. He wanted them all. He *needed* them all. He daydreamed about them hour after hour in his cell, and things came to sit in his mind such that he could not embark on his life as a fully-fledged human being if they did not embrace him as a son, a brother and a father. Only if he could witness his virtuous self through their eyes, it seemed, through *all* of their eyes, could he leave the black places in his past behind.

'The first thing I must do when I get out of here is sit down with my mother and beg for forgiveness, and forgive her in turn,' he told me once. 'If she is past that stage, if she can't forgive me, I don't know whether I'll cope.'

'I must be a father to Glynnis,' he told me on another occasion. 'What will I do if she won't accept me as a father? Maybe she's given me my last chance already. If that happens, I won't be able to get up in the morning.'

'I must make amends with my foster-mom,' he said the following day. 'She is the only one who watched over me from when I was a baby, right through school, right through all my shit. She is old now. She has diabetes. Her leg was amputated a couple of years ago. She hasn't come to visit me during this sentence because she can't move around. But before this sentence, she came to visit me in jail every time. She never gave up on me. She is like my memory. She is the only one who has seen my whole life.'

Until his release, he had only one tool with which to rebuild his family: the payphone in the corridor outside his cell, which ate up the credit on his phone card at an alarming rate. It was, of course, not nearly adequate. He would speak to his foster-mother, his sister Anne, his daughter Glynnis, trying desperately to condense the extraordinary things that had happened to him during the last four years into a brief conversation. At the other end of the phone, the excitement in his disembodied voice was unfathomable; it smacked of madness, of *tronk malheid*, of a man who had been locked up too long.

Shortly before his release, I visited Glynnis in Mitchells Plain. 'When I was at school,' she told me in a tone of studied indifference that failed to conceal the depth of her bitterness, 'I would tell people my father was in the army and was always away. When that didn't work any more, I said he was dead.' She stopped at 'dead' and said nothing for a long time, allowing the word to echo.

As I was leaving, she told me to give Magadien a message: 'Tell him not to come and see me the day he is released, or the day after, or even the following week. I don't want this man coming to tell me he suddenly wants to be my father. If he did that, I think I'd throw him out. If he's serious, he's going to have to earn it, and that will take a long, long time.'

As for Gadija, her love, I was soon to learn, had wilted under her son's persistent hatred. 'He is not going to stay in my house,' she told me. Then she lowered her tone and squeezed the words out in a whisper: 'I don't trust him.'

His place in his siblings' lives, I learned, was far less fraught. He was their brother and they were fond of him; but they had long ago learned to think of him as a benign absence. It was as if he was a ghost who occasionally, unexpectedly, donned a flesh-and-blood body. They would enjoy him while he lasted, barely think of him when he disappeared.

At the centre of the future he imagined during his last months in prison were the Benjamins. They were to be his real test, the nuclear family he was to love and care for. He was adamant that he was going to live in their home from the day he was released. 'My sons are there,' he told me. 'I must raise them.' That they were not his blood sons was irrelevant to him. 'Johaah's dad died when he was in the womb, and he has been calling me daddy since he could talk. I am his father, as much as I am Glynnis's and Noes's. As for Jumat, his father's family lives in Mitchells Plain. They play no role in bringing him up. Without me, he does not have a real dad.'

About eighteen months before his release, Faranaaz came to see him and he told her to stop making the trip to Pollsmoor. 'The Benjamins are dirt poor,' he told me. 'And they are typical coloureds. They buy everything on credit and go broke. So there is a TV, a video machine, but no food on the stove, no money for school fees. I told Faranaaz that spending the money to come to visit me was irresponsible. She must rather buy supermarket coupons so the kids get a good meal every day.

'Faranaaz was furious. She said I didn't want to see her any more because I was having an affair. It's ironic. I had been so unfaithful to her in the past. But I'd been in prison since 1998, and I hadn't slept with anybody.

'A couple of months later, I learned she was having an affair with a gangster, a 28. He was buying his drugs from the Firm, and one day he vanished with his drugs without paying for them. Some people from the Firm came round to the house asking for money. There was no money. So they beat Faranaaz up, and Johaah had to hide, otherwise they would have beaten him up as well, maybe killed him, who knows?

'I wanted to kill her. If she had come to visit me after I heard that news, I would have strangled her. Here I was, in prison, leaving the gangs behind and trying to build a normal family, and she brought the fucking gangs into the house, endangering the life of our child.'

The irony is cruel. For years Magadien had treated Faranaaz with hair-raising callousness, and for years she had stuck it out. Now, just as he was becoming the sort of man who might make a good husband, she snapped. She had had to wait too long.

When Magadien went on his speaking tour to Ladismith, Uka paid him a fee of R500. He asked Jansen to give it to the Benjamins. 'Eid was coming up and the boys needed new shoes,' he told me. 'And straight after that, Johaah's school fees were due. That's where the money was meant to go.'

When I arrived in Cape Town in January 2003, having not seen Magadien for a month, I walked into his cell and found him slumped on his bed, his head buried in his chest. 'I phoned Manenberg last night,' he told me in a broken voice. 'There are no shoes for the boys, and there is no money for Johaah's school fees.

'I dreamed last night about escaping. Anne once said I can come and live in a wendy house in her yard. I was dreaming of doing that, of running away from being a family man. Sometimes it seems too hard. My son can't pay his school fees and I have no money. I am going to live in a fucked-up household and I don't have the means to fix it. How can I live in a house with a woman who doesn't mean anything to me any more? How am I going to send the kids to school? I am already missing prison and I haven't even left yet. Things are safe here. There is food. There are thick walls no tornadoes will ever knock down.'

*

In February 2003, less than four months before Magadien's release, Johnny Jansen went on extended leave. The day after he left, the knives came out for William Steenkamp. Jansen had made enemies during his five-and-a-half years at the helm of Pollsmoor Admission Centre. It was in part because he was a zealous reformer. Many of his staff resented his ethereal talk of rehabilitation. As far as they were concerned, they were the custodians of thugs and scum; talk of human souls was not only barking mad: it was dangerous – it put staff at risk. Jansen also had enemies because there were people who coveted his job; at the end of apartheid, there had been a scramble for position among old Popcru members. Those who lost out willed him to fail. And finally, Jansen was a patriarch: he suffered no fools and scorned those who disagreed with him. For his enemies, his absence was a time for catharsis, a time for envy and resentment to do its work. So they turned on his golden boy, William Steenkamp, and hammered him with a ferocity that should rightly have been reserved for Jansen himself.

Magadien had been due a weekend visit to his family. He was scheduled to leave the prison on the evening of 8 March and return on the tenth. The day after Jansen left, he was informed that his weekend out of prison had been postponed indefinitely. He was also informed that he would have to re-apply to keep his single cell.

'I am nearly finished here and they think there is still time to destroy me,' he complained. 'They want to keep me from my family so that I become unstable. They know what it means for a prisoner to wait for his first weekend in five years, and then be denied it at the last minute. And then they want to throw me into the communal cells on D Floor with the gangs, in the hope that I'll be provoked to stab someone. When Mr Jansen comes back, they want to be able to smile at him and say: "Your Steenkamp fucked up. He's here for another two years."'

Magadien fled. He applied to be transferred to Pollsmoor Medium C, the pre-release prison at the other end of the prison grounds.

'I don't think I have the stomach for this,' he told me. 'I'm feeling so vulnerable. I'm going out soon and I'm shit scared. If they want me to fuck up badly enough, I will fuck up. I don't trust myself. Besides, Medium C is a pre-release prison. You get weekends when you want them; I'll be able to prepare my family for my release. And you get to work every day, to prepare you for a job on the outside.'

He moved to Medium C on 4 March 2003, three months and five days before the completion of his sentence. It was not what he had expected. Johnny Jansen's Admission Centre had sheltered him from the arbitrary violence that still reigned in some of South Africa's prisons, nine years after the end of apartheid. At four o'clock on his first morning at Medium C, the staff conducted a raid on the communal cell in which he had been housed. They found his coin collection – half-cent pieces from the 1960s, pennies and shillings from before he was born, British pence and Italian lire given to him by visitors from abroad. In January, the Department of Correctional Services had banned money from the prisons. The warder who found his coin collection reminded Magadien of the new regulation, and slipped the collection into his pocket.

'I started reasoning with him,' Magadien told me the first time I came to visit him at Medium C. 'I told him he could see for himself I couldn't buy anything with these coins.' The warder sneered at him, chuckled and walked off.

There was another raid on Magadien's second night. He stood outside for an hour in the autumn cold, and when he finally returned to his cell he discovered that a R20 phone card was missing. He told the warder who had searched his belongings, a Mr Kloppers, and before he had finished speaking, Kloppers took his baton off his hip and struck Magadien on the back of the head.

When we met, he bowed his head low to show me the red welt. 'That's the first time in my life I haven't fought back,' he told me.

'If I'd fought back, he would have charged me with assault. I would have gone back to Admission Centre for another two years. So instead I said, "Fine, you win. You keep the phone card and you get to hit me on the head. You're the boss." It was the most self-control I have ever shown in my life.'

Despite the fact that he was now in a pre-release prison, his applications for weekends out all went unanswered. So did his applications to work during the day. The prison's regulations allowed each inmate one phone call per week. He was stranded, out of contact, with nothing to do all day.

As at Admission Centre, he could not eat prison food. But here, there were no warders prepared to buy him fruit from the outside. He lost weight. He broke out in an angry rash – from his neck, across his back and onto his stomach. He developed a hacking cough. He asked to see the doctor but only a nurse would see him; she gave him cough mixture. I bought him a bottle of multi-vitamins. I slipped them into his pocket when nobody was looking; accepting a parcel from the outside was a punishable offence.

Just a few weeks earlier, he had been the hero of Jansen's Admission Centre, the man who had scrambled out of the abyss and was going to change the world. Now, he was a wreck. When I came to see him, his eyes clawed at me gratefully. He kept looking at the clock behind my head. 'Another 15 minutes, and then you're gone. And sanity with you.'

*

He was due to be released on Monday 9 June. Three days earlier, I learned that Annie Mekka was dead. She had died the previous Monday and had been buried on the Wednesday. Nobody had bothered to tell Magadien.

I phoned his sister, Anne. We had never met. I introduced myself, explained that I had been spending time with her brother in Pollsmoor, and said I was sorry her mother had died. There was a long silence.

'I didn't know how to get hold of him,' she finally said, as if I had hurled an accusation at her. 'I didn't even know whether he was in Pollsmoor.'

I was going to see Magadien the following day. A journalist is not meant to tell his subject that his foster-mother has died. A journalist is meant to watch. I imagined myself sitting with Magadien for an hour, keeping my knowledge to myself.

'I'm going to see him tomorrow,' I said. 'I'll tell him about your mom.'

'Tell him,' she instructed me, appropriating my decision. 'Tell him I told you to inform him.'

I told him the moment we sat down. We were in the visitors' courtyard, a bare space with concrete floors, high walls and a scattering of plastic chairs and tables. Around us, orange-overalled inmates sat with their lovers, parents and children. We were surrounded with awkwardness, with men discomfited by the unaccustomed presence of loved ones.

He said nothing for a long time, his face quite emotionless. It was one of those peculiar silences when you know what the other person is thinking: David Cornelius; nobody had told him about David's death either.

'Seems they're making a habit of it,' he said finally. 'Seems I need to give them a piece of my mind.'

I said nothing, and another three or four minutes passed in silence.

'I knew she was going to die during this sentence,' he said, 'ever since she was diagnosed with diabetes. I gave them Mr Jansen's phone number about eighteen months ago so that I could be informed immediately. I didn't want to miss the funeral. I needed to be there when she was lowered into the ground.'

We began speaking about Gadija. 'I'll go and talk to her when I get out,' he said. There was coldness in his voice now. 'I will explain to her how I feel. I will ask for her forgiveness, but only once. If she is not prepared to give it to me, I will just move on.'

'You have many things to ask her,' I said, 'like who your father is.'

'No,' he replied, 'I have nothing to ask her. If I ask her that, she won't take it as curiosity; she'll take it as making trouble. I've been here before. It's always the same.'

PART THREE

GOING HOME

21
MANENBERG

The small coffee table in the living room was cluttered with the accoutrement of Magadien's welcome. There was biryani and heavily curried chicken and curried rice and curried meat balls, all on a bed of lettuce, tomatoes and pickled cucumber. Magadien was late. The food was covered with an embroidered fly net.

A delegation from Uka had gone to pick him up from the release centre in Mitchells Plain. They were meant to have arrived at about eleven in the morning. It was lunch time now.

Jumat, Faranaaz's 14-year-old son, sat opposite me in the living room, the net-covered feast between us. I watched an afternoon soap opera on the television. He grinned broadly at me and said nothing. The rest of the Benjamins seemed to be avoiding the living room. Only Johaah wandered in and out occasionally.

The Benjamins were all unemployed at the time and thus all at home. Magadien's two sisters-in-law and their respective husbands, his two brothers-in-law, his parents-in-law. Eight adults, no work. And, of course, Faranaaz. They lived their lives in densely packed layers extending from the front of the house to the back of the yard: Mr and Mrs Benjamin in the front bedroom; Magadien's sister-in-law Leila and her husband and child in the back bedroom; everyone else in wooden wendy houses that filled every spare space in the back yard. There was also a chicken coop and a dog.

I got up, walked onto the front porch and talked to the dog. Mrs Benjamin watched us from the other end of the porch. She said her husband was a dog-lover. At the sound of his name, Mr Benjamin appeared from behind the house. He grinned broadly at me, revealing toothless gums. We spoke about dogs, and about his move to Manenberg 35 years ago. He said he had lived in the southern suburb of Wynberg before the apartheid removals had chased him away.

'Were your white neighbours happy to see you go?' I asked.

'No,' he replied, somewhat shocked by the question. 'They were sorry.'

I got my road map from my car and he showed me where he used to live.

'We were in a little coloured pocket. The street one side was rich whites. The street the other side was *lanie* coloureds. The *lanies* came to our shebeens to buy beer, but they wouldn't drink with us. They went straight home and drank behind closed doors.'

He used the end of his fingernail to point to a street corner on the map.

'That's where Mrs Arnold lived. She was a fat, white Afrikaans woman who used to come over to the coloured section to smoke cigarettes in the afternoon. At about four or five she'd say, "*Fok, ek moet huis toe gaan*, if my husband knows I've been here he'll *moer* me." We laughed because Mr Arnold was very small and thin.

'When we left, Mrs Arnold cried, all the way down her fat cheeks onto her chin.'

*

Magadien and his entourage finally arrived. It consisted of Johnny Jansen's daughter Leslé, who worked full-time for Uka, her husband, and a middle-aged man called Mr Pitt. He was introduced to me as Uka's treasurer. He said nothing all afternoon. Magadien was wearing a brand-new pair of black shoes, a gift from Uka, he told me later. As soon as the party arrived, Mrs Benjamin ushered us into the sitting room and took the netting off the food. Mr Benjamin came in and sat down, but the rest of the family retreated. It was just the guests, Magadien and his father-in-law. Nobody said anything. The television was loud.

The flies hovered around the newly naked food. Leslé tried to coax the family to come in and eat. They smiled politely and remained outside. Eventually, Mr Pitt got up and helped himself to a modest plate. Then, after a respectable pause, Leslé's husband, then Leslé, then me.

The relentless discomfort in the Benjamins' living room came from two sources. First, we were a bunch of middle-class people in a poverty-stricken Manenberg home. The Benjamins seldom leave Manenberg. They can't afford to. The centre of Cape Town is only

15 km away. Jumat had been there once. Mrs Benjamin hadn't been there for five years. Their connection with the rest of the world was their television set. We arrived in their living room like creatures from a foreign planet.

But also, there was the question of why the net-covered biryani was sitting there in the first place. Every man in the Benjamin family over the age of 18 had been to jail. There was nothing unusual about Magadien's journey. And besides, as far as most of the household was concerned, his connection to their family was thin – just an estranged wife. So they were asking themselves for what purpose these strangers were being fed biryani. The truth is that the feast was Mrs Benjamin's doing. She was trying to make a point; she wanted Magadien to get back together with Faranaaz. And she had gotten licence to make her point because she was the only member of the household with a steady income; the family was humouring the whims of its breadwinner. Everyone except Faranaaz. She had taken flight. She was nowhere to be seen.

Finally, Magadien himself eased the tension. He called the family together, and they responded obediently this time. We all squeezed into the living room, and he stood before us and made a speech.

'My mother has just died,' he said in Afrikaans. 'Yet I have come out of jail to the love of a family.' He turned to Mrs Benjamin. 'Mama, I am so grateful, if I carry on speaking I will cry.'

She beamed at him benevolently. 'We love you. Maybe you did bad by other people, but not by me. I like you. I like your manner. You are a gentleman.' The Uka people smiled and I smiled and Magadien stared at his new shoes.

*

That night, Magadien slept in one of the wendy houses in the back yard. He shared a bed with Johaah. Faranaaz and Jumat slept in the house. It was mid-winter, and there was just a thin strip-plank wall between him and the cold; he went to bed wearing all the clothes he owned and spent the night wide awake, his teeth chattering. The following morning, Leila gave him a plate of fried eggs and bread. He managed about half of it. Leslé came to pick him up to do Uka work. His bail conditions stipulated that he only leave his home for a couple of hours on Saturdays and Sundays. During the week, he required special permission to walk past the

Benjamins' front gate, and only for work. Leslé had had to apply to his parole officer for permission to take him. In the following months, I, too, would have to phone his parole officer every time I wanted to take him somewhere.

Leslé drove him to a high school in Steenberg, just a stone's throw from Pollsmoor. He spoke to the kids about finishing school and living a clean life. He told them horror stories about the big prison they saw from their classroom window. The work was unpaid; Uka had not yet raised a salary for him.

In the afternoon, Magadien and I drove around the Cape Flats. At about four, just before rush hour, we found ourselves on an elevated stretch of the freeway overlooking the ghettos of Hanover Park and Heideveld, where Magadien had grown up. There were the rows of weather-beaten tenement blocks with staircases on the outside, separated by stretches of urban veld – the world Magadien had inhabited as a child. Next to them, the tenement blocks with stairs on the inside – a new neighbourhood, a different planet; when Magadien had described Margie Smith and her family's double-storey flat, he had spoken with visceral hatred. Then the rows of free-standing houses, freshly painted and cheaply manicured – a strained attempt at suburbia, the intended signs of prosperity signifying a great deal of effort. Then the low-roofed factories with their tall chimneys and their relentless face brick.

To me, these were all gradations of sameness. To Magadien, every part of this vista bar one was once a place of foreigners – *sturvies*, pretend-*sturvies* and factory owners. It took the bitterness of unadulterated envy to mark these distinctions so boldly. The heavy parochialism of Magadien's childhood was animated by sheer destructiveness.

'How are you feeling?' I asked.

'I've got jet lag.' He looked at his watch. 'It's lockup time. The corridors are empty in Pollsmoor. Two days ago, it was time for me to read a bit, watch some TV, then sleep. It's amazing that it will be rush hour in a few minutes, that for the last five years, it has been rush hour now every weekday. I have to ease back into it. We must go home so I can sleep.'

We got off the freeway and headed down Landsdowne Road towards Manenberg. I told him I had enjoyed Mrs Benjamin's biryani.

'Early this morning, there was a knock on the front door and I answered,' he said. 'It was a woman from across the road. My mother-in-law had borrowed money from her for my welcome. She wanted to know where her money was. I felt terrible. It was for me. I'm not earning a cent. The old lady is putting food on my plate.'

During the following weeks, I watched the workings of the Benjamins' domestic economy. Once every few days, Mrs Benjamin walked six kilometres to the spice market in Athlone and then walked back laden with spice. She laid her merchandise out on a table in the living room, opened her front door and sat on the porch.

She marks her spices up by about 20%; her neighbours could go to Athlone and get their spices for the same price she does. But getting to Athlone from Manenberg costs either a taxi ride or a three-hour return walk; by buying from Mrs Benjamin, her clients save either money or time.

She opens her front door at about eight in the morning and waits. By nightfall, she has usually made enough to put dinner on the table. Sometimes not: sometimes the family eats bread and butter. Mr Benjamin spends the afternoons smoking Mandrax on the field opposite the house. I was too polite to ask whether he dips into the household budget to buy his buttons.

I watched Mrs Benjamin sitting on her porch and wondered what prevented her from starting a proper business. She is the only seller of quality spices on her block. She has a captive market. Between savings and loans, she could surely get together the few hundred rand required to stock her business properly, to get enough capital to earn something decent.

The Benjamins, I discovered, do borrow liberally, far too liberally. But they seldom invest their debt into the old lady's spices. There are the expenses you would expect: school fees to pay and new shoes to be bought for Eid. Every appliance in the Benjamin home was bought on credit: the monthly bills are beyond their means; the telephone is cut off periodically. And then there is another expense, perhaps the most crippling of all: getting out of the ghetto. The video machine breaks and there is no repair shop in Manenberg. They go to a place in Grassy Park, 15 km away. The video machine doesn't come back. They must go to Grassy Park to get it. Leila is pregnant and must go to the hospital in town for a check-up. Johaah is picked to play in the local soccer team and must go to Cape Town to buy football boots.

The Benjamins are defeated every day by the travesty of Cape Town's town planning. To live their lives, they need to leave their ghetto, move around their city. They are poor; it is just too expensive. The price of movement is their ruin.

The Benjamins are scorned for their poverty. Magadien's mother and some of his siblings despise them. 'Magadien married into rubbish,' they tell me. 'That is why he went back to jail.'

Magadien's family is poor, but they are far better off than the Benjamins. They all finished school. They all work. His sisters married men with apprenticeships and trades. Their kitchens have tiled floors and boast clean, melamine surfaces. Their fridges are full.

'Why couldn't Magadien have married Margie Smith,' Gadija told me the day I met her. 'She is such a decent girl.'

The heart of the accusation against the Benjamins remains unspoken. It is that they lack self-care, that they allowed this to happen. They are scorned so bitterly because they are too close to home, because the same could have happened to the Wentzels; there but for the grace of God …

Marrying a Benjamin is not something Magadien's family finds easy to understand. He had the opportunity to go up, but he decided to go down. *Daar's iets fout met sy kop* – he's not quite right upstairs.

22

A SISTER AND TWO OLD BASTARDS

On Magadien's fourth day out of prison, I took him to visit Zubeida, one of his half-sisters. We knocked on her kitchen door and when she saw it was her brother she threw her arms around him and kissed him enthusiastically on the cheek. She sat us down at the kitchen table, took a giant chocolate cake out of its tin, and offered us coffee, chocolate cake and toffee apples. I had learned by now that one judges a ghetto home by its kitchen; Zubeida's kitchen was large and immaculate. Its melamine shone. Zubeida herself went well with her kitchen. She was broad-boned and pretty. She wore a pink t-shirt and blue jeans.

She treated her brother like a good-natured old dog who had unexpectedly wandered into the house; she jibed him affectionately.

'You will be back inside in three months,' she said with a grin. 'You always are.'

'I won't,' he replied. 'Not this time.'

'Oh, but you will.'

'I'll bet you breakfast. If I am a free man three months from today, you will buy me breakfast.'

He stopped smiling, put a heavy look on his face, and switched from Afrikaans to English. He tried to tell her what he had been through these last five years. It didn't come out quite right.

'I was one of the most powerful prison gangsters in this province,' he said. 'I could click my fingers and somebody would die. I gave it all up. I risked my life to give it all up. I'm a nobody now, and getting there is the bravest thing I have ever done.'

As she listened, she took in the way his clothes sat on his body.

'You're so thin,' she commented. 'Do you have AIDS?' She asked the question with a smile on her face, but she was neither joking nor being insensitive. There was love and care in her eyes.

The question unnerved him. He mumbled in reply. 'No. I just couldn't eat prison food.'

'What did you do for sex? Boys?'

Again, her bluntness discomfited him. 'Sometimes,' he murmured. 'But there were girls in prison too.' He had recovered. There was mischief in his eyes. 'Bronwen, Mandy, Melissa.'

She frowned. She didn't understand.

'They're transvestites,' I explained.

She scrunched up her nose and looked nauseous. 'I'm serious. When were you last tested for AIDS?'

I marvelled at the ease with which she asked him about his sex life and his health, and the way she mitigated her bluntness, which could so easily have been crass and clumsy, with grace. I was soon to learn that there is a chasm between the men and the women of Magadien's family. The women are emotionally articulate; they do not hesitate before saying what is in their hearts.

The next time we visited Zubeida was lunch time on a Sunday. Magadien, Zubeida, her husband and I were in the kitchen. Her kids were playing Sony Play Station in their bedroom. There was a commotion outside, the excited voices of children and adults mingled together. We all went onto the street to see what was happening. Except for Magadien. He went into the kids' room and played Sony Play Station.

A crowd of about seventy was making its way through the neighbourhood. The atmosphere was mildly carnival, as if a troupe of jesters had unexpectedly come to town. At the front of the procession, two elderly men were dragging two younger men down the street by fistfuls of their baggy pants.

'They stole a video machine from a family up the road,' someone in the crowd explained. 'They are being taken to be punished in front of their parents.'

We followed the crowd. A couple of blocks on, it stopped outside a house and the two elderly men marched one of the youngsters inside and slammed the front door shut. They emerged a few minutes later, the young man's head sunk in shame into his chest, blood oozing from his mouth and nose. He covered his face with his hands, as if his blood was like nakedness and had to be concealed.

'Why is he bleeding?' Zubeida's daughter asked.

'Because they smacked him, my love,' she replied.

Then Zubeida turned to me. 'This happens all the time,' she said, 'but it does no good. They should call the police.'

The crowd disappeared as quickly as it had emerged. The spectacle was over. Just the two shamed boys were left on the street.

Zubeida thought some more. 'But if the police were called, they would go to prison and come out even worse. So maybe the answer is to shoot them.'

'But then your brother would have been shot long ago,' I said.

She raised her eyebrows in shock. 'Ja: it's too complicated.'

*

On Magadien's first Sunday morning out of jail, we went to Hanover Park, to the street where he spent his teenage years, where Quinton and the late Annie Mekka had lived, and where the Never Worry Bastards were born. We went to Anne's house, Magadien's only 'full' sibling, and his one-time ally in his war against Quinton. She wasn't home; she was at church. Her husband, Brian, who had grown up on that street with Magadien and Anne, was basking in the sun in the front yard, sitting on a low stool, the back of his head leaning lazily against the wall of his house.

He was a carpenter; he built cupboards and drawers for the cabins on luxury yachts. He complained that the rand was overvalued and that his employers were losing their American clients. He was dry and sardonic. He never smiled, but was never serious. He would not lift the back of his head from the wall. He just sat there and looked at Magadien mischievously through squinted eyes.

I told him his wife was a good woman, spending her Sunday mornings in church. He looked at me quizzically, trying to work out whether I was terribly earnest or just had a poor sense of humour.

'Going to church,' he finally said with studied dryness, 'does not make you good.'

Magadien started telling him about his time in Pollsmoor. Brian listened without comment until Magadien mentioned that he had had his own cell and a television set.

Brian raised his eyebrows in displeasure. 'That's ridiculous.

That's my fucking taxes you were spending.' He closed his eyes and took in some more sun. 'When you go back next time, I'll personally see to it that you are thrown into a communal cell. I will go to Pollsmoor myself to see. I'll take a day off work to do it. If you have your own cell, I'll go on a tax strike.'

Someone called Magadien's name from the gate. It was Jack, Magadien's soul mate of his teenage years. They were the most adventurous of the Never Worry Bastards. They were the ones who began breaking into factories and *sturvy* houses.

He could barely stand up straight. He leaned precariously against the Van Roois' fence. His eyes were deep in the back of their sockets. A thick film of spittle had gathered around the corners of his mouth. He asked Magadien for money. Magadien laughed; he was quite literally penniless. Jack looked queryingly at my car, as if to say: 'If you arrived in that, you have money.' Magadien shrugged and laughed again. We continued our conversation with Brian. Jack tried to listen for a while. He couldn't follow. He stumbled back into the street.

We said goodbye to Brian and went to a house across the road where Stan Landman lived, another of the original Never Worry Bastards. He was overcome with emotion when he saw Magadien. He threw his arms around his old friend and hugged him for a long time, shutting his eyes tight.

He invited us into his house. His mother was in the kitchen making lunch. She eyed Magadien warily.

'So you're back for a few weeks,' she said caustically.

It was the kitchen of a poor family; tiny and dark and lined with very old wooden cupboards. Stan ushered us into his bedroom and made a great fuss of closing his door. It wouldn't close. He wedged a chair in front of it.

He sat down on his bed, picked up a three-quarters empty bottle of Old Brown Sherry and took a long swig. I realised for the first time that he was drunk. He began a long, incoherent monologue: 'My life is fucked up. I used to be great. I used to be clever. I don't have a life. I don't have a girlfriend. I had a girlfriend, but then she fucked off. The bitch. I've got a job, okay, but my best friend is this.' He pointed at his sherry bottle. He stared at Magadien pleadingly, as if his old friend had come out of the prison to save him. He kept looking at the closed door nervously, as if his mother was eavesdropping.

'Ja,' Magadien said. 'You were the smartest of all of us, and now you're treating your life like an old rag. You're …'

'I was the smartest, the natural leader, and now look what's happened to me. I've been cursed by an evil God.'

He looked at me suspiciously. 'What's wrong with you? Why won't you drink my sherry? Do you want a coke? What do you want from me?'

Going home, I told Magadien that his friends seemed more fucked-up than he'd ever been. 'No matter how bad things got for you,' I said, 'it seems you always had presence of mind. You were a 28. You had pride.'

'Ja,' he replied. 'And they had everything going for them. They both got a trade. They never went to prison. I need to talk to Uka. They want me to help strangers. I need to tell them that I must help the people around me as well. I can't only help strangers when the people I grew up with are wasting away.'

He saw something in my rear-view mirror and told me to stop. I looked round. In the distance, an old man was crossing the road. He wore a cloth cap. His back was stooped. He stared at the ground as he walked. He appeared to be overly timorous, as if he expected someone to stop him and make trouble.

'Quinton,' Magadien said.

23
GADIJA

We went to see Gadija in the late morning on a weekday. She and Magadien had not laid eyes on each other in five years. One could tell from the exterior of her house that she was a good deal poorer than her daughters. An old wooden fence sheltered her home from the street. Its door had no hinges; we lifted it off the ground to open it. There was overgrown grass in the driveway and a wrecked old bakkie, long out of use. In the back yard, a dog was tethered to a pole. He barked at us indignantly.

We knocked on the door for a long time and then Magadien tried the handle; the house was unlocked. We stepped into a small, dark room with posters of Bruce Lee, pin-up girls and British football stars. It was the bedroom of Gadija's youngest, Waleed. He was 21. Later, when I got to know him, he wanted to take me to underground drag-racing tournaments held in deserted lots at three in the morning.

We stepped into the only other room in the house. It was big enough to host a king-size bed and a pedestal. Gadija and her husband Victor were under the covers, watching a small black-and-white television set. It was immediately apparent that she was Anne's mother: the same broad cheekbones, the same wide forehead, her eyes tough but generous. She smiled at Magadien absently, in a manner that suggested he came to visit her every morning, and invited us in. She was wearing a thin linen nightdress. For a brief moment, she was thrown by the prospect of greeting a stranger in her nightclothes, but only for a moment. She smiled at me graciously, sat up in bed with great poise, and apologised for the state she was in. 'I've got asthma,' she said. 'Not feeling myself today.' I was about a metre from her bed. She stretched out her arm, took my hand, drew me towards her and kissed me on the cheek.

I immediately thought of the Gadija Stephen Sampson had conjured for me – of how hard she played, of how she had dazzled a serious young boy with her capacity to live.

She asked Magadien how he was. Her tone was neutral. The moment she addressed him, he was transformed. He was a young boy, a whinging, unhappy young boy. He complained that the Mekkas hadn't bothered to tell him that Annie was dead, that he should have been at the funeral, that he needed to be at the funeral, that they had forgotten him once again. He was babbling. I was reminded of the day the minister came to Pollsmoor and Magadien had not been given a turn to speak, of how he had stamped his foot in front of Johnny Jansen like a child who has had his toy stolen. He wasn't going to stop until she gave him solace. She interrupted him, but not to comfort him.

'Ja,' she sighed. 'I'm also having problems with your sisters. This one fights with that one, and they try to get me involved. I'm too tired. I turned 60 last year. I can't be a parent like that any more.'

She brushed Magadien aside and put her hand on my forearm. 'Tell me about you,' she said.

I told her. I told her I had had a long conversation with Stephen Sampson.

'Shame,' she said. 'Poor Stephen. He left a message for me the other day. He said he was under great stress. He was at the end of his tether. His mother still won't leave him alone. Denise is a bitch.'

'Seems that way,' I said.

'I brought that boy up,' she said. 'Denise did fuck all. Excuse my language, but it's true. When Stephen wanted to tell someone he was gay, he didn't come to her; he came to me. I said to him: "My boy, you must be what you want to be, and you must go and tell your mother who you are, and she must accept it. If she doesn't, I'll step in because I've got a whole lot of dirt on that bitch."'

She stopped talking and stared at Magadien.

'This one's just like his father,' she said. I felt excitement well up in me. She was going to say something tender. 'He stops on every corner,' she continued, 'and wherever he stops there's a new baby.'

*

Gadija grew fond of me very quickly. Whenever I visited, she kissed me warmly on the cheek and patted the chair next to her bed for me to sit down. (She was always in bed.) She gave me a pen for Christmas. She kept forgetting my name; she called me Stephen. She insisted that I come to her husband's birthday party. At the party, several young girls clung to me the whole night. Three asked me to take them to Johannesburg and marry them.

'White arse,' I overheard one of Gadija's neighbours saying. 'They go crazy for white arse.'

I didn't like the attention she gave me in Magadien's presence. I started going to see her alone.

'I want you to know the truth,' she said on our first morning alone together. 'I want to tell you why Magadien is the way he is.' She lined up several cigarettes on her bedside table; she was preparing for a long morning.

'We must start with my story,' she said. 'Magadien's story starts from my story. My childhood was a terrible childhood. Everything I ever did for my kids was to stop them having the childhood I had. When I opened my eyes as a baby, I never knew my mother. She was already out of my life. I woke up behind my grandmother's back. She was the only one who gave me love and security. Not my father.

'We lived in the Strand. My father and my uncle had just come back from the war. They were in a terrible state, all the men who came back from the war. They drank. There was no work for coloureds. It was the beginning of apartheid. In those days, you were allowed to take fish out the sea. That's what my uncle and father did. They got fish out the sea and sold it. Crayfish, fish, perlemoen.

'When my grandmother died, I was in my early teens. After that, we were lost children; my father never had time for us children. Me and my cousin were standing and watching my grandmother's coffin go away. My father's sister said: "What are we going to do with the kids now?" We were standing there not knowing what was going to happen to us, or which side we were going to. My aunt, she was married to my father's brother; she worked as a cook at a hotel in Somerset. She said: "If this is what's going on, I'll take them. I'll take them all." We were very young. Me, my sisters, my cousins.

'But things weren't better at my uncle's place. He was drinking heavily. So was my father. It was like they were drinking water.

My uncle used to abuse my auntie and we used to have to go and hide at a neighbour's place.

'We were turning into young women now. We needed this and that. My uncle wasn't interested. Then I ran away from home. I was not yet sixteen. The reason I ran away, my uncle took a sjambok to me. I had gone with friends without telling him. When I came back, he took a whip and split my back open. I ran to my auntie and showed her. She scolded him. The next day, everything was blank. I just knew I had to run away. I didn't know where. My uncle tried to stop me, but my friend came with a bike and put me on the bike. My cousins all came to the station to say goodbye. I was still fifteen. I couldn't take it no more. There was no mother love, no father love. I went to my father and told him I'm running away. You know he actually gave me train fare. He gave me money to run away. You tell me, what father would give his daughter money to run away? No human being who has love for his child would do that.'

She went to stay with a cousin who worked for a white family in the inner-city suburbs of Cape Town. Her cousin kept a lookout for work. After a few weeks she told Gadija of a young family in Tamboerskloof called the Sampsons. They had a young son. Another child was on the way. They needed somebody to look after their children.

'I took the job immediately,' Gadija told me. 'I was still a child myself, and I had to look after two children. Denise was never around. She kept saying her nerves were shot and she had to go overseas. I brought up the children.

'I was a still a child. The Greens used to go out all evening. I was lonely. I was looking for the love I had never had. And I met David Cornelius, the caretaker at the building where the Greens lived. He was also young, eighteen, nineteen. But he knew what he wanted. He wanted girls, one after the other. Automatically, we got together. And so I had Magadien. I was going for seventeen. He was born at the Somerset Hospital in Green Point. I had nowhere to take him, so the Sampsons kindly allowed him to stay with me there. I gave him the name Magadien. Norman gave him the name Darryl. They showered him with love, gave him everything he needed. He got the things the other children didn't want. Clothes, cots, prams. They were all the best quality, still like new.

'I couldn't keep Magadien and my job. It wasn't possible. By the time he was three months old, it was too much. He wasn't a newborn any more. He needed attention. I thought, I must find a proper home for my boy. I had met a woman called Hanna and I asked her if she knew of anyone who could look after him. She introduced me to Annie Mekka. I met her, and introduced her to my people. My people liked her. They agreed to pay for something every month to look after him. Annie agreed. Annie's husband, Johnny, agreed. He worked in the ship. Went away for three months all the time.'

'Who are "your people"?' I asked.

'My people? The Sampsons. I call them my people because they took me as their own. They stood by me in thick and thin. I'm talking about Norman, and his father, Harry. Not Denise. She was a cow from day one. Harry loved me as a daughter. Norman loved me as a sister.

'You know, Harry bought me a car. Before I could drive it, Norman took it to the gym and drove it into a wall. There was a terrible fight. Norman and Harry screaming at each other like the roof was going to fall down. I never got to drive that car.

'Harry also wrote me into his will. He was going to leave me quite a sum. And then, after I left David, I decided to marry this fellow Khan – I was pregnant by him. I told the Sampsons. They called a big family meeting. The whole *fokken* family was there. And the old man started with me. He said this Khan is a rubbish. He's no good. Harry had my best interests. He could see things much better than me. I was still young. I said, no, I'm marrying him. I'm carrying his child. Harry slammed his fist. He said the family could look after my child. He said if I married Khan, he would cut me out of the will. He did. I never got a cent when he died.

'So, there was fighting and hugging, like there is with all families. Denise aside, the Sampsons were the only family I ever knew. When Anne was born, three years after Magadien, and also by David – this is before I met Khan – I gave her to the Mekkas as well. But Harry was there for her the whole time. Anne and Harry have the same birthday. Every year, he would say to me: "Bring your child." Anne would come and Harry would take her shopping. He would go to the most expensive shops in town and buy her whatever she wanted. I was proud. My children wanted for nothing.'

Gadija stopped. She excused herself and went to the bathroom. She came back and drank a glass of water. She lit a cigarette, took a handful of tissues from her bedside table and put them on her lap; she was preparing for tears.

'You understand I was satisfied with what I had done for my kids. My circumstances were tough, but I had made sure they would never have the childhood I had. I worked myself to the bone for them. Through all Denise's shit, I carried on working for her. I wiped her children's bums and gave them their medicine. I grew to love them. They called me mommy. It was for *my* kids that I loved these two other children. My kids had a good home. Annie was a golden person with a golden heart. They called her mommy and called me by my name. That hurt me. But I put them in her care and I know I did the right thing.

'When did Magadien become a bad egg? I'm sorry to say this, but it was while he was under Annie's wing. First, the government gave her her papers and she had to move from town to Heideveld. Then Johnny died and she moved to Hanover Park, with my help, mind you; I went to Norman, and Norman organised with the government that she get a place in Hanover Park.

'And then Quinton moved in. Quinton was a hell of a piece of work. We've made our peace now, but he was a pig back then. The kids were suffering under him. When he came, Annie started neglecting the children, but she was still collecting the government money. I had a hell of a fight with Annie. I stood in the street outside her house, and I said Quinton must go. Quinton came out. I picked up a brick. I wanted to *donder* the bastard on the head. Unfortunately, I missed him, and I broke Annie's window. I made a hell of a scene.

'Magadien hated Quinton, and Quinton hated Magadien. He started rebelling against Quinton, and Quinton started rebelling against him. Magadien started smashing people's windows and stealing Annie's linen to buy drugs, and stealing Annie's money. He was running with gangs. The police caught up with him.

'I was there for him. I was always there for him. I went to Norman, like I always did, and Norman asked what he must do. I said let him be sentenced to a caning. Let them give him a bloody good hiding and then we'll see what's what.

'It didn't help. He started with his nonsense again. Annie complained to me and I went to Norman. The police caught up with him again. This time, I sent him to a boys' school. It didn't work. He was too clever to be in a boys' school. He was always brilliant at school. He lasted there three months and I took him out.'

As I listened to Gadija, I felt for Magadien. He had gotten himself into Bonnytown using his own guile: it had probably been the deftest act of his childhood. Now, everyone had appropriated his time in 'the boys' school' for their own purposes. For his siblings and his childhood friends, it was evidence that he was congenitally criminal: it had all started before puberty. For Gadija, it was testimony to the fact she had always been there for him, that she had done her utmost to save him. It occurred to me that of all the motives that propelled Magadien to cooperate so enthusiastically with the writing of this book, this was the most important: he wanted to rescue his history from the tongues of others.

'When Magadien finished school,' Gadija continued, 'we didn't give up on him. No, Norman was a saint of a man. He gave Magadien money to go to university. Magadien was so brilliant at school. It was Norman's dream that Magadien would become an attorney like him. But he went to the college for only three months. Then he went to jail.'

'Magadien said he wasn't convicted of a crime that time, it was ...'

'Ja, it was because of the riots. He was involved with the students: burning tyres and throwing stones and God knows what. He went to Victor Verster. Norman tried to get him out, but it was the government, they were fighting the government, and nobody can get you out for that.

'When he came out, he went to stay with Annie. He started smoking buttons, theft, stealing from Annie, from me, from Quinton. He got involved in the Never Worry Bastards. He was back in prison soon. They took him to a jail somewhere in the country. I don't remember where. Me and Annie went to visit him.

'After that, Magadien started drifting away from me. I started drifting away from him. I couldn't help him any more.'

'What was happening with you and the Sampsons in the mean time?' I asked.

'I stuck it out with Denise as long as I could. She was a cow. She was no mother to her children and no wife to her husband. Norman was like a pup in her hands. At any rate, one day enough was enough and I gave her a piece of my mind.

'We had a hell of a fight. She told me I was stealing her children. "How dare you allow them to call you mother," she said. I said: "If you were their mother you would be there 24 hours a day. You don't care about your husband. Your children were still in nappies when I brought them up. I sacrificed my own children. When there is a problem at school, a blood nose, who do they run to? Me, not you. No, you go overseas, because your nerves are shot. How can your nerves be shot? You sit on your fucking arse."

'She told me to fuck off and never come back. I said, fine. I left that day.

'At any rate, Norman and I kept in touch all the years I was away. When there was a problem with the kids, I phoned him. A few years later, after they were divorced, I went back to Denise to run her house.

'That ended when me and Denise had a hell of a fight there. It was Stephen's birthday. He was maybe nineteen, twenty. He was in college. He wanted to invite a few gay friends. Denise was overseas. He asked me to give him a Muslim pot – biryani, curry. I thought, everybody needs a life. She would never have allowed it. He took the gap because she was overseas. Joanne, Stephen's younger sister, gave us away. She didn't like gays. She didn't like what was going on. So she told Denise when she came back.

'The moment she was back, she started with me. "You use my money for corrupting my son. You nasty fucking witch. You must fuck off." I was in a hell of a state. I was having problems with my own life. I was nearly nine months pregnant, and my husband was moving in with another woman. I said, "I'll fuck off, forever this time. But listen to me lady. Listen to my words: don't come cry by me if Joanne disappoints you. You are always looking down on Stephen, but don't be surprised if Joanne disappoints you."

'I packed my bags and never came back. I phoned just once, years later, to see how Stephen was doing; I was worried about him. On the phone, she was so nice, pretended nothing had happened, said I must come and visit, that Stephen always speaks about me.

'When I came to visit, she told me her sob stories. Joanne had married a man who looks exactly like her father and had turned the children against their grandmother. I said: "Do you remember what I told you? Stephen was gay and you pushed him away. Now Joanne has pushed you away. Now you can feel what it's like. Me and Stephen were always the outsiders. You sort it out. It has nothing to do with me. My only concern is Stephen."'

'And Magadien?' I asked.

She turned away from me. Her body heaved. I watched her profile as the tears rolled down her cheeks. She fumbled for a tissue and slowly wiped her eyes.

'You know, he phoned me from prison a couple of years ago and begged me for my forgiveness. I said: "My child, I have forgiven you long ago." And it's true. I meant it. But I also want your book to tell the truth. Norman and me walked the world for that boy. He threw it back in our faces. I sacrificed my youth for my children. I worked like a slave. I lived in the claws of a bitch. Against all the odds, when I had no decent home to give them, I found another one for them. It was all thrown back in my face. He stole from me, all these years, from me, a poor woman. My own *fokken* son. Where is his heart?'

'When did Anne and Magadien find out that you were their ...'

'They knew!' she snapped. 'They knew from the start!' It was the only time she lost her poise in my presence. 'Anyone who tells you different is a liar.'

*

In the weeks and months to come, Magadien visited Gadija every weekend. She neither welcomed him, nor threw him out. She would look him up and down. 'You're looking well,' she would say. 'Are you all right?' That is as tender as she got, in my presence at any rate.

I asked him whether he spoke openly with her about his anger toward her.

'We speak,' he said, 'in our own sort of way.'

'What do you speak about?'

'We speak.'

24
DOGGY-BAG

In early July, the Western Cape's schools adjourned for the winter holidays; the work Magadien had been doing with Uka in the schools was suspended. His bail conditions stipulated that if he had no work, he was to stay at home during the week, all day every day. He confined himself to his wendy house in the back yard. Faranaaz was in the main house; it was her domain; he was avoiding her. Her boyfriend, the man who had absconded with a stash of buttons belonging to the Firm and had thus brought the wrath of violent men to the Benjamins' home, had been arrested for drug possession and was in Pollsmoor. So Faranaaz was home most days.

Mrs Benjamin was oblivious to the patently obvious; to her mind Faranaaz and Magadien were always on the brink of reconciliation. She brought him a pile of toast in the mornings and a plate of curry in the evenings. He battled to swallow the food his mother-in-law gave him. He felt it was an unacknowledged dowry payment, an advance reward for getting back together with Faranaaz.

'When I'm sitting in my wendy house,' he told me, 'I see in my mind Mrs Benjamin sitting on the front stoep waiting for people to come and buy her little packets of spices. She is carrying the house. She is carrying me. Whenever she brings me my plate, I know how much it has cost her. It makes me feel like a crook.'

School holidays meant that Jumat and Johaah were at home during the day. Johaah is a shy, intensely silent boy. He and Magadien appeared to communicate like two mute people – with gestures, body language and eye contact. But when Johaah did address Magadien he called him 'daddy'. Indeed, he had decided long ago to make Magadien his father; he was the one who had quietly begged Magadien to remarry Faranaaz back in the mid-1990s, when Magadien got his job at City Glass. Johaah and Magadien became family to each other by the force of mutual will.

Jumat, on the other hand, kept his distance; he made a point of addressing the new man in the house as 'Uncle Magadien'.

'He is making choices,' Magadien told me. 'I respect that. Johaah's father died while he was still in the womb. I am the only father he has ever known. Jumat still has a father, even though he is hardly ever around. So I understand that he is figuring things out for himself. That's okay. I'm here. When he needs me I'll be here for him.'

In the weeks following his release, Magadien and I would go on daily excursions – to Hout Bay to see Tokkie Jonkers's parents; to the Strand to revisit his life there; to the Centre for Conflict Resolution in town to see Michelene Benson, the woman who had been his counsellor in Pollsmoor. When asked about his family, he would talk about his four children. By July, Jumat was still calling him 'Uncle', and his responses to questions began to change; now, when people asked after his family, he said he had three children. He was constantly shuffling, adjusting. The gap between the family he had invented in Pollsmoor and the real, independent people he met on the outside – people with their own ideas about his place in their lives – grew by the day.

Indeed, nothing on the outside was quite as he had imagined it in Pollsmoor. Gadija accepted him into her home whenever he visited, but she was visibly wary; the cathartic reconciliation he had pictured from the sanctuary of his prison cell vanished into the realm of fantasy – where it had always belonged – whenever he saw her. His sisters were kind to him when he visited, but it was not often – every couple of weeks or so; for the rest of the time, they played little part in his life. As for his children – the ones with whom he did not share a roof – the combination of his bail restrictions, his poverty and his fear kept them elusive. He seldom had the freedom of movement or the money to venture to the Strand; he had not been able to locate Noes yet. He had spoken to Glynnis on the phone, but the frostiness in her voice had served as a caution; he did not visit her.

As for the Benjamin home in Manenberg, he felt increasingly like an interloper. He was penniless, entirely dependent on the largesse of a poverty-stricken family. He was never going to get back with Faranaaz; he wondered for how long their generosity would last.

Even the question of retrieving his name, by which he had set so much store when he was in prison, proved inordinately complicated. To the Benjamins, Gadija and the people he knew in the Strand, he was Magadien. Yet whenever we walked into a Christian household – like the Jonkers' flat in Hout Bay, or the homes of his childhood neighbours in Hanover Park – people called him Darryl. At the Centre for Conflict Resolution and among the members of Uka, he was William Steenkamp, the man they had met at Pollsmoor. On the few occasions we met an ex-convict on the street, he was JR. The manner in which he had lived his past had set so much of his future in stone; he was coming to learn that one cannot reinvent oneself without reinventing the people around whom one has lived a life; he was no alchemist.

On one of our day excursions, he was addressed by all four of his names in the space of a few hours, as we drove from one slice of his life to another. I asked him how much it bothered him.

He shrugged. 'I have been out a month. It is early days. This is what I was expecting.'

*

He still had Uka, the prospect of daily work about which he was passionate, the prospect of earning a living. But by mid-July, as he sat in his wendy house waiting for the new school term to begin, he sensed that something was wrong. 'I can't put words to it,' he told me. 'It's just a vibe: a bad vibe.'

He was right. In the week the province's schools opened, Johnny Jansen's daughter, Leslé, came to fetch him again. The work with the school kids resumed. But no sooner had it begun than it ground to a halt. Meetings were set up with various foundations to raise a salary for Magadien; the meetings were cancelled, or postponed, or missed completely.

He phoned Jansen and scheduled a time to see him. He borrowed money from his sister-in-law, got a taxi to Pollsmoor, and arrived at Jansen's office at 11 am, two hours early. He waited in the prison lobby, watching people come and go.

'A group of 28s walked in,' Magadien told me. 'I knew them all well. They had come to visit an inmate. They called me over and talked. *"Nei, broer, jy's nou a vry man. Kom smoggel met die ouens."* They were inviting me to sell buttons and crack in Elsies River. If I went with them, I knew that within a week I'd be driving a car and have a wallet full of cash. I could arrive home one day with a new wardrobe for Johaah. I could give Mrs Benjamin money for rent, food and to get the telephone reconnected. I kept my head down. I tried not to think about it.'

At ten past one, Jansen emerged from his office. He announced that he had to cancel: an unexpected meeting.

I am not sure precisely how Magadien's relationship with Uka finally ended: whether he told them he was too poor to work for free, or whether they stopped bringing work his way. There were acrimonious meetings. There was much mutual bitterness. By August, it was over. He had severed ties with them completely. He has hardly seen Johnny Jansen since.

His relationship with the prison head had been dangerously filial. What he called his 'Change', was, I believed, tied inexorably to his newfound father. I expected that losing Jansen would break him. I thought he would throw a childish tantrum, full of spite and hatred for his faux-father. I thought he would kick his new world to pieces, end up back in Pollsmoor, and smile treacherously at Jansen from behind the bars.

'Who would win if I did that?' he asked me when I put this scenario to him. 'You think I'm going to ruin my life in order to prove a point to him? You think I'm that fucking stupid? You disappoint me. You've underestimated me.'

He was speaking as much to himself as to me. He enjoyed my provocation. He enjoyed having a part of himself externalised: a real figure onto whom he could unleash his polemic.

'A year ago,' he said, 'I would have told you that Mr Jansen was the most important person in my life, that I would trust him with anything. A year is not a long time, and look what has happened now. I have learned that people come and go; it is myself I have to live with. If the principles by which I want to run my life are only alive because of other people, I'm fucked. I may as well book myself back into Pollsmoor now, and tell them it's for the crimes I'm going to commit soon.'

'No matter how many Johnny Jansens come and go …' I started encouragingly.

'Ja,' he interrupted, 'and no matter how many Jonny Steinbergs come and go.'

It was a subtle accusation. It was August 2003. I had told him that my research would be ending in February 2004. After that, I would not be coming to Cape Town much any more. Like Jansen's interest in Magadien, mine too would dissipate.

What he did next was breathtaking. At times I thought it excruciatingly sad, at times disturbingly heroic. Penniless and largely housebound, he decided to go it alone, to fabricate his own private change agency from the material within his reach. On a Tuesday morning in August, he got permission from his parole officer to go to town for a morning, borrowed taxi fare, and went to the Centre for Conflict Resolution. He asked if he could use a computer and a printer. He made an A4 advertisement announcing the formation of a youth group. He called it the Tornado Stallions. He printed a few dozen copies, went back to Manenberg, and handed them out door-to-door. The advertisement was addressed to parents. It promised to take their children off the streets, away from the drug corners and the shebeens, and to show them Cape Town. Membership was to cost R5 per month.

'I've scheduled a few activities for the coming months,' he told me. 'I want to take the kids hiking, to show them this city's mountains. I want to take them to Camps Bay beach, to show them this city's ocean. I want to take them to the Company Gardens in town, where Johnny Mekka first took me, to show them Cape Town's historic sites, to tell them that their ancestors built this city that they never get to see. I want to form a soccer team for boys and a softball team for girls. To you, maybe it seems like small things. You must understand that these kids live in the most beautiful city in the world and they never get out of their ghetto. How can they ever live normal lives if they never see their city, if they never know that the beauty and the history is theirs too?'

By late September, he had 30 kids signed up and enough money for a single outing.

'I postponed the trip to the beach,' he told me. 'It was going to be cheaper to go hiking. So I decided to take them to Rhodes Gardens. We had enough money either for taxi fare or for cool drinks. We made a decision together: we are here for exercise, not for a taxi ride. So we jogged all the way to Rhodes Gardens, about twelve kilometres. We had a wonderful afternoon there. I read the names of the indigenous flowers to them. Then we walked back. It was dark by the time we got into Manenberg.'

I was in Johannesburg on the day of the Tornado Stallions outing. I imagined this wiry, middle-aged man, jogging purposefully through Cape Town's streets, a pack of teenagers diligently in tow, off to see nature. I was reminded of his first weeks at

Pollsmoor in 1998, after his betrayal of the Morrises; how he had paced the length of the prison, single-minded in his determination to mend the wreckage the Number had become. I wondered whether this penchant for quixotic projects was to be his salvation or his destruction.

There were other works of healing available to him, also without pay. In Pollsmoor, he had befriended a warder – a Mr Arendse – who coached the prison's juvenile rugby team. Occasionally, Mr Arendse would pick Magadien up from Manenberg and take him to Pollsmoor to give the young rugby players a motivational talk about the hazards of crime. I joined him on one of these outings.

The youngsters sat in a huddle at Magadien's feet on the Pollsmoor rugby field. The field is near the bottom of Pollsmoor's premises and offers a panoramic view of the prison and the landscape that surrounds it. Magadien spoke against the backdrop of the wide face-brick, the turrets and the vast expanse of barbed wire, and behind it, the magisterial height of Ou Kaapse Weg, the cars climbing the mountain pass like metallic ants. The things that framed him lent him authority; his voice seemed to come from the landscape itself.

He was smooth, self-assured. He spoke with the hint of a knowing smile on his face. He had left the hell his life had become in Manenberg; he lifted himself into a never-never world of performance.

'A gangster has two choices,' he told his audience. 'Prison or ...'

'Death,' the boys replied obediently. They knew the line by heart. It reminded me of arithmetic tables.

'I used to think warders and whites were my enemies,' he continued. 'You know what? I was inventing enemies for myself. The real enemies were within me. My demons. I used to think I was attacking warders and whites, hurting them. But they went home to their normal lives. I was the one left in prison at night. I was the one destroying my life. I was the one who was hurt.

'When I stopped destroying myself, life became easy. It became light. Think of soccer heroes like Benni McCarthy and Quinton Fortune. They are also from the ghettos. If they had made the wrong choices, they would be sitting here with you, listening to me. Nobody would ever have known about their talent. They would have been wasted.

'Five years ago, warders and whites were my enemies.' He grinned, savouring his story's irony. 'Now, most of my friends are warders and whites.'

I gazed at the prison and the mountain, and listened to Magadien's words. They left me feeling listless and depressed. Was I reading too much into his speech? He seemed to be saying that you have a choice; either you covet whites and middle-class coloureds, and you destroy what they have: or you covet whites and middle-class coloureds, and you befriend them in order to have what they have. Those are the realms of possibility.

He was dreaming before his audience, a painful, private dream. His words painted a fantasy he had been nurturing for five years. He had befriended whites and *sturvies*, and he had failed.

*

Then there was his love life. He lived it almost entirely in his head, but its imaginative energy was sparked by fragments of his real life. He understood his romantic imaginings as a monumental process of preparation.

He is an inveterate flirt. In the presence of a woman to whom he is attracted, he resorts to tactile boyishness. He touches, teases. His seriousness vanishes and is replaced by mischievous innuendo. His attention is trained on his body and its meanings; he is possessed by the single-minded acquisitiveness of a hunting teenager.

There was Lenza, the neighbour of Gadija's whom he had courted back in 1996. She had a four-year-old daughter now. Once, driving past her house, we saw Lenza's daughter standing at the front door. Magadien blew her a kiss. She smiled broadly, put her hand to her mouth and blew an extravagant kiss back. Lenza was watching from a corner of the courtyard. She giggled and shook her head.

I have not met a child who does not adore Magadien. To a young mother, he is ineluctably compelling.

Then there was Landa, who lived in the block opposite the Benjamins. Like Lenza, she was young, in her early twenties. At night, he would watch television with her and her family in their living room. He would kiss her good-night on the cheek, go back to his wendy house in the Benjamins' back yard, and write about Landa and Lenza in his diary.

I had given him his diary as a 43rd birthday present while he was still in Pollsmoor. He had requested it; he had taken his current diary from the papers beneath his bed and shown it to me. It was a wildlife diary printed by the Parks Board, each page adorned with zebras, buck and antelope. 'A social worker who visited the prison gave it to me,' he said. 'She's sweet. The animals are pretty. But where the fuck must I write my thoughts? The animals are in the way. I want you to bring me a big fucking diary with lots of blank space. I've got lots of thoughts.'

Now, six months later, he was using his diary to practise the arts of romance; it played host both to fantasy and to a kind of emotional training regimen. In his daily entries, he consummated the flirtations he was kindling in his real life. His writing was not erotic; it barely touched on sex. It imagined his relationships after they had been consummated, how he would feel in the presence of a woman, how he would learn to love. He sensed dimly that he would have to teach these things to himself in the solitude of his wendy house, his son asleep beside him.

He knew that the stakes were very high, that his romances would have to remain on paper until he was ready; his life was too precarious to tolerate a premature foray into love. He sensed it was here that things might unravel: in the realm of intimacy.

He did not know when he might be ready; how does one begin to judge these things? All he knew was that he was still formally married to Faranaaz, that he lived under her parents' roof, and that his parole conditions forced him to sleep there every night. His circumstances sheltered him from the things he feared. He waited, and he wrote.

On a Thursday in late August, he got permission from his parole officer to spend the morning in town. He returned at lunch time. Mrs Benjamin was waiting for him on the front porch. She was dangling his diary by its page marker.

'We had a hell of a fight,' he told me. 'I said she had no business reading my diary. She said it was very much her fucking business; I was being unfaithful to her daughter. I told her it's not possible to be unfaithful with a pen and a piece of paper, and that anyway, I had told her from the beginning that I was going to divorce her daughter. I had never lied.

'I went into my wendy house and stayed there the whole afternoon. I was shaking and sweating. That night, my mother-in-law called me for dinner like I was a dog. She whistled and slapped her hand against her thigh like I was a dog.

'I took the plate and put it in the fridge. I went to bed hungry. The next day, I opened the fridge, looked at my food, and closed the fridge again. That afternoon, I fed it to the dog. There was no supper for me that night. Hassan, my brother-in-law, gave me half of his plate. I ate it like a thief.'

From that day on, there was a silent war of attrition between Magadien and the Benjamins. They would not throw him out, and he would not leave. They sniped at one another, passively and vindictively.

'The other day, I walked into the living room,' he told me, 'and suddenly there was silence. They had been talking about me. They don't politely change the subject. They just sit there and say nothing. I feel like I have a disease they might catch.'

Some evenings, Magadien would find himself alone in the living room and switch on the TV. 'Out of the blue, they now urgently have to watch TV; not the channel I was watching – another channel. So I go to Landa's house to watch TV. When I get back, they scowl at me, as if to say: "You have been sleeping with Landa."'

'I know you don't have a cent,' I said to Magadien. 'I know you can't walk out of there tomorrow and rent a place of your own. But why do you stay? The people around you loathe you. That can't be good. And you're creating a situation where you're a prisoner again. You wait to be dished up food. The people who give you your food are like warders; they don't care about you. Sometimes they forget to feed you. Sometimes they forget on purpose. The more I think about it, the more it scares me that you have found yourself in a situation where you are like a prisoner again.'

'Where must I go?' he asked. 'To Zubeida or to Anne? How long will it be before their husbands start to hate me? I'll just be this mouth that has to have food shovelled into it. Food costs money. They already work too hard.

'Must I go to my mother? Must I sleep on the floor next to Waleed's bed? Must I sleep in my mother's bed with her husband? You've seen how small their house is.

'At the moment, my options are Manenberg or the Firm. Either I am a prisoner in that house or I sell drugs. I'm not going to sell drugs. I'd rather be a prisoner.'

He began to look for work. He went back to the Centre for Conflict Resolution and asked Michelene to help him compile a CV. He could glaze and he could lay bricks. He was prepared, for the first time since his release, to contemplate manual work. It was a far cry from the spiritual vocation he had so confidently expected during his last months in Pollsmoor.

He walked Cape Town, going into factories, shops and warehouses, and handing out his CV. He walked up and down Bree Street and Loop Street, then moved across town and into Buitenkant Street, then into the old District Six. He began to walk home along Main Road, through Lower Woodstock and Salt River. In Salt River, he stopped handing out his CV and window shopped at the warehouse and discount stores. He began fantasising; he began playing 'what if ...?'

'What if I earned R2 000 a month? What would I buy first? School shoes for Johaah, and new soccer boots? Something for Glynnis when I go to say hello. Fifteen rand a day on food. How much would I have left?'

By the time he arrived in Manenberg in the early evening, he had learned dozens of prices by heart. He had divided his imaginary salary into five categories, and worked out that he would save R400 a month. 'Because Noes, when I find her,' he explained, 'will have needs. Like school fees. She must finish school. And because she is a young woman now; she is 16. Young women need things.'

He gave himself a day's break and then caught another dawn taxi to town. He spent the day walking back to Manenberg again, handing out his CV along the route.

He was never going to get a job this way. He had put his prison record on his CV.

'People said I was mad to do that,' he said. 'But I would be mad not to do that. How can I start with a deception yet again? You know as well as I do how it would end.'

Finding work was much easier when his object was to steal.

*

When Magadien and I met at Pollsmoor, we agreed that there would be no exchange of money between us. From my side, I did not want to buy a poor man's story. Having thousands of strangers read an intimate account of one's life is not an easy business. A person's motivations in submitting his life to a writer are always opaque, always, in the end, unknowable, even to himself. I did not want to mix money into these motivations. His invitation to his inner sanctum had to come for free; he could not be the recipient of a bribe.

Since his release from jail, I had been visiting Cape Town every six weeks. Each of my trips lasted about ten days. In prison, he was fed by the state. Outside, he was destitute. If I had refused him a cent, he would not have starved. He filled his stomach most days without my help.

But aside from being a journalist and his subject, we were two human beings together. One had money and the other was penniless. The idea that no money exchange hands became utterly perverse. And so we broke our rule, but only a little. For the duration of my visits, I bought him three meals a day. I also bought him a tracksuit and a pair of shoes for Johaah.

It was a strange and uncomfortable compromise. A rich man walks into the life of a very poor one and gives him scraps. But if he gives more, what is the cost? However honourable his intentions, he is in essence bribing the poor man to share his story with the world.

The last Thursday of July was also the second-last day of one of my periodic trips to Cape Town. I had not seen Magadien all day; the working hours had been taken up with several other appointments.

I spent the early evening sitting in a bar in Kloof Street, watching a cricket match between South Africa and England. My cellphone rang; the Benjamins' land line number came up on the screen. It was more than unusual. Calls to cellphones are expensive. They would never have allowed Magadien to phone me unless something awful had happened.

I answered the phone and Magadien muttered at me inaudibly.

'I can't hear you,' I said.

'I say we don't have power,' he replied. 'The money has run out for power. We can't cook. And we've got no butter. Nobody in Manenberg has butter to loan us.'

I said nothing. There was a long silence.

'There is nothing for dinner,' he continued, 'only dry bread. There is a pregnant woman in the house.'

His voice changed suddenly. He adopted a new tone. It was very familiar; I had heard it many times before, but not from him.

I had heard it in the voices of other Pollsmoor prisoners, men who had looked me in the eye and not seen a human being there, only an opportunity.

'What did you have for lunch today?' he asked in his new voice.

'Toasted cheese and tomato sandwiches.'

'No,' he replied. 'You're lying. You went to a nice restaurant today: one of the ones where they charge R50 for a bowl of spaghetti. Do me a favour. Bring me something nice tomorrow. Bring me a doggy bag from your fancy restaurant. I'll share it with my family.'

I switched off my phone and stared blankly at the cricket match on the television screen. I felt no empathy, just deep anger. After all we've been through, I thought. And you want to reduce things to this. Has it come to this? Perhaps I had been dreaming all along; perhaps this is indeed the price that is paid when a rich man gets too close to a poor man.

*

The following day, when I went to Manenberg to see him, he behaved as if nothing had happened. The voice was gone. He was jovial, pleased to see me.

I stared at him coldly.

'What's the matter?' he asked.

'Don't fuck with me again.'

'I wasn't fucking with you. I was hungry.'

'Ja, you were hungry. But that doesn't give you licence to fuck with me.'

'Don't you know a joke when you hear one? Don't you understand how I joke?'

I said nothing. He turned his back to me, stared into the distance for a long time, then sighed deeply. He offered me his hand.

'Peace,' he said. 'Let's have peace between us. It's not nice when you're unhappy. Because I like you, my friend. You know I care for you very much.'

I drove away feeling miserable. Today, he had needed to repair the bond between us with the same urgency that had compelled him to break it last night. I felt I was taking my place among the likes of Norman Sampson and Johnny Jansen – the hated, beloved whites and *sturvies* of Magadien's life.

25
NOES

In mid-July, Magadien found Noes. It had been a tortured quest. We had spent two afternoons wandering through Rusthof, the Strand's coloured township, going from one door to the next, asking everyone and anyone if they knew where she was.

It was only after we found her that I discovered why the search for Noes had been so difficult. Magadien had known all along where she lived: with Josephina, her aunt and legal guardian. She had been living there ever since her mother was murdered in the early 1990s. What Magadien had not told me is that Josephina was unhinged. If Noes's father had appeared out of the blue asking to see his daughter, Josephina would have thrown him out the house and called the police. So he avoided her house. He was hoping to find Noes elsewhere, out of Josephina's sight.

He dragged me along his laboured, circuitous route to his daughter, and eventually, towards the end of our second trip to the Strand, we were given an address on Webb Street, the house of Noes's closest friend. We hooted and watched the front door. Two teenage girls appeared, one tall and elegant, the other diminutive and baby-faced. They were both carrying large mugs of coffee. Magadien got out of the car and smiled at them.

'Daddy!' the shorter girl shouted. She dropped her coffee mug, sprinted to the gate and flung herself into Magadien's open arms. She was 11 years old the last time she had seen him – another lifetime.

On the way to the Strand, Magadien had been agitated and nervous.

'What the fuck do I know about having a sixteen-year-old daughter?' he asked. 'I'm shitting myself.'

But once she was in his arms, he knew what to do, and he did it with admirable grace. They disentangled, and Magadien leaned against the car. When he spoke to her, she turned her gaze from him and directed her answers down the empty street. Gently, he put his hands on her shoulders until she turned and looked up into his face. She was no more than five feet tall; she spoke in a tiny voice, the voice of a girl half her age.

He was wonderful with her: demonstrative, quietly excited; he gently squeezed answers about the last five years from her. What he heard was obviously upsetting, but he betrayed none of it. He maintained his benign attentiveness throughout.

She told him that she did not go to school any more, that she never finished standard nine. She was expelled for swearing, fighting and smoking. She said these things matter-of-factly, as if describing her day. He nodded slowly and told her she would go back to school one day, that it was of the utmost importance.

He asked if she had a boyfriend and she nodded.

'How old is he?' he asked.

'Nineteen.'

He started to ask more and then checked himself. He smiled at her sheepishly: 'I know you know this,' he said. 'But I'll be a stupid old man and say it anyway. Please be careful, my love. It's easy to fall pregnant. It's even easier to get sick and die.'

She averted her gaze and giggled. 'Daddy!' Her fingers played nervously with her chin.

'Please, Noes. I'm serious.'

'Yes, Daddy,' she replied obediently in her small girl's voice.

He put his arm round her shoulder and walked her down the street. I could not hear what they were saying, but I watched. She was smiling and blushing. The warm, adult attentiveness she was receiving delighted her. But she did not know what to do with it. She couldn't stop giggling.

They returned to the car. Magadien took out a scrap of paper and wrote down two phone numbers.

'This one's mine, in Manenberg,' he said. 'If there is ever any problem, you must phone. And when there isn't a problem, when you just want to talk, you must phone. I'm on parole. I can't come to visit whenever I like. But I'll come whenever I can.

'And this number,' he continued, 'this is Glynnis, your big sister. She is in Mitchells Plain. I want you to make me a promise, just one promise, nothing else. Please phone her.'

We drove off and Noes stood in the middle of the street and waved.

'Why Glynnis?' I asked.

'Noes is living in hell,' he replied. 'You haven't met her aunt yet. She must get out of this place and go back to school. But I can't do it. If I try to take Noes, Josephina will go mad. There'll be a hell of a custody battle. I'm on parole. I'll lose.

'But I know Glynnis. If Noes phones her, she will tell Noes to come and visit her. They've never met, but she will be curious about her little sister. And when she sees Noes, she will love her. She'll discover that Noes is living in hell, and she'll never go back. Glynnis will send her back to school.'

I nodded. It seemed like several deductions too many.

He read the scepticism in my face and smiled at me. 'I'm a pauper living in the house of people who hate me. This is the best I can do. This is my plan.'

*

Sure enough, Noes phoned Magadien in mid-August. She had been speaking to her older sister on the phone every day. Glynnis had invited her to spend a long weekend. Would Magadien come to the Strand to fetch her?

We drove through the town towards Josephina's house. Rusthof is laid out in a perfect grid. The place is bare: no parkland, no empty spaces, no foliage – only the occasional gigantic bluegum. The bareness makes the symmetry offensive, as if the same street has multiplied itself from the highway all the way down to the sea.

To the north and east, the towering peaks of the Hottentots Holland stare down into the township. The houses on Josephina's street are tiny and square, smaller than a communal cell in Pollsmoor. The mountains and the big ugly trees accentuate the smallness; as if the houses could be blown away by a sneeze.

Noes was standing outside Josephina's house. She greeted us nervously as we walked past her.

We knocked on the front door and walked in. Josephina was a colossal woman; she was crammed into one of the two double beds that were the house's only furniture. The rest of the household was assembled around her as if the place was a makeshift amphitheatre and she was about to sing. Three small children and a young woman with an infant in her arms sat on the other bed. The woman was smoking a cigarette over her baby's head. There were three men in the room, and they all stood against the far end of the second bed. They were all in their twenties and wore the uniforms of gangsters: baseball caps worn with the peaks backwards, earrings, sleeveless shirts and Number tattoos on their shoulders.

We weren't two feet into her home when Josephina launched herself into a tirade. She screamed in a seamless torrent, barely taking a breath. She remained flat on her back, shouting up at the ceiling.

Noes was fucking up her life, she screamed. She wanted to tell Magadien what a lying little girl Noes was. She wanted to explain to Magadien exactly how it fucking came about that Noes left school. Noes came home one day without her bag. She claimed she had lost it. There were a whole lot of books in it, books that Josephina had just fucking bought for her. Josephina was a poor woman; she did not buy books to be lost. Josephina went to see the principal. He said Noes had thrown away her fucking bag; she didn't want to go to school any more. Noes smoked buttons. You could smell it on her breath. Noes had been hanging out with a girl called Florence. Florence was evil. She was a sangoma. She was sleeping with a married man.

With monumental effort, Josephina threw her duvet aside to expose her leg. It was covered in a plaster cast. Florence and Noes put a spell on her, she said. They made her stumble and break her leg.

She showed Magadien a scar on her arm. She kept having accidents, she said. Noes and Florence were trying to kill her. Noes kept telling her she was not her real mother. She had sacrificed half her life for that ungrateful little bitch, and now Noes was telling her she was not her real mother. There was no fucking way Magadien was going to take Noes to see Glynnis. Noes didn't bother to ask for permission. And in any case, Noes had packed her bag as if she didn't intend to come back.

Josephina stopped as suddenly as she had started. She put her leg back inside the duvet, adjusted her pillows and stared at the ceiling. Magadien had been listening meekly all the while. Now he shook his head, stepped outside and asked Noes to come in. She didn't want to. Magadien coaxed her.

She walked tentatively through the front door, and her presence was too much provocation for Josephina. She launched her complaint again, louder than before, this time shifting with great effort onto her side so that she could see the little bitch who was ruining her life. Noes stared at her with childish defiance, walked outside and lit a cigarette. The young woman on the second bed watched angrily, put down her baby and followed Noes outside.

'You're acting all strong because your dad is here,' she shouted at Noes. 'When he's gone, I'm going to *moer* you. *Jy gaan kak!'* 'You're going to shit off!'

'Ja, meisie,' Josephina contributed from her bed. *'Jy gaan kak!'* 'Yes, my girl: you're going to shit yourself!'

Magadien managed to coax Noes inside again. He placed her in front of Josephina and started lecturing her. 'How dare you tell Josephina she is not your real mother,' he said half-heartedly. 'She is your mother, and she always will be. She has been bringing you up since you were three. And how dare you not ask her permission to visit Glynnis?'

It worked like magic. Josephina calmed. She went through the motions of hurling a little more abuse at Noes, but was soon boring herself. She waved us away: silent consent; Noes could leave with Magadien.

Josephina turned to face the wall, as if Noes's departure was too disgusting to watch. The rest of the household stared at Noes stonily: Josephina's silent chorus.

On the trip to Glynnis's house in Mitchells Plain, Noes sulked. She had no idea that the lecture Magadien had given her was feigned and tactical, that its only aim had been to get her out the house. All she knew was that her dad had suddenly appeared in her life again, that he was warm and empathetic one day, a heartless ally of her aunt's the next. She sat on the back seat, commiserating with herself from within the depths of her child's world, railing against the arbitrary whims of the adults who controlled her life. Magadien, who was in the passenger seat, turned round and tried to talk to her. She stared out the window, refusing to make eye contact. She didn't say a word the entire journey.

Glynnis was not home. We left Noes with Margie's husband. Magadien had been free more than two months now; he still hadn't seen Glynnis.

*

A few days later, Magadien got a call from Glynnis.

'How dare you!' she shouted. 'Noes doesn't have proper shoes. She only has slipslops. You've been out of jail two months and you haven't bought her a pair of shoes. All her possessions she fits into a plastic bag. She doesn't go to school. Why haven't you put her back in school? What kind of father are you?'

'Is she still with you?' Magadien asked meekly.

'No. She went back to the Strand this morning.'

Magadien did not tell her he had no money to buy shoes, nor that his home was a rickety wendy house and that he was living in it on borrowed time. On the few occasions he had appeared in Glynnis's life, he had done so with money. He had been wearing good clothes and had bought her little gifts.

He did not tell her that it was not so, that he had nothing. He was too ashamed. In his imagination, fatherhood and poverty did not go together. If he was to reconcile with his daughter, he believed, he could not open the discussion by declaring he was destitute.

'Glynnis acts strong,' he told me. 'She acts like she can shout at me, one adult to another. She thinks she's learned to live life without a father. But there's a very angry child in her. There's a part of her that hates me more than she can say.'

*

In late October, Magadien got a call from the Strand. Josephina had thrown Noes out; she was sleeping in a different house every night, moving from one friend to another.

When I saw Magadien, he was ashen-faced.

'A young girl can't live like that in a place like Rusthof,' he said. 'It's a matter of time before she is beaten up or raped. We have to fetch her now.'

'Where will she live?' I asked.

'We'll get there,' he said. 'We'll get there.'

On the way to the Strand, we stopped in at Gadija's place. Outside the house, Magadien told me that Gadija had been sick. A week ago, she had an asthma attack during the night; she had been rushed to hospital.

Gadija was indeed very sick. She lay flat on her back and looked weak and miserable. Usually delighted to see me, today she barely gave me a glance.

Magadien explained his dilemma.

'There is no space for her here,' she replied weakly. 'If there is anywhere she can stay, it is with your aunt in Macassar. But you will have to explain yourself to her. All these years, you've never been around. When her husband died, you weren't there for the funeral. Maybe she'll take your daughter. Maybe she won't.'

She was exhausted, battling to pay attention. I could not help myself remembering that she too, Noes's grandmother, was once a miserable 15-year-old from the Strand, living in a house with no love. By the time we left, she was asleep.

We drove to the Strand and found Noes at Josephina's sister's house, another little matchbox on the same street. Josephina's sister's name was Fi. The family resemblance was striking; she looked just like Josephina, but where Josephina's face was plastered with torment, hers was serene and jovial.

Noes sat on Fi's bed looking relaxed. There was a mellowness about the house, an aura of sanity. She and Fi were watching television: a rugby world cup match between Wales and the All Blacks. The image jumped and flickered and the sound disappeared periodically. Fi sent her husband, Isaac, onto the roof to adjust the aerial.

'And now?' Isaac shouted from the roof.

'Turn!' Fi shouted.

'And now?'

'Turn.'

The image kept jumping and flickering. The sound kept vanishing.

A group of small children gathered outside the house, pointed up at Isaac stumbling round his useless aerial, and laughed their heads off. Noes went outside to watch and started laughing as well.

Josephina's house was about 150 metres down the street. I watched her making her way towards us. Her bulk alone made the journey difficult. Her plastered leg made it a veritable marathon. She swung the leg in a wide loop, as if drawing a circle around every footstep. By the time she reached Fi's house, her forehead was covered in beads of sweat.

She took a moment to catch her breath, walked into the house and began to remonstrate. But it was half-hearted this time. She was going through the motions. Her eyes darted around nervously; she lacked confidence.

Noes had been coming home at 12 at night, at one in the morning, she told her audience. Her friends were bad news. She had found a condom in Noes's bag, a fucking condom.

She cupped her forehead in her hand and her monologue trailed off.

'I can't any more,' she said plaintively. 'I'm too tired.'

Noes glared at the television.

Magadien listened with visible emotion. He stared at the floor and quite literally gritted his teeth. When Josephina finished speaking, he asked Fi if he could use her phone; he called the Benjamins.

'Please Mama,' he begged. 'I am pleading with you. You are the only one who can help me. Let me just bring her round so you can meet her.' He was grovelling at the feet of his enemy. Given what had passed between them, nothing from Mrs Benjamin would come for free, I thought to myself. He was bringing another woman's daughter into the house, no matter that the rival was long dead. He would pay her back, not in money, but in the currency of their war of emotional attrition.

*

On the journey back to Manenberg I watched Noes in the rear-view mirror. She was trying to take command of the language of her body, to send herself the right signals. She stared defiantly into the middle distance, shoring up her steel, preparing for adversity. It wasn't working. She rummaged through the supermarket packet that contained her worldly possessions, found a t-shirt, held it up to her mouth and bit on it.

When we arrived at the Benjamins' house, she started putting her shirt back in her packet, thought better of it, and held it to her mouth once more. She walked inside, clutching it like a treasure. Nobody greeted her. It was as if she was invisible. She stuck close to Magadien, never allowing herself to trail more than a couple of footsteps behind him.

That evening, I phoned Magadien.

'I took her for a walk to show her Manenberg,' he said. 'I spoke to her quietly. I said there is no shouting in my wendy house, no hitting. Johaah has just turned 18 and I have never hit him in my life. But he behaves. He is up at four every morning and he is home early every night. I gave her ground rules. I said I want her home at 10 pm, and I want to meet the people she goes out with. I asked her if this was fair. She said it was.'

Mrs Benjamin kept her silence during the following days. She neither greeted Noes, nor made any mention of her. It was understood that Magadien would be responsible for feeding her.

'From now on,' Magadien told me, 'I must make food for myself, Noes and Johaah.'

'Why Johaah as well?'

'Because if I feed her and not him, there will be waves. He'll feel like he's being excluded because my daughter is in the house now. We must all eat together.'

'Where will Johaah sleep?'

'With his mother. It is too much to ask him to sleep in the same bed as me and Noes.'

I was to stay in Cape Town another three days. I gave Magadien enough money to feed the three of them for a week.

'This is not sustainable,' I said. 'How are you going to keep putting food on her plate?'

'I know how to make plans,' he told me encouragingly. 'I've been through a lot worse than this.'

*

I spent Christmas and New Year in a small mountain village in the Eastern Cape, out of cellphone range. When I got back home to Johannesburg, there were several SMSs from Magadien on my phone. I called him.

'I have just had the most miserable Christmas of my life,' he told me despondently. 'My last five Christmases were in jail and they were all better than this.'

'What happened?'

'Noes is back in the Strand, with Josephina. Mrs Benjamin threw her out the house. Every time Noes walked out the front door the Benjamins would shout and scream and say she was running with the Americans. They bashed on my door and told me my daughter was being a slut and sleeping with gangsters.'

'Was she running with the Americans?'

'The boys in this block belong to the Americans,' he said. 'You can't live in Manenberg and not talk to gangsters. Faranaaz can run with a drug dealer, and attract violent men to this house, and that is okay. But if Noes talks to some boys on the street corner, they want to throw her out the house.

'Last week, they dragged her back home by her hair. They took out a belt, put it in my hand, and told me I had to beat her. I said no and they told me I was a useless father, I was fucking up my daughter. They said if I didn't hit her with the belt, they would. So I did. I had told her there would be no hitting in my house, and I hit her. I don't know how many time I've looked back at my own childhood and promised myself never to raise a hand to a child. Afterwards, I told her I loved her.

'She had to get out of here. Even I know a little bit about bringing up children. They were driving her to gangsters. They were making her defiant. If you shout at a child the whole day and night for sleeping with gangsters, she will sleep with gangsters. I was losing control. So I took her back to Josephina.'

'How was that?'

'Josephina had missed her. When she saw Noes she hugged her and cried. I've been speaking to Noes on the phone every day. She says things are quiet in Josephina's house. No shouting. They talk nicely to her.'

There was a long silence.

'How are you holding up?' I asked.

'I miss her terribly,' he replied. 'I think about her every second of the day.'

26
DARRYL

When Magadien was released from jail in June 2003, Joanna Flanders Thomas, the woman who had run the sensational change workshops among the gangsters on D Floor, had been away in the United States. Less than a week after his release, Magadien and I found ourselves driving through the outskirts of Hanover Park. He suggested that we stop at Anne's place; perhaps she was home from work.

When we arrived at the house, Anne's son came rushing out.

'There's someone on the phone for you,' he told Magadien.

It was Joanna. She was calling from Philadelphia. She had phoned on the off-chance that she would find him there.

He came back to the car dazed.

'This is only the second time I've been to this house since my release,' he said, grinning from ear to ear. 'Why did she phone now?'

He looked at me closely.

'Do you believe in coincidence? A coincidence like this? What were the chances that this would happen: one in a thousand?'

We drove in silence for a while. He stared out onto the road in wonderment.

'This is a message,' he said finally. 'Joanna is in my future. That's the meaning of this. I must listen to the meaning.'

Since the day she had come to him with the news that the Benjamins had survived the tornado, Joanna's place in his mind had been associated with a world of symbols and portents. Back then, the signs had been apocalyptic; God had torn Magadien's prospective home from its foundations, warning him that his deficit in the book of judgment was running off the page. Now, Magadien was back in the world, it was indeed crumbling about him, and the sign Joanna had brought him was an intimation of hope.

As the year wore on, he would speak of Joanna from time to time. She was not back yet; she was back now, but she was taking a recuperative holiday in Namibia; she was back from Namibia, but she and Magadien had not seen each other.

These were desperate times for Magadien. As the weeks turned into months, the haunting feeling that things would never change came to sit with him. On bleak days, he was taken by flights of fancy. He had met an executive at a large blue-collar recruitment agency, for instance; the executive had agreed that Magadien would run life and vocational skills workshops for hundreds of contract workers; he would pay Magadien R4 000 a month. Other days, other fancies. Once, Magadien took a crumpled cellphone advertisement from his bag. 'For only R2 999,' the advertisement read, 'you can start your own mobile phone service.'

'I'm going to go to the bank tomorrow,' he told me. 'They will lend me R3 000. I am going to go into business.'

Joanna was always among these painful dreams. 'She was there for me when I thought my world had literally been demolished. She will be there for me again.'

*

In early November, I arrived in Cape Town having not seen Magadien in six weeks. It was about the time that Noes began her brief stay at the Benjamins' place in Manenberg. Magadien and I went on what had become a customary long stroll through the streets of the ghetto, a posse of curious children in tow. Whenever I went to see him, I would arrive to a small army of little people; they hovered about him like flies around the ears of a big serene dog. On our long walks across the ghetto, they would always follow us in droves, eyeing Magadien's every gesture with fascination. They adore him; he draws them like a magnet.

'I've been seeing Joanna,' he said. 'I've been going to her church in Athlone every Sunday for the last month.'

I asked him something about the leader of the congregation, the priest.

'There is no priest,' he said. 'Anybody can get up and speak. I have been speaking a lot, about my past, my change, my difficulties since I've been out of jail. They're making me strong. They're giving me love. Since I've been going to church, I've been sleeping well every night. I'm at peace with myself, even with the Benjamins. They can treat me like shit and I turn the other cheek. I have no dreams about going back to prison any more, no dreams about crime. For the last week, I have been walking Cape Town looking for work, walking the soles of my shoes down. The church gave me the strength to do that.'

I asked him whether he had become a Christian.

'I was waiting for that question,' he replied. 'I knew you were going to ask it. I go there for spiritual enrichment. There's no use splitting hairs over what to call God.'

'What do you call yourself at church: Darryl or Magadien?'

'Darryl.'

'And are you still Magadien among Muslims?'

'I'm Darryl everywhere. I've told my mother I am Darryl. She doesn't like it, but she's come to accept it.'

We walked some more and he said nothing for a long time.

'I'm finished with the Muslim religion,' he said finally. 'There's too much hypocrisy. Here the Benjamins are in the middle of Ramadan, fasting every day, but they stab me in the back.'

*

On a Saturday afternoon in late January 2004, Magadien and I drove to a community parkland area in the northern suburbs to attend a family day organised by his church. It was one of those quasi-rural facilities with goats and sheep, a braaiing area, a swimming pool and an open field for cricket and soccer games.

In the parking lot outside there was a brand-new BMW, a Mercedes and several respectable-looking middle-market cars.

'*Sturvies*,' I said.

'Ja,' Magadien replied. 'But wonderful *sturvies*. Wonderful people.'

We walked into the parkland; before us was one of those universal middle-class scenes from everywhere and nowhere – women sitting on deck chairs, men gathered around a braai, children playing volleyball. The only distinction was the absence of drugs. The men around the braai held soft drinks in their hands, rather than beers, and the women on the deck chairs gesticulated with cigarette-free hands.

I was introduced to some of the church elders: an insurance

salesman, a headmaster, an estate agent. They were all in their thirties and forties, young men with young families.

Magadien had spoken to me about a church elder by the name of Simon. I found him lighting a braai and introduced myself to him. He wore shorts, a fresh t-shirt and a wide floppy hat: a suburban man's weekend kit. We shuffled around one another for some time, mutually cautious. He told me the church was called the Community Bible Fellowship. It was established 17 years ago when about three dozen members of a mainstream evangelical church had broken away to form their own congregation.

'Seventeen years,' I said. 'That's a long lifespan for a congregation outside the institutional mainstream.'

'Yes,' he replied, 'but we have been through bad moments. Some of the church elders have emigrated. Younger and less experienced people like me had to pick it up. There was a bit of a wobble.'

'Why did you break away from the mainstream church?' I asked.

'For two reasons, mainly. Because they did not believe in the equality of women, and because, well, because we believe that Jesus is our Saviour and brought the Good News.'

'You mean that proselytising is mandatory for Christians, and the mainstream church didn't …'

'Well, something like that. Our congregants are messengers.'

I liked Simon, if for no other reason than that he resisted all the stereotypes of a proselytising Christian. He was reserved and somewhat cold. When he spoke, he did so sparingly and with extreme care; I imagined that in business he was fastidiously prudent and unreservedly tough. I imagined that he considered himself wise to the ways of the unscrupulous. For the half-hour or so that we spoke, he almost resisted asking me a single question about my beliefs. Just once: 'I am not sure what role God plays in your life, but …' and then he went on to something else. He framed the comment in a way that I did not have to answer.

Speaking of messengers and converts, we got onto Magadien. Darryl was making good progress, Simon said, but there was still some way to go. 'We have had other experiences of ex-gangsters, difficult experiences. It's not straightforward.'

And so, the church welcomed Magadien, but it was cautious and watchful. On this Simon expressed himself with delicate diplomacy.

'It is difficult to know where to strike the right balance,' he told me. 'On the one hand, Darryl has no income and must support his family. On the other, we don't want to make his relationship with the church one of dependency. That is not good for either of us. And that is also something,' he added pointedly, 'that you might be asking yourself. We don't know, for instance, what he is getting from you.'

'How are preparations for his baptism going?' I asked.

'He has expressed enthusiasm about being baptised, and that is very good. But perhaps it is a little too early. He smokes cigarettes. We do not take issue with that. But he was on drugs for a long time. We need to monitor his progress.

'You see,' he continued, 'when you are baptised, you are immersed in water. It symbolises the death of your past self. Obviously, it is not a literal death. How can you get rid of your whole past just like that? But we do want to know that you have moved some distance before you are baptised.'

For the half-hour or so that Simon and I spoke, Magadien circled us in a wide arc. He was never closer than fifty metres from us, but he watched like a hawk. Eventually, he succumbed to his anxiety, abandoned his vigil, and came to join us. Simon excused himself.

'What the fuck were you talking about for so long?' he asked me suspiciously. 'You journalists: talk, talk, talk.'

For the rest of the afternoon, he was exquisitely meek. He did not speak unless spoken to, and when he answered, he did so with studied deference.

I left the parkland that afternoon unsure what to think of Magadien's new adventure. The church had become his ballast; without it, the ideas that had moved him so profoundly in Pollsmoor would surely become ethereal and unreal, and eventually evaporate. Unemployed, penniless, unable to be a proper father: these are circumstances in which ideas of moral renewal begin to seem absurd. The church was a real, concrete place, a place he could enter to submit himself to the rigours of harsh moral evaluation, a place that would excommunicate him if he strayed. It was as if he was strapping himself to his seat in the midst of a journey that had become intolerable.

And indeed, a few days after the church's family event, he took himself to a community centre on the Cape Flats and enrolled in an addiction programme; he had given up drugs and alcohol long ago, but he wanted to quit cigarettes. 'I'm the only shithead in that entire congregation who smokes,' he said.

Yet there was something about his relationship to this new, ascetic discipline that echoed unpleasantly. The echo was that of the age-old relationship between the coloured ghetto man and the coloured middle class. The church regarded him with caution. Its belief told it that everyone can be delivered from evil. But it was also deeply wary of the world in which Magadien had spent his life. They were uncertain about how to read him, a little suspicious of his intentions. The relationship between the *skollie* and the *sturvy* has so often ended badly. There is something in the *sturvy's* gaze that wills the *skollie* to play his devious part.

*

I started calling him Darryl. Sixteen months ago – another lifetime – he had introduced himself to me as Magadien. Arriving at that name had been an act of will, a painful assembling of an identity. So was this. Only this time, the process by which he had found himself a name was marked by the unforgiving lessons he had learned since his release. Everything he had grasped had slipped through his fingers. Fatherhood, missionary work, a salary, his own home: every coordinate of the life he had imagined during his hey-day at Pollsmoor had proved elusive. When the ground beneath your feet keeps cracking up, the idea that your identity is something you retrieve, a datum you gather from the truth of your past, becomes empty and meaningless. He had learned that how he was to understand himself was a matter of pragmatic choice, not discovery. Of all the strands of life that drifted past him, he grasped the few that appeared to be solid; he adjusted himself accordingly and hoped for the best.

Driving through the Flats on an afternoon in early February 2004, he took out his ID book and glared at it disparagingly.

'My birth certificate was lost long ago,' he said. 'This identity document was made for me by the prison authorities when I voted in 1994. It says I was born on 8 March 1963. But Anne was born in December 1963. How could I have been born nine months before her? My mother would have to be a machine. Am I three years older than Anne, or four? I don't remember; it is one of the two.

Some days my mother says I was born in 59, some days she says 1960. This ID book is a lie. What will happen if I get a job on this ID book and someone finds out it is not my real birth date? Or a driver's licence, or a bank account, or a fucking divorce? Will I find that I'm still married to my wife? When I was underground, all my records were lost, even my prison record. How can that be? It's as if I was erased while I was underground. Erased forever. I try to get back into the legitimate world, the world of records, and all I have to show for myself is this.' He waved his faulty ID document in my face.

'I went to talk to my mother about it,' he continued. 'She told me that when I was born she had registered me as Magadien Darryl Martin Wanza. Not Wentzel, Wanza. That was her family name. Where did Wentzel come from? How did Wanza become Wentzel? When I was growing up, I was always aware of this Wanza name hovering in the background. But my name was Wentzel since I can remember. There was so much other confusion about who I was that it didn't occur to me to ask anyone.'

He dismissed the whole matter with an irritable wave of the hand. 'If I get obsessed with it,' he said, 'I'm just going to drive myself mad. You know, when I first started cooperating with you on this book, these things were important to me. They're not any more. I have to think of the present and the future now. I have to leave the stuff I don't need behind. Now, this book is important, not for me, but for my children and grandchildren. I want them to have a record of all the things I have been. There will be plenty rumours floating around. I want to be in a position to answer their questions.'

*

In December 2003, a member of the Community Bible Fellowship congregation found Magadien a temporary job with a large blue-collar recruitment agency. They provided scores of unskilled contract workers to many of Cape Town's factories and businesses. He was assigned to work at an enormous bakery in the industrial district of Maitland. The job lasted three weeks.

Some time after his work there had ended, he took me to Maitland to visit the bakery. The woman who had found him the temporary job was employed there as a receptionist. With some difficulty, she managed to convince the security guards at the gate to let us in.

As we made our way towards a bridge that overlooked the factory floor, a block of solid heat slapped us in our faces. Below us, a massive assembly line snaked its way across a space about a hundred metres long. Workers wearing paper sanitary hats were dispersed along the length of its body.

Magadien's job had been to feed the oven. The temperature at his work station was 49°C, the humidity 84%. In his first couple of hours on the job, he had dehydrated; nobody had told him to keep drinking water. During the week, he fell ill; he had a hacking cough and a blistering headache. He dragged himself out of bed each morning to return to work.

He was paid R130 a week, usually for four days' work, sometimes five. R20 went to his weekly train fare. R80 went to Mrs Benjamin. He was left with R30 a week to feed himself and Noes, just about enough for two loaves of bread a day.

From outside the factory gate, the place resembled a caricature of Dickensian unhappiness: a wide, low-slung building of no particular colour stretching across the length of a block. The façade facing the street was entirely windowless, as if the building's interior harboured treasures or shame. Around the perimeter of the factory premises, two layers of tall, sturdy fence, topped with coils of barbed wire. Three or four white security guards paced authoritatively behind the fence, armed with two-way radios and outsized limbs.

Out on the street, people waited and lingered. Some sat in jagged circles on the pavement. Others stood at the fence and stared inside. Two young men ventured to within a few yards of the factory gate, attracting the attention of one of the security guards within. He walked up to the gate and hammered it with his fist. '*Hamba!*' he said. 'Fuck off.'

Magadien motioned to the people lingering outside.

'They're waiting for work,' he said. 'Some of them come at five in the morning. Others sleep on the pavement during the night. On a lucky day, some of them are picked to do one shift. But even after the shift is chosen, the rest wait. You can come here any time of the day or night – they will be here.'

He stood aside, offering me this world for contemplation; he treated it like an evidentiary exhibit.

'Usually,' he continued, 'they pick the blacks and ignore the coloureds. Blacks are prepared to work for nothing and don't complain. Us lighter-skinned people talk back too much.'

He spoke philosophically, as if he was doing a voiceover for some documentary. But the image of the timeless job-seekers that had accosted him every morning as he walked through the factory gates had clearly stirred something powerful in him. He was waiting for it to boil and overflow and become words.

We drove from Maitland to the centre of Cape Town, parked at the entrance to the Company Gardens, and made our way down its central pathway. He said nothing, but the spectacle of the factory gates stood so vividly in his imagination, it was as if he was painting it in the empty space in front of us.

'I am so full of ideas,' he said at last, 'I think I'm going to explode. Those people outside the bakery: are they human beings? How often must you sleep on the pavement outside a factory before you lose your humanness forever?

'My people are sick, so badly sick, and so many of them sick, that sometimes it's all too much to fit in my head.

'For the last week, I've been going to a shebeen every night, not to drink, but to watch. There's this eighty-year-old woman who goes there every night; she shuffles there on her walking-stick. She sits there smoking and drinking with the young people. She drinks the cheapest fucking wine; it's not fit for human beings. It's black and disgusting. You could use it as petrol in your car. The other night I sat with her, and I said: "Ma, why do you come here every night?" She looked at me and said: "It's the only time I get any peace."

'There's this other guy at the shebeen; he also comes every night. He's so fucked up he can't wash himself. No one can stand the smell. The other night, we had to take off his clothes and wash him. He stood there in this fucking tub, naked as the day he was born, with no shame, like a little child.

'My people are sick. How can you live in a world where when you take your girlfriend for a walk, you are always looking behind your shoulder?' He began to dart around the Company Gardens pathway, ducking phantom predators. 'On the Cape Flats,' he continued, 'even the dogs are scared of human beings.'

He thought of the bakery and the broken people in the shebeen, and the two mingled in his head.

'The coloureds are still the slaves of this province,' he said. 'During the week, they work for nothing. On weekends, they kill each other. The province is prepared to come and pick up the corpses. That's all their job is.'

*

In early 2004, several 'temptations', as the church would say, presented themselves in Magadien's life. He was walking through Manenberg one afternoon; a BMW with darkened windows stopped alongside him. The back door opened and three men jumped out and greeted him warmly. They were all 28s from Elsies River; he knew them well from prison. Elsies River was the stronghold of the the Firm in the northern districts of the Cape Flats. He wondered what had brought them to his section of Manenberg; it was Americans' turf. They asked him where he lived and offered to give him a lift home.

Late the following night, Johaah came to Magadien in his wendy house and told him that there were people outside who wanted to see him. He went into the street and found a spanking-new Mercedes Benz parked outside the house. The driver got out and motioned for Magadien to get into the back. He stepped into the car and found himself sitting next to a famous man, famous in the northern ghettos at any rate. His name was Arnie; he was a senior member of the Firm responsible for managing a large swathe of Elsies River.

'He took about ten sheets of Mandrax tablets out of his bag and offered them to me,' Magadien said. 'I said no. Arnie said okay, took a couple of hundred bucks out his pocket and gave it me.

'It was okay to say no. It wasn't really a serious offer. The Americans sell buttons in my area of Manenberg, not the Firm. If I had started selling here, I would have to cut my prices below the Americans' prices. Then the Americans would have started with me. And if they'd done that, the Firm would have to step in and risk people to defend my market. It made no sense.

'What was really happening was that he was acknowledging me. He was saying: "You're a senior 28. You did not come to us when you got out of jail, but we've found you and you are one of us. There's always a place for you." It was a gesture.'

'It was a double-edged gesture,' I replied. 'And it worries me. As long as you mind your own business, it's okay with them. But when you, as a senior 28, start speaking out against the Number, then your business is their business. When we started this book, you thought that you were going to become a prominent public speaker, that when you spoke out against the gangs you'd have a whole organisational infrastructure behind you, that when the book was published your views would already be known to the gangs. But actually what's happened is that you're just an unemployed man living in a wendy house. When this book is published, you'll be vulnerable.'

Whenever I raised concerns about his security, he responded angrily.

'Before I met you,' he said, 'I risked my life in prison, standing up for Joanna, starting Friends Against Abuse. Every day, I was talking out against the Number and I was sleeping every night next to men with knives. You weren't there. You'd never met me. It had nothing to do with you. What makes you think it has anything to do with you now? Must I live my life in a way that will make *your* conscience feel better? You've spent a long time with me now. You've known for a long time that I've been cooperating with you for my own reasons. I need to fight. If this book doesn't help me to fight, it will have been a waste of time.'

'It *is* my business,' I said. 'You have dreams of being a martyr. Sometimes you think life is too difficult and you dream about going down in a hail of bullets. You think your spirit will still be there, watching your funeral, with everyone so proud of you. You won't be there. Your flesh will be rotting in your coffin; that's all.'

'You're pathetic,' he replied sharply. 'Sometimes I think you've taught me so many things. Other times I think you're just pathetic. You'd rather I was miserable and unemployed, but safe. You'd rather that when I die, there is nothing left on this earth to remember me by.'

*

Some time in late January, I asked him how Gadija was doing.

'I haven't been to Heideveld in three weeks,' he replied. 'I've been in trouble with the Americans there. If I go back, I'm going to have to hurt somebody.'

At Christmas time, Landa had given Magadien her cellphone. It was broken. She didn't have the money to fix it. A cousin of his brother-in-law's called André told Magadien he fixed cellphones for a living, and offered to take it. André lives a few houses away from Gadija. He was in the Americans. He was also a *laaitie;* he was young, had never been to jail, and was of a junior rank.

'After about a week,' Magadien told me, 'I went to André to fetch my cellphone. He had sold it. I told him if he didn't give me another one I was going to break his fucking face.

'That night, I went to see my mother. When I was walking home, André and about six of his friends popped out from nowhere. André put a gun in my face and told me he was going to kill me. I walked away. There were seven of them and one of me. I just told them to fuck off and walked away. I haven't been back to Heideveld since then.'

'What will they do to you if they see you?'

'That's not what I'm worried about. I'm avoiding André because if I see him I'm going to stab him. André is a member of my family. He sees my mother every day. If I make a scene with him, I'll be an outcast. I've spent seven months trying to show my family I'm peaceful.'

'Why will you stab him?'

'He's a *laaitie*. He pulled a gun on me. And I was the one who was wronged.'

'That doesn't answer my question.'

'That's how things are. I live in the ghetto; you don't. The ghetto has rules.'

'Like what rules?'

'You've never met my brother-in-law Shamil. You've never met him because he doesn't live with the Benjamins. He lives round the corner. He's deep in the 28s, a soldier. He's very committed. The other night he was walking home and this American *laaitie* stopped him in the street and said, "*Wie is jy*?" – "Who are you?" Shamil started to *sabela* with him, and he saw that this *laaitie* didn't know how to *sabela*. He didn't know what he was talking about. Shamil told him to move out the way and he said no, so Shamil took out a knife and stabbed him. He laid charges. Shamil had to get out of Manenberg. So there's an example of the rules you asked about.'

'You're talking like you're still a gangster.'

'No. If I was still a gangster, I would go and visit my mother whenever I like. And if André stopped me in the street, I'd fuck him up. I'm avoiding seeing my own fucking mother because I'm trying not to make trouble. A gangster would laugh at me for that.

'On Sunday, there's a big family gathering at my mother's place. The whole family will be there. Including André. I'm not going. I'm going to go to my mother in advance and apologise and tell her why. I don't have a cent in my pocket. There will be as much free food there as I can eat. I'd get to see all my sisters at the same time; that hasn't happened in years. I'm going to stay locked up in my wendy house instead.'

*

That Sunday morning, Magadien and I went to a Community Bible Fellowship service in Athlone. The church was housed in a modest building: a simple hall attached to a triple-storey block. The block housed the beneficiaries of a church programme for marginalised women. They were trained in simple craft skills, and ran a cooperative.

We arrived shortly before the service was to begin. A young chubby man stood at the front of the congregation. He was holding a microphone to his mouth, had closed his eyes tight, and contorted his face into an expression of intense bliss. Wide sweat stains ringed his armpits. 'God has not failed me yet,' he chanted, pointing his face to the heavens and shaking his head in wonder. 'In all my years, God has not failed me yet. Can you name a time in your life God has failed you? No, God has not failed me yet.' A gentle melody on the piano accompanied his incantations.

The congregation sang a few hymns and then Simon stepped to the podium to deliver a sermon. Wearing a jacket and tie, he addressed the worshippers in the same manner in which he had spoken to me when we met; he was slow and studious, quite deliberately uncharismatic; he chose his words with extreme care, explaining each ritual with lean simplicity. He said that the bread he was to pass around the congregation represented the body of Christ, and the grape juice represented his blood. He explained that these were symbols, not real bodies or blood.

At the end of his sermon he asked if anyone in the congregation had something 'burning' that they needed to share. An elderly man rose. He pointed to the elderly woman beside him.

'Everyone knows that my wife has had a so-called setback,' he began. His voice was shaky. 'She begins chemotherapy on Thursday. I say "so-called" because the enemy lies,' he continued, a note of enthusiasm entering his voice. 'The enemy likes to demoralise us and upset us.' Murmurs of approval drifted from the congregation. 'That's why they like to talk about "so-called" setbacks. This so-called setback is just another station along the way. We can only come through it stronger.'

A woman seated next to me began nodding vigorously. She squeezed her eyes shut. 'The enemy lies,' she murmured. 'He always lies.'

*

In the car on the way back to Manenberg, Magadien was silent. I could feel his depression, but I did not know what had triggered it. I asked him and he said nothing.

Back in the church, he had cut a strange figure. He was cleanly shaven and wore smart grey slacks and a collared shirt. He looked, I guess, like a middle-aged working-class man dressed for church. I had never seen him like that before. He usually wore jeans and a t-shirt.

During the church service, he had sat quietly by himself in his grave, nondescript clothes. Afterwards, he had gotten up and walked across the hall with bowed head and hands in pockets; he had greeted people politely, answered questions briefly, and left.

We stopped at a red light. It turned green and I hesitated for a moment. There was a minibus taxi behind us. Its tyres screeched, it lurched beside us and the driver stuck his fist out the window and hurled a volley of expletives at me before speeding away.

Magadien shook his head. 'You asked me what the matter is.' He pointed at the disappearing taxi. 'That's what the matter is. We have just been in the presence of God, and two minutes later, we come out to this. We have come from a place of peace and driven out into madness. Whenever you are happy, someone is angry with you. Whenever you are angry with someone, he wants you to be happy. Everything is violent, violent, violent. Just sharing the same planet with other people is violent, violent, violent. If that man had gotten out of his car, I would have done something terrible to him. And then he would have come to look for me to shoot me.

And I would have died because he couldn't wait two seconds at the fucking traffic light.'

We drove the rest of the way home in silence. I parked outside the Benjamins' house, turned and looked at him. 'It's not just that things are violent. Something's the matter. What is it?'

'Everything,' he replied. 'In the last few minutes, I have thought about everything, and it's all wrong. In an hour's time, there will be a family gathering at my mother's house. That fucking *laaitie* cunt is going to be there stuffing his little mouth and I will be locked in my wendy house. There is free food waiting for me and I am staying here. I'm so fucking *nice* I want to be sick.'

'I don't have to go now,' I said. 'Should we go out for lunch?'

'No, we shouldn't go out for lunch. It would make me sick. I want to be alone.'

27
GLYNNIS

Out of the blue, Glynnis made contact with Magadien. It was the last week of January 2004. They had not spoken since the previous August, when she had scolded him for not taking care of Noes. In the space of two days, she sent four text messages to his cellphone, asking him to phone her back. Magadien didn't have money to make calls from his cellphone. He watched the messages appear on his screen, one after the next, and eventually, at the end of the second day of messages, borrowed R10 and phoned her back.

She was furious. She demanded to know why he had taken so long to return her calls. Aware that he was fast running out of airtime, and in any case shy to announce that he was broke, he ignored her demands and asked her what she wanted. Of all things, she wanted money. He told her he would come to her house the following day.

The next morning, a couple of hours before his appointment with his daughter, Magadien and I were walking through the centre of Cape Town when she sent him another text message. This time, we called her back from my phone.

'My daddy told me he's coming to see me this morning,' she said to me. 'Is he lying?'

'No,' I replied. 'I'm driving him. We're about to get into the car.'

'Do you promise?'

'I promise, yes.'

'Good. Now I have the word of an honest man.'

*

I had met Glynnis about a year before, while Magadien was still in jail. She had no idea who I was when I phoned, had not imagined that anybody would write a book about her absent, criminal father. I announced myself and asked if I could see her.

'Are you free now?' she asked.

'Yes.'

'Then come. Come right now.' And she gave me directions to her house. I was struck by her decisiveness, her urgency.

She lived at the time in a rented room in the Mitchells Plain suburb of Westridge. It was immaculately ordered and neat, as if nobody lived there, as if it was a museum, not a home – a distilled exhibition of a Mitchells Plain bachelor flat.

She ushered me into her room with lightly-worn courtesy and offered me a seat. She was strikingly beautiful: extremely thin, like her father, delicately framed, and short. She wore her hair tied back from her face, as if she knew her prize possessions were her eyes: murky brown and enormous, much too big for her slender face, lending her an astonishing intensity.

She sat silently, waiting for me to announce my business. I told her I was writing a book about her father, that she, even through her absence, was a significant person in his life, that I had wanted to meet her.

'And to write about me?' she asked sharply.

'Yes. Inasmuch as you are his daughter, I want to write about you.'

She looked at me thoughtfully. 'That's okay,' she said finally. 'You can write about meeting me today. What has my daddy been saying about me?'

I marvelled at the economy of the exchange she had just negotiated. I was to write about her; she was to receive a report about Magadien: a fresh report – I had been with him that very morning.

As I began to talk, I felt a little like Magadien must have when he spoke to disbelieving family members from the public phone in the corridor outside his cell. Trying to express the profundity of what he had been through without sounding trite was an uphill battle. I felt the inadequacy of my words the moment they left my mouth.

I told her of his remorse – about Margie, about Glynnis herself – of his determination to win her trust and become a father, even this late in life, of his painful awareness that it would be gruellingly difficult.

She stared at me with her enormous eyes. I couldn't figure out whether they were cold or just thoughtful. 'You know, my mother, Margie, she must have been very in love with him when she was young. She's a wonderful human being.' She rolled her eyes cynically. 'I guess we all make mistakes.

'But, you know, it lives with her, the things he has done to her. I don't know what went on between him and my mom back then. But I know she is still scarred from it. She will never say a bad word to me about him, because he is my daddy. But sometimes, when I hug her, I feel her withdraw into herself, or step away from me, and I know it's about him; she's still suffering from the ways he hurt her.'

'And you?' I asked.

'I'm okay. Maybe because I stopped thinking of myself as someone with a father a long time ago. I've maybe seen him five times in my life. If I passed him on the street, I don't think I'd recognise him.'

She said these things matter-of-factly, but she could not hide her emotion. For the first time, she lowered her eyes and began speaking to the hands resting in her lap.

'You know, at school, when people asked me about my father, I'd say he was in the army. And when that didn't work any more, I said he was dead.' She paused, and allowed the word to linger. And then, in case I didn't get it: 'I said, like, that my own father was dead.

'He phoned me from jail about a year ago. He begged me to forgive him. He said I was his princess. His princess!' She shook her head dismissively. 'He said he'd be there for my 21st birthday last year, that he'd be there when I became an adult. It's a big thing, you know. He said he hadn't been there for my childhood. Now he was going to be here for me for the rest of my life. I took him seriously, you know.'

'He thought he'd get a weekend out,' I replied. 'His application was turned down.'

'But he must be honest with me,' she said sulkily. 'He mustn't lie.'

She laughed cheerlessly. 'He says I must forgive him. Forgive him for what? For not being my father? I forgive him. I was cross with him when I was younger, but I'm not any more. Like I said, if I saw him, I probably wouldn't recognise him. I've made my peace with him.'

I felt a surge of empathy for her, with the hurt she was trying so hard to conceal.

'He's a member of a gang, hey?' she asked me.

'Ja: the 28s.'

She looked at me blankly. 'My daddy wrote me a letter a while ago, telling me I am his princess, asking me to forgive him. And then he told me about the things he'd done in his gang. I mean, it's disgusting; why does he think I want to know these things?'

'To come straight with you? To tell you who he's been, so he can start an honest relationship with you?'

'When's he getting out?'

'In June.'

'He mustn't come and tell me I'm his princess. I've been his princess too many times before. His words mean nothing. If he comes to me the day after he's released, I'll throw him out. If he comes to me a week after he's released, I'll probably still throw him out. He must take it very, very slow. He can't just be my daddy because he suddenly thinks his whole life has changed. He can't just click his fingers to make me his daughter. We must take it slow.'

I nodded. That was, indeed, the most sober commentary on Magadien's Big Change I had heard.

I asked her to tell me a little about herself. She said she had worked briefly as a teacher. Now, she was a waitress at an up-market hotel in Cape Town. She began explaining the protocol of five-star service with an expert's confidence, like a pianist describing how she plays a familiar score: how to approach the table, when to offer more wine, the intuitive balance one must strike between attentiveness and respectful distance. She was, I imagined, a particularly good up-market waitress; I pictured her fine attention to detail, to etiquette, her instinctive capacity to read the habits and whims of people foreign to her.

'Is the money good?' I asked.

'You know, Jonny,' she replied, 'my boss is making me into a racist.' She opened her shoulders wide and gesticulated with indignation. 'I don't want to be a racist! At the beginning, he was paying all the coloured girls less than the white girls, even though the white girls didn't have a clue what they were doing. We had to teach them from scratch.'

'What did you do?'

'I put my foot down. I put a stop to it. And now he hates me. He's looking for a reason to fire me. It's a matter of time. I swear, that man is making me into a racist.'

I told her I wanted to meet Margie.

'Come,' she said. 'Let's go.' And we walked the two kilometres or so between her room and Margie's house.

It was late afternoon. The streets were full of people returning from work. She appeared to greet every last one of them, all the way to Margie's house, always with her impeccable, well-brought-up courtesy.

Margie wasn't home. Just her husband was there – the man Magadien had stalked and terrorised many years back, when he discovered that Margie had left him while he was in jail – and Margie's younger daughters. Glynnis's stepfather was affable, warm. He and Glynnis were light and gentle with each other. Her younger sister said she needed money for a school outing. Glynnis took out her wallet and gave her sister a R20 note. And that is the image of her I was left with for the following year: a powerful young woman, more together than Magadien had ever been, walking into the world with great clarity, but also with confusion; an adult with unfinished childhood business still swirling in her head.

*

It was now a year later, and Magadien and I were driving out to Mitchells Plain, answering Glynnis's angry summons. She was back at Margie's house now. A few months earlier, the restaurant at which she worked had changed hands and the contracts of the coloured waitresses had not been renewed. She was staying with Margie to save money while looking for a new job.

This was, by Magadien's own reckoning, perhaps the most important day since his release from prison; his estranged daughter had asked, indeed, demanded, to see him. As with Noes a few months earlier, he found himself in the passenger seat of my car, making his way towards an uncertain fatherhood.

Given the significance of the day, I wondered at his choice of clothes. Usually, he wore a nondescript t-shirt and a pair of jeans. Today, he dressed like a gangster: a thin vest that paraded his tattoos, a gaudy pair of reflector sunglasses with thick silver frames, a heavy, garish earring in each ear. Why now, I wondered. Why is this the man he wants to introduce to Glynnis after so many years?

'You look like you're going to put a gun in my face and take my car,' I joked.

He laughed. 'Why must the bad guys monopolise good clothes?'

We parked across the road from the house and walked through the open front door to find Margie washing dishes in the kitchen. She was large and doughty, wore a thin cotton working uniform and a scowl on her face. Her scowl was reserved for Magadien. She cursed under her breath, studiously avoided greeting him, and went into the back of the house to call Glynnis. Magadien and I sat down in the lounge. Margie returned a moment later, and Magadien grinned at her cheekily.

'Where's your manners?' he asked her, still grinning. 'Don't we get coffee?'

'Coffee?' she asked indignantly, looking him in the face for the first time. '*Kak!*'

She went back to the kitchen, still mumbling under her breath, rinsed a dish, put it on the rack, came back into the lounge, and asked me how I had my coffee.

'And me?' Magadien asked, as she made her way back to the kitchen. 'What about me, fatty?' He turned to me. 'Don't you think Margie's fat?'

'*Pasop!*' she replied from over her shoulder. 'Watch it!'

Glynnis emerged from the back of the house. Once again, her hair was tied back from her face, and her large eyes took Magadien in. This time, the emotions they expressed were quite clear. They were intensely curious. And they were generous; they wanted to love. She went up close to him and traced a finger down his biceps. He flinched; the unexpected physical contact unnerved him.

'You should get rid of your tattoos,' she said.

'No,' he replied indignantly.

'But they're terrible. You must show that you're leaving that behind.'

'What do you want me to do: pretend my past never happened? You think that's healthy?'

'Ja, but ...' her voice trailed off. It was a good answer.

Margie returned with two cups of coffee, one for me, the other for Magadien. She gave him a mischievous smile.

Glynnis sat down opposite her father, leaned forward in her chair, and looked at him closely. 'What happened with Noes?' she asked. 'Why did she go back to the Strand?'

'My in-laws threw her out,' he replied.

Glynnis nodded. 'Because she's another woman's daughter.'

'No. Because they don't like me. They were punishing me.'

'You have to give people time,' Glynnis said. 'They still think of you as a criminal. It takes time to show people you've changed.'

'No, it's not that. It's that I won't reconcile with their daughter.'

Glynnis shot him an irritable look. 'Then why are you still there?' she asked, raising her voice. 'You can't be around people who don't make you feel good. It's bad for you. It's a stupid thing to do.'

Magadien shrugged. 'I'm not leaving.'

'You know what it says in Corinthians,' she said. 'Don't be a thorn in other people's side.'

'Ja,' he replied, 'but you know what it says in Matthew?'

'Ja, ja: thy shall love thy neighbour as thyself. But you must see that what you are doing is stupid.'

And so they went at it for a good ten minutes, sparring, their weapons drawn from a bottomless armoury of biblical quotations, this father and daughter who had not laid eyes on each other in more than five years.

As their battle ground on, I grew increasingly annoyed with Magadien. Here was his daughter, perhaps the most significant person in his life, trying to communicate with him, and his only response was to drown her in obfuscation.

I did what a journalist should never do; in a fit of frustration I told her what he should have at the beginning. 'Maybe,' I said, 'he still lives with the Benjamins because he can't afford to leave.'

She nodded, taking it in, then resumed lecturing him. 'Move in with your mother, or your sister, or somewhere. Just a room, where you don't have to pay rent. Start small. You can't start right to the top. You have to build slowly.'

He nodded stubbornly, like a reluctant child taking advice from a parent. It was a strange inversion.

'So,' Glynnis said coldly, 'you don't have money for me, do you?'

'No.'

She slammed her fist against the arm of the chair. 'There you go again. I am so angry with you. Not because you don't have money for me. Because you lied to me.'

'I didn't lie to you.'

'I phoned to ask you for money. You said yes.'

'I didn't say yes. I said I'd come and see you.'

'But that implies yes. Don't play games.'

'You're playing games. You're saying I said something I didn't. I said I'd come and see you.'

'So, you're poor. So what? Why couldn't you just *say* that? Why couldn't you say: "Glynnis, I wish I could help you, but I'm too poor"? At least that would have been honest. Why must you lie to me?"

'Glynnis, listen to me. I didn't lie. I said I was coming, and I'm here. Aren't I here?'

And so it continued. They went on and on at each other, arguing the meaning of the words 'I'll come and see you', until the semantics of their argument felled them both, and the conversation died a slow, tortured death.

There was a long silence. And then Magadien broke it.

'The other night,' he said, 'someone very close to Colin Stansfield came to me.'

'Who's Colin Stansfield?' Glynnis asked irritably.

'Who's Colin Stansfield? He's the richest fucking gangster in this province. They wanted me to work for him. I could have come to visit you in a BMW today, with money falling out of my pockets.'

She stared at him glumly. Perhaps she didn't understand. Or perhaps she was just annoyed with his indirectness, his clumsiness. I wish he had said it differently. I wish he had told her that she had phoned him to ascertain whether he could be a proper father, that she had done so by asking for money, that he could have bought her love, that she had tempted him to buy her love, that it would have been easy, but that he won't – he won't do it that way.

'You know,' he said, 'I am a man. I have needs. For five years in prison I didn't fulfil my needs. Now I am under the same roof as my wife, but I don't sleep with her. And I haven't slept with anyone else, because it's not right.'

He stared at his feet. He knew it hadn't come out right.

'Shame,' Glynnis replied sarcastically. 'You poor man. You have needs.'

Margie chipped in from the kitchen with a dismissive snort.

It was time to go. Glynnis asked for a lift to a friend who lived at the other end of Mitchells Plain. The three of us drove off together.

Sitting in the car, Magadien next to me, Glynnis's face in my rear-view mirror, I realised that I had just seen a part of Magadien, a part of the essence of Magadien, I had never seen before. Hour after hour we had sat in his cell, walked the streets of Manenberg, driven the length and breadth of Cape Town, and he had talked and talked and talked. He had spoken of himself with such urgency, with such exquisite emotion, that I had been mesmerised. I realised only now that he could talk like that *about* his life, not *in* his life. Confronted with the presence of his mother, of whom he had thought and talked until he had cried in pain, he was mute. Face-to-face with Glynnis, whom he loved with a degree of rue-fulness no father should experience, he had been unable to tell her that he was poor, that he was struggling, that he loved her more than he could express.

The gangster clothes he had chosen to wear today; the blurting out to Margie that she was fat; the clumsy, jerky sentences about his sex life: these, I realised, were delivered with great pain; they were a substitute for communicating.

I had never really entered Magadien's world. He had fabricated from our relationship an adjunct to his world, a separate chamber. He could talk to me the way he did because I was not a flesh-and-blood human being from his life, but an abstraction, a blank canvas on which he was free to paint. Back here, in the rooms of his real life, he was no artist. Here, his seductive brushstrokes gave way to cryptic, hesitant squiggles. Here, things came slowly and painfully.

My thoughts kept returning to his choice of clothes. Was he simply forcing Glynnis to deal with his past, as he himself had intimated? I think the signs he was sending her were much more delicate than that. His earrings and his shades were, perhaps, a kind of protective muti, a shield. 'If you reject me,' he seems to have been reminding them both, 'I have another "family" to whom I owe allegiance. I can go back there.'

We arrived at Glynnis's friend's house and Glynnis invited us inside. In the lounge, Magadien and his daughter resumed their debate about the meaning of the words 'I'll come and see you'. Glynnis's friend nodded supportively whenever Glynnis spoke, and shook her head politely whenever Magadien spoke. We left after about ten minutes.

Glynnis walked us to the car. As we were leaving, she touched him on his shoulder once again. 'You must come and see me soon,' she said. 'And you must spend more time here next time. Why must you leave so quickly?'

We drove out of Mitchells Plain in silence.

'How are you feeling?' I asked finally.

'This has been the best day since my release,' he declared. 'My greatest fear was that she'd reject me. She didn't. I'm full of hope. I haven't been so full of hope since the day I walked out of jail.'

'But she fought with you from the moment you walked through the door.'

'Ja, she fought with me. That is her way. She's like me. She's stubborn. But she likes me. She's giving me a chance. If she didn't like me, she wouldn't have fought with me. She would have thrown me out. Why do you think she invited us in to her friend's place? She wanted to show off her father, warts and all.'

He is right, I thought to myself. He understood his daughter far better than I did. In the privacy of his own thoughts, his grasp of the people he loves is lucid and subtle.

'So where to from here?' I asked.

'Where to from here? You ask that question like I have the sort of life where I can see a week into the future. Where to from here: we're driving back to Manenberg; I'm going to make myself a cup of coffee, sit in the sun outside my wendy house, and think nice thoughts about my daughter. Then we'll see.'

AFTERWARDS

From the very beginning of our collaboration, Magadien and I made a firm agreement that I would not pay him. After he was released from jail, and things did not go right for him, we stuck to that agreement, even though, in these new and unpleasant circumstances, there were times when it seemed perverse.

From my side, the idea of paying him for his cooperation, especially now that he was struggling, did not sit right. It is not that the material would somehow be truer if it came for free, nor that our relationship would be purer. In painting a portrait of a struggling man, one is already involved in a transaction, irrespective of whether money changes hands. Its terms are troublingly opaque, the stakes inordinately high. The struggling man grants you immense power, the power to describe both his dignity and his humiliation to an audience of vicarious and perhaps unsympathetic strangers, people who would have no right to eavesdrop on his life under normal circumstances. That is his side of the bargain.

Mine is not as easy to define. What is he getting from me in return? He knows, dimly, that he has lived the treacherous life of a man in the margins, that he wants the world he has shunned and that has shunned him in turn to recognise him, to gasp at the pain he has suffered and at the fortitude he has exercised. But that is a terribly abstract and uncertain reward. Can he be sure that this is what he will get, or how he will feel if it finally arrives? He is, in the end, a gambler. He is not entirely certain of what it is he wants until he sees it, until he has already cast his die. He must wait until the book is published and read before he can understand what it is that he has received.

I did not want to reduce this complicated transaction to something simple and unpleasant; I did not want to buy the things he was offering me for a loaf of bread. It seemed ominously close to a poor person accepting money from a doctor to have some experimental surgery performed on his body.

Yet the moment the writing was done, and Magadien had read much of the manuscript and a publication date had been set, our arrangement seemed wrong to me. I had spent 18 months extracting his story from him, and I was taking it away, leaving him, quite literally, with nothing. Perhaps if he had had a job, a home, some food on his table, things would have been different. Despite the firmness of the convictions I had held before, leaving penniless a man about whom I had grown to care a great deal was wrong.

So, in the end, he did take away something concrete and measurable from our encounter; the day our collaboration on this book ended, I offered him 10% of the royalties I would make from it. He accepted, began by taking 10% of my advance, and used it to capitalise a small business, doing what Robin Morris once taught him – cutting and fitting glass.

I phoned every once in a while and asked how the business was doing. Things were tough, he told me. There are broken windows all over Manenberg, but few people have money. Most asked him to work on credit. He refused.

The bulk of his work had come from members of the Community Bible Fellowship congregation. A headmaster contracted him to repair windows at his school. There were other projects in the pipeline. He was not yet earning a living. He and the reserved, doughty Simon had drawn up a business plan. Perhaps his work will begin to support him, they said, if we keep at it and stay alert: perhaps a few months from now.

But as time went by, the phone calls became more despondent. As I write, in June 2004, what little business he had at the beginning has dried up; the tools he bought lie idly under his bed. He remains as destitute as he was the day he walked out of jail. 'Perhaps next year …' he says hollowly.

When he looks back on our relationship a few years from now, I wonder what he will see. Perhaps I am to take my place among the *sturvies* and whites who once flitted in and out of his life; people who were seduced by his story for a time, tried to help, and then moved on. Perhaps, even as we go through the motions of speaking on the phone, my voice will remind him that there is no crossing the boundary, that it was always an illusion. Between *ndotas* on one side, and whites and *sturvies* on the other, there is a wall too high to climb.

*

He did, in the end, demand that I uphold my end of the literary bargain. It came in the form of a phone call in mid-2004, a couple of months after I had completed the research.

'You know,' he told me on the phone, 'I have a problem with something in the book.'

'Which part?' I asked.

'It's not anything that's there,' he said. 'It's something that's not there. You know me. You know how much I hate unhappy endings. They make me depressed. Right now, I'm walking to the train station. I'm holding this cellphone in my right hand. In my left hand, I am holding the hand of a young woman. You never met her. But I'm holding her hand.

'Remember, my friend, remember when we first met, and we spoke in my cell, I told you about my dream. I wanted a white picket fence, and a fiancée, and we would walk through the streets holding hands, and we'd stop and look at things and smile together, and we'd go home and shut the door and make love.'

'I remember,' I said.

'This is it,' he continued, 'real love, no strings attached. She had issues, which I understand. Others treated her badly. I told her I will love her 'til my dying days.'

He asked me to hold on a moment, and then she was at the other end of the line. 'I'm so embarrassed,' she said. 'I'm going to kill him.'

Magadien again, laughing: 'I'm over the moon. I feel like shouting from the top of Table Mountain. Do you understand?'

'It sounds wonderful,' I said. 'Congratulations. May it last.'

'I knew you'd understand, brother. I knew because you are my brother. You know what it means to me. You know my heart.'

AFTERWORD

By MD Wentzel

I dedicate my role in this book to all gang members and inmates who want to change their lives and are caught in the myth that tells them that to change is to die. Change isn't about dying, it is about what you want for the future. A future in prison or in a gang has no benefits, no pension and no medical aid; all it has is pain and suffering. Wake up, and take charge of your lives and all the responsibilities that await you.

Change is possible. Change begins with you.

I also dedicate this book to the following organisations and people:

Community Bible Fellowship (CBF)
Centre for Conflict Resolution (CCR)
Department of Correctional Services (DCS)

But mostly to Mr JJ Jansen and family; Mr CG Malgas and family; Mrs Joanna Flanders Thomas and family; Mrs Michelene Diane Benson and family; Stan Henkelman and staff; Chris Giffard; Estelle Malgas; and Noxi and Sally in the library at CCR for their support and friendship.

To my family: Milly and Nadine; my mom; my sisters Anne, Nazley, Shana, Layla, and my brothers Ebrahiem (Khaki) and Waleed; my daughters Glynnis and Vanecia (Noes) for whom I was not there when they needed me most, when they needed a father in their lives. I hope that one day I'll make them proud. My son Johaah for giving me the best gift a man could ask for, a grandson, Junaid, who is my life; now I will have the chance to see a small child grow up to become what he wants, as long as it is for the best.

To all the inmates and gang members: crime doesn't pay, rehabilitation is the only way. Think about your kids and families, and forget about a past of pain.

To the schools and educators: your duty is to learn and to teach and to see growth.

Last but not least: my friends Dullah, Bennie, Chris, Charra and Lappies, and the ladies: Zizi, Fouzia, Shirley and Penny.

God bless all those who read this book written by my brother and friend Jonny Steinberg: thank you for giving me the opportunity to tell my story, a story untold.

May God be the judge of this book.

BIBLIOGRAPHY

Books, articles, unpublished manuscripts

Badroodien, Azeem 'Race, Crime, Welfare and State Social Institutions in South Africa from the 1940s', in *Social Dynamics* vol. 25 no. 22, 1999, pp 49-74.

Beaumont, Gustave de and Tocqueville, Alexis de *On the Penitentiary System in the United States and its Application in France*, trans. Francis Lieber, Carbondale and Edwardsville: Southern Illinois University Press, 1964 (first published in 1833).

Beyers, CJ *Dictionary of South African Biographies* vol. 3, Pretoria: HSRC, 1977.

Bosman, Herman Charles *Stone Cold Jug*, Cape Town: Human and Rousseau, 1999 (first published in 1969).

Breytenbach, Breyten *The True Confessions of an Albino Terrorist*, London: Faber and Faber, 1984.

Bundy, Colin '"Action, comrades, action!" The politics of youth-student resistance in the Western Cape, 1985', in Wilmot James and Mary Simons (eds) *The Angry Divide: Social and Economic History of the Western Cape*, Cape Town and Johannesburg: David Philip, 1989, pp 206-217.

Canetti, Elias *Crowds and Power*, trans. Carol Stewart, Penguin: London, 1992 (first published as *Masse und Macht*, Hamburg, 1960).

Chisholm, Linda 'Crime, Class and Nationalism: The Criminology of Jacob de Villiers Roos, 1869-1918', in *Social Dynamics* vol. 13 no. 2, 1987, pp 46-59.

Coetzee, JM *Giving Offense: Essays on Censorship*, Chicago: University of Chicago Press, 1996.

Conover, Ted *New Jack: Guarding Sing Sing*, New York: Vintage, 2001.

Corry, TM *Prison Labour in South Africa*, Cape Town: Nicro, 1977.

Cronjé, Geoffrey *Voogdyskap en Apartheid*, Pretoria: Van Schaik, 1948.

Cronjé, Geoffrey et al *Regverdige Rasse-Apartheid*, Stellenbosch: Christen-Studenteverenigingsmaatskappy, 1947.

Fagan, Eduard 'S v Nero en 2 Ander', in *Stet* (3)1, February 1985, 22-26.

Friedman, Steven (ed) *The Long Journey: South Africa's Quest for a Negotiated Settlement*, Johannesburg: Ravan Press, 1993.

Gear, Sasha and Ngubeni, Kindiza *Daai Ding: Sex, Sexual Violence and Coercion in Men's Prisons*, Johannesburg: CSVR, 2002.

Ghirardo, Diane *Architecture After Modernism*, London: Thames and Hudson, 1996.

Giffard, Chris 'The Prisons Transformation Project in Western Cape Prisons', seminar presented at the Centre for the Study of Violence and Reconciliation, Johannesburg, October 2001.

Giffard, Chris 'Out of Step? The Transformation Process in the South African Department of Correctional Services', dissertation submitted in partial fulfilment of the degree of Master of Science in Criminal Justice Studies, Scarman Centre for the Study of Public Order, University of Leicester, 1997.

Giliomee, Hermann *The Afrikaners: Biography of a People*, Cape Town: Tafelberg, 2003.

Goffman, Erving *Asylums: Essays on the Social Situation of Mental Patients and Other Inmates*, London: Penguin, 1973 (first published in 1961).

Goyer, KC; Saloojee, Yusuf; Richter, Marlise and Hardy, Chloe 'HIV/AIDS in Prison: Treatment, Intervention and Reform', submission to the Jali Commission of Enquiry on behalf of the AIDS Law Project and the Treatment Action Campaign, March 2004.

Grann, David 'The Brand: How the Aryan Brotherhood became the most murderous prison gang in America', in *The New Yorker*, 16 and 23 February 2004.

Haysom, Nicholas 'Towards an Understanding of Prison Gangs', Institute of Criminology, University of Cape Town, 1981.

Hobsbawm, Eric *Bandits*, New York: Pantheon Books, 1981 (2nd edition).

Hofmeyr, Isabel 'Building a Nation From Words: Afrikaans Language, Literature and Ethnic Identity, 1902-1924', in Shula Marks and Stanley Trapido (eds) *The Politics of Race, Class and Nationalism in Twentieth Century South Africa*, London and New York: Longman, 1987.

Howard, Ebenezer *Garden Cities of Tomorrow*, London: Faber & Faber, 1970 (first published in 1898).

Jacobs, James B *Stateville: The Penitentiary in Mass Society*, Chicago and London: Chicago University Press, 1977.

Jensen, Steffen 'Claiming Community – Negotiating Crime: state formation, neighbourhood and gangs in a Capetonian township', PhD dissertation submitted to International Development Studies, Roskilde University, Denmark, September 2001.

Jensen, Steffen 'Discourses of Violence: coping with violence on the Cape Flats', in *Social Dynamics* vol. 25 no. 2, 1999, pp 75-97.

Jeppie, Shamil 'Leadership and Loyalties: The Imams of Nineteenth Century Colonial Cape Town, South Africa', in *Journal of Religion in Africa* 26(2), 1996, pp 139-162.

Joyce, James *Finnegans Wake*, London: Penguin, 2001 (first published in 1939).

Keswa, Rodney 'King Nongoloza Made Men of Women', in *Sunday Times Extra*, 26 September 1976.

Keswa, Rodney 'The King Recruits New Gang in Jail', in *Sunday Times Extra*, 3 October 1976.

Keswa, Rodney 'I Saw a Jail Gang Execution', in *Sunday Times Extra*, 17 October 1976.

Keswa, Rodney 'Secret Salutes Ex-Cons Give a Jail Boss', in *Sunday Times Extra*, 24 October 1976.

Keswa, Rodney 'Rival Spoilers Were Recruited in Prison', in *Sunday Times Extra*, 7 November 1976.

Kinnes, Irvin *From Urban Street Gangs to Criminal Empires: the changing face of gangs in the Western Cape*, Pretoria: Institute for Security Studies, 2000.

Le Corbusier, Charles *The City of Tomorrow and its Planning*, London: John Rodker, 1929.

Leggett, Ted *Rainbow Vice: The Drugs and Sex Industries in the New South Africa*, Cape Town: David Philip, 2001.

Lewis, Gavin *Between the Wire and the Wall: A History of South African 'Coloured' Politics*, Cape Town and Johannesburg: David Philip, 1987.

Lodge, Tom *All, Here, and Now: Black Politics in South Africa in the 1980s*, Cape Town: David Philip, 1991.

Lötter, JM and Schurink, WJ *Gevangenisbendes: 'n Ondersoek met spesiale verwysing na nommerbendes onder Kleurlinggevangenes*, Pretoria: RGN (Verslag S115), 1986.

Lötter, JM 'Prison Gangs in South Africa: A description', in *South African Journal of Sociology*, 19(2), 1989, pp 67-75.

Malcolm, Janet *The Silent Woman: Sylvia Plath and Ted Hughes*, New York: Vintage, 1994.

Malcolm, Janet *The Journalist and the Murderer*, New York: Vintage, 1990.

Mandela, Nelson *Long Walk to Freedom*, Johannesburg: Macdonald Purnell, 1994.

Martin, Denis-Constant *Coon Carnival: New Year in Cape Town, Past and Present*, Cape Town: David Philip, 1999.

Mathiesen, Thomas *The Defences of the Weak*, London: Tavistock, 1965.

Matshikiza, John 'Stuck Between Paradise and the Dark', in *Mail & Guardian*, 28 August 1998.

Morgan, Rod 'Imprisonment: Current Concerns and a Brief History since 1945', in Mike Maguire, Rod Morgan and Robert Reiner (eds) *The Oxford Handbook of Criminology*, Oxford: Clarendon Press, 1997.

Mumford, Lewis 'The Garden City Idea and Modern Planning', in Ebenezer Howard *Garden Cities of Tomorrow*, London: Faber and Faber, 1970, pp 29-40 (first published in the 1946 edition of Howard's book).

Nasson, Bill 'Political Ideologies in the Western Cape', in Tom Lodge *All, Here, and Now: Black Politics in South Africa in the 1980s*, Cape Town: David Philip, 1991.

Nasson, Bill 'Oral History and the Reconstruction of District Six', in Shamil Jeppie and Crain Soudien *The Struggle for District Six, Past and Present*, Cape Town: Buchu Books, 1990, pp 44-66.

Nasson, Bill "She preferred living in a cave with Harry the snake-catcher': Towards an Oral History of Popular Leisure and Class Expression in District Six, Cape Town, c 1920s-1950s', in Philip Bonner, Isabel Hofmeyr, Deborah James and Tom Lodge *Holding Their Ground: Class, Locality and Culture in 19th and 20th Century South Africa*, Johannesburg: Ravan Press, 1989, pp 285-308.

Nasson Bill 'Book Review of *Buckingham Palace District Six*, by Richard Rive', in *Social Dynamics* 13(2), 1987, pp 86-88.

Newton-King, Susan 'The Labour Market of the Cape Colony, 1807-1828', in Shula Marks and Anthony Atmore *Economy and Society in Pre-Industrial South Africa*, London: Longman, pp 171-207.

Pinnock, Don 'Ideology and Urban Planning: Blueprints of a Garrison City', in Wilmot James and Mary Simons (eds) *The Angry Divide: Social and Economic History of the Western Cape*, Cape Town and Johannesburg: David Philip, 1989, pp 150-168.

Pinnock, Don 'State Control and Street Gangs in Cape Town: towards an understanding of spatial and social development', MA thesis, University of Cape Town, 1982.

Pinnock, Don *The Brotherhoods: Street Gangs and State Control in Cape Town*, Cape Town: David Philip, 1982.

Pinnock, Don 'District Six: Historical Vignettes', in *South African Outlook*, January 1980, pp 9-11.

Pinnock, Don with Douglas-Hamilton, Dudu *Gangs, Rituals and Rites of Passage*, Cape Town: African Sun Press, 1997.

Rive, Richard 'District Six: Fact and Fiction', in Shamil Jeppie and Crain Soudien *The Struggle for District Six, Past and Present*, Cape Town: Buchu Books, 1990, pp 110-116.

Rive, Richard *Advance, Retreat: Selected Short Stories*, Cape Town and Johannesburg: David Philip, 1989.

Rive, Richard 'Growing up in District Six', in *South African Outlook*, January 1980, pp 6-8.

Rive, Richard *'Buckingham Palace', District Six*, Cape Town: David Philip, 1986.

Rive, Richard *Emergency*, Cape Town and Johannesburg: Ravan Press, 1988 (first published in 1964).

Schärf, Wilfried 'The Impact of Liquor on the Working Class: The Implications for the Structure of the Liquor Industry and the Role of the State in this Regard', MA thesis, Faculty of Social Sciences, University of Cape Town, 1984.

Schreiner, Olive *Thoughts on South Africa*, Johannesburg: Ad Donker, 1992 (first published by T Fisher Unwin, 1923).

Schurink, WJ 'The World of the *Wetslaners*: an analysis of some organisational features in South African Prisons', in *Acta Criminologica* vol. 2 no. 2, 1989.

Schurink, WJ, Schurink, E and Lötter, JM 'Numbers gangs in South African prisons: an organisational perspective', paper delivered to the 17th Annual Society Congress, University of Natal, 1986.

Seekings, Jeremy *The UDF: A History of the United Democratic Front in South Africa, 1983-1991*, Cape Town: David Philip, 2000.

Shell, Robert *Children of Bondage: A Social History of the Slave Society at the Cape of Good Hope, 1652-1838*, Johannesburg: Witwatersrand University Press, 1994.

Soudien, Crain 'District Six: from protest to protest', in Shamil Jeppie and Crain Soudien *The Struggle for District Six, Past and Present*, Cape Town: Buchu Books, 1990, pp 143-180.

South African Institute of Race Relations *A Survey of Race Relations in South Africa, 1985*, Johannesburg: SAIRR, 1986.

South African Institute of Race Relations *A Survey of Race Relations in South Africa, 1980*, Johannesburg: SAIRR, 1981.

South African Institute of Race Relations *A Survey of Race Relations in South Africa, 1979*, Johannesburg: SAIRR, 1980.

South African Institute of Race Relations *A Survey of Race Relations in South Africa, 1978*, Johannesburg: SAIRR, 1979.

South African Institute of Race Relations *A Survey of Race Relations in South Africa, 1977*, Johannesburg: SAIRR, 1978.

South African Institute of Race Relations *A Survey of Race Relations in South Africa, 1976*, Johannesburg: SAIRR, 1977.

Sparks, Richard, Bottoms, Anthony and Hay, Will *Prisons and the Problem of Order*, Oxford: Clarendon Press, 1996.

Standing, André *The Social Contradictions of Organised Crime on the Cape Flats*, Pretoria: Institute for Security Studies, 2003.

Sykes, Gresham M *The Society of Captives: A Study of a Maximum Security Prison*, Princeton: Princeton University Press, 1958.

Van Houten, Stephen 'The Prisons Transformation Project: Understanding psychological trauma in the prison context', paper submitted to Parliament's Portfolio Committee on Correctional Services, August 2001.

Van Onselen, Charles *The Small Matter of a Horse: The Life of 'Nongoloza' Mathebula, 1867-1948*, Johannesburg: Ravan, 1984.

Van Onselen, Charles *New Babylon, New Nineveh: Everyday Life on the Witwatersrand*, Johannesburg: Jonathan Ball, 2001 (first published in two volumes in 1982).

Van Zyl Smit, Dirk 'Change and Continuity in South African Prisons', in Robert Weiss and Nigel South (eds) *Comparing Prison Systems: Toward a Comparative and Internal Penology*, Sydney: Gordon and reach, 1999, pp 401-426.

Van Zyl Smit, Dirk 'Prisoners' Rights', in *South African Human Rights Yearbook*, vol. 5, Durban: Centre for Socio-Legal Studies, 1995, pp 268-280.

Van Zyl Smit, Dirk *South African Prison Law and Practice*, Durban: Butterworths, 1992.

Van Zyl Smit, Dirk 'Adopting and Adapting Criminological Ideas: Criminology and Afrikaner Nationalism in South Africa', in *Contemporary Crises* 13, 1989, pp 227-251.

Vidal, Gore *Palimpsest: A Memoir*, London: Abacus, 1996.

Western, John *Outcast Cape Town*, 2nd edition, Berkeley and Los Angeles: University of California Press, 1996.

Court Cases

Rex vs Mkosi Mkemeseni and 16 Others, Witwatersrand Supreme Court, 17 August 1915.

S vs Nkombisa, Cape Supreme Court, May 1974.

S vs Malgas and 6 Others, Cape Supreme Court, May 1975.

S vs Mombevu and 2 Others, Cape Supreme Court, April 1976.

S vs Marthinussen and 3 Others, Cape Supreme Court, September 1977.

S vs de Kock and 13 Others, Cape Supreme Court, June 1978.

S vs Pietersen and 2 Others, Cape Supreme Court, November 1978.

S vs Chavulla and 4 Others, Cape High Court, February 1999.

Chavulla and 4 Others vs S, Supreme Court of Appeal, February 2002.

Commissions of Inquiry

Report of the Commission Appointed to Enquire into the Johannesburg Prison, Pretoria: Government of the Transvaal, 1905.

Lansdown Commission, *Report of the Penal and Prison Reform Commission*, 1947.

Viljoen Commission, *Commission of Inquiry into the Penal System of the Republic of South Africa*, 1976.

Van Greun Verslag, *Ondersoek aangaande Toestande in die Brandvlei-gevangenis*, February 1972.

Van Dam Committee *Report of the Committee of Inquiry into Events at the Barberton Maximum Security Prison Barberton on 20 and 30 September 1983 and Related Matters*, May 1984.

Kriegler Commission, *Commission of Inquiry into Unrest in Prisons Appointed by the President on 27 June 1994*, Pretoria: February 1995.

Government Papers

Department of Justice, *Annual Report for the Year 1910*

Department of Justice, *Annual Report for the Year 1911*

Department of Justice, *Annual Report for the Year 1912*

Department of Justice, *Annual Report for the Year 1913*

Department of Justice, *Annual Report for the Year 1914*

Historian's Material Lodged in University Archives

The Molepo Collection (early 1980s), Afrikaner Library, University of the Witwatersrand, Johannesburg.*

* This is a collection of material lodged at the library by Charles van Onselen after the completion of his histories of the early Witwatersrand.